The German-Hebrew Dialogue

Perspectives on Jewish Texts and Contexts

―

Edited by
Vivian Liska

Editorial Board
Robert Alter, Steven E. Aschheim, Richard I. Cohen, Mark H. Gelber,
Moshe Halbertal, Christine Hayes, Moshe Idel, Samuel Moyn,
Ada Rapoport-Albert, Alvin Rosenfeld, David Ruderman, Bernd Witte

Volume 6

The German-Hebrew Dialogue

Studies of Encounter and Exchange

Edited by
Amir Eshel and Rachel Seelig

DE GRUYTER

ISBN 978-3-11-068373-8
e-ISBN (PDF) 978-3-11-047338-4
e-ISBN (EPUB) 978-3-11-047160-1
ISSN 2199-6962

Library of Congress Cataloging-in-Publication Data
A CIP catalog record for this book has been applied for at the Library of Congress.

Bibliographic information published by the Deutsche Nationalbibliothek
The Deutsche Nationalbibliothek lists this publication in the Deutsche Nationalbibliografie; detailed bibliographic data are available on the Internet at http://dnb.dnb.de.

© 2019 Walter de Gruyter GmbH, Berlin/Boston
This volume is text- and page-identical with the hardback published in 2018.
Cover image: Dani Karavan, *Mifgash*, 2004–5. Water, grass, white Carrara marble, red bricks, text; 1.5 × 4.5 × 4.5 m. Villa Lemm, Berlin, Germany. Photo: © Studio Dani Karavan
Typesetting: Compuscript Ltd., Shannon, Ireland
Printing and binding: CPI books GmbH, Leck
♾ Printed on acid-free paper
Printed in Germany

www.degruyter.com

Contents

Rachel Seelig with Amir Eshel
Editors' Introduction —— 1

Part One: German-Hebrew Exchange in Modernist Literature

Abigail Gillman
Not like Cherries, but like Peaches: Mendelssohn and
Rosenzweig Translate Yehuda Halevi's "Ode to Zion" —— 19

Maya Barzilai
The Flowers of Shame: Avraham Ben Yitzhak's Hebrew-German
"Revival" —— 41

Na'ama Rokem
Dan Pagis's Laboratory: Between German and Hebrew —— 61

Rachel Seelig
Stuttering in Verse: Tuvia Rübner and the Art of Self-Translation —— 77

Giddon Ticotsky
Vera Europa vs. *Verus Israel:* Modern Jews' Encounter with
Europe in Light of Lea Goldberg's *Encounter with a Poet* —— 105

Stefanie Mahrer
Texts and Objects: The Books of the Schocken Publishing
House in the Context of their Time —— 121

Galili Shahar
איכה/Ach: Lament and Being in Hebrew and German —— 143

Part Two: German-Hebrew Encounters in the Arts Today

Ruth Ginsburg
"I write bilingual poetry/in Hebrew and in silence" —— 159

Freddie Rokem
Before the Hebrew Notebook: Kafka's Words and Gestures in Translation —— 177

Yael Almog
Europe Will Be Stunned: Visualization of a Jewish Return —— 197

Amir Eshel
"In His Image": On Dani Karavan's Artwork in Germany —— 211

Tal Hever-Chybowski
***Mikan ve'eylakh* (From this Point Onward), translated by Rachel Seelig —— 241**

Mati Shemoelof
The Berlin Prize for Hebrew Literature (excerpt from a novel in progress), translated by Rachel Seelig —— 253

About the Authors —— 261

Rachel Seelig with Amir Eshel
Editors' Introduction

1 Opening the dialogue

> Meine Muttersprache ist nicht die Muttersprache meiner Mutter. Die Muttersprache meiner Mutter ist nicht die Muttersprache ihre Mutter. Die Mutter Sprache ihre Mutter ist nicht die Muttersprache und so weiter. Und So viel viel weiter. (Tomer Gardi 2016, 91)
>
> [My mother tongue is not my mother's mother tongue. My mother's mother tongue is not the mother tongue her mother. The mother tongue her mother is not her mother tongue and on and on. And so much much more on.]

Fragmented, ungrammatical, some might say "improper," *Broken German* is not only the title of Israeli writer Tomer Gardi's latest novel but also the language in which it was written. As a hopeful for the 2016 Ingeborg Bachmann Prize, Gardi was the dark horse in what has been described as the most diverse group of nominees in the prize's thirty-nine year history, with five out of fourteen authors claiming non-German citizenship or ancestry (including the winner, British-Ghanaian novelist Sharon Dodua Otoo). Yet unlike all of the other nominees, Gardi, a native of Kibbutz Dan and resident of Tel Aviv, neither lives in a German-speaking country nor speaks German perfectly. His nomination for the Bachmann Prize points to a loosening of norms surrounding the aesthetics and politics of German. Is "proper German" (*reines Deutsch*) no longer a prerequisite for receiving one of the highest German literary honors? This was the question on everyone's mind at the Festival of German-Language Literature in Klagenfurt, Austria.

The question is deceptively simple. Today, with three and even four generations of Turkish migrants and "post-migrants" calling Germany home, and swaths of immigrants and refugees entering the country every year, most recently from Syria, the country that Helmut Kohl once famously declared "not an immigration land" (*kein Einwanderungsland*) is now remarkably multicultural and multilingual. In light of the demographic changes – as well as reactionary opposition to these changes from the Radical Right – the notion of "proper German" has become highly controversial. According to Klaus Katsberger, the judge who nominated Gardi for the Bachmann Prize, "broken German" constitutes an important alternative to this hegemonic concept. In his view, Gardi's ungrammatical idiom is the language of newcomers and a powerful symbol of Germany's emerging "welcome culture" (*Willkommenskultur*). "One should have more faith in German literature," Katsberger argues, "*It succeeds where European politics fails*. Providing a home to the refugee and to linguistic immigration, which arrived long ago and live among us, is among [this literature's] greatest tasks" (Katsberger 2016).

Katsberger's remarks reflect a shift in the critical reception of writing by so-called *Ausländer* (foreigners) in the last half century. It is certainly a departure from the reactions provoked by Paul Celan's receipt of the Georg Büchner Prize in 1960, which betrayed abiding anti-Semitic sentiments in describing the poet's hermetic language as the product of an "alien" (*Fremdling*) from the "eastern outskirts of the German-language domain" (Eshel 2004, 59). In the post-reunification era a similar argument about language was attributed to Turkish-German migrant writers such as Emine Sevgi Özdamar, the first non-native German speaker to receive the Bachmann Prize in 1991. One critic of Özdamar's play *Karagöz in Almania* (1982) declared, "Broken German is tantamount to bad theater," while another, commenting on Özdamar's Bachmann-Prize submission, condescendingly praised the "awkwardness" (*Unbeholfenheit*) of the language as a sign of its "authenticity," ignoring the deliberate nature of Özdamar's language errors (Jankowsky 1997, 267). Today, twenty-five years since reunification and Özdamar's Bachmann Prize victory, writers who consistently expand the horizon of the German language and the sphere of German literature are respected, indeed celebrated around the globe. Yoko Tawada's ascendance to global literary recognition is but one indication of this tendency (Galchen 2016).

Tomer Gardi, neither a native German speaker like Celan, nor a migrant to Germany like Özdamar and Tawada, is seen not as an illegitimate interloper but as emerging talent worthy of consideration. During the judges' discussion at the Bachmann Prize competition, Hildegard Keller summed up the state of affairs with a comment that mimicked what she called Gardi's "poetic pidgin," saying, "German belongs to everyone. German belongs also to me. I can Bachmann Prize!"

Gardi's self-confident arrival on the German literary scene signals not only a transformation in German attitudes toward writing by so-called *Ausländer* but also a change in Israeli attitudes toward Germany and the German language. It is therefore an appropriate point of departure for the present volume, which is devoted to exploring the fraught yet fruitful relationship between German and Hebrew cultures, two cultures long viewed as separate or even as diametrically opposed. The essays gathered here call into question the prevailing belief, which gained purchase in the wake of World War II and the Holocaust, that there was no space for German in Israeli culture, just as there remained no trace of Hebrew in German culture. The notion that German and Hebrew could occupy the same cultural space seemed unfathomable, even anathema.

During the early years of Israeli statehood, German became taboo, despite the fact that it had been the lingua franca of thousands of Jewish immigrants and possibly the most commonly heard language in the coffeehouses of the *yishuv* during the 1930s and 1940s (Halperin 2015, 46). At the Hebrew University of Jerusalem, German language instruction was banned in 1934 in response to the ascent of the Nazi regime, even though roughly fifty percent of the faculty at the time were either native German speakers or trained in German universities. It was not until 1953, following the signing of a reparations agreement between Israel and West Germany, that German courses were reintroduced at the university (Weiss 2014). Even after the establishment of diplomatic relations between West Germany and Israel in 1965, the relationship between the two cultures remained tense. German, once celebrated as a vehicle of *Bildung,* came to be linked in the nascent Israeli imagination with Hitler's regime; the language of Goethe and Schiller was now tied to the perpetrators of the Holocaust.

In recent years, however, the relationship between German and Israeli cultures has evolved from one of mutual estrangement to one of mutual fascination. Government-sponsored academic exchange programs, joint startup ventures, national film board collaborations, not to mention the sheer increased mobility of students and young professionals, have impacted this relationship profoundly. Whereas Germans growing up in the shadow of World War II were largely unfamiliar with Jews and Jewish culture, their children are now traveling to Israel as volunteers and exchange students and immersing themselves in the Hebrew language and Israeli culture. And whereas Israelis born to Holocaust survivors tended to boycott all things German, their children now flock to Berlin, where a growing Israeli expat community has taken root.[1] These nomadic Germans and Israelis share liberal values and view increased exchange between their cultures as an important response to rising ethnic nationalism and right-wing extremism in both Germany and Israel. More than seventy years since the end of World War II, the rift between Germans and Israelis, especially those who came of age in the post-Cold War era, has begun to narrow.

---

[1] Official estimates of Israelis living in Berlin range from 5,000 to 15,000. It is difficult to determine a precise figure, since many enter Germany with European passports, and Israel's Central Bureau of Statistics does not identify as emigrants anyone who returns to visit Israel within a year of departure. For a sociological study of the Israelis in Berlin phenomenon, see Oz-Salzberger 2001; Yair 2015. For further demographic information, see Alon 2015.

2 German-Hebrew studies

A major outgrowth of increased exchange between Germany and Israel within the academic arena is the subfield of "German-Hebrew Studies." Moving beyond concepts of rupture, trauma and collective memory that long have dominated German-Jewish Studies, while challenging the Zionist frame that has long defined the study of modern Hebrew literature and Israeli culture, this new area of scholarship focuses on relational concepts such as migration, bilingualism, dialogue and translation, concepts that refer less to the boundaries between cultures than to the ways in which such boundaries are traversed. *The German-Hebrew Dialogue: Studies of Encounter and Exchange* is the first book dedicated to sketching out the parameters of this emerging field. The idea for the volume, which follows a number of scholarly gatherings, articles and journal issues on the subject, stems from a workshop convened at the Hebrew University of Jerusalem in 2015, entitled "The German-Hebrew Dialogue in the Multilingual Era." Expanding the focus of the workshop, which focused primarily on literature, the present study brings together essays on literature, film, art, theater and intellectual history that reveal the manifold ways in which German and Hebrew cultures have intersected from the Enlightenment until the present day.

If German-Hebrew Studies constitutes a "subfield," under which disciplinary rubric does it fall? The question does not have a simple answer. As the hyphen indicates, German-Hebrew Studies is by definition interdisciplinary, and thus disrupts and decenters the boundaries by which various fields are defined. First, it adds a crucial new layer to German-Jewish Studies, which generally has been restricted geographically to German-speaking lands and chronologically to the pre-World War II period. German-Hebrew Studies points to the ways in which encounters between these two cultures emerged during the eighteenth century and have persisted – albeit in a dramatically altered fashion – until today. The interlinguistic, intercultural dialogue between German and Hebrew dates back at least as far as Moses Mendelssohn, the father of the eighteenth century *Haskalah* (Jewish Enlightenment), whose Bible translation (1780–1783), written in High German but transcribed in Hebrew characters for a broad public of Jewish readers, not only marked the beginning of linguistic assimilation for Jews in Germany but also foreshadowed the linguistic "hybrids" that are beginning to emerge with greater frequency in contemporary literature (Eshel and Rokem 2013, 1).

The adoption of German and assimilation into German society that Mendelssohn's Bible translation was intended to promote did not result in a permanent rejection of Jewish languages, as is often assumed. During the early decades of the twentieth century, many post-assimilation German Jews expressed interest in Jewish languages, specifically Hebrew and Yiddish, as sources of the

Jewish tradition and cultural cohesion that they feared had "dribbled away," as Franz Kafka lamented in his famous letter to his father (Kafka 1966, 81). Kafka's Hebrew notebook is just one concrete example of the fascination with Hebrew that emerged during this period of Jewish renewal. Another more symbolic example can be found in Martin Buber's address at the 1909 Congress for the Hebrew Language in Berlin. The paladin of Jewish renewal, Buber would soon translate the Hebrew Bible into German together with Franz Rosenzweig, yet admitted defeat when called upon to speak publicly in Modern Hebrew: "Unfortunately, I must speak about the Hebrew language in a foreign tongue, as I am not able to think in the Hebrew language and I do not want to translate my thoughts, which are thought in the foreign language, into my own but less known language" (Brenner 2013, 13). Else Lasker-Schüler took a different tack when the poet Uri Zvi Greenberg requested to translate some of her poems from German into Hebrew, to which she shot back incredulously, "But I have *already* written them in Hebrew" (Brenner 1996, 138). Kafka, Buber and Lasker-Schüler regarded Hebrew as their "own" tongue, even if it was less familiar than German, the "foreign language" in which they spoke and wrote exclusively. As they grappled with questions of native language and national identity, they turned to Hebrew as an imagined language of origin while facing the conundrum that Kafka summed up as "the impossibility of writing German and the impossibility of writing differently" (Kafka 1977, 289).

While early twentieth-century German-Jewish writers expressed fascination with Hebrew as the wellspring of a dormant Jewishness, Hebrew (and Yiddish) writers of the interwar years were strongly influenced by German literature and culture. Writers such as Michah Yosef Berdichevsky, Hayim Nahman Bialik, S.Y. Agnon, Avraham Ben-Yitzhak and Leah Goldberg (to name just a few) wrote and published not only in German-speaking cities but also about these cities. A flurry of new research on interwar Hebrew and Yiddish cultures identifies Berlin and Vienna as two leading centers, or temporary "enclaves," in which an expressly diasporic Jewish literary modernism developed (Brenner 2015; Nethanel 2013; Pinsker 2011; Schachter 2011; Seelig 2016). Scholars interested in the transnational, multilingual nature of Jewish modernism increasingly resist the division of Hebrew and Yiddish literatures, their exclusion from the study of European modernism, and the conflation of Hebrew with Zionism and the State of Israel. Their work casts doubt on the monocultural nationalist narrative that has governed the study of Hebrew culture by drawing attention to the various European centers in which Hebrew literature developed alongside Jewish writing in Yiddish and other languages during the first half of the twentieth century.

This new body of scholarship reflects a growing discourse on "diasporic Hebrew," a concept that celebrates intercultural exchange and linguistic pluralism. Insofar as it contributes to this discourse, German-Hebrew Studies corresponds to another area of Hebrew literary scholarship that rejects monolithic conceptions of "Israeli Hebrew" by drawing attention not only to lost European heritage languages such as German, Yiddish and Russian but also to the suppressed heritage languages of Mizrahim (Jews of Middle Eastern and North African descent), especially Arabic and Ladino (Hochberg 2007; Levy 2014). With increasing scholarly efforts to expose a wealth of cultural and linguistic origins and influences the multiplicity of voices that make up Israeli society slowly is coming into clearer view.

The Holocaust of European Jewry changed the relationship between German and Hebrew cultures irrevocably. But the relationship was not cut short. German-Jewish culture persisted after World War II in the newly formed state of Israel, with German-Jewish writers and thinkers such as Werner Kraft, Gershom Scholem, Else Lasker-Schüler and Ilana Shmueli continuing to write German in the Jewish State. Some writers who once had expressed a purely symbolic fascination with Hebrew actually began writing bilingually in both German and Hebrew, such as Arieh Ludwig Strauss, whose oeuvre has garnered renewed interest in recent years (Barouch 2016; Seelig 2016). Strauss is remembered not only as a bilingual poet but also as a prominent Hölderlin scholar and influential teacher; his lectures on Hebrew literature and world literature at the Hebrew University of Jerusalem strongly impacted the next generation of Hebrew writers, including Yehuda Amichai, Tuvia Rübner and Dan Pagis, likewise native German speakers. Although these writers are associated with the so-called "Statehood Generation," the first crop of Hebrew writers to produce ostensibly "national literature" in vernacular Hebrew, their abiding attachment to German betrays the inherent limitations of such designations (Gold 2008; Rokem 2010).

Whereas early statehood writers often concealed German behind a veneer of "native" Hebrew, more recent Israeli fiction reflects the process of coming to terms with Germany and the German language and its relationship to Israeli culture. The semi-autobiographical protagonists of Chaim Be'er's *Lifney ha-makom* ("Upon a certain place," 2007) and Yoram Kaniuk's *Der letzte Berliner* ("The last Berliner," published in German translation in 2001 and then in the original Hebrew in 2004) travel to Germany as representatives of Israeli culture, where they are forced to grapple with the German-Jewish past. The experimental novelist Yoel Hoffmann, meanwhile, demonstrates the manner in which German has been pushed to the margins of Israeli society by incorporating German words and phrases (alongside Yiddish, Arabic and the occasional Hungarian) – accompanied by explanatory notes in the margins – directly into his ostensibly monolingual Hebrew texts (Barzilai 2014).

Writing "between" Hebrew and German, or between Israel and Germany, these writers represent the movement of languages across linguistic and national borders. This brings us to the third area to which German-Hebrew Studies contributes, namely the study of migration, diaspora and transnationalism. Tomer Gardi's *Broken German* exemplifies the fluidity of linguistic and national borders in the age of globalization. The epigraph of this essay, which was included in Gardi's submission for the Bachmann Prize, is on the surface a simple (albeit grammatically flawed) statement about language, but in fact it refers to the aftereffects of ongoing migration, the repeated transmutation of the mother tongue (*Muttersprache*) from one generation to the next in an age defined by mobility and mass migration. As the epigraph suggests, the seemingly narrow topic of German-Hebrew exchange may be regarded as emblematic of a much larger wave of linguistic migration and subsequent cultural transformation. Perhaps "subfield," then, is not the correct term, since German-Hebrew Studies contributes to several different disciplinary categories while also calling into question the ways in which these categories are demarcated and divided. Indeed, what makes German-Hebrew Studies so rich is that fact that it reflects on the crossing of borders while itself crossing borders.

3 Between Berlin and Tel Aviv

German-Hebrew exchange is not merely a topic of academic fascination but rather a thriving aspect of contemporary German and Israeli cultural life, particularly in the wake of increasing Israeli migration to Germany, especially to Berlin. Indeed, "Israelis in Berlin" has become a kind of catchphrase in its own right, eliciting a wide range of reactions in the media. Some Israeli politicians and public personalities have lambasted young Israelis for choosing to "return" to the country responsible for the destruction of twentieth century Jewish life in Europe. Former Minister of Finance Yair Lapid, for instance, expressed utter incredulity and disdain over the willingness of these young migrants to "throw the only country the Jews have in the trash just because life is easier in Berlin." Evidently, the choice of Berlin has touched a nerve. As *Ha'aretz* editor Aluf Benn commented sardonically, the Israeli establishment sees Israeli immigration to the German capital, of all places, as "the ultimate failure of Zionism" (Rudoren 2014). This tension reveals a growing rift between mounting Zionist nationalism and the desperation and disenchantment of a generation of secular young Israelis who associate Germany with future opportunities rather than with the traumatic past.

The controversy provoked by Israeli migration to Berlin points to another rift in Israeli society, namely between *Ashkenazim* (Jews of European origin) and *Mizrahim* (Jews of Middle Eastern and North African origin). *Mizrahi* Jews residing in Berlin feel alienated by the incendiary critiques of a Jewish "return" to Germany, since they descend not from Holocaust victims or survivors but from Jews who emigrated or were exiled from Muslim lands, for whom Arabic and Ladino, rather than German and Yiddish, represent repressed heritage languages. Mati Shemoelof, a *Mizrahi* journalist, activist and writer based in Berlin, co-organizes the Poetic Hafla ("party" in Arabic), a monthly event for multilingual literary readings, spoken-word poetry and interdisciplinary performance art that takes place at various venues throughout the city. Organized by Israelis but attended by guests of various national backgrounds, the Poetic Hafla reflects Shemoelof's belief that Berlin is not simply a city once conquered by Hitler or divided by a menacing wall but rather a liberal environment in which linguistic, cultural and religious identities can be negotiated openly, indeed, a city where walls can and should be toppled. Berlin, for *Mizrahi* writers like Shemoelof, must not be reduced to its blighted past but rather viewed as the city of a hopeful future.

It is not only the city but also its language that is capturing the imagination of a growing cohort of young Israeli writers, some of whom take up German as a language of composition, as in the case of Tomer Gardi, or as a metalinguistic preoccupation. Whereas Gardi writes "broken German" in Latin letters, Shemoelof experiments with code-switching, occasionally incorporating transliterated German fragments into his Hebrew writing:

איש שרייבה היבראיש
איש כותב עברית
דו פראגסט וארום שרייבה איש היבראיש אין ברלין
וואלה, אני לא יודע

[Ish shreibeh Hebreyish/ A man writes Hebrew/ Du fragst varum shreibeh/ ish hebrayish in Berlin/ *Wallah*, I don't know] (Shemoelof 2016)

Another Israeli poet, Almog Behar, who does not actually speak German but claims a connection to it as one of the languages of his grandparents (along with Arabic, Ladino, and Dutch), incorporates quotes from Hebrew translations of German texts by writers such as Gershom Scholem and Paul Celan as part of his ongoing critique of "Israeli Hebrew" and the suppression of Jewish heritage languages. Not unlike the early twentieth century German Jews who felt a connection to Hebrew despite their limited familiarity with the language, contemporary Israeli writers like Behar claim a connection to German despite their tenuous grasp of the language.

In a sense, Israeli writers looking to German and Germany are working to salvage the multilingual tradition of their predecessors. This is how Tal

Hever-Chybowski describes the mission of his Berlin- and Paris-based Hebrew literary journal, *Mikan ve'eylakh* ("From here onward"), whose mission statement heralds "the return of diasporic Hebrew to here – to Europe, to Ashkenaz, to Berlin – not just to the site of its destruction but also a place that was once one of the greatest centers of the diasporic republic of Hebrew letters." Hever-Chybowski views his journal as part of a broader movement of "non-hegemonic, intercultural, interlingual literature."[2] In a similar vein, the Berlin-based journal *Aviv*, also founded in 2016 by a German, Hanno Hauenstein, and an Israeli, Itamar Gov, is aimed at "renew[ing] the relationship between the Hebrew and German language and culture" by showcasing art, literature, and journalism that present "linguistic diversity as enrichment and bilingualism as a gift."[3]

Well before the new crop of "Israeli Berliners" began writing in and about German, German writers of both Jewish and non-Jewish origin began to investigate Hebrew and Israel as a kind of imagined second home. For example, Maxim Biller's short story "Land der Väter und Verräter" ("Country of fathers and perpetrators," 1994), set in Haifa's Mount Carmel neighborhood, seamlessly incorporates Hebrew words such as "Shuk" (market) and "Allijah" (immigration to Israel), while Katharina Hacker's *Tel Aviv: Eine Stadterzählung* ("Tel Aviv: tale of a city," 1997) conveys intimate details of living in Tel Aviv from the perspective of a young, non-Jewish German woman. The increased mobility of Germans and Israelis and attendant decline of inherited stigmas have facilitated new forms of bilingual exploration and expression. For these cultural nomads, the relationship between German and Hebrew is no longer confined to conventional binaries of victim/perpetrator and exile/homeland, but rather serves as a source of creativity and transnational identity.

While contemporary literature produced in German and Hebrew tends to expose a two-sided trajectory between disparate cultural spaces, cross-cultural collaboration and inter-linguistic exchange increasingly takes place in the world of cinema. A watershed achievement in this field was Eytan Fox's *Walk on Water* (*Lalekhet 'al ha-mayim*, 2004), produced in Israel and premiered to great acclaim at the Berlin Film Festival. The film tells the fictional story of Eyal, an Israeli Mossad agent hired to assassinate a former Nazi, who poses as a tour guide and befriends his target's grandchildren, Axel and Pia (Pia now lives on a kibbutz, and Axel has arrived to visit her from Germany). Although the film unfolds primarily in English, the dialogue often weaves seamlessly between German and Hebrew.

---

2 See the mission statement on the journal's website: http://mikanve.net/wp/ (10 January 2017).
3 See the description on the magazine's website: http://avivmag.com/en/ (10 January 2017).

In the last ten years since Fox's success, there has been a veritable renaissance of German-Israeli film co-productions, many dedicated to exploring postwar German-Israeli relations, including Arnon Goldfinger's *The Flat* (2012), Ester Amrami's *Anderswo* (2014) and Mor Kaplansky's *Café Nagler* (2016). Perhaps the most interesting of these films in terms of linguistic and cultural exchange is *Anderswo* (meaning "elsewhere"), about a romantic relationship between Israeli Noa (Neta Riskin) and German Jörg (Golo Euler). The relationship is put under pressure when Noa leaves their home in Berlin to visit her ailing grandmother and Jörg follows her unannounced. Although he manages to find common ground with Noa's mother (played by Hanna Laszlo) thanks to a mishmash of German and Yiddish, he is tone deaf with respect to Israeli gallows humor. When Noa's brother, Dudi, mentions that the grandfather of the German football star Bastian Schweinsteiger died in Auschwitz, Jörg is perplexed. "He fell from a watchtower," says Dudi without cracking a smile, eliciting nothing but a blank stare. "It was a joke, man," Dudi quickly adds.

Although the relationship between Noa and Jörg survives such awkward moments, cultural tensions persist and some things are inevitably lost in translation. The culture gap forms the heart of Noa's floundering academic research project, a "dictionary of untranslatable words," featured throughout the film in a series of short linguistic "excursions" in which immigrants from China, Korea, South America, Russia and Israel attempt to explain untranslatable words from their native languages. Yet, as the movie clearly demonstrates, this gap also serves as fertile ground for artistic engagement and the creation of new narratives and works of art – indeed, the very fabric of an emerging German-Hebrew, German-Israeli shared life and culture. While the generation of Schweinsteiger's grandparents may have lived or served in the grim locations where many Jews were murdered, their grandchildren and great-grandchildren tell each other stories about their divided and shared histories, creating herewith new literature, cinema and even new families. Katharina Hacker's more recent novels, *Eine Art Liebe* (2003) and *Skip* (2015) are just one example of what is a clearly discernable, broader trajectory.

4 Chapter overview

The following essays are divided into two parts. The first part, "German-Hebrew Exchange in Modernist Literature," concentrates on twentieth-century German-Hebrew literary exchange, while Part Two takes up contemporary topics. The essays gathered in Part One coalesce around questions of translation, bilingualism and linguistic migration. Abigail Gilman's contribution spans the Enlightenment era to the early twentieth century in its comparison of Moses Mendelssohn's and Franz Rosenzweig's translations of the medieval Hebrew poet Yehuda Halevi. Gillman argues that working with poetry, specifically with Halevi's most famous poem, the Zionide, shaped both philosophers' vocation as translators and served as a stepping-stone on the path that led both to translate the Hebrew Bible.

Several of the essays that follow take up the topic of self-translation. Using newly discovered materials from the archive of Avraham Ben-Yitzhak (born Avraham Sonne), Maya Barzilai explores the interplay of German and Hebrew in the poet's modest yet seminal oeuvre. By tracing common motifs in poetic drafts and fragments produced in both languages, Barzilai demonstrates an "interlingual poetic dialogue" that reveals a profound tension between fin-de-siècle Viennese decadence and the Zionist conception of Hebrew as the "language of revival." Another poet whose archive betrays a continuous, non-linear movement between German and Hebrew is Dan Pagis, the subject of Na'ama Rokem's essay. Through close-reading of two archival documents written in German, a translation of the poem "In the Laboratory" (*Ba-ma'abadah*) and a letter addressed to the Austrian poet Ernst Jandl that includes two poems of homage, Rokem offers an intimate portrait of Pagis's bilingual "laboratory," her metaphor for the process of self-translation that creates space for experimentation, uncertain outcomes and multiple contingent paths. The process of self-translation is likewise the focus of Rachel Seelig's essay on Tuvia Rübner, a contemporary and close friend of Pagis. Seelig takes as her point of departure the concept of "stuttering" as both a leitmotif and an aesthetic strategy that calls into question monolithic notions of fluency and challenges the conventional binary categories of translation theory.

While the above essays focus specifically on translation and bilingualism in the works of individual poets, two of the essays in Part One examine cultural-historical events and trends through the genres of memoir and book history. Giddon Ticotsky presents a new reading of Leah Goldberg's *Encounter with a Poet* (*Mifgash 'im meshorer*, 1952), inspired by the life and work of Avraham Ben Yitzhak, as a prism for the encounter of East European Jews with German and Austrian modernism during the first of the twentieth century. He argues that Jewish writers who hailed from the "periphery" of the German *Kulturkreis* saw themselves as scions of *Vera Europa* (the true Europe), identified strongly with German culture and sought to preserve it as part of their collective memory. Stefanie Mahrer turns to the wider field of book publishing as an index for German-Jewish cultural continuity in a transnational context. Her study of the Salman Schocken Publishing House (*Schocken Verlag*) traces the venture's trajectory from Berlin to New York and Jerusalem and discusses its role in promoting Jewish cultural literacy, facilitating collaborations between Jewish publishers and non-Jewish artisans and resisting the policies of the National Socialist Regime. Finally, the last essay in

Part One provides a kind of poetic coda and spiritual mediation on bilingualism, the loss of language, loss and mourning. Focusing on the lexically distinct yet vocally similar words איכה and *Ach*, Galili Shahar considers the ways in which words of despair, in both Hebrew and German, are reduced to mere sounds, cries and breath. The pairing of these words, which are utterly emptied of meaning, allows German and Hebrew to meet, as Shahar puts it, "at a place of lingual poverty."

In the second part, "German-Hebrew Encounters in the Arts Today," we move from discussions of literary modernism and twentieth century German-Jewish and Israeli culture into the twenty-first century and recent discourses surrounding contemporary art. Ruth Ginsburg proposes a fresh approach to the poet Almog Behar's notion of "multilingual Hebrew," a concept that implicitly critiques hegemonic "Israeli Hebrew" by remaining open to the past and to silenced Jewish languages. While most scholars interested in Behar's work have emphasized his *Mizrahi* origins and critique of the suppression of Arabic as a Jewish language, Ginsburg examines two poems that betray Behar's relationship to German, a language he does not speak but that he regards as an equally integral aspect of his family history, the site of collective memory and acknowledged rupture. Freddie Rokem transports us into The Ruth Kanner Theatre Group's experimental theater performance, *The Hebrew Notebook – And Other Stories by Franz Kafka*, commissioned in 2013 in honor of the 120th anniversary of the National Library of Israel, where the notebook is now housed. A non-traditional performance consisting of recitation (in both German and Hebrew), interactive performance and collective storytelling, *The Hebrew Notebook*, Rokem argues, investigates the mechanisms of translation between languages and cultural contexts while offering a cultural critique of the dominant Israeli Hebrew culture.

The focal point of Yael Almog's essay is Yael Bartana's experimental film trilogy, *And Europe Will Be Stunned*, which mirrors the classic Zionist theme of "return" to the Land of Israel in its portrayal of an imagined "Jewish return to Europe." Almog shows how Bartana, an Israeli artist based in Berlin and Amsterdam, critiques established Zionist narratives and memorial practices while taking part in the broader discourse on migration, integration and xenophobia currently underway in Europe. Transnational artistic production is a central theme of Amir Eshel's essay on the Israeli artist Dani Karavan, whose work combines sculpture and architecture with natural topography and literary sources, often from the Hebrew Bible. Focusing on some of Karavan's major public works in Germany from the 1970s to the present, Eshel examines the role of Hebrew names in facilitating a meaningful aesthetic experience that invites the viewer to reflect on the German and Jewish past as well as on broader ethical and political dilemmas of modern history. Drawing on the philosophies of Martin Heidegger and

Hannah Arendt, Eshel presents Karavan's works in Germany as a crucial expression of the relationship between German and Hebrew and as a case study for investigating the German-Hebrew junction in the arts. Both Almog and Eshel show how politically aware and internationally active artists such as Bartana and Karavan not only erect bridges between Israeli and German/European cultures but also move beyond hermetic discussions of national identity to take part in the transnational discourse on the politics of memory.

The volume concludes with previously unpublished translations of texts by two leading representatives of the new Israeli culture in Berlin. The first is the introduction to the inaugural issue of the Berlin- and Paris-based Hebrew literary journal *Mikan ve'eylakh* (From here onward), written by Founding Editor Tal Hever-Chybowski. This programmatic essay endorses the concept of "world Hebrew" (*'ivrit 'olamit*), a term that encompasses both spatial and temporal dimensions (the Hebrew adjective *'olami* means "worldwide," "universal" and "eternal") and highlights the reach of the Hebrew language and Hebrew literature throughout the world and across generations. Calling into question "the myth of the death of Hebrew," Hever-Chybowski makes a powerful plea to salvage the diasporic origins and legacy of Hebrew by celebrating the continuity of literary production in cities like Paris, London, New York and Berlin. Pride of place is given to Berlin, the cradle of *Ashkenaz*, not only as a historical site of cultural transfer and transformation since the period of the *Haskalah* but also as the location where most of the essays and literary works gathered in the journal were written and edited.

The volume closes with a literary contribution by Mati Shemoelof (published here in English translation), an excerpt from his novel in progress, *The Berlin Prize for Hebrew Literature*. Whereas Hever-Chybowski's essay concentrates on the relationship between Hebrew and the languages of *Ashkenaz*, German and Yiddish, Shemoelof's piece introduces us to the inner world of Chezi Morad, a Berlin-based Israeli writer of Iraqi origins who feels snubbed by the Eurocentric mainstream Israeli literary establishment, and his German girlfriend, Helena, who is coping with the psychological aftermath of a miscarriage. Shemoelof's writing takes us into the most intimate quarters of this striving and struggling Berlin couple, offering a restrained portrait of love and loss, compassion and inevitable misunderstanding. Taken together, Hever-Chybowski's essay and Shemoelof's literary excerpt reveal the dynamism and diversity of Hebrew culture in Berlin, which spans not only a vast historical spectrum, extending from the days of Moses Mendelssohn to the present, but also the ethnic and cultural spectrum that encompasses Hebrew, German, Yiddish and Arabic, literary languages cultivated in the diaspora and nourished by one another.

The essays gathered in this volume do not exhaust the parameters of the broad, emerging field of German-Hebrew Studies, but they gesture at the depth and breadth of an ongoing and constantly evolving encounter. Indeed, the twentieth and twenty-first centuries alone account for four generations of writers and artists whose creative consciousness bears the imprint of multilingual, transnational exchange between German and Hebrew, two languages and cultures that are anything but separate.

Works cited

Alon, Tal. "The most comprehensive survey about Israelis in Germany reinforces the image: secular, educated – and leftwing." *Spitz Magazine* (December 2015). http://spitzmag.de/webonly/7238 (9 January 2017).

Barouch, Lina. *Between German and Hebrew: The Counterlanguages of Gershom Scholem, Werner Kraft and Ludwig Strauss*. Berlin, Boston & Jerusalem: De Gruyter & Magnes University Press, 2016.

Barzilai, Maya. "Translation on the Margins: Avraham Ben Yitzhak and Yoel Hoffmann." *The Journal of Jewish Identities* 7.1 (2014): 109–128.

Brenner, Michael. *The Renaissance of Jewish Culture in Weimar Germany*. New Haven: Yale University Press, 1996.

Brenner, Michael. "Between Triumph and Tragedy: The Use and Misuse of Hebrew in Germany from Mendelssohn to Eichmann." *Prooftexts: A Journal of Jewish Literary History* 33.1 (Winter 2013): 9–24.

Brenner, Naomi. *Lingering Bilingualism: Modern Hebrew and Yiddish Literatures in Contact*. Syracuse: Syracuse University Press, 2015.

Dohrn, Verena, and Gertrud Pickhan. *Transit und Transformation: Osteuropäisch-jüdische Migranten in Berlin 1918–1939*. Göttingen: Wallstein Verlag, 2010.

Eshel, Amir. *Zeit der Zäsur: Jüdische Lyriker im Angesicht der Shoah*. Heidelberg: Universitätsverlag Heidelberg, 1999.

Eshel, Amir. "Paul Celan's Other: History, Poetics, and Ethics." *New German Critique* 91 (Winter 2004): 57–77.

Eshel, Amir, and Na'ama Rokem. "German and Hebrew: Histories of a Conversation." *Prooftexts: A Journal of Jewish Literary History* 33.1 (Winter 2013): 1–8.

Estraikh, Gennady, and Mikhail Krutikov. *Yiddish in Weimar Berlin: At the Crossroads of Diaspora Politics and Culture*. Legenda: Oxford, 2010.

Galchen, Rivka. "Imagine That: The Profound Empathy of Yoko Tawada." *The New York Times*, 27 October 2016. http://www.nytimes.com/interactive/2016/10/30/magazine/yoko-tawada.html?_r=0 (5 January 2017).

Gardi, Tomer. *Broken German*. Graz & Wien: Droschl, 2016.

Gold, Nili Scharf. *Yehuda Amichai: The Making of Israel's National Poet*. Waltham: Brandeis University Press, 2008.

Halperin, Liora. *Babel in Zion: Jews, Nationalism, and Language Diversity in Palestine, 1920–1948*. New Haven: Yale University Press, 2015.

Hochberg, Gil. *Jews, Arabs, and the Limits of Separatist Imagination*. Princeton: Princeton University Press, 2007.

Jankowsky, Karen. "'German' Literature Contested: The 1991 Ingeborg-Bachmann-Prize Debate, 'Cultural Diversity,' and Emine Sevgi Özdamar." *The German Quarterly* 70.3 (Summer 1997): 261–276.

Kafka, Franz. *Letter to his Father. Brief an den Vater*. Trans. Ernst Kaiser and Eithne Wilkins. New York: Schocken Books, 1966.

Kafka, Franz. *Letters to Friends, Family, and Editors*. Trans. Richard and Clara Winston. New York: Schocken Books, 1977.

Katsberger, Klaus. "Wir schaffen das!" *Die Zeit,* August 19, 2016. http://www.zeit.de/kultur/literatur/2016-08/literatur-migration-tomer-gardi-broken-german (9 March 2017).

Levy, Lital. *Poetic Trespass: Writing between Hebrew and Arabic in Israel/Palestine*. Princeton: Princeton University Press, 2014.

Nethanel, Lilach. "David Vogel's Lost Hebrew Novel, *Viennese Romance*." *Prooftexts: A Journal of Jewish Literary History* 33.3 (Fall 2013): 307–332.

Oz-Salzberger, Fania. *Israelis in Berlin*. 1. Aufl. Frankfurt am Main: Jüdischer Verlag im Suhrkamp-Verlag, 2001.

Pinsker, Shachar. *Literary Passports: The Making of Modernist Hebrew Fiction in Europe*. Stanford, CA: Stanford University Press, 2011.

Rokem, Na'ama. "German-Hebrew Encounters in the Poetry and Correspondence of Yehuda Amichai and Paul Celan." *Prooftexts: A Journal of Jewish Literary History* 30.1 (Winter 2010): 97–127.

Rudoren, Jodi. "An Exodus from Israel to Germany, a Young Nation's Fissures Show." *The New York Times,* October 16, 2014. https://www.nytimes.com/2014/10/17/world/middleeast/in-exodus-from-israel-to-berlin-young-nations-fissures-show.html?_r=0 (9 March 2017).

Schachter, Allison. *Diasporic Modernisms: Hebrew and Yiddish Literature in the Twentieth Century*. New York: Oxford University Press, 2011.

Seelig, Rachel. *Strangers in Berlin: Modern Jewish Literature between East and West, 1919–1933*. Ann Arbor: University of Michigan Press, 2016.

Shemoelof, Mati. *Germanit shvurah fun ayn yuden dikhter* ("Broken German by a Jewish poet"). *Ha'okets,* September 23, 2016. http://www.haokets.org/2016/09/23/ דיכטאר-יודן-אין-פון-שבורה-גרמנית / (9 March 2017).

Weiss, Yfaat. "Rückkehr in den Elfenbeinturm: Deutsch an der Hebräischen Universität." *Naharaim: Zeitschrift für deutsch - jüdische Literatur und Kulturgeschichte* 8.2 (2014): 227–245.

Yair, Gad. *Love is not Praktish: The Israeli Look at Germany* (Hebrew). Tel Aviv: Kibbutz Meuchad/Poalim, 2015.

Part One: **German-Hebrew Exchange in Modernist Literature**

Abigail Gillman
Not like Cherries, but like Peaches: Mendelssohn and Rosenzweig Translate Yehuda Halevi's "Ode to Zion"

אני כנור לשיריך I am a harp to your songs

In my research on the history and practice of translation in German Jewish society, I relish the (rare) occasions when translators explicitly address the choices of their predecessors. At such moments, translators who pride themselves on their originality reveal an awareness of their historicity. A famous example is Franz Rosenzweig's provocative essay, "Der Ewige: Mendelssohn und der Gottesname" of 1929, in which he argues, in essence, that Moses Mendelssohn *got God's Name wrong* in his Pentateuch translation of 1780–83: the proper name of the biblical God (Tetragrammaton) should not be rendered *der Ewige* (the Eternal One), since this appellation is too abstract, too Calvinist, too cold.[1] Rosenzweig's dispute with Mendelssohn had a polemical subtext: rejecting *der Ewige*, which had been adopted in so many subsequent Jewish Bibles and prayer books, was part of an effort to dissociate the Buber and Rosenzweig Bible translation from its precursors, and distinguish their method from the scholarly and aesthetic approaches to translation that had dominated the one-hundred-fifty-year-long history of German Jewry.

A less well-known chapter in the dialogue between these two towering philosopher-translators of Hebrew scripture concerns their reception of a third figure: the towering philosopher-poet of medieval al-Andalus, Yehuda Halevi. This essay takes as its starting point the irresistible fact, noted as such by Dominique Bourel, that both Mendelssohn and Rosenzweig published German translations of Halevi's most famous poem, the Zionide ציון הלא תשאלי (hereafter referred to as Ode to Zion; Bourel 2007, 145–146). Comparing their translations of just the first eight lines of Halevi's poem enables us to flesh out the radically different approaches to translation which also underlie their German versions of the Hebrew Bible – two of the most famous and influential Bible translations in Jewish history.

The cherries and peaches in my title come from a passage towards the end of Rosenzweig's *Nachwort* (Afterword) – the essay included as an afterword to both editions of poems by Halevi in German. Rosenzweig wonders how

---

[1] Originally published in Elbogen and Bergmann 1929, 96–114; also published in *Zweistromland*.

he might lead the reader to enjoy the poems not like cherries, but like peaches; "nicht wie Kirschen, sondern wie Pfirsiche":

> Wie konnte ich den Leser dieser Übersetzungssammlung verhindern, sich als Leser zu benehmen, mit anderen Worten, wie konnte ich ihn dazu bringen, die Gedichte nicht wie Kirschen, sondern wie Pfirsiche zu verspeisen, also nicht das nächste schon anzufangen, wenn er noch das vorige kaum herunter hätte, sondern jedes hübsch einzeln und mit Bedacht und mit der Vorstellung: so bald gibts nun vielleicht keins wieder.
>
> [...]
>
> Also den Leser aus einem Leser und Vertilger zu einem Gast und Freund des Gedichts zu machen. (Rosenzweig 1927, 167–168)
>
> [How could I prevent the reader of this collection of translations from behaving as a reader, in other words, how could I bring him to consume the poems not like cherries but like peaches, that is not to begin the next one when he still has hardly finished the previous one and with deliberation and with the idea: perhaps there will not be one like this again so soon.
>
> Thus, to change the reader from a reader and a consumer into a guest and friend of the poem.] (Galli 184)

Rosenzweig urges his reader not to read Halevi's poems one after the other, in haste, but to savor and "befriend" each one. Cherries, moreover, are native to Germany; peaches were an imported fruit, like the exotic lemons in Mignon's song from Goethe's novel.[2] A translator who favors peaches over cherries prefers a foreignizing approach to a domesticating one – the difference, in a word, between Rosenzweig and Mendelssohn. But I also wish to call attention to something important which Mendelssohn and Rosenzweig have in common. Both cherries and peaches have a hard kernel, which corresponds to the religious core of Halevi's artistry. Albeit in different ways, both translators sought to acquaint their readers with this "God-kissed" poet, to use Heinrich Heine's phrase, this "great Jewish poet in Hebrew," as Rosenzweig called him; and, through poetry, to Judaism.[3]

*****

---

[2] I thank Liliane Weissberg for this observation. Mingon's song begins, "Kennst du das Land, wo die Zitronen blühn, / Im dunkeln Laub die Gold-Orangen glühn, / Ein sanfter Wind vom blauen Himmel weht, / Die Myrte still und hoch der Lorbeer steht, / Kennst du es wohl? / Dahin! Dahin /Möcht ich mit dir, o mein Geliebter, ziehn!" Mignon is a character in Goethe's novel *Wilhelm Meisters Lehrjahre* (1795–1796).

[3] I thank Peter Cole for the idea of "Judaism through poetry."

Jews the world over admired and engaged with the medieval poet, physician and philosopher known to us as Yehuda Halevi (Toledo, 1075 – Alexandria, 1141). Halevi is regarded as the exemplary Hebrew poet, and mythologized as the first Jew who travelled to the Land of Israel not simply as a pilgrim, "to visit Jerusalem and the other holy sites and return, but rather to die there and mingle his body with the stones and soil of the land of Israel" (Scheindlin 2008, 4). Until the nineteenth century, Halevi was known for the Arabic philosophical dialogue *Kitab-al-Khazari*[4] (translated into Hebrew as *Sefer ha-Kuzari* in 1506), and also, by the Ode to Zion, which had been incorporated into the Ashkenazi liturgy for the Ninth of Av. Only in the mid-nineteenth century was the corpus of religious and secular poetry – Zion poems, wine songs, riddles, panegyrics and epithalamia, written in Hebrew in Arabic genres and meter – collected and published by Samuel David Luzatto. Translation into a vast array of languages proliferated. One of Halevi's most recent English translators, Peter Cole, writes that "Yehuda HaLevi is perhaps the most famous and certainly the most revered of all the medieval poets"; "[t]he poetry Halevi wrote is prized for its fusion of a pure Hebrew lyricism and religio-historical concerns" (2007, 143, 144). The poems lament past troubles and also contemporary ones. As well acquainted as he was with Arabic and Castilian poetry, "his muse spoke to him in the old and sacred language of the Bible,"[5] and his poems exemplify the *shibbutz* (German: *Musivstil*), "the use of recognizable scriptural verses or fragments of verse," whether as "charged" literary allusions or more "neutral" ornaments in poems (Cole 2007, 542–543).[6] Late in his career, Halevi developed reservations about the Jewish adoption of Arabic poetics. "He continued composing in the classical style in the last years of his life, but also began experimenting with an alternative poetics that would de-Arabize Hebrew verse and return it to exclusively Jewish sources" (Cole 2007, 144).

Like many Halevi elegies, the poem under discussion "combin[es] an ode to Zion with a lament for its fall," even as it ends with a prayer for the redemption of Jerusalem (Weinberger 1998, 131). It "won special distinction and many imitators" throughout Jewish history who copied its form and in particular the rhetorical question with which the poem begins (Weinberger 1998, 131; also 186 and 400).

---

4 The complete title is *The Book of Refutation and Proof in Support of the Abased Religion*.
5 Gottheil 1906. In this respect Halevi was an heir to Saadiah Gaon, who also composed liturgy that emphasized biblical language (rather than poetic embellishments, rabbinic sources and midrashim, and folklore, thought to be more entertaining to the congregation), and whose hymns contained didactic elements and philosophical themes.
6 See Cole's informative explanation of the technique in his Glossary (Cole 2007).

Among Ashkenazi Jews, the Ode to Zion was the best-known of the *kinot* (dirges or elegies lamenting historical persecutions and martyrdoms). It was also widely known during the Ottoman period, in South Asia and the Mediterranean Basin. French-German poets imitated Halevi in their dirges written after the murder of Jews in the Rhineland in the twelfth century. The most famous Jerusalem song of the twentieth century, Naomi Shemer's "Yerushalayim Shel Zahav" (Jerusalem of Gold) of 1967, crafted its refrain from the eighth line of Halevi's Ode: *ha-lo' le-khol shirayikh, 'ani kinor;* am I not, for all your songs, a harp?

Among German Jewish intellectuals, our two translators' fascination with Yehuda Halevi was hardly anomalous. From the beginning of the *Haskalah*, Halevi took on an additional role as the most famous representative of Sephardic Judaism that became the adopted heritage, the usable past *par excellence*, of modern German Jewry. His work and biography touched on, or directly influenced, the worlds of liturgy, philosophy, poetry, classical religious thought and popular literature, as well as debates over the role of Hebrew in bilingual Jewish diaspora and Zionism. The German Jewish engagement with medieval Hebrew poetry was part of a quest for new paradigms of Jewish cultural production in the German language. As Ismar Schorsch argues (with particular reference to synagogue liturgy), "Without the embrace of Sephardic culture, the rebellion against Ashkenaz was hardly possible"; drawing inspiration from abroad made it possible to create a rupture with the immediate, local past (1994, 78). What this means for our purposes is that between Mendelssohn's translation of 1755 and Rosenzweig's of 1922 there existed an enormous corpus by nineteenth-century Hebraists and scholars of *Wissenschaft des Judentums* who translated and edited medieval Spanish-Hebrew poems and *piyyutim* (liturgical poems) and regarded them as superior to their native Ashkenazi *piyyutim*.[7] Groundbreaking publications included Michael Sachs' 1845 collection, *Die religiöse Poesie der Juden in Spanien* (2nd ed. Berlin 1901), and the very first German-language divan: Abraham Geiger's *Divan des Casteliers Abu'l-Hassan Juda ha-Levi* (Breslau 1851; Schirmann 1938–1939, 360–367). The roster of scholarly works noted in Heinrich Brody's preface to *Die neuhebräische Dichterschule der Spanish-Arabischen Epoche* (Leipzig 1905) includes pioneering studies by Delitszch, Dukes, Zunz, Kaempf, and Sulzbach. In Berlin in 1894, the Hebrew periodical of *Ha-ḥevra mekitze nirdamim* (The Society to Awaken the Sleepers) began to publish Brody's editions of the poems in consecutive volumes. By 1920, in Chaim Schirmann's estimate, there were seventeen different German translations of the Ode to Zion. Halevi's overall import

---

[7] Ismar Schorsch argues that this was part of the effort to introduce the Sephardic pronunciation of Hebrew into the new German synagogue (1994, 76–78).

in German Jewish culture may be summed up by Gustav Karpeles' paean in the preface to an 1893 edition of the Diwan (which included two different renderings of the Ode to Zion):

> In *Jehudah b. Samuel Halevi* (arabisch Abul Hassan ibn Allavi, 1086) hat die Entwickelung des in der neuhebräischen Litteratur maßgebenden Princips ihren Höhepunkt erreicht; er ist das dichterisch verklärte Bild der jüdischen Volksseele in ihrem poetischen Empfinden, in ihrem geschichtlichen Ringen, in ihren patriotischen Stammesgefühlen und in ihrem weltgeschichtlichen Martyrium ohne Gleichen. (Karpeles 1893, 1)

> [In Yehuda b. Samuel Halevi (Arabic: Abul Hassan ibn Allavi, 1086) the development of the authoritative principle of modern Hebrew literature has reached its apex; he is unrivaled as the poetically transfigured image of the Jewish people's soul in their poetical feeling, in their historical struggle, in their patriotic clannishness and in their world-historical martyrdom.]

Even within these broad trends, the translations of Mendelssohn and Rosenzweig merit special attention. Translating Halevi's poetry was a stepping-stone on the path that led these two philosophers, after philosophy, to translate the Hebrew Bible; moreover, their experience with Halevi's poetry shaped their vocations as translators. Mendelssohn's career as a Hebrew translator began with the *kinah*, followed (after a fifteen-year hiatus) by translations of biblical poetry (Song of Deborah in Judges 5, Song of Songs, Psalms) and finally, the Pentateuch. Rosenzweig began by translating liturgical texts – Grace after Meals ("Tischdank"), *Kaddish d'Rabanan* ("Lernkaddish"), *Kol Nidre*, and the Sabbath liturgy for Friday night ("die häusliche Feier"). He then turned to Halevi's poetry, translating almost one hundred poems, and following that, at Buber's invitation, he translated the Hebrew Bible.[8] To engage with poetry was the mark of a true German intellectual; no less was the aspiration to be a "harp to [Zion's] songs," in the words of the Ode to Zion, the ultimate credential of the Jewish poet. That being said, to become the German harp of Halevi's intricately crafted Hebrew songs meant something quite different for Mendelssohn and Rosenzweig. Mendelssohn approached the poem as a Romantic, amplifying its imagery and elevating its form so as to align with modern tastes. Translating Halevi gave wings to Mendelssohn's own poetic imagination; his version reads like a German ode in free rhythms. Rosenzweig took the exact opposite approach: he used translation to highlight the poem's liturgical character and theological essence. As a rule, he retained the strict meter and rhyme scheme of the original Hebrew. Rosenzweig

---

[8] On Rosenzweig's career as a translator, see Mach 1988, Galli 1995, Askani 1997, and Benjamin 2009.

aspired to transform Halevi's Diwan back into a book of *Kinot* – literature back into liturgy.

****

Moses Mendelssohn, translating in 1755, called his version of the poem "Elegie an die Burg Zion gerichtet" (elegy to the fortress of Zion); Franz Rosenzweig, translating in 1922, called it "An Zion" (to Zion). Here are the first eight lines of the sixty-eight-line elegy in Hebrew, followed by Nina Salaman's English translation:

- - v - - v- - - -v- -v-
- - v - - v- - -v- - - -

צִיּוֹן הֲלֹא תִשְׁאֲלִי לִשְׁלוֹם אֲסִירַיִךְ
דּוֹרְשֵׁי שְׁלוֹמֵךְ וְהֵם יֶתֶר עֲדָרָיִךְ
מִיָּם וּמִזְרָח וּמִצָּפוֹן וְתֵימָן
שְׁלוֹם רָחוֹק וְקָרוֹב שְׂאִי מִכֹּל עֲבָרָיִךְ
וּשְׁלוֹם אֲסִיר תַּאֲוָה נוֹתֵן דְּמָעָיו כְּטַל
חֶרְמוֹן וְנִכְסַף לְרִדְתָּם עַל הֲרָרָיִךְ
לִבְכּוֹת עֱנוּתֵךְ אֲנִי תַנִּים וְעֵת אֶחֱלֹם
שִׁיבַת שְׁבוּתֵךְ אֲנִי כִנּוֹר לְשִׁירָיִךְ

> Zion! Wilt thou not ask if peace be with thy captives
> That seek thy peace – that are the remnant of thy flocks?
> From west and east, from north and south – the greeting
> "Peace" from far and near, take thou from every side;
> And greeting from the captive of desire, giving his tears like dew
> Of Hermon, and longing to let them fall upon thine hills.
> To wail for thine affliction I am like the jackals; but when I dream
> Of the return of thy captivity, I am a harp for thy songs. (Salaman 1928, 3)

Moses Mendelssohn seems to have been the first person to translate the Ode to Zion from Hebrew into German, though he may have been acquainted with the *kinah* in Yiddish translation.[9] Of course, in the mid-eighteenth century, the Ode was not yet an anthologized poem, but a piece of liturgy. According to Werner Weinberg, Mendelssohn's translation was published five times in the eighteenth and nineteenth centuries, in liturgical and literary contexts (1985, LXXV). Though a minor work in the context of Mendelssohn's oeuvre, the "Elegie an die Burg Zion

---

[9] Werner Weinberg believes that Mendelssohn copied the poem from a book of *Kinot* from 1696. It is possible he knew it from Yiddish *Kinot* books of 1698 and 1718. See Weinberg 1985.

gerichtet" becomes significant when we consider that it bridged two periods of Mendelssohn's career when he was intensively engaged with poetry and translation: the mid 1750s, when his literary career took off, and the late 1770s and early 1780s, when he translated Hebrew scripture.

About the first of these periods: according to Altmann and Bourel, Mendelssohn originally translated the poem in 1755–1756 for the literary periodical *Beschäftigungen des Geistes und des Herzens* edited by Johann Georg Müchler (Altmann 1973, 774 n.37). Müchler, a scholar and translator, was the co-founder of a society for scholars and authors in Berlin, a circle of belles-lettres that included G.E. Lessing, Friedrich Nicolai, and poet Karl Wilhelm Ramler. "In a way," writes Altmann, "Mendelssohn had become the poet laureate of the Berlin Jewish community" (1973, 69). He twice reviewed the most important scholarly work on Hebrew poetry, Bishop Robert Lowth's *De sacra poesi Hebraeorum* (1753, 1757). Mendelssohn not only translated from Hebrew into German; he wrote in Hebrew and German and translated *into* Hebrew. He co-founded the Hebrew periodical *Kohelet musar* (preacher of morals) out of a desire to inspire a Hebrew language renaissance. In that journal, he published his Hebrew translation of the first nine stanzas of Edward Young's poem "Night Thoughts" (1742–1746). In a famous letter of 1756, Mendelssohn also expresses his desire to write poetry, if "Madame Metaphysics" would forgive him (Altmann 1973, 66). Mendelssohn was also familiar with the *Kuzari*. Adam Shear speculates that Mendelsohn studied the *Kuzari* with his teacher, the maskil Yisrael Zamosc, in Berlin in the 1740s and 50s (Shear 2008, 223–224). Mendelssohn quoted the Kuzari in *Kohelet musar*, and twenty-five years later, he incorporated Halevi's ideas about the sacred origins of the Hebrew language (originally drawn from the Midrash) in his Preface to the Pentateuch translation, as well as in other parts of his Pentateuch commentary.[10] Andrea Schatz explains that in the *Kuzari*, Mendelssohn found support for his eventual conclusion that Hebrew language texts in a bilingual Jewish diaspora would have to be accessed through translation. But what can the translation of Halevi's *kinah* teach us about Mendelssohn's evolving views of Hebrew, and of translation?

Mendelssohn's "Elegie to the City of Zion" is part paraphrase, part imitation (in John Dryden's classification). In the following excerpt, which corresponds to

---

[10] "Mendelssohn and others used the *Kuzari* to argue for the importance of Hebrew – picking up pre-maskilic uses of the *Kuzari* extending back to Renaissance Italy (but also to Ashkenazic figures such as Isserles)" (Shear 2007, 288).

the first eight lines cited above, I underline language that is not anywhere present in the Hebrew:

"Elegie an die Burg Zion gerichtet. Aus dem Hebräischen."

> Vergißt du, Zion! Der Deinen,
> Die sclavisch <u>in Fesseln ietzt schmachten</u>?
> Des Ueberrests jener <u>unschuldigen</u> Heerde,
> <u>Die vormals in deinen ruhigen Thälern geweidet</u>?
>
> Nimmst du den Frieden nicht an,
> Mit welchem sie Dich von allen Seiten begrüßen,
> <u>Dahin sie ihr Treiber zerstreuet</u>?
>
> Den Gruß eines <u>in Fesseln noch</u> hoffenden Sclaven,
> Dem <u>wimmernd</u> die Zähren, wie Tropfen
> Des <u>nächtlichen</u> Thaues auf Hermon herabrollen.
> <u>Zufrieden</u>. Könnte sein Thränenbad nur Deine <u>verlassene</u> Hügel befeuchten.
>
> <u>O! Seine Hoffnung sinket noch nicht</u>;
> Ietzt da ich dein Elend beweine,
> <u>Gleiche ich</u> der <u>nächtlichen</u> Eule,
> Und wenn mir von deiner Erlösung geträumt,
> Wird <u>mein frohes Gemüth</u>,
> Die Harfe deiner <u>freudigen Dankl</u>ieder.

Mendelssohn composed his version of 1753 in free rhythms – a style characterized by the absence of rhyme, regular verse lengths, and metrical patterns. The notion that poetic language contains its own natural rhythm was novel at the time. In fact, according to Wolfgang Kayser, it was Friedrich Klopstock who first wrote German verse in free rhythms in the 1750s, in particular for poems that address God within nature, such as the famous ode "Frühlingsfeier" of 1759 (1981, 53). Halevi's verse was written in Hebrew quantitative meters; Mendelssohn's verse is heavily dactylic ("freudigen Danklieder").

As striking as his departure from the meter are the liberties Mendelssohn took with vocabulary and imagery. The opening German words "Vergisst du, Zion! Die Deinen..?" ("Do you, Zion, forget your own...") already paraphrase the Hebrew opening words, "Do you not inquire after [the] welfare [of]."[11] Moreover,

---

[11] When Johann Gottfried Herder revises Mendelssohn's version of the poem, he takes Mendelssohn's vocabulary but composes elegiac distichs, restoring to the poem its sublime structure. He also changes the tense of the opening question ever so slightly, to wit: "Hast du vergessen der Deinen, die jammernd schmachten in Fesseln?" rescuing the awkward opening by way of the rhyme *vergessen* and *Fesseln* (Herder 1792).

Halevi repeats the word *shalom* (peace; greeting) in three different phrases all linked by alliteration: *tishali liSHLOM; dorshey SHLOMekh; SHALOM' se-I*, and *SHLOM* recurs in line five; but Mendelssohn uses *Frieden* only once, in line five. In lieu of repetition, he elaborates the pathos by adding adjectives, adverbs and flowery images. Instead of "captives" (Hebrew, line one) he writes "ones who slavishly languish in chains." The sad tone turns pastoral when the "remnant of your flock" is depicted as "innocent herds" that "formerly grazed in your still valleys." The phrase "Tears like dew" is elaborated by way of six different "liquid" words: *Tränenbad, befeuchten, herabrollen, Zähren, Tropfen, beweinen*. On the other hand, rather than enumerate the four directions (as do Halevi and the Bible), Mendelssohn summarizes, "from all sides to which their herders dispersed them." Perhaps he thought he would improve the poem by continuing the trope of the people as a flock (Hebrew, line four).[12] These herders, "Treiber," also introduce a perpetrator of the exile, although the Hebrew offers no reason why the people of the diaspora languish.

Finally: Mendelssohn smoothes out the paratactic effects. To this end, he adds an entire verse at the beginning of stanza four, "O! Seine Hoffnung sinket noch nicht," perhaps in order to prepare readers for the turning point, the introduction of the lyric self. In a similar vein, the words "gleiche ich" turn a metaphor into a simile.

The fulcrum of these first fourteen lines is the phrase "mein frohes Gemüth," "my happy disposition / temperament" (line sixteen), in lieu of the Hebrew "I" (*ani*). With this emotional description of the lyric self, as with the other additions and expansions, Mendelssohn's translation foregrounds the poetic imagination as the true harp, or instrument of these "joyful" songs to Zion. What is the source of this joy? It is no surprise to find good poetry in the Bible. But to have evidence that Jews living in the medieval diaspora had a poetic imagination – that the "frohes Gemüth" can produce "freudige Danklieder" even in Al-Andalus – is truly a cause to rejoice.

***

---

[12] With regard to "improving" this poem: Mendelssohn actually omits two verses later in the poem, because he didn't think they fit in; his publisher Christian Gottlob Meyer filled in the ellipsis. His explanation included as a postscript to the 1778 Hebrew-letter version begins, "Reader, do not be surprised that two stanzas were not translated. This was not due to the translator's fatigue, but rather, because the poet (*m'konen* = writer of the *kinah*) skipped from topic to topic. He began comparing Israel to a herd of sheep, then spoke of them as grasping the edge of the garment, leaving the initial image..." (Mendelssohn 1972, 368).

The nucleus of Franz Rosenzweig's "An Zion," announced in the first line, is the phrase "Joch tragen" (to bear a yoke). The turn of phrase is significant for two reasons: first, the word "tragen" announces the dominant rhyme scheme, "-agen"; second, the yoke signals the translator's subjugation to form, rhyme, and meter – a theme also alluded to in line 8 ("zu Deinen Liedern zu schlagen"), a rare instance in which Rosenzweig actually departs from the literal sense. He does so, in my view, to suggest that translation, like poesis, is about the regular beating, counting out of the song.

An Zion

Zion! nicht fragst Du den Deinen nach, die Joch tragen,
    Rest deiner Herden, die doch nach Dir allein fragen?
West, Ost und Nordsturm und Süd, – o laß von ihnen den Gruß
    Dessen, der fern ist und nah, von ringsher Dir sagen.
Gruß des, den Sehnsucht umstrickt, des Träne wie Hermons Tau;
    O sänk' auch sie hinab zu Deinen Berghagen.
Wein ich dein Leid, Schakal werd ich; träum ich Dich fronbefreit,
    Bin ich die Harfe, zu Deinen Liedern zu schlagen.

Rosenzweig's version is closer to the Hebrew in every respect than Mendelssohn's. Whereas Mendelssohn elides the initial image of Zion inquiring after the welfare of her captives, Rosenzweig crafts a chiasm, [niCHt] FRAGEN naCH / naCH… FRAGEN, to mirror the Hebrew *do you not inquire after us…who inquire after you?*, and places the sonorous "Du den Deinen" in the middle.[13] The word "FRonbe-FReit" is an ingenious rendering of Halevi's "SHiVaT SHVuTekh," a highly unexpected phrase that means "the return of your captivity" (not "of your captives") alluding to Psalm 126. (Mendelssohn uses "Erlösung"). *Fronbefreit* evokes (*Frondienst*), the term for slavery in Luther's German Bible, and mimics the paranomasia of the Hebrew; the consonants appear in reverse order in "HaRFe."

Mendelssohn expands eight Hebrew lines into seventeen; Rosenzweig's translational practice was about contraction, *tsimtsum:* fitting the poem back into its original Hebraic mold of 34 distichs alternating 13 and 14 syllables, masculine and feminine cadences.

Rosenzweig first mentions translating "the great Zionide" in a letter to Gertrud Oppenheim of November 30, 1922.

---

[13] Interestingly, "fragen nach" is also used in the first Yiddish version by Leib ben Chayim haSofer (Dessau 1698).

> Verse sind auch wieder entstanden, die dir aus der Kasseler Vorlesung (Wesen des Judentums) bekannte große Zionide (68 Zeilen mit 34 Reimen auf agen) und eins auf das Metrum [....]¹⁴ und den Reim ab ab 1. Cd cd cd ab ab 2. Ef ef ab ab bis 5. Lm lm lm ab ab. Etsch!
>
> [Verses have also arisen again, the great Zionide (68 lines with 34 rhymes on "-agen") known to you from the Kassel lecture (Essence of Judaism), and one on the meter [....] and the rhyme ab ab 1. cd cd cd ab ab 2. ef ef ab ab to 5. lm lm lm ab ab. Ha!]

That he included the rhyme scheme and meter in this letter, and also boasted about thirty-four verses with an – *agen* terminal rhyme, tells us something about his priority as a translator. The approach to form was justified as a condition of the first word "Zion!", because the initial apostrophe to "you, Zion" determined the rhyme scheme. Why? In Hebrew, the possessive suffix is "rayikh," where "r" belongs to the root of the Hebrew word, and "ayikh" indicates possession. So: *asirayikh* (your captives) *adarayikh* (your flocks), *shirayikh* (your songs). Because each rhyme word contains "you" or "your" within it, rhyme, as Rosenzweig says, is not the "grout" but the "bricks" of the poem, "das Baumaterial selbst" (Rosenzweig 1927, 87). Rosenzweig rhymes lines 1,2,4,6,8: *tragen, fragen, sagen, Berghagen, schlagen;* in doing so, he imitates an important feature of medieval prosody, "tsimud," a rhetorical term that refers to the juxtaposition of words that are either perfect homonyms or share similar sounds, often to virtuosic effect.

Mendelssohn's version did not rhyme; Rosenzweig elevated rhyme to a philosophical and theological principle, one not, however, appreciated by his contemporaries. Gertrud Oppenheim called the poems "mit Reimlexicon zusammengeschustert," as if the translator was simply having fun with a rhyming dictionary (Rosenzweig 1979, 963 n. 2). A more serious criticism was voiced by the poet Ludwig Strauß. When Strauß' father-in-law Martin Buber asked him his opinion of Rosenzweig's Halevi book, Strauß called the translations "künstlich und gewunden" artificial and distorted (18 June 1924; Rübner 1990, 87). Strauß objected to the formalist approach to translation practiced by Rosenzweig, Stefan George and many others, which he deemed overly simplistic. Strauß was particularly offended by Rosenzweig's comment in the *Nachwort* that translators of Halevi who didn't replicate the meter were nothing but "lazy" (Rübner 1990, 87).[15]

---

14 I am unable to reproduce the metrical guide that Rosenzweig sketched at this place in his letter.

15 Rosenzweig's cavalier attitude to prior translators of the Zionide comes through in another letter written almost one and half years after his letter to Oppenheim (May 15, 1924): "Ich vergass, Sie um Herders, Mendelssohns und Bialiks Zioniden zu bitten; ich kenne sie alle nicht. Vor allem Herders" Rosenzweig 1979, 961.

But it was one of these "lazy" translators who apparently inspired Rosenzweig to produce his own version of Halevi's poems in the first place: the Rabbi and literary writer Emil Cohn (1881–1948).[16] Rosenzweig refers to Cohn as his negative inspiration in a letter to Martin Buber (January 6, 1923): "Moreover, I translated a slim volume by Halevi with an afterword and notes.... The rhyme and meter have been replicated precisely. This whole [project] owes its appearance to Emil Cohen (given to me by Michael), which offended me to such a degree that verses emerged."[17] What was it about Emil Cohn's *Diwan* of 1921 that made Rosenzweig angry enough to produce translations of his own? Perhaps it was the fact that Cohn rendered the Zionide in unequal verses (cola) and stanzas (in a manner reminiscent of Goethe's *Sturm und Drang* poem "Prometheus"), and placed the lyric subject, rather than Zion, front and center: "Hear them, hear me as well!" Cohn's translation of Halevi's eight lines expanded to twenty-two German verses divided into three stanzas (10+6+6):

> Zion, willst du nimmer wieder
> Die verbannten Kinder grüßen,
> Sie, die letzten deiner Herde,
> Die dich immer wieder grüßen?
> Osten, Westen, Süden, Norden,
> Alle Nähen, alle Weiten—
> Horch, von allen fernsten Borden
> Grüßt es dich:
> Höre sie, Zion!
> Höre auch mich!
>
> Armer Gefangener ich,
> Ich mit meinem Sehnen,
> Hermonstau meine Tränen!
> Hermonstau?—O wären sie's nur,
> Daß ihrer Tropfen Spur
> Deine ewigen Höhen benetze!

---

16 Cohn (1881–1948) is the author of the Hebrew play *Letter of Uriah*. From 1925–1936 he served as the rabbi of the Grunewalder Synagogue in Berlin. He immigrated to the United States in 1939.
17 "Außerdem habe ich ein Bändchen Halevi übersetzt mit einem Nachwort und Anmerkungen....Reime und Metren sind genau nachgebildet. Das Ganze verdankt seine Entstehung Emil Cohn (den mir Michael schenkte), über den ich mich so geärgert hab, dass daraus Verse wurden" (Rosenzweig 1979, 878).

Ich aber, ein Tier der Wüste,
Kann nur heulen ob deinem Falle;
Nur, wenn im Traume die Zukunft mich grüßte:
Heimwallende Scharen – zum Liedeshalle
Meine Schmerzen alle,
Zur jubelnden Harfe waren. (Cohn 1921)

Cohn's was the most recent example of a long tradition of German free renderings of Halevi initiated – one might argue – by Mendelssohn in 1755. Ironically, Cohn believed that he, too, was rectifying a long tradition of bad Halevi translations; in his preface, he states that he began the twelve-year process of translating the *Diwan* in the manner of "freie Nachdichtung," but eventually concluded that rather than use the poetry to inspire his own creativity, he would use translation to try to do justice to the medieval singer (*diesem Sänger selbst zum Rechte zu verhelfen*), given the inadequacy of all extant translations (Cohn 1921, 139). Cohn's self-understanding notwithstanding, Rosenzweig identified him as representative of the tradition of *Nachdichtung,* which his own translations aspired to counteract – a position he spells out in detail in the *Nachwort*[18] to the translations.

***

Rosenzweig's *Nachwort* combines a translator's apologia with an excursus about the history of Bible translation in Germany. The latter, the excursus, is often cited, since Rosenzweig praises Martin Luther as the exemplary German translator – the "religious genius" who became a "world-historical person" through translation. Only in the essay's more technical second half does Rosenzweig celebrate

---

18 The *Nachwort* was oddly sandwiched between the poems and the notes (*Anmerkungen*), rather than placed at the back of the second edition, titled *Jehuda Halevi: Zweiundneunzig Hymnen und Gedichte* (Lambert Schneider, 1927). Rosenzweig grouped the poems in four categories of his own devising: *Gott, Seele, Volk, Zion*; this was his own twist on the custom of dividing them according to genre. He took the prerogative to assign each poem a German title that reflected his understanding of its central idea; Hebrew titles (first lines) could be found in the *Anmerkungen* and in a second, three-page index at the very back of the book, paginated from right to left. Like every anthologist of Halevi, Rosenzweig references the editions of Luzatto and Brody in his notes. In another respect, the *Anmerkungen* broke with convention; rather than philological comments or biblical references, the notes relate to the poems as tangents, touching upon an essential matter but ultimately moving in unexpected, Rosenzweigian directions. The complex interconnection and idiosyncratic arrangement of the three components of the book became undone in the *Gesammelte Schriften* (ed. Raphael Rosenzweig, 1984), and even in Martin Buber's 1933 *Schocken Bücherei* edition of twenty poems (Jehuda Halevi. *Zionslieder. Mit der Verdeutschung von Franz Rosenzweig und seinen Anmerkungen*. Berlin: Schocken Verlag, 1933).

the *Jewish* religious genius, the poet-philosopher Yehuda Halevi, in defense of his own unusual technique.

Rosenzweig makes the fundamental point already in the first paragraph: "Grundsätzlich war meine Absicht, wörtlich zu übersetzen... [Basically my intention was to translate literally...]" (Rosenzweig 1927, 153; Galli 169). He mentions "Herr [Emil] Cohn," in passing, but, perhaps with an eye towards a broader readership, attacks the "patron saint" of *Nachdichtung*, the classical philologist Wilamowitz, known for making ancient texts understandable (*Verständlichermachen*; Rosenzweig 1927, 154).

By the end of the *Nachwort* he arrives at the astounding claim that all Jewish poetry in exile, by its very nature, resists domestication – "Alle jüdische Dichtung im Exil verschmäht es, dieses ihr Im-Exil-Sein zu igno, rieren [All Jewish poetry in exile scorns to ignore this being-in-exile]." He thereby constructs an imperative for his own foreignizing approach. Throughout the essay, he insists that foreignness is innate to Halevi's verse, which he describes using words such as "Unnatürlichkeit" (unnaturalness) "unnachbildbar" (non-reproducible), "Fremdheit" (foreignness) (Rosenzweig 1927, 161; Galli 177).

An important aspect of the foreignness (at least to modern ears) is the poet's well-known "Musivstil" (mosaic style): the incorporation of scriptural phrases and liturgical words that is the signature accomplishment of medieval Jewish poetry. Rosenzweig notes that Halevi's texts exemplified, in their time, what the Italians have in Dante and the Russians in Dostoevsky, and though he does not mention it, what the Germans have in the Luther Bible, namely, "diese glückliche Einheit nun von Sprechen und Denken... [this fortunate unity of speech and thought]" (Rosenzweig 1927, 162; Galli 178). Halevi drew allusions (*Anspielungsgehalt*) from the full landscape of biblical literature and playfully embedded them in his verse; they are not ornaments, they are the warp and woof of his language. As anyone who studies the poems in Hebrew knows, "das Zitat ist hier ganz und gar nicht ein schmückendes Anhängsel sondern es ist der Zettel für den Einschlag der Rede [Here the quotation is by no means an adoring pendant, rather it is the label for the envelope of his speech]" (Rosenzweig 1927, 162; Galli 178).

Yet another source of foreignness is word choice. Rosenzweig states emphatically – though perhaps with some false modesty – that the translator is not a ruler, but an obedient servant: "Er hat nicht das Recht, sich von dem eigenen, ihm eigenen Wort tragen zu lassen, er muß jedem fremden Wort nachgehn [He does not have the right to allow himself to be carried by his own word, the word personal to him. He must reproduce word for word as they are given to him]" (Rosenzweig 1927, 163; Galli 179). Literality is the translator's imperative. This is the point that Ludwig Strauß called a "mechanical nihilistic" theory of poetic form. When discussing word choice, Rosenzweig denigrates the average German speaker, claiming that his knowledge of German language reaches only back as far as Heine's *Buch der Lieder*, and that he barely knows Hölderlin's hymns and Goethe's *Westöstlicher Diwan* – two important models for Rosenzweig's project.

But all of these imperatives (word choice; biblical allusion; meter) pale in comparison to that which dictates Rosenzweig's approach to rhyme, which, from his vantage point, was the most misunderstood aspect of Halevi's poems, both by average readers and connoisseurs. One reason that rhyme is misunderstood is ignorance about Hebrew; another is ignorance about poetry. Rosenzweig recounts the following anecdote: "Ich fragte vor Jahren einmal einen Freund nach dem Metrum der Zionide, die er von Kindheit an alle Jahre am 9. Ab zu sagen gewohnt war; er antwortete, er habe oft schon danach gesucht, aber es sei keines vorhanden, es seien freie Rhythmen! [Years ago I asked a friend once about the metre of the Zion songs which he was accustomed to recite since childhood every year on the Ninth of Av. He answered, he had often tried to find it, but none was there– they were free rhythms!]" (Rosenzweig 1927, 165; Galli 1995, 181).

The *Nachwort* builds to the crucial question: just because a poet subjects himself to these rules – rhyme, meter, *Musivstil* – must the translator artificially recreate them? Rosenzweig answers the question definitively with a defense of Halevi's originality: the characteristics which make Halevi a stranger to us, *unnatürlich*, have nothing to do with historical context; they form the core of his originality, which entailed *using formal patterns and repetition to express truth and love*. The bottom line is that these poems were not written to be anthologized in a divan; there was no *Reimnot*, no external compulsion to rhyme. The Ode to Zion was a liturgical poem to be chanted and responded to in the synagogue; this was not *l'art pour l'art*, but "Zweckkunst" (art with a purpose) (Rosenzweig 1927, 166; Galli 183). As with all liturgy, the essential matter was repetition and recurrence, both within the liturgical text and across the Jewish calendar, year after year. Moreover, in Rosenzweig's view, repetitive patterns – rhyme, rhythm, meter, refrain, and acrostic – are inspired by truth, on one hand, and by the feeling inspired by that truth: love of God. "Wie letzthin überhaupt die Wiederholung die große und einzige Form ist, die der Mensch zum Aussprechen seins ganz Wahren hat [As in the final analysis repetition is altogether the great and only form which man has for expressing what is entirely true for him]" (Rosenzweig 1927, 167; Galli 183). And, finally, with respect to love: Rosenzweig claims that Halevi's liturgical poems are ultimately love poems, but not of the Christian, Romantic sort. They are not the kind of love poems found in Heinrich Heine's *Dichterliebe*, in which love comes to an end at the end of the song cycle (or where, arguably, there was never love in the first place, only the word "love").¹⁹ This kind of love never tires, never becomes old: "Im Munde des Liebenden wird das Wort der Liebe nicht alt…" (Rosenzweig 1927, 167). Rosenzweig might have quoted Elizabeth Barrett Browning: "How do I love thee? Let me count the ways." Counting the ways is in any case the intent behind Rosenzweig's mis-translation of line eight of the Ode to Zion: "Bin ich die Harfe, Zu deinen Liedern zu schlagen [I am the harp playing to your songs]" (Galli 164).

***

Rosenzweig identified translation – and liturgical poetry – with "Knechtschaft" (servitude). For Mendelssohn, by contrast, translation liberated the "frohes Gemüth" (joyous disposition). This very exuberant poetic spirit also infused Mendelssohn's translations of biblical texts in the 1770s and 1780s. I cite three examples:

First: Mendelssohn's German translation of the *kinah*, first published in 1755–1756, reappeared over two decades later as one of three sample translations printed in "Alim l'trufah" (leaves for healing), the 1778 prospectus printed to attract subscribers for the Pentateuch project. The poem, printed this time in Hebrew script and facing the original Hebrew, was printed at the very end of the prospectus which also included a preface by Mendelssohn's collaborator Solomon Dubno; Exodus 1–2; and another "poetic" pericope, Numbers 24–25. According to an editorial postscript, the *kinah* was included there only to fill up some blank pages – just "by chance" (Mendelssohn 1972, 363). Correspondence suggests that the true motive was to advertise Mendelssohn's skill as a translator of difficult (poetic) language, and also, to legitimate Hebrew-German (and Jewish-German) translation as a promising cultural activity, one with relevance also to the religious sphere of Bible translation.²⁰

Second: Mendelssohn's excitement about poetry found its way onto the actual pages of the Pentateuch translation. The first poem in the Hebrew Bible, Lamech's little speech to his wives Adah and Tzilah (Genesis 4:23–24), provides an occasion for Mendelssohn to extol Hebrew poetry and explain its mechanics,

---

19 Rosenzweig's deprecation of Heine's poetry is a topic for further study. What he did Rosenzweig think of Heine, and of Heine's verse epic in four parts, *Jehuda ben-Halevy* written in Paris in 1851? Heine was the consummate rhyming poet, above all, as an expression of irony, existential (and real) homelessness, and the collapse of idealism.

20 This subtle message is signaled by the fact that the German version of the poem, facing the Hebrew version, is published (like the Be'ur itself) in Hebrew letters. Mendelssohn's poem had of course appeared in Müchler's periodical in Latin characters, which means that it travelled in the opposite direction as the Be'ur, which began in Hebrew characters and was reprinted soon thereafter in Latin letters.

referring to Bishop Lowth's theory of biblical parallelism.[21] The speech is rendered in verse within the translation, and Mendelssohn's commentary on the poem stands out in the page layout. (Buber and Rosenzweig were not the first translators to attend to cola!) Poetry stands out even more vividly in the pages leading up to the Song of the Sea (Exodus 15). For the first time in the history of (Jewish?) biblical exegesis, a commentator explicated the formal aspects of biblical poetry (Altmann 1973, 410–412). Mendelssohn compares biblical, Greek, and Roman verse forms, arguing that the latter two produce poetry meant for the "ear." By contrast, the biblical poet cares about the content; the heart, not the ear. Mendelssohn bemoans the loss of the music that must have accompanied the Psalms, but emphasizes that modern readers can still appreciate the characteristics of biblical *Dichtkunst*: short phrases with few words; pauses in rhythm which give the hearer time to reflect on the meaning; the superiority of word over syllable, content over form. Mendelssohn's excursus on Exodus 15 is so long that he has to apologize, though he adds that he might have gone on forever.

Third: Scholars tend to view Mendelssohn's Psalms translation as a different kind of project than the Pentateuch, claiming that the former was an artistic project for Christian scholars, and the latter a pedagogical project for his Jewish compatriots. Incorporating his earlier translation of the Halevi poem into his career as a translator allows us to interconnect these two projects, the artistic and the scholarly/pedagogical. Mendelssohn began translating the Psalms in 1770, a decade before turning to the Hebrew Bible. In his preface, he presents the Psalms as the fruit of a ten-years labor: "die Frucht einer mehr als zehnjährigen Arbeit" (Mendelssohn 1972, 6). But which kind of fruit were these Psalms – peaches, or cherries? Mendelssohn's apologia confirms that translating poetry was first and foremost an imaginative enterprise, not a scholarly one.

> Ich habe die Psalmen nicht in ihrer Ordnung, nach einander weg, übersetzt, sondern wählte mir einen Psalm, der mir gefiel, der zu der Zeit mit der Lage meines Gemüths übereinkam…. Lies du eben so, mein Leser! Wie ich geschrieben habe; wähle dir einen Psalm wie er grade um die Zeit mit deinem Gemüthszustande übereintrifft: vergiß auf eine kurze Zeit alles dessen, so du von diesem Psalm bey Uebersetzern, Auslegern und Paraphrasten gelesen hast; lies meine Uebersetzung, und urtheile! (Mendelssohn 1972, 6)
>
> [I did not translate the Psalms in order, but I chose a Psalm that pleased me, that matched my current state of mind…. Reader, read them in this spirit! As I have written them; choose a Psalm that corresponds to your state of mind: forget for a short time everything that you have read about that Psalm from translators and commentators; read my translation, and you be the judge!] (My translation)

---

[21] Lamech's speech and Proverbs 27:6 demonstrate the two types of parallelism discussed by Lowth.

When a translator notes that he chose poems randomly and the reader should do the same – pick whichever poem speaks to us in a given moment – he is saying, "consume them like cherries, rather than peaches;" Mendelssohn's Romanticism shines through. He closes by repeating his instructions to read the Psalms uncritically, without bias, as he translated them.[22]

Interestingly, Franz Rosenzweig also started out translating Halevi's poetry in an unsystematic manner; the initial selection was "persönlich," "zufällig" (personal, accidental). The Halevi collection as a whole was a random selection (*Zufallsauswahl*; Rosenzweig 1927, 166), until a clear, guiding idea took over:

> Es kommt im Übersetzung immer irgendwann ein Augenblick, wo die Scheidewand zwischen Gedicht und Übersetzung, und sei es nun für einen Augenblick, fällt. Um dieses Augenblicks willen übersetzt man, wenn man es auch selber nicht weiß; aber dieses Augenblick ist auch die Schranke, die einen in der Auswahl beschränkt.
> Das Zufällige der Auswahl verlor sich dann im Laufe der Arbeit. (Rosenzweig 1927, 166)
>
> [There always comes in translating a moment when the dividing wall between poetry and translation falls down, if only for a moment. For the sake of this moment one translates, even if one does know it oneself; but this moment is also the barrier which restricts one in the selection.
>
> The accident of the selection got lost then in the course of the work.] (Galli 182)

It was neither chance nor temperament that determined the selection of poems, but success. Ultimately, chance was replaced by the dogma of repetition, both within a given poem and across the poems. Rosenzweig's defensive of repetition as the only "form" that can do justice to truth sums up his own poetics. He insisted thereafter that he had approached this body of poetry unromantically, as one who, no less than the poet himself, is a "Knecht," a servant of an inner religious vision. Rhetorically, Rosenzweig's final comment above enhances the self-portrait of a translator who started out as a child of his time, but then overcame his age *in himself*. Rosenzweig announces this agenda explicitly in one of the final Notes in his Halevi book, commenting on another well-known poem, "My Heart in the East, my self, in the outermost West," which he titled "Zwischen Ost und West" (between East and West). Here, Rosenzweig identifies most personally with Jehuda Halevi's legacy as a mediator between Occident and Orient;

---

[22] "Kurz! ich glaube, ohne kritische Vorutheile [sic] übersetzt zu haben; wünsche ohne kritische Vorurtheile gelesen und beurtheilt zu werden, und verspreche, ohne kritischen Eigensinn, Belehrung anzunehmen" (Mendelssohn 1972, 6–7).

his longing for Zion; and his rejection of Western Judaism. Rosenzweig writes, "Halevi's longing for Zion, the split of the person between East and West... is a turning point in the history of Jewish exile":

> aber Jehuda Halevis einsames Seelenschicksal ist das erste Feuerzeichen der neuen Bewegung, die dann, nur mit der einen, doch stärkenden Atempause des nachmendelssohnschen Jahrhunderts, in der die führende Westjudenheit den Zusammenhang radikal zu verleugnen suchte, bis in unsre Gegenwart trägt. (Rosenzweig 1927, 243–244)

> [...but Jehuda Halevi's lonely spiritual destiny is the first beacon of the new movement which than carries on to our present, only with the one yet invigorating breathing space of the century following Mendelssohn, in which the leading Western Jewry sought radically to deny the connection.] (Galli 264)

***

Both Mendelssohn and Rosenzweig understood that to translate poetry was to work in the artistic and spiritual heights of language. Poetry was a realm outside of philosophy and critique. Halevi's poetry was proof positive that Hebrew as a holy language could be fertile and alive in the diaspora, and thus, both Mendelssohn and Rosenzweig proudly gave Halevi's elegy a new life in the German language.

In the eighteenth century, a translator of liturgical and biblical poetry could claim the mantel and the prestige of a German poet; it follows that Mendelssohn privileged the poetic sections of the Bible, viewing them as the choicest gems within scripture. In the twentieth century, in turn, Rosenzweig's servile, neo-classical approach to poetry could not but end in a return to prose. After all, a good half of the Halevi book was in prose – not only the Afterword, but also the Notes, which were more like prose poems, or mirror-images of the poems in prose. As a practitioner of translation, Rosenzweig fancied himself a *Knecht*, "*asir taáva*" or captive; but Rosenzweig's imagination flowers in the Notes. The Notes would convert the poems from cherries into peaches, and the reader, from a casual consumer into a "guest and friend" of poetry – (not a poet) – because they opened up the poems' intellectual and religious core. In this vein, Rosenzweig broke off his work translating Halevi to collaborate with Martin Buber on the Bible translation. Perhaps it is by a similar logic that Buber and Rosenzweig insisted that, appearances notwithstanding, the proper genre of Hebrew scripture was prose.

The heart of the matter for both translators is that, as Rosenzweig states, "Yehuda Halevi was a great Jewish poet in the Hebrew language." Thus I conclude, in the spirit of Rosenzweig's epigram by the German-Greek translator Friedrich Leopold von Stollberg – "Oh dear Reader, learn Greek and throw my translation into the fire." Oh dear Reader, learn Hebrew and throw Rosenzweig, Herder, Cohn, Geiger, Mendelssohn, and all the rest, into the fire!

Works cited

Baron, Salo. *A Social and Religious History of the Jews*. Vol. 7. New York: Columbia University Press, 1958.
Benjamin, Mara H. *Rosenzweig's Bible. Reinventing Scripture for Jewish Modernity*. Cambridge: Cambridge University Press, 2009.
Bialik, Chaim Nachman. *Shirim be-yidish, shire yeladim, shire hakdashah: mahadurah mada'it be-livyat mevo'ot ve hilufei nosah*. Ed. Dan Miron. Tel Aviv: Dvir, 2000.
Biemann, Asher D. *Dreaming of Michelangelo: Jewish Variations on a Modern Theme*. Stanford, CA: Stanford University Press, 2012.
Bourel, Dominique. *Moses Mendelssohn. Begründer des modernen Judentums*. Trans. Hörst Brühmann. Zürich: Ammann Verlag, 2007.
Cohn, Emil. *Ein Diwan*. Berlin: E. Reiss, 1921.
Cole, Peter, ed. and trans. *The Dream of the Poem. Hebrew Poetry from Muslim and Christian Spain 950–1492*. Princeton: Princeton University Press, 2007.
Delitzsch, Franz. *Zur Geschichte der jüdischen Poesie: vom Abschluss der heiligen Schriften Alten Bundes bis auf die neueste Zeit*. Leipzig: Karl Tauchnitz, 1836.
Elbogen, Ismar, Judah Bergmann and Simon Bernfeld, eds. *Gedenkbuch für Moses Mendelssohn*. Verband der Vereine für jüdische Geschichte und Literatur in Deutschland. Berlin: M. Poppelauer, 1929.
Galli, Barbara Ellen. *Franz Rosenzweig and Jehuda Halevi. Translating, Translations, and Translators*. Montreal: McGill-Queens University Press, 1995.
Geiger, Abraham. *Divan des Castiliers Abu'l – Hassan Juda ha-Levi*. Breslau: J.U. Kern, 1851.
Gottheil, Richard, Max Schloessinger and Isaac Broyde. "Jehuda Ha-Levi." [1906] Jewish Encyclopedia.
Halevi, Jehuda. *Zionslieder. Mit der Verdeutschung von Franz Rosenzweig und seinen Anmerkungen*. Berlin: Schocken Verlag, 1933.
Herder, Johann Gottfried. "Über Denkmale der Vorwelt," *Zerstreute Blätter* 4 (1792)
Karpeles, Gustav. "Einleitung." *Divan des Jehuda Halevi. Eine Auswahl in deutschen Uebertragungen*. Berlin: Hugo Schildberger, 1893.
Kayser, Wolfgang. *Geschichte des deutschen Verses*. 3rd ed. Munich: Francke Verlag, 1981.
Losch, Andreas. "'Der Ewige' als Synthese des Stern. Der Gebrauch des Gottesnamens 'der Ewige' bei Franz Rosenzweig." *Naharaim* 9.1–2 (2015): 195–215.
Mach, Dafna. "Franz Rosenzweig als Übersetzer jüdischer Texte: Seine Auseinandersetzung mit Gershom Scholem." *Der Philosoph Franz Rosenzweig: Internationaler Kongreß, Kassel 1986*. Ed. Wolfdietrich Schmied-Kowarzik. Freiburg & München: Verlag Karl Alber, 1988.
Mendelssohn, Moses. *Gesammelte Schriften, Jubilaeumsausgabe*. Vol 14. Ed. Werner Weinberg. Stuttgart: Friedrich Frommann, 1972.
Mendelssohn, Moses. *Gesammelte Schriften, Jubilaeumsausgabe*. Vol. 10.1. Ed. Werner Weinberg. Stuttgart: Friedrich Frommann, 1985.
Rosenzweig, Franz. *Gesammelte Schriften. Briefe und Tagebücher*. 2 Vols. The Hague: Martinus Ninjhoff, 1979.
Rosenzweig, Franz. *Jehuda Halevi. Zweiundneunzig Hymnen und Gedichte*. Berlin: Verlag Lambert Schneider, 1927.
Rübner, Tuvia, ed. *Briefwechsel Martin Buber - Ludwig Strauß 1913–1953*. Frankfurt a.M.: Luchterhand, 1990.

Salaman, Nina, trans. *Selected Poems of Jehudah Halevi*. Philadelphia: Jewish Publication Society of America, 1928.
Schatz, Andrea. *Sprache in der Zerstreuung: Die Säkularisierung des Hebräischen im 18. Jahrhundert*. Göttingen: Vandenhoeck & Ruprecht, 2009.
Scheindlin, Raymond P. *The Song of the Distant Dove. Judah Halevi's Pilgrimage*. New York: Oxford University Press, 2008.
Schirmann, Chaim. "Translations of 'tzion ha-lo tishali' of Yehuda Halevi." *Kiryat ha-Sefer* 15 (1938–1939): 360–367.
Schorsch, Ismar. *From Text to Context. The Turn to History in Modern Judaism*. Hanover: Brandeis University Press & University Press of New England, 1994.
Shear, Adam. "Juda Halevi's Kuzari in the Haskalah." *Renewing the Past. Reconfiguring Jewish Culture from al-Andalus to the Haskalah*. Ed. Ross Brann and Adam Sutcliffe. Philadelphia: Pennsylvania University Press, 2003. 71–92.
Shear, Adam. *The Kuzari and the Shaping of Jewish Identity 1167–1900*. Cambridge: Cambridge University Press, 2008.
Weinberg, Werner. "Einleitungen." *Moses Mendelssohn, Gesammelte Schriften, Jubilaeumsausgabe*. Vol. 10.1. Ed. Werner Weinberg. Stuttgart: Friedrich Frommann, 1985. IX-XCIII.
Weinberger, Leon J. *Jewish Hymnography. A Literary History*. London: Littman Library of Jewish Civilization, 1998.

Maya Barzilai
The Flowers of Shame: Avraham Ben Yitzhak's Hebrew-German "Revival"

Between 1903 and 1930, the Galician-born poet Avraham Ben Yitzhak published a dozen modernist Hebrew poems. Despite this meager poetic yield, Ben Yitzhak was recognized by his contemporaries and by later writers and critics as an innovative and influential poet.[1] Already in 1909, the Hebrew poet Ḥaim Naḥman Bialik lauded Ben Yitzhak in a letter sent to his hometown, Przemyśl, for his "synthesis of the prophetic and the modern" and for the originality of his "style and form."[2] The Hebrew writer Leah Goldberg provides, in her memoir of the poet, an assessment of the unique qualities of Ben Yitzhak's writing. She notes his precise lexicon that draws from the Bible but "resounds in the spaces of the world of the future." His poetry exhibited "a new linguistic musicality," with its unrhymed lines, free rhythm, and use of Sephardic accentuation at a time when the Ashkenazic accentual-syllabic meter still reigned. Ben Yitzhak revolutionized Hebrew, for Goldberg, because "he was the first Hebrew poet whose watch-hand showed not only the specific Jewish time, but the hour it was for world literature" (Goldberg 1952, 57–58). Subsequent generations of poets also saw Ben Yitzhak's Hebrew musicality as set in a universal – that is, a modern European – key. In 1960, Natan Zach essentially echoed Goldberg's idea that there was no time-lag in Ben Yitzhak's case: his modernist Hebrew poetry, "rooted" as it was "in the soil of another poetry," fully corresponded to contemporaneous developments in European literature (Zach 6.10.1960, 7–8). Ben Yitzhak has also been remembered as a cosmopolitan Viennese café-dweller who befriended the likes of Elias Canetti, Richard Beer Hofmann, and Hermann Broch, and developed a German "oral modernism, an art that is all process" (Kronfeld 1996, 15).

When considering the newness and forward-looking aspects of Ben Yitzhak's poetry, we need to take into account his linguistic points of departure.

Acknowledgment: I am grateful to Rachel Seelig for her astute comments and careful editing.

---

1 According to the literary critic Dov Sadan, "His few poems were received, at the time, with amazement; the best readers knew them by heart; words of praise and acclaim were written about them" (1963, 75).
2 Central Zionist Archives – henceforth CZA – A165/6.

DOI 10.1515/9783110473384-003

The poet's ability to write in a Hebrew that was synchronized with "world literature" was also an outcome of his rich literary life in the German language. Ben Yitzhak's papers, discovered soon after his death in 1952, reveal that throughout his years of sporadic publication in Hebrew, the poet continued writing in both German and Hebrew, as well as expressing himself, though more infrequently, in and against his native Yiddish.[3] The poet's diaries contain notes in German and Hebrew, often interweaving the languages on the same page and even mid-sentence. More importantly, up until the mid-1920s Ben Yitzhak wrote poetic drafts and fragments in the two languages, and translated his and others' writing between Hebrew and German.[4] Thus his German modernism was not only oral but also written, significantly overlapping with his modernist Hebrew poetry.[5]

When closely examined, this interlingual poetic dialogue defies any clear notion of a language of origin or of a stable translational relationship. It is not a "horizontal" self-translation between European languages of equal status, but its verticality also cannot be clearly mapped; Ben Yitzhak translated in both directions and German, while more prestigious and dominant, was, for Zionist writers of his generation, less desirable than the Hebrew that they acquired through much effort.[6] In certain instances, Ben Yitzhak translated back and forth more than once – the 1910 poem "*Mizmor*" ("Psalm") most likely had its origins in the German poem "Gesang" ("Song"), and it was in turn translated by the poet back into German in 1915 as "Dem Dichter" ("For

---

[3] In his Hebrew notes for lectures delivered in the 1910s, Ben Yitzhak considers Yiddish to be disconnected from the Jewish people's spiritual life and "national value," a severely deficient language in which true creativity cannot take place (CZA A165/3).

[4] In 1950, after the discovery of Ben Yitzhak's notebooks, Prague-born Zionist journalist Robert Weltsch wrote to German-born Zionist Georg Landauer that a fuller edition of the poet's writings is now potentially publishable, including his "very beautiful" German poems, since "in his time in Vienna, Sonne appears to have lived entirely in German lyric" (CZA A165/19). Ben Yitzhak's translations into Hebrew include poems by Rainer Maria Rilke and Friedrich Nietzsche, and he also translated Bialik into German.

[5] Born Avraham Sonne in 1883, the poet grew up in Przemyśl speaking Yiddish and German (and possibly also Polish). As an adolescent he began studying modern Hebrew in the Sephardic pronunciation under the tutelage of Eliezer Meir Lipschütz, a Zionist scholar and educator from Lemberg/Lvov in Galicia who immigrated to Palestine in 1910. Letter exchanges between the two reveal that Ben Yitzhak's early Hebrew publication were self-translations from his German poetry (Barzilai 2014, 112–113).

[6] On the differences between symmetrical or horizontal translations among languages of widespread and relatively equal status and vertical translations among asymmetrical languages of divergent dominance and spread see (Grutman 2013).

the Poet") (CZA A165/5). In other cases, it remains unclear which version of the same poem was drafted first, thus challenging the notion of an "original" or primary language. Furthermore, Ben Yitzhak wrote several free-standing German poems and fragments that stand in dialogue, through shared imagery and poetic devices, with his Hebrew poems, published and unpublished. The poet's archive also contains drafts of prose works, essays, and even a screenplay in German, revealing that Ben Yitzhak experimented with multiple genres and forms in this language.[7]

This essay fleshes out Ben Yitzhak's bilingual poetics by tracing shared motifs and forms of address across clusters of poems in both languages. Coming into his own as a writer in the immediate fin-de-siècle period in Vienna, where he resided between 1908 and 1933, Ben Yitzhak absorbed and reworked several modernist aesthetic developments – first, the restrained impressionist mode of conveying the fleeting sense impressions that the external world makes on the eye/I; second, Ben Yitzhak's writings, especially when taking his unpublished drafts into account, also exhibit symbolist, decadent, and expressionist tendencies (Hever 1993, 60–61). His was a "restrained expressionism," wrote Zach on the basis of the published Hebrew poems (Zach 1960). Critics such as Hannan Hever have further examined the more explicitly expressionist poetry that Ben Yitzhak wrote in Hebrew and German but never published.[8] In tandem with his experimentation in impressionism and expressionism, Ben Yitzhak also wrote in a bleak note, influenced by European decadence; his poetry conveyed a sense of decline even when written in the language of revival.

Repeated evocations of flowers, for instance, enabled Ben Yitzhak to work through his relationship to the romantic tradition; while representing (feminine) youthfulness and purity, his flowers are also colored with the shame and decay of a decadent aesthetic. At the same time, Ben Yitzhak's specific Hebrew terms for flowers evoke and call into question the Zionist rhetoric of regeneration, revealing how the writer's European-decadent sensibility stood at a cross-linguistic tension

---

[7] (CZA A165/5). The screenplay, entitled "Schiff Staatenlos" ("Ship Stateless"), was most likely composed after World War I (Barzilai 2013, 125–129).
[8] As Hannan Hever has shown, the poet's Hebrew drafts, such as those for the poem "*Bodedim omrim:*" ("A Few Say:"), reveal that he also wrote in an expressionist mode, creating dynamic, and politically-responsive collages, in contrast to his more philosophical and impressionist published writings (Hever 1993, 99–100). Ben Yitzhak's unpublished *German* oeuvre bears further evidence to the persistence of an apocalyptic-expressionist strain in works composed during and after World War I (Barzilai 2013, 114–115).

with his Hebraism. Similarly, the image of the majestic robe recurs in both German and Hebrew poems, conveying a decadent sense of the end of a royal lineage and offering a symbolist experience of ecstatic encounter with the boundless divine. The latter viewpoint finds its expression, again, in the Hebrew terms that allude to the biblical robe of God and the priestly robes. When read side-by-side, the drafts of poems in Hebrew and German reveal Ben Yitzhak's intricate triangulation of biblical allusion with modern Hebrew poetics *and* German literary precursors and contemporaries. He draws on Lamentations in order forge a modern Hebrew poetic language that conveys an acutely contemporary mood of decline and cultural pessimism.

Throughout these fragments, translations, and published poems, address and apostrophe to female subjects or feminized objects provide Ben Yitzhak's poems in German and Hebrew with a sense of voice, invocation, and eventfulness. His writings are often directed both inward and outward, addressing and describing another, at times with an urgency conveyed through the apostrophic "Oh" or "*ho*" ("O" in German and Hebrew, respectively). The notion of apostrophe proves useful for interpreting not only Ben Yitzhak's dialogues with other poets but also the intrapoetic conversations between his Hebrew and German versions. Despite the decadent sensibility that permeates his writing, Ben Yitzhak's constant movement between languages and his addresses within poems and across poems generate a sense of rich activity that cannot be delimited to one particular ideological and aesthetic framework. Rather than merely enhance the lyricism of his poetry, Ben Yitzhak's use of apostrophe and address across his oeuvre draws attention to the linguistic and political tensions that informed the poet's writing in the early decades of the twentieth century.

1 A lingual flowering

In an undated German-language note, Ben Yitzhak acknowledged the contribution of the Jewish Enlightenment (*Haskalah*) to the process of Hebrew language revitalization. The poet depicts the "wonder" of the "old tongue of religion" that introduced, via the *Haskalah*, the message of a new world-sentiment to the ghetto. In Ben Yitzhak's words, the rejuvenated *maskilic* Hebrew language "blossomed like flowers after the night, and the shower of its blossoms fell upon the gloom of the frozen." The flowers of Hebrew here symbolize light (day) and renewed life; they are also the flowers of *Haskalah*, considered a mode of combating the darkness of the supposedly enclosed and petrified pre-modern Jewish world. These flowers constitute a "wonder" since it is precisely the old language (Hebrew) that in Europe becomes an instrument for change and renewal, unlike the petrified Yiddish of the "ghetto."

The prophetic calling of the *Haskalah* was, therefore, no "lifeless rationality," but a kind of awakening to life.⁹

The trope of revival as flowering was prevalent in the early twentieth century. It appears, for instance, in Bialik's 1907 essay "*Shiratenu ha-tse'ira*" ("Our Young Poetry"), which discusses the new generation of Hebrew writers that had recently emerged. Bialik describes these young poets, including Ya'akov Kahan, Ya'akov Steinberg, and Zalman Shneour, as concerned with the eternal and individualistic themes of "life and death, love and hatred, nature and the human soul," rather than with the collective and its needs for representation. He compares them to "white flowers" that have blossomed on the ancient tree of Hebrew literature, flowers whose continued existence and ability to bear future fruit remains undetermined (Bialik 1954, 234). In just a few years' time, Ben Yitzhak would be counted among these same poets. His published poetry also meditates on nature, life and death, the cosmos, and avoids nationalist themes and pathos, focusing on the "silence" that "will blossom from [the] lips" of the "blessed."¹⁰

Floral images and verbs connoting blossoming are ubiquitous in Ben Yitzhak's Hebrew oeuvre; yet these flowers are suggestive of death and the passing of youth, rather than of revival. In 1912, the young poet published his poem "*Kintot ha-yom*" ("Day's Decline") in Aḥad Ha'am's Hebrew journal *Ha-shiloaḥ*. The poem opens with the following stanza:

בִּשְׁקֹעַ מְדוּרוֹת-חַיֵּינוּ הָאֲדֻמּוֹת
נָסִיר מֵעַל מִצְחֵנוּ זֵר-הַחֲגִיגוֹת
פְּרוּעַ-הֶעָלִים וְהַשּׁוֹשַׁנִּים הַנּוֹשְׁרוֹת,
וְאַחַר דּוּמָם נֵרֵד אֶל הַנְּהָרוֹת.

The crimson fires of our lives fading
we lift the festival wreaths from our brows
with their unkempt leaves and falling petals,
and then, in silence go down to the rivers.

(Ben Yitzhak 2003, 30–31)

---

9 "Man kann die Haskalah blächeln, ihr kindhaftes Vertrauen – lebloser Rationalismus war sie nicht. Denn in ihr schlug sich ein verdüstertes Auge verjüngt auf. Es müsste schon ein sonderbarer Rationalismus sein der sich an der Prophetie erbaut. Und doch war dem so. Die Propheten waren ihre Erwecker. Aber wunderbar, die hebräische Sprache die alte Religionsprache wie viele meinen wollen, war der Bote eines neuen Weltgefühls im Ghetto mit den neuen Forderungen kam ihr verjüngstes Leben, sie...blühte wie Blumen nach der Nacht, und ihr Blütungen kam über die Dusterkeit der Erstarrten" (CZA A165/5).
10 While Ben Yitzhak's published poetry does not directly address historical events and nationalist themes, his unpublished writing in Hebrew and German contains references to the Zionist movement and to World War I. On his political writing in Hebrew, see (Hever 1993, 122–155). On his literary engagement with World War I, see (Barzilai 2013).

The first word of the Hebrew poem, "*bi-shkoʻa*" ("fading" or "sinking"), is a term of decline, reminiscent of the sunset: the redness of the fires subsequently evokes the end of days and not their bright burning. The Hebrew verbs "*nasir*," "*noshrot*," and "*nered*" convey the downward motions of removing wreaths, falling flowers, and the procession "down to the rivers". The last line of the entire poem depicts the "moaning" of "black lyres," linking the rivers of the first stanza to the streams of Babylon, portrayed in Psalm 137 as a site of exile, mourning, and the cessation of song.

In this poem, the flower is one of the prominent symbols of exilic decline. The removal of the festival wreaths coincides with the falling of *shoshanim*, a biblical term for flowers that also appears in Song of Songs and Psalms ("*la-menatseaḥ ʻal shoshanim*," "For the lead player, on *shoshanim*," Psalms 69:1 in Alter 2007, 236). In the second stanza, the speaker observes in the "reddish twilight" how "white flowers" come, carried on the face of the water from a "joyful garden," representing "our youth" that is drifting by. As in other poems by Ben Yitzhak, here too the poet attempts to capture the brief period between the waning of life and its utter disappearance; spring and youth are evanescent and will be soon forgotten. The white flowers are not a symbol of a delicate revival, as in Bialik's essay, but of evanescent youth and the passage of time ("our youth has drifted past"). In another poetic fragment, Ben Yitzhak even rhymes the word spring, "*aviv*," with the verb "to forget him," "*shekhaḥtiv*" (Ben Yitzhak 2003, 46–47).

Writing about decline in the Hebrew language, Ben Yitzhak was attuned to developments in European literature, but also had to negotiate the ideological dictum "that the new Hebrew literature should be a literature of national renewal reflecting and shaping actual national realities and the eternal national spirit of the Jewish people" (Bar-Yosef 1994, 150). As Hamutal Bar-Yosef explains, this optimism of the Zionist ethos – and Ben Yitzhak was a committed Zionist who worked, in the post-World War I period, for the Zionist Organization in London – functioned at cross-purposes with the desire to stand on equal ground with contemporary European literature that was "saturated with an atmosphere of pessimism, subjectivism, and amorality" (Bar-Yosef 1994, 151; Hever 1993, 123). When we consider, however, the pessimism of the exilic Psalm, it becomes evident that Ben Yitzhak modernized the Hebrew language by merging ancient tropes with a fin-de-siècle aesthetics.

Two short fragments, one written in Hebrew and published posthumously, and the other composed in German, both concerning ars poetical flowers. When read side by side, these fragments delineate a poetics of German-Hebrew address. The central image that the two pieces share is that of a "flower of shame," or a flower colored by shame, the cause of which remains unknown. They stand in conflict with the notion of a more positive Hebrew flowering and Zionist regeneration. This common image across German and Hebrew drafts reveals how Ben Yitzhak experimented with the expression of the same poetic idea in different languages, rewriting the notion of shameful flowering.

הוֹי שׁוֹשַׁנַּת הָעֲמָקִים לִבְנַת בּשֶׁת

O lily of the valley the whiteness of shame

(Ben Yitzhak 2003, 50–51)

An ein Schneeblümchen (?)

Oh Blume der Scham im Schnee
Wie ist die Sonne fern
Rein und bleich vor Weh
Oh Du ihr früher Stern

To a little Snow-flower (?)

O flower of shame in the snow
The sun appears so far
Pure and pale with woe
O you, her former star

(CZA A165/22)[11]

The unpublished German text dates back to 1924, and the Hebrew fragment was written toward the end of the same year (Ben Yitzhak 1992, 70). Both were composed after Ben Yitzhak had all but ceased to publish Hebrew poetry and can thus be understood as retrospective comments on the potential of modern poetic expression in Hebrew. The rhymed German "An ein Schneeblümchen" and the condensed, haiku-like Hebrew line are both addresses to flowers, linking shame and whiteness. In Jewish tradition, to shame someone in public is "to whiten their face" (*halbanat panim*), an act that the Babylonian Talmud likens to murder (bBM 58:2). The "lily of the valleys" (*shoshanat ha-'amakim*) is one of the beloved's names in the Song of Songs. While this flower became "the very epitome of blossoming in the symbolism of the Bible" and appears "in prophetic visions about the restoration of Zion to her former glory," Ben Yitzhak connects the white

---

[11] Ben Yitzhak himself added the question mark within parentheses at the end of the title. All translations of the German poems from Ben Yitzhak's archive are mine.

blossoming of the lily to shame thus playing down the idea of restoration (Bloch and Bloch 1995, 148–149).[12]

When read alongside the German stanza, the shameful whiteness of the *shoshana* becomes colored, as it were, by the whiteness of Europe's snowy landscapes, where both texts were written. But while the reference to snow in German only indirectly evokes whiteness, in Hebrew Ben Yitzhak uses the word "white" in a possessive structure that concretizes, as Hannan Hever has shown in other instances, the color-adjective (1993, 65–66). The attribution in German of "purity" and "paleness" to the flower plays, moreover, on the tension between the European association of whiteness with female purity and innocence and the Jewish linkage between whiteness and public shaming. When read side-by-side, the two drafts reveal how the use of similar words in different languages ("white" or "shame") complicates the process of "semiotic transformation," since these words carry different connotation in each language.[13] In other words, the shame of the "pale" flower in the snow only makes sense when read alongside the Hebrew draft, since only in Hebrew are shame and whiteness idiomatically connected. The whiteness of shame must therefore be understood as an interlingual, German-Hebrew, European-Near Eastern construct, and the affect of shame itself as linked to the flowering of Hebrew poetry in the European context.

Not only shame and whiteness but also night and day are confounded in the German stanza through the link between star and sun. When compared to a star, the flower in the snow further upends the relative positions of heaven and earth. Considering that the word for sun in German, *Sonne*, is Ben Yitzhak's own surname, the line "wie ist die Sonne fern" ("the sun is seen so far") points to a more personal relationship between the poet and his German subject

---

[12] For instance, in Hosea 14:6–8, God exclaims: "I will be as the dew to Israel, he shall blossom as the *shoshana*." In Song of Songs 2:1, the lover declares that she is a flower: "I am the rose of Sharon, / the wild lily of the valleys" ("*Ani ḥavaẓelet ha-sharon shoshanat ha-'amakim*"). Peter Cole follows Ariel Bloch and Chana Bloch in his translation of *shoshanat ha-'amakim* as "lily of the valley," but this flower has also been translated as "lotus," "hyacinth," or "narcissus" (1995, 54; 2003, 51). In present-day Hebrew, *shoshana* means rose, as translated by Ilana Pardes in her study of the Song of Songs (2013, 59).

[13] The Bulgarian translation theorist Alexander Ludskanov developed the term "semiotic transformation" to suggest that since the same word has different connotations in different languages, translators need to distill the significance of the term and find an equivalent that conveys the same notion, even when not using a similar word (Bassnett 2014, 28–29).

matter. In pursuing the Hebrew language and its lilies, Sonne has ostensibly traveled poetically, if not physically, to far off lands; his German poetic yield is but a "former star" of a glowing Hebraist sun. Nonetheless, just as distant stars continue to revolve around the sun, so the connections between *Schneeblümchen* and *shoshana*, German and Hebrew, persist. Thus, for instance, the flower in the frozen snow of the German poem evokes the image of Hebrew as "a flower after the night," rejuvenating the petrified European Jewish existence. The contradictory name of the "snow-flower" calls into question, however, the dichotomy between a frozen past and revived future, suggesting the possibility of a diasporic flowering.

In all these ways, the two fragments in Hebrew and German seem to address each other, not only their respective flowers. The canonical and prestigious "lily" comes into dialogue with the rarer, and more rarefied, "snow-flower," and the poetic device of apostrophe heightens this exchange. Apostrophe, the address to an inanimate, dead, or otherwise absent object/other renders the addressee more "present, animate, and anthropomorphic," according to Barbara Johnson (1986, 30). For Jonathan Culler, apostrophe, likewise, makes "the objects of the universe potentially responsive forces," and this dialogue with the universe reconciles subject and object as a willful act that is "accomplished poetically" (2002, 139, 143). William Blake's famous apostrophe to a flower, "O Rose, thou art sick," both anthropomorphizes the rose and shows a deeper concern for this supposedly inanimate object. The reversal of spatial and perceptual categories in the German fragment discussed above enacts the passion of apostrophe as a form of animating dialogue, and this dialogue carries forth into the Hebrew poem and back.

"Oh Blume" and "*hoy shoshana*" enact an interlingual calling that also establishes Ben Yitzhak's voice as one that moves between languages, albeit within the muted and fragmentary realm of unpublished lyric. Apostrophe, Culler reminds us, "makes its point by troping not on the meaning of the word but on the circuit or situation of communication itself," and this communication, as we have seen, takes place, for Ben Yitzhak, across poems in different languages (2002, 135). The affect of shame can be understood in this instance not only in the sense of deflowering, echoing Blake's poem, but also as an expression of embarrassment concerning lyric expression in multiple languages. Ben Yitzhak's call to these Hebrew and German flowers portrays Hebrew's modern blossoming, moreover, as a painful and even shameful form of impossible purification. These flowers are linguistically and culturally tainted, in other words, by the presence of other languages and contexts that disrupt the ideal of national monolingualism. Hebrew's flowering rests upon translation as rewriting, a process that can never be fully completed and that animates an ongoing interlingual dialogue, both public and private.¹⁴

Another unpublished fragment, dated 23–24 February 1926, expresses a similar sentiment:

כָּכָה הָיוּ רֵאשִׁית גַּעְגּוּעֵינוּ:
כְּעָנָף פּוֹרֵחַ לְנֹכַח שַׁחַר
כִּפְרָחִים
כִּדְרָאוֹן אֶרֶץ מְלֵחָה.

This was the start of our longing:
Like a flowering branch before the dawn
Like flowers
Like the shame of a barren land.

(Ben Yitzhak 2003, 62–63)

Through multiple similes, Ben Yitzhak compares the sentiment of longing to flowers and to the "shame of a barren land." The last line conveys the futility of flowering, alluding to a biblical passage in which the prophet Jeremiah tells those who no longer believe in God that they shall live in a "salty" (*melekha*) or barren and "uninhabited" land (Jeremiah 17:6). Although the object of the speaker's longing remains unclear, the fragment juxtaposes flowering and barrenness, suggesting that this particular flowering branch might not yield fruits. Bialik, in the essay discussed above, asked whether the flowers of new Hebrew poetry will "yield fruits and fruits of fruits or will the first storm carry them away and scatter them like chaff?" (1954, 234). The image of a fruit implies a particular telos for the flowering, whereas Ben Yitzhak's art was one of sowing without any expectation of reaping, as he wrote in his last-published poem, "Blessed Are They Who Sow and Do Not Reap" (2003, 43). Chana Kronfeld describes this Hebrew poetic endeavor as a refusal "to constitute his minor modernist project as productive ... resisting reterritorialization, identity, and income" (1996, 17). Kronfeld considers the choice to write and publish in Hebrew as "the ultimate act of modernist oppositionality." It denied Ben Yitzhak entry to the modernist canon

---

14 André Lefevere considers all translation a form of rewriting, whereas for Menakhem Perry it is the particular process of "autotranslation" that enables a writer to undertake "bold shifts from the source text," blurring the boundaries between translation and rewriting. When systematic, such shifts can "serve as powerful indicators of the activity of [translational] norms" governing the relationships between the two languages and their literatures. (Lefevere 1992, 9–10; Perry 1981, esp. 181). This activity of translational norms is necessarily charged, for Lawrence Venuti, with "ideological force," since these norms are "produced and enlisted in cultural and political agendas" (Venuti 1998, 29).

in which he belonged and which he critiqued. This external, dialogic tension with German modernism manifested itself, however, also in an internal conversation between German and Hebrew poems. Laced with shame and inhibition, the German-Hebrew dialogue allowed Ben Yitzhak to develop his "minimalist, pared down expression," as well as his aesthetics of process, rather than reaping. (Kronfeld 1996, 16).

2 Arrested translation

The idea that apostrophe and address work across poems to establish a multilingual poetics – and not only within the confines of a single poem – can help elucidate Ben Yitzhak's self-translations as well. As Susan Bassnett maintains, "the concept of the original in self-translation is far more fluid than in other kinds of translation, and indeed raises doubts as to whether an original can be said to exist at all" (2013, 20). Bassnett even encourages us to reconsider the necessity of the term "self-translation" and to interpret the writer's work more holistically as a series of rewritings, at times across languages, in which a point of origins is often lost or unknown (2013, 24). Taking up the case of Dan Pagis's German and Hebrew drafts of the same poem, Na'ama Rokem likewise claims that the poetic draft constitutes "a series of crossroads that offer multiple possibilities," revealing the pursuit of translation as "a *process* rather than a *product*" (2015). Ben Yitzhak's unpublished writings provide us with a glimpse into the open-ended nature of translation experiments in German and Hebrew. His rewritings not only unsettle any stable hierarchy or chronological relationship between these two languages, but also show that this practice of self-translation was inherent to his poetics of non-productivity and restraint.

A case in point is the 1913 poem "*Malkhut*" ("Royalty") that exists in Ben Yitzhak's archive as an incomplete bilingual draft, written on a single piece of paper. Because both language versions of this poem appear side by side, the direction of translation remains unclear, suggesting a process of interlingual experimentation. In addition, both drafts flank a German-language letter that, through its address to a young woman, stands in dialogue with the mode of poetic address to a female other, the figure of night, in the German and Hebrew lyric drafts. Signed in the published Hebrew version "Venice, 1910," "*Malkhut*" also needs to be read in relation to the German tradition of poetic writing about Venice, from Goethe through Nietzsche, to Rilke and Trakl. This complex web of textual relationships underscores the co-presence of German and Hebrew writings in Ben Yitzhak's creative process and the importance of German for his "minor modernism" in Hebrew (Kronfeld 1996, 17).

Both Hebrew and German versions of "*Malkhut*" open with the decline of royalty expressed by the downward sweep of a heavy crown and robe. Through the Hebrew verb "*yishtefu*," to spill, the robe's train comes to resemble the water of the sea; similarly, the first-person description of royal decline fluidly transitions into an image of a moaning sea.

הַיּוֹם יִדְעַךְ בַּעֲטַרְתִּי
יַכְבִּיד הַזָּהָב עַל מִצְחִי
שׁוּלֵי מְעִילִי יִשְׁטְפוּ עַל פְּנֵי מַעֲלוֹת הַשַּׁיִשׁ
מַה יֶּהֱמֶה הַיָּם בִּפְאֵר יְגוֹן הָעֶרֶב

Day flickers and dies in my crown,
the gold weighs on my brow;
my robe's train spills over the marble stairs
and the sea moans
into the splendor of evening's despair.

(Ben Yitzhak 2003, 33)

Der Tag verglimmt in meiner Krone
Der goldne Reifen beschwert mir die Stirn
Mein Gewand wallt den Marmor hinunter
Was rauscht das Meer in weher Abendpracht

The day's glimmer goes out in my crown
The golden hoop weighs upon my brow
My robe flows down the marble
How the sea roars in the pained glory of evening

(CZA A165/5)

In the Hebrew, the word for "marble stairs," "*ma'alot*," evokes the biblical term for stairs (as in Kings 1:19), but also the term for ascent, referring to the pilgrimage to the Temple. The association with the Temple is strengthened through term "*shuley me'ili*," "my robe's train," referring to the clothing that Aaron, as a Temple priest, is instructed to prepare and don (Exodus 28:34 and 39:25).[15] But instead of ascending to a position of royalty or of connection with the divine, the poem's speaker is weighed down by his golden crown. His robe also spills in a downward motion, enhanced in the German version through the words "wallt ... hinunter" ("flows down"), suggestive of flowing water and thereby linking robe and sea, also with the help of the forceful motion implied by "hinunter."

---

15 In Isaiah's vision, the "edges" ("*shulav*") of God fill the divine hall (Isaiah 6:1). I am grateful to Yosefa Raz for this allusion and for the reference to the *Shekhina* in the poem's title.

The German first stanza corresponds, moreover, to an undated German poem found in Ben Yitzhak's archive in which the same term for "robe" (*Gewand*) appears. The train of the soul's robe in this German poem is also described as dragging, and then resting upon stones.

> Jetzt wölben sich
> in breiten Bogen
> die Verse
> zu errichten der Seele
> ihren Feiertag
>
> Die lange ihr Gewand
> schleppte im Staub
> und an den verlassenen
> Steinen schlief.
>
> Now the verses
> curve into a broad bow
> to erect for the soul
> its holiday
>
> The train of her robe
> drags in the dust
> and rests on the forsaken stones.
>
> (CZA A165/5)

In this self-reflexive poem, poetic verses are animated, creating broad bows, possibly rainbows, that celebrate the soul. The second stanza, however, turns from the sky and its joyous creation to the earth and the soul's robe, the train of which drags in the dust. The poem ends, as do several of Ben Yitzhak's Hebrew poems, with muteness, or the cessation of song: "Mute like her / and flowers-forgotten" ("Stumm wie sie / und blütenvergessen").

Although "*Malkhut*" resembles this ars poetical draft, it begins with the image of declining royalty, rather than ending at this point. Indeed, the tone of "*Malkhut*" dramatically changes as the speaker turns to address, rather than merely describe, his interlocutor. As Tuvia Rübner has suggested, the Baroque qualities of the first stanza, reminiscent of the work of Hugo von Hoffmanstahl, including the golden hues of sunset and crown and rich materials of the robe and marble, are reduced, in the second stanza, to a starker, black and white opposition (Rübner 1986, 317–318). The poem shifts from a decadent and static scene of solipsistic decline to an unfolding relationship with the feminine other who, through the elements of wind and voice, potentially opens the way for expression and resurgence or rising. The Hebrew *ruaḥ* (wind, but also breath or spirit, in biblical Hebrew) the impermanent-eternal medium evoked in other Ben Yitzhak poems of the same period such as "When Nights Grow White," lifts the black hair of the addressee, trailing it across the white marble stairs upon which she is seated. Unlike the heavy priestly or royal mantel, the hair does not drag or fall but is carried in the air, full of motion.

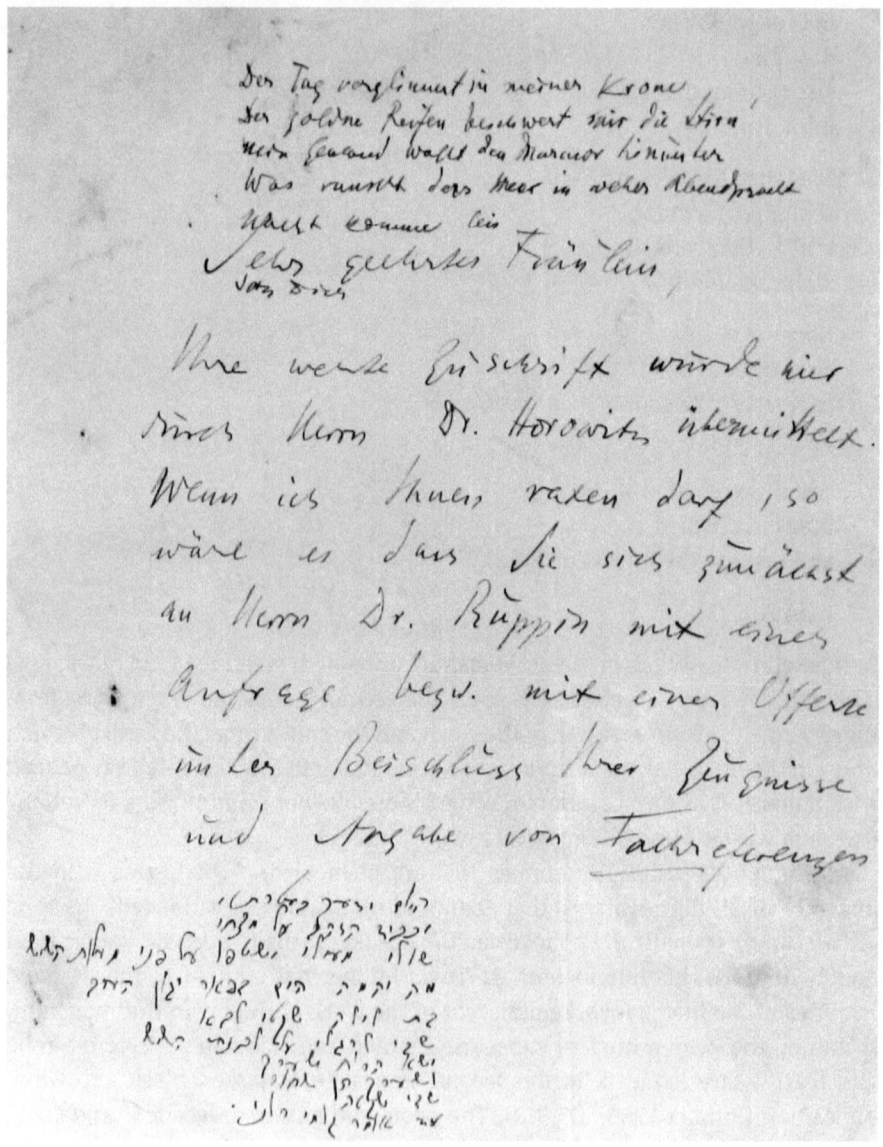

Fig. 1: Manuscript of Avraham Ben Yitzhak's *"Malkhut"* in German and Hebrew (Central Zionist Archives, Jerusalem, A165/5).

In the bilingual draft, the second stanza is represented in German by two lines only, which, like the addressee's hair, trail into the draft of the letter: "Nacht komme leis / Setz Dich" ("Night come quietly / sit down"). A fuller version of the same stanza appears in the Hebrew draft, although it is also missing one line – "Now the waters swell—" – when compared with the 1913 published poem.

בַּת לַיְלָה שְׁקֵטִי לָבֹא
שְׁבִי לְרַגְלַי עַל לִבְנַת הַשַּׁיִשׁ
יִשָּׂא הָרוּחַ שְׂעָרֵךְ
וּשְׂעָרֵךְ הֵן שָׁחוֹר
[—הִנֵּה גָאוּ הַמַּיִם]
שְׁבִי שְׁקֵטָה
עַד אֹמַר קוּמִי רֹנִּי.

Daughter of night come quietly
sit at my feet on the marble's whiteness
the wind will lift your hair
in all its blackness
[Now the waters swell—]
be still
until I say, rise and sing.

(Ben Yitzhak 2003, 33)

The title of the Hebrew poem, "*Malkhut*," alludes to the Kabbalistic *sephira* (emanation) associated with the *Shekhina* (the immanent divine presence), and the poem concludes with a command, or call, to the daughter of the night, a combined Lilith and *Shekhina* figure, to "rise" and give a ringing "cry."[16] This utterance is both postponed and immanent, "*ad omar*," "until I say."

The phrase "*kumi roni*" ("Rise, sing" in Peter Cole's translation) can convey two opposed meanings in biblical Hebrew: most commonly *roni* suggests a return to life through joyous song (as in the Psalms), but it can also be a call of anguish, as in Lamentations.[17] The combination of the two verbs in "rise and sing" alludes directly to Lamentations 2:19, where daughter-Zion, "*bat-tsiyon*," is addressed and told to "arise" and "cry out at night," to "pour out [her] heart like water / In the presence of the Lord!" (Stein 1999, 1756). The verb *roni* connotes here weeping, rather

---

[16] The title "*Malkhut*" also alludes to Ibn Gabirol's famous liturgical poem "*Keter Malkhut*" ("The Kingly Crown").
[17] See, for example, *Jeremiah* 31:7 where the verb "*la-ron*" unambiguously connotes happiness and rejoicing. In *Proverbs* 1:20 and 8:3 the same verb is used in association with the voice of wisdom, describing wisdom shouting in the streets ("חכמות בחוץ תרנה / ברחובות תתן קולה").

than rejoicing. Furthermore, in verses 18–19 of this second Lamentations chapter, the word "night" appears twice ("*yomam va-layla*" and "*kumi roni ba-layla*"), thus strengthening the connection of Ben Yitzhak's poem to this particular biblical passage through the figure of *bat layla*, daughter night.[18] For Gershom Scholem, writing only a few years after Ben Yitzhak composed these drafts, lamentations is the language of destruction and silence that, in Lina Barouch's words, "equally mourns the 'Fall' of language and grants hopes for its redemption" (Barouch 2010, 2). By distilling the phrase "*kumi roni*" from Lamentations 2:19, Ben Yitzhak similarly laments language itself, allowing "the infinity of silence" to follow this phrase that ends the Hebrew poem (Scholem quoted in Barouch 2010, 24).

As a text mourning the destruction of Jerusalem and the Temple that is recited on the day of commemoration for this destruction (*Tish'ah be-av*), Lamentations provides the Jewish correlative to the Viennese fin-de-siècle sense of decline in the first stanza. It transports European decadence into a mythic key, while also raising questions regarding the very language in which one might voice lament for a culture and its icons. We might associate the first half of the poem in German with fin-de-siècle decadence – here literalizing the Latin *decadere*, to fall or sink – and the second half in Hebrew with the urgency of language revival. For Rübner, Ben Yitzhak contrasts the falseness of royalty and its dying beauty with the mourning of the black-haired daughter of the night, suggesting a religious awakening that is held in check (1986, 318–319). But this division into the German-influenced and the biblical-influenced stanzas – graphically represented by the trailing off of the German stanza on the piece of paper – neglects the Temple motifs already present in the first stanza, particularly in the Hebrew version. I suggest, instead, that this particular lamentation could only be heard through an act of translation, even when this translation remains in the margins, ultimately relegated to silence.

Friedrich Nietzsche's 1888 Venice or "Gondola" poem is an important intertext for Malkhut in its entirety. In a conversation with Leah Goldberg, Ben Yitzhak mentions this poem as one of his favorite works by Nietzsche and he also discusses its last line – "Hörte mir jemand zu?" ("Was anyone listening?") – as a question that has not received an answer or echo because of the destruction of the culture from which it arose (Goldberg 1952, 30). Dated "Venice 1910," Ben Yitzhak's poem, like Nietsche's, consists of two stanzas, and the golden crown of the first stanza is reminiscent of Nietzsche's depiction of singing as "golden drops." In both texts, moreover, the speaker is situated at the edge of the water, listening to the sound of the sea, in Ben Yitzhak's case, and to the music carried across the "quivering expanse," in Nietzsche's (2007, 29–30).

---

18 Semantically, the addition of *bat* to a place name does not signify the daughter of that place, but personifies the place itself as daughter. Accordingly, I translate *bat layla* as daughter night (Berlin 2002, 10–12).

In Nietzsche's poem, the animated soul of the speaker responds to the sound of song, "Gesang," coming from afar, with its own private song, but it is unclear whether anyone hears the soul's music. In view of the German "Venice" song, we might approach the two figures in *"Malkhut"* as two aspects of one being, the speaker and his soul or muse. This intimate division finds another echo in the presence of both Hebrew and German drafts on the same piece of paper, as though one were the reflection of the other. Richard Block reads Nietzsche's poem as "the impossibility of the self to escape its own dialectical or metaphysical enclosure." He claims that while initially the speaker dissolves into Venice and its music, ultimately the external environment disappears and the speaker cannot move across the bridge or find the other but remains within a circle of self-questioning and self-mirroring (Block 2005, 207, 209–210). Ben Yitzhak's counterpart is, likewise, an instrument of song, if not a literal one as in Nietzsche's poem. Still, while "daughter night" is told to "come quietly" and "sit quietly," she is also ordered to "rise, sing." The poem does not cast doubt on the possibility of this song as a public utterance, even when it is postponed.

This layering of Jerusalem Temple imagery, Lamentations, and Nietzsche's Venice finds its literal and material equivalent in the presence of the two versions, German and Hebrew, on the piece of paper preserved in the archive. The presence of both German and Hebrew drafts complicates the call within the poem to *bat layla* (daughter night) or *Nacht* (night). Hesitating between German and Hebrew, Ben Yitzhak scribbled the two incomplete poems on the margins of a drafted letter, the status of which remains undetermined. The text of the letter is centrally situated on the page, with the German poem written above it and the Hebrew below. In the letter, Sonne advises a young woman to apply to Dr. Ruppin, presumably the German-Jewish Zionist leader Arthur Ruppin, with an inquiry or offer supported by testimonials (possibly certificates) and professional references.[19] Addressed to a young woman, but in a formal, non-poetic register of German, the letter provides advice on future action by the addressee. As such, it stands in implicit relationship to the address to the female figure in the poem itself.

If the speaker of the poem calls upon daughter night to "rise and sing," this deferred call for a form of rejuvenation enacts Ben Yitzhak's own commitment to the Zionist enterprise. Ben Yitzhak participated in several Zionist Congresses and was sent, in 1917, by the Zionist Committee to investigate the situation of Jews in areas of Polish and Russian occupation. Joining the Zionist Confederation in London in 1919, he was appointed secretary of the Palestine section, and later

---

19 The letter in German reads as follows: "Ihre wende Zuschrift wurde mir durch Herrn Dr. Horowitz übermittelt. Wenn ich ihnen raten darf, so wäre es dass Sie sich zunächst an Herrn Dr. Ruppin mit einer Anfrage bezw. mit einer Offerte unter Beischluss Ihrer Zeugnisse und Angabe von Fachreferenzen" (CZA A165/5).

became the main secretary of the Confederation's administration. Ben Yitzhak was critical, however, of the "hyper-political" and, in his view, financially irresponsible behavior of central factions in the Zionist movement. He resigned in 1921, after the group with which he was affiliated, headed by Julius Simon and Neḥemia de-Lima, published a highly controversial report advocating the economic solvency and efficiency of the Jewish settlement in Palestine (Hever 1993, 122–128).

In view of this biographical background, the very presence of the (accidental) German letter infuses the universal lyric language of Ben Yitzhak's poetry with a specific time, place, and political horizon. "*Malkhut*," published more than a decade prior to Ben Yitzhak's resignation, is indirectly linked, through this draft, to the poet's political engagement and to Ruppin himself, who became director of the Palestine Office of the World Zionist Organization in 1908. On the one hand, the image of the end of royalty and the potential for the new rising of the daughter create a poetic equivalent to Ruppin's turn to Palestine and his practical organizational activities to settle Jews in this land. On the other hand, Ben Yitzhak himself remained in Vienna until 1938, when forced to leave, ceasing to publish his Hebrew poetry and expressing, even in this poem, a sense of hesitation and mourning. Considering the possibility of song in a bilingual context, Ben Yitzhak uses translation as a means to promote Hebrew modernism without advocating a blithe rejoicing in any language.

Drawing on an entourage of female figures/muses – *bat layla*, *Nacht*, and the *Fräulein* of the letter – Ben Yitzhak mediates between German and Hebrew and their different modes of address. He predicates the possibility of song, even if this song is a lamenting cry, on the address to this Other who must herself then rise and sing. In contradistinction to the notion of apostrophe as constitutive of the lyrical voice, of the poet's "I," the role of the poem's speaker as public mediator is brought to the fore with the help of the letter's act of non-lyrical communication and of address to another who is capable of response; he is the one who transmits the song to others, just as he passes the letter and its female subject from Dr. Horowitz to Dr. Ruppin. The formal-official register of the German letter stands in contrast, nonetheless, to the intimacy of the German poetic line, "Night come quietly," and to Ben Yitzhak's use of the informal "du" in the poem, in contrast to the letter's formal "Sie" address. In these ways, the presence of the letter alongside the two poetic versions draws our attention away from poetic self-constitution and towards the processes of mediation and translation between languages and registers, as well as between the political and the poetical spheres.

***

The work of language revival was, for Ben Yitzhak, a translational and interpersonal one, always addressed to another entity, a "you," to a different language, place, and time. In the mid-twenties, moreover, the poet attempted to write in his native Yiddish, implicitly retracting his earlier depreciatory attitude towards this language.[20] The way in which his oeuvre has been canonized to this day – only in Hebrew, as lyric poems and fragments of lyric – thus obscures the multilingualism inherent to Ben Yitzhak's efforts to reshape the Hebrew language itself. As Walter Benjamin writes in "The Task of the Translator," "the language of translation envelops its content like a royal robe with ample folds. For it signifies a more exalted language than its own and thus remains unsuited to its content, overpowering and alien." The superfluous nature of translation, its unsuitability to the original, elevates the language of translation and retains its foreignness, rather than merely emphasizing the kinship between languages and their ability to approximate each other (Benjamin 1996, 258, 256–257). Ben Yitzhak's poems depict the shame of flowering and the decline of royalty in the context of rewriting, shoring up the poetic act as a form of translation that retains its foreign and exalted nature. We can thus read his decadent aesthetic not only as a reflection of his times, but also as a sign of his German-Hebrew poetics. Hebrew, the central language of Ben Yitzhak's published expression, was unsuited in many respects to the European contents of his verse; it also emerged through a process of self-translation. The result was an affect of shame for poet and readers alike. And, perhaps because of this shame, the excesses of Ben Yitzhak's translational poetics have not been discussed and his archive "drags in the dust." Ben Yitzhak's Hebrew and German poems address each other, however, and not only their internal female addresses. They point to a new, interlinguistic mode of reading that is attentive to the ample folds of poetry's own robes.

Works cited

Alter, Robert. The Book of Psalms: A Translation with Commentary. New York: W.W. Norton & Company, 2007.
Bar-Yosef, Hamutal. "Romanticism and Decadence in the Literature of the Hebrew Revival." *Comparative Literature* 46.2 (1994): 146–181.
Barouch, Lina. "Lamenting Language Itself: Gershom Scholem on the Silent Language of Lamentations." *New German Critique* 37.3 111 (2010): 1–26.
Barzilai, Maya. "The Poetics of Statelessness: Avraham Ben Yitzhak after World War I." *Naharaim* 7.1–2 (2013): 111–130.

---

20 Ben Yitzhak drafted a Yiddish poem beginning with the line *"velt (vi) bistu shoyn avek geshtorbn!"* ("world [how] you have already died away!"), dating it 1 December 1925, one day after the composition of the posthumously published Hebrew poem *"met ha-'olam hitporer shildo"* ("The world has died"). For a discussion of the two poems, see (Barzilai 2014).

—. "Translation on the Margins: Hebrew-German-Yiddish Multilingualism in Avraham Ben Yitzhak and Yoel Hoffmann." *Journal of Jewish Identities* 7.1 (2014): 109–128.
Bassnett, Susan. "The Self-Translator as Rewriter." *Self-Translation: Brokering Originality in Hybrid Culture*. Ed. Cordingly, Anthony. London: Bloomsbury, 2013. 13–25.
—. *Translation Studies*. London: Routledge, 2014.
Ben Yitzhak, Avraham. *Collected Poems*. Trans. Cole, Peter. Jerusalem: Ibis, 2003.
—. *Kol ha-shirim*. Ed. Hever, Hannan. Tel Aviv: Ha-kibbutz ha-me'uhad, 1992.
Benjamin, Walter. "The Task of the Translator." *Walter Benjamin: Selected Writings*. Eds. Bullock, Marcus and Michael W. Jennings. Vol. 1. Cambridge: Harvard University Press, 1996. 253–263.
Berlin, Adele. *Lamentations: A Commentary*. Louisville: Westminster John Knox Press, 2002.
Bialik, Ḥaim Naḥman. "*Shiratenu ha-tse'ira*." *Kol kitvei Ḥaim Naḥman Bialik*. Tel-Aviv: Dvir, 1954. 230–235.
Bloch, Ariel A., and Chana Bloch. *The Song of Songs: A New Translation with an Introduction and Commentary*. New York: Random House, 1995.
Block, Richard. "Falling to the Stars: Georg Trakl's 'In Venedig' in Light of Venice Poems by Nietzsche and Rilke." *The German Quarterly* 78.2 (2005): 207–223.
Culler, Jonathan. "Apostrophe." *The Pursuit of Signs: Semiotics, Literature, Deconstruction*. Ithaca: Cornell University Press, 2002. 135–154.
Goldberg, Leah. *Pegisha 'im meshorer: 'al Avraham Ben Yitzhak Sonne*. Merḥavya: Sifriyat po'alim, 1952.
Grutman, Rainier. "Beckett and Beyond: Putting Self-Translation in Perspective." *Orbis Litterarum* 68.3 (2013): 188–206.
Hever, Hannan. *Periḥat ha-dumiya: shirat Avraham Ben Yitzhak*. Tel Aviv: Ha-kibbutz ha-me'uhad, 1993.
Johnson, Barbara. "Apostrophe, Animation, and Abortion." *Diacritics* 16.1 (1986): 28–47.
Kronfeld, Chana. *On the Margins of Modernism: Decentering Literary Dynamics*. Berkeley: University of California Press, 1996.
Lefevere, André. *Translation, Rewriting and the Manipulation of Literary Frame*. London: Routledge, 1992.
Nietzsche, Friedrich Wilhelm. *Ecce Homo: How to Become What You Are*. Trans. Large, Duncan. Oxford: Oxford University Press, 2007. Print.
Pardes, Ilana. *Agnon's Moonstruck Lovers: The Song of Songs in Israeli Culture*. Seattle: University of Washington Press, 2013. Print.
Perry, Menakhem. "Thematic and Structural Shifts in Autotranslations by Bilingual Hebrew-Yiddish Writers: The Case of Mendele Mokher Sforim." *Poetics Today* 2.4 (1981): 181–192.
Rokem, Na'ama. "The Translator's Laboratory: A Draft from the Dan Pagis Archive." http://perspectives.ajsnet.org/translation-issue/the-translators-laboratory-a-draft-from-the-dan-pagis-archive/ *AJS Perspectives*. 2015 (29 June 2016).
Rübner, Tuvia. "*Ha-tamid bli omer: 'al Avraham Ben Yitzhak*." *Meḥkarei yerushalayim be-sifrut 'ivrit* 9 (1986): 311–323.
Sadan, Dov. *Ben din le-ḥeshbon*. Tel-Aviv: Dvir, 1963.
Stein, Rabbi David E. Sulomm, ed. *JPS Hebrew-English Tanakh*. Philadelphia: Jewish Publication Society, 1999.
Venuti, Lawrence. *The Scandals of Translation: Towards an Ethics of Difference*. London: Routledge, 1998.
Zach, Natan. "*Lifney sha'ar 'im ne'ila (le-shirat Avraham Ben Yitzhak)*." *Davar* Hotza'at davar, 6.10.1960: 7–8.

Na'ama Rokem
Dan Pagis's Laboratory: Between German and Hebrew

Like many other Hebrew poets, Dan Pagis was not a native speaker of the language in which he wrote. He belongs to a group of authors who were born in German-speaking Europe in the first half of the twentieth century and who became important Israeli poets of the state generation (other prominent examples are Yehuda Amichai, Nathan Zach and Tuvia Rübner, who is discussed by Rachel Seelig in this volume.)[1] After his arrival in Israel in 1946, Pagis adopted a Hebrew first name and preferred not to write or speak about his experiences during the war or his prewar life. He devoted his academic career to the study of medieval Hebrew poetry and to the recovery of the modernist Hebrew poetry of David Vogel. His own Hebrew poetry is written primarily in a deceptively simple vernacular idiom, a Hebrew spoken by Israelis in their everyday lives.

However, there is evidence that Pagis did not leave the German language entirely behind him. For example, Pagis turned to German in annotating and organizing the drafts of the prose poems posthumously collected and published under the title *Father*. In those drafts, the German language seems to represent some kind of super-ego that hovers above the poems, asking questions such as: "take out? If it stays, it could be less symbolic, even if it's all true" (Pagis 1991, 380).[2] In other cases, Pagis's German seems to constitute a subtext or a linguistic subconscious that lurks beneath the Hebrew text. Anne Birkenhauer, one of Pagis's German translators, has argued that her translations bring such subtexts to light, revealing alliterations and word plays that constitute a kind of German shadow to the Hebrew poem. An apposite example is the poem "Draft of a Reparations Agreement," which responds to the German term "Wiedergutmachung" (literally: making good again) by ironically promising that "Everything will be returned to its place/ [...] The scream back into the throat./ The gold teeth back to the gums./ The terror" (Pagis 1989, 35). As Birkenhauer notes, Pagis's wry comment on the German terminology remains implicit in the Hebrew version of the poem and becomes explicit only when it is translated into German (Pagis 2003, 270).

---

[1] See also Eshel (1999); Ezrahi (2000); and Shabat-Nadir (2016).
[2] Hannan Hever has since published a facsimile of the drafts of *Father*, which reveals how important and prevalent the use of German is to Pagis's writing. The drafts merit a much more detailed and close analysis than I can provide here (Hever 2016, appendix).

The two archival documents I discuss in this article are further evidence of Pagis's ongoing engagement with the German language, but they do not fit neatly within either of the two aforementioned models. Instead of hovering above the text or lurking behind it, here the German language is a medium for dialogue and reflection. I begin with a draft of a letter that Pagis wrote to the Austrian poet Ernst Jandl, which is accompanied by two poems written in homage to him. While there is no evidence that the letter was completed and sent to its addressee or that the author planned to share the poems with other readers, I maintain that they provide a glimpse of an experiment or an exploration that becomes possible by virtue of switching into German. This "laboratory" between the languages is a space for the author to reflect on the contingency of his personal circumstances, his language choice, and his writing. This metaphor is borne out in the second case presented here, which is a draft of Pagis's translation of his own poem, "In the Laboratory," into German. Here, the author uses the translation process to reconsider his text and contemplate the different possibilities opened up by it. The process of self-translation, which remains unfinished, allows Pagis to multiply the meanings of his poem, rather than pin down one "correct" reading. This opens up a space that is a poetic and linguistic "laboratory" of sorts, in which the poet can engage in experiments. Attempting to access this experimental space, I read the poem and its incomplete translation as a reflection on fate, history and human freedom.

The private, unfinished nature of both documents – the unsent letter and homage to Jandl and the self-translated poem – thus presents a challenge, but also an opportunity. On the one hand, it is difficult to talk of authorial intention and to analyze choices made, when the ultimate choice was to keep the text from the eyes of readers. On the other hand, both cases present a valuable glimpse of the author's work process through the corrections and revisions that remain evident on the page. I argue that both documents can be read as statements on the condition of bilingualism itself, specifically the bilingual condition of a German-speaking Holocaust survivor in Israel. In the uncompleted translation process, the reader finds a space between German and Hebrew that is not governed by the teleology of the history of the survivor, as the relationship between the two languages is typically depicted in the Israeli context. In the conventional Israeli narrative, German was necessarily abandoned in the wake of the Nazi destruction, and Hebrew was its inevitable successor. Pagis's incomplete translation, with its divergent possibilities, opens a space of multiple contingent paths rather than one inevitable path.

Self-translation is emerging as a productive subfield within translation studies. Anthony Cordingley has argued that self-translators are endowed with "stereolinguistic" sensibilities, which allow them to perceive their different languages and cultures from the outside, and always in relation to one another. He explains: "self translators share with many other writers from the margins the tendency to subvert the possibility that their writing affirms a singular national culture or literature. [...] Hybridity characterizes not only many self-translators' external and textual environments but the internal bilingual and bicultural space out of which their creativity emerges" (Cordingley 2013, 2–3). Jan Hokenson and Marcella Munson use the image of stereoscopy as well, proposing that in the case of self-translated texts it is not productive to focus on the differences between source and target, as translation scholars often do, but rather to "start from a point closer to the common core of the bilingual text, that is, within the textual intersections and overlaps of versions" (Hokenson and Munson 2014, 4). Indeed, the documents presented here call for a stereoscopic reading that takes into account both the German and the Hebrew perspective without positing the primacy of either. Through such a reading, we gain a better understanding of Pagis's multilingualism and of his relationship to the historical conditions that had formed him between German and Hebrew.

1 *Zettelchen* in a bottle

Around 1985, Pagis penned a letter to the Austrian poet Ernst Jandl and attached two poems to it. Jandl, who was born in in Vienna in 1925, began publishing experimental poetry inspired by Dada and concrete poetry in the early 1950s; he was also a translator, who rendered in German seemingly "untranslatable" texts such as the nonsense poems of Gertrude Stein. In frequent public readings, he appeared as a charismatic and whimsical figure. It is hard to know exactly when Pagis encountered his work and the nature of his engagement with it. Dada and nonsense poetry did not have much traction in the Hebrew literary scene, and Pagis's writing was no exception. The letter and the poems that he addressed to Jandl seem to have been written as much for private purposes as they were intended to initiate an actual conversation. Indeed, there is no evidence that he ever sent them. Bracketing the question of an actual dialogue between the two authors, however, I read these documents as evidence of the productive space of possibility that Pagis found between German and Hebrew. In his missive to Jandl, Pagis uses the German language not only as a means of communication but also as a medium for thinking about the nature of the poem as a communicative act. He does so firstly by engaging with Jandl's avant-garde poetry and second by offering his own vision of the poem as a kind of letter in a bottle, a message that precariously seeks an addressee, but may not find him.³

Of course, it is not a coincidence that this is the topic of a German-language missive written by a Hebrew poet. The letter implicitly addresses the contingent and indeterminate nature of communication across languages and translation between them, and in particular the precarious relationship between German and Hebrew, the two languages that seem, in the wake of the Holocaust, to be positioned on two sides of an un-crossable and untranslatable abyss. The very existence of the letter could be read as counterevidence to this perception, showing as it does that the Hebrew poet continued to read and engage with German poetry and felt the need to communicate with a German writer in German. But the text of the letter shows much more than that. It indicates that switching into German provided Pagis with an opportunity to reflect on contingency itself: on the fact that no historic or biographical event, or even an event such as the writing or the reading of a poem, is necessary and inevitable. In other words, by writing the letter Pagis asserts his freedom within historical circumstances, a freedom embodied by the creative act of writing a poem.

Since the letter has not been published previously, I quote it here in full:⁴

Jerusalem

Sehr geehrter Herr Jandl,

Ihre Gedichte und ihr Sprachgefühl haben mich schon vor Jahren fasziniert, und jedes neues Buch von Ihnen, und auch einzelne Gedichte, die ich in Zeitschriften fand, waren immer ein Fest für mich. So geht es natürlich vielen anderen Lesern, aber ich möcht...[e] ich befinde mich ich gehöre zur Grupp...[e] zu Ihren Verehrern außerhalb des deutschen Sprachgebiets und ich schreibe hebräische Gedi...[chte] höre Sie dreifach: in Ihrer ursprünglichen Stimme (eine Aufnahme von einer Lesung hat mir das auch bestätigt), in einer tiefen Über...[setzung] oberflächlichen Übersetzung, und wenn ich so sagen sozusagen auch in eine[r] Tiefübersetzung. Schon in den sechziger Jahren Ich selbst schreibe hebräisch (einige Gedichtsbände, davon auch drei in Englisch und viele verschiedene mittelalterliche Studien, nach Beruf nach bin ich Mediävist in Jerusalem). Aber Ihre Auge von den... Meine Gedichte sind weit von den...in...gar nicht nahe Ihren oberflächlich gehört oder gelesen, gar nicht nahe an den

---

3 I am deliberately paraphrasing Paul Celan's formulation in his Bremen Prize speech, following the connections between Pagis and Celan established in the work of Eshel (1999) and Ezrahi (2000).
4 Hadas Shabbat-Nadir discovered this document, and the poems that accompany it, and has generously shared them with me. Ellipses represent words that I was not able to decipher. Round brackets are in the original, square brackets are my additions/clarifications. I thank James McCormick for help with deciphering some of the words. The handwriting in all of the archival documents presented in this article is not always entirely decipherable and some uncertainty remains about some of the details.

Ihrigen, aber in Wahrheit habe ~~in der Tief[e]~~ habe ich viel von Ihnen gelernt. Schon ~~und schon~~ vor vor vielleicht 20 Jahren ~~schrieb ich zwei deutsche~~ schrieb ich auch zwei deutsche Hommage Gedichte für Sie (eben nicht in meinen gewohnten damaligen oder jetzigen Stil). ~~und aber~~ war aber zu schüchtern Sie damit zu belästigen. Wir haben zwei gemeinsame bekannte (T. Carmi las mit Ihnen, auch Amichai), aber ich dachte mir: du wartest bis du einmal Ernst Jandl irgendwo triffst. ~~dann~~ Nun war ich sogar zweimal in Wien ~~im~~ Neujahr und 1984 ~~vor einen viertel? Jahr wusste aber nicht~~ konnte Sie aber nicht erreichen. ~~hätte aber gerade~~ und nahm die zwei Zettelchen wieder nachhause mit. ~~Nun aber habe ich~~ als ich zufällig in Deutschland war hörte ich ~~auf Umwegen und gerade~~ im ~~deutschen~~ [...] Rundfunk ein kurzes Interview ~~mit Ihnen und sagte an~~ mit Ihnen und ~~sagte mir: aber das war~~ kann nicht mehr warten: ich muß Ernst Jandl zu seinem Geburtstag gratulieren. ~~(Schon Sie...Aber ich denke auch...~~ (Aber Sie sind selber schuld daran) ~~Aber~~ Hier sind ~~die zwei Zettel die ich Sie schon vor~~ die so viele Jahre gewartet haben, ~~und auch [...] darauf~~ fast wie meine mittelalterliche MSS in denen ich meisten[s] schreibe ~~aber du siehst sogar...gestehe das ist aber bloß fan mail Sie sind bestimmt sehr beschäftigt, und ich wollte Ihnen nur~~

[Dear Mr. Jandl,

Your poems and your feeling for language have fascinated me for years, and every new book by you, and even individual poems that I have found in journals, were always a celebration for me. Of course, this applies to many other readers, but ~~I want [...] I am located in~~ I belong ~~to a group of~~ to your admirers outside of the German language realm and ~~I write Hebrew po ... [ems]~~ hear you in three ways: in your own original voice (a recording of a reading confirmed this for me), in a ~~deeper trans...[lation]~~ superficial translation, and ~~if I may say~~, in a sense also in a deep translation. ~~Already in the sixties~~ I myself write in Hebrew (a few volumes of poetry, among which also three in English, and ~~many~~ various medieval studies, by profession I am a Medievalist in Jerusalem). ~~But your eye of which...~~ My poems are ~~far from... not at all close to yours~~ heard or read superficially, not at all close to yours, but in truth I have ~~in depth~~ I have learnt a lot from you. Already ~~and already before~~ approximately 20 years ago ~~I wrote two German~~ I even wrote two German homage poems for you (not in my usual style, then or now). ~~And but~~ I was, however, too shy to burden you with that. We have two mutual acquaintances (T. Carmi read with you, also Amichai), but I thought to myself: you'll wait until you meet Ernst Jandl somewhere. ~~Then~~ Now I have even been to Vienna twice, in the New Year and in 1984 ~~a quarter of a year ago, but I did not know~~ but was unable to reach you. ~~I would have~~ and took the two slips of paper back home with me. ~~But now I have~~ When I happened to be in Germany, I heard ~~on a detour and in German~~ [...] radio a short interview ~~with you and said to~~ with you and ~~said to myself: but that was~~ can no longer wait: I must congratulate Ernst Jandl on his birthday (But you yourself are to blame for that) ~~But~~ here are the two notes ~~that I already before for you~~ that have waited so many years, ~~and also for~~ almost like my medieval manuscripts in which I mostly write ~~but you can even see... admit that this is nothing but fan mail you are surely very busy, and I only wanted~~][5]

Pagis introduces himself to Jandl as a loyal admirer of his poetry. He immediately clarifies that, although he has long been fascinated by Jandl's linguistic

---

[5] Unless otherwise indicated, translations from the German are my own, with the help of Rachel Seelig.

sensitivity and has celebrated the arrival of every one of his new poems, he is not a reader like any other. Making this distinction sets off a series of hesitations and self-corrections. The intention of the formulation that Pagis ultimately lands on – "ich gehöre zu Ihren Verehrern außerhalb des deutschen Sprachgebiets" – is entirely clear, of course. As a writer who lives in Jerusalem, Pagis is located "outside of" the German-speaking realm. But, there are a number of ironies that emerge from the statement as he ends up formulating it, and they are sharpened by the words that he crosses out on the way to this formulation. First, there is the assumption that most of Jandl's readers are within the German world, making Pagis the exception. And yet, Jandl's writing assiduously deconstructs the German language and brings it into contact with other languages that are allowed to interfere with it, inviting non-German readers to take part in the game (Stuckatz 2016).

Jandl's poem "Calypso" is a good example. It begins: "ich was not yet/ in brasilien/ nach brasilien/ wulld ich laik du go/ wer de wimen/ arr so ander/ so quait ander/ denn anderwo". Jandl's playful language-mixing leads to a fantasy about understanding multiple (perhaps even all) languages: "als ich anderschdehn/ mange lanquidsch/ will ich anderschdehn/ auch lanquidsch in rioo" (Jandl 2016, 98). Or perhaps it is more accurate to say that these lines make a claim for universal intelligibility via the medium of a bastardized English: if German can be creolized and turned into a variant of English, surely so can Brazilian Portuguese, allowing the visitor to understand at least something and to make himself understood. Most importantly, the borders between languages are blurred and the idea of a pure German, or a pure German-speaking realm in which Jandl's poems are received, is deconstructed.

Thus, Pagis's clarification that he is found outside of the neat confines of the German "Sprachgebiet" comes across almost as a private joke: "just like your poems themselves," he might add. Furthermore, by writing the letter in German, Pagis in fact re-inserts himself into the German-language space from which he has claimed to be removed. Indeed, Pagis struggles to find the adequate German words to describe his existence outside of German. He starts out by expressing a wish ("ich möchte…"), but rather than completing it he turns to locate himself ("ich befinde mich"). When that too turns out not to be a viable way of expressing his condition, he turns to the term "gehöre" – I belong – and starts out by imagining a group that might form this belonging. At the end of these multiple hesitations, it may not be surprising that Pagis settles on the emphatic statement that what defines him as a reader of Jandl is his existence outside of the space of the German language.

But, Pagis proceeds to clarify, rather than simply constituting a form of exclusion, his place "outside" the German language is in fact a privileged position, which allows him to hear Jandl in three different ways: in the poet's "original voice," in a "superficial translation," and in a "deep translation." This trifold distinction is illuminated by what comes after it in the letter. At this point, Pagis introduces himself to Jandl as not only a reader of his poetry but also a fellow poet and a scholar of medieval literature. And he must now perform a delicate balancing act: on the one hand, claiming symmetry between himself and his fellow poet; and, on the other, marking the difference between them. What emerges is their affinity on yet another level. Not only are Pagis and Jandl both poets, but in both cases Pagis also emphasizes the distance between superficial and deep understanding. "Superficially heard or read," Pagis's poems are completely different than Jandl's; but in fact, he professes, "I have learned a lot from you." Interestingly, in this case the word depth – "Tiefe" – is struck out, as if Pagis is hesitating precisely at the point of establishing this affinity with Jandl and showing that just as he can hear Jandl in a superficial and a deep translation, so too can his poems be heard superficially or deeply. It seems to me that Pagis is interested here not so much in making a distinction between poetry that does or does not have "depth," but rather in the precarious nature of the poem as a missive that claims to be understood or understandable. In other words, the claim for depth, here, is not a self-assured claim to status as a poet, but rather the intimation of an abyss that looms close at hand. Jandl courts this precariousness by deconstructing language, and Pagis tells him he too is always close to it because of his position as an intermediary between languages. The fact that these two languages are German and Hebrew lends the abyss an existential dimension, because Pagis is not only an intermediary but also a survivor and it is the very fact of his survival that allows him to be an intermediary. When he tells Jandl that he hears his poems on several levels at once, through the mediation of his removal from the German language, he is asking his interlocutor to think together with him about the circumstances that have created this removal.

Pagis's concern about the reception of his poems – not only whether they are read "deeply" or "superficially" but whether they can be read at all – is entirely concrete at this moment. He now mentions the two poems he has written in homage to the admired poet, adding an elaborate account of his attempts to share them with Jandl. Before I comment on this account, let me first present the poems themselves, which are attached to the letter in the archive and are both dated "Jerusalem, 1971." The first one seems to have been written in response to Jandl's visit in Jerusalem – though it remains unclear whether this is a historic visit or one that Pagis imagined – and it revolves around puns and alliterations with the poet's name:

> Hommage
>
> Ernst Jandl:
> Er ist verneinend das geheimste Ja
> ~~auch~~ [...] wir ehren ihn
> in diesen Windundsteinjerusalem
> ergebenst fernst
> Hier lacht er uns gesund
> doch
> denn erst im Sternwien
> wird Jandl ernst.
>
> [Homage
>
> Ernst Jandl:
> He is negative of the most covert yes
> ~~also~~ [...] we honor him
> in this Wind-and-stone-jerusalem
> sincerest and most distant
> here he laughs us healthy
> yet
> for only in Starry-vienna
> Jandl becomes earnest.]

Pagis contrasts between his own hometown and that of his addressee, which he renames "Windundsteinjerusalem" and "Sternwien," a gesture that seems to give starry Vienna the advantage over the stony, windy city of Jerusalem. Indeed, the poem focuses on the honor and the benefit arising from Jandl's visit, which brings the stormy city a relief in the form of healing laughter. The visit is embodied in the sounds that cross over from Jandl's name and into the poem: the repeated j, n, d, st and nst sounds of lines 2–4. This echoes a favorite strategy of Jandl's, the building of strings of assonances such as the string of o's and s's that makes the famous poem "Ottos Mopps." Pagis's poem ends with the Austrian poet's return to his home and his true identity. Here he becomes Ernst, becomes earnest, leaving the reader to ask: who was he when he "laughed us healthy"? Other questions the reader might ask are: what is the relationship between the sound play of the first part of the poem and the pun, based in the homophony between the name Ernst and the adjective earnest, that concludes it? And, what is the relationship between the different contrasts constructed in the poem (Vienna and Jerusalem, the no and the yes of the phrase "verneinend das geheimste Ja," assonance and homophony)?

The second poem, in contrast to "Hommage," does not name its addressee explicitly, though it extends Pagis's engagement with Jandl's poetic style. Proceeding from a concrete image of a storm, the poem turns into a soundscape of repeating g's, n's and w's:

Gewitter

O heiter Regenstand,
o Gegenstand und Wind
und Wand –
der Widder mit dem Sturmhorn
und dummen Widerstand,
nimm ihn aufs Korn, den Hund!
So bist du endlich windstill
hebst die Hand
so weich und wund und
unverwandt

und
unverwandt.

[Tempest

Oh serene state of rain
oh thing and storm
and wall –
oh ram with the storm-horn
and stupid resistance
stick it to him, that dog!
now you are finally still
raise your hand
so soft and sore and
steadfast

and steadfast]

Following Jandl's model, Pagis constructs the poem by creating sound-concatenations that are not immediately (or perhaps not at all) decipherable semantically. Thus, "Regenstand" leads to "Gegenstand," which leads to "Widerstand;" but the last also echoes "Wind," "Wand" and "Widder," and leads to the alliteration of "weich," "wund" and "unverwandt" in the final lines. The repetition of "unverwandt" seems to instantiate one sense of that word – steadfastness, or fixedness – a sense underscored by the echo with "Wand" (wall) and further relating to the idea of "Widerstand" (resistance). But "unverwandt" can also be read as the opposite of "verwandt" (related) and thus its repeated appearance at the end of the poem can be read also as a comment on the distance between speaker and addressee, the alienation felt by the speaker toward the language in which the poem is penned, or simply the lack of an apparent relation between the different words that comprise the poem.

In fact, the two poems are not merely difficult to understand. Rather, they are *about* the very difficulty of understanding; they confront the reader with a semantic barrier that cannot be overcome (a fixed and steadfast wall, if you will). And this, in some sense, is what Pagis is talking about when he provides Jandl with a detailed account about the difficulty that the two notes – the two "Zettelchen" that he seems to have been holding on to for over a decade – have had in making their way to their addressee. This part of the letter reflects Pagis's fundamental interest in the precarity that attends the poetic missive, an interest closely tied to his interest in crossing between German and Hebrew and to his engagement with Jandl's writing.

After he admits that he had previously been too shy to share the two poems with Jandl, Pagis shares an anecdote that borders on the surreal about his attempts to deliver them to their addressee. Having waited for years until he would "meet Jandl somewhere," he had taken the two notes with him to a visit in Vienna in early 1984 but had to take them back home with him. The second attempt is also motivated by a journey: "When I happened to be in Germany, I heard a short radio interview and could no longer wait: I had to congratulate Ernst Jandl on his birthday." Pagis's mention of the trip to Germany seems to hold the potential for a longer story, which he decides not to tell. What remains are the beginnings of it that are struck out, making for an incomplete, ungrammatical sentence: "When I was in Germany I heard ~~on a detour and precisely in German~~ radio a short interview." One can only speculate what detour Pagis may have taken on his visit to Germany, but he seems to be relieved to have discovered Jandl's voice along the way. The account of the unsuccessful attempts to bring or send the poems to Jandl culminates with Pagis's fantasy that the two notes with his poems on them are like the medieval manuscripts that are the object of his academic interest. This can be seen as a wishful thought, that their addressee will see them as a lost treasure and will read them with philological attentiveness. But it is also another loaded gesture to history, as if Pagis is telling Jandl that the crossing between German and Hebrew can only happen if historical awareness is maintained.

Will Pagis's poems arrive at their destination and be read by Jandl? While in some sense the letter itself provides a response to the question ("here, with this letter, once it reaches you, the poems as well will have arrived"), in another sense it is written precisely to question whether this is possible. Even if the poems do arrive, Jandl's poetry has deconstructed the very idea of transmission and transmissibility to such a degree that Pagis's missive to him now exists in a realm of radical contingency, an experiment with uncertain results. But, to reiterate, it is not a coincidence that this (imagined) conversation is happening with a *German* poet. As we shall now see, for Pagis this sense of contingency was closely tied to his stereoscopic, bilingual vision, activated in the laboratory of self-translation.

2 The translator's laboratory

Pagis's archive contains a number of attempts at self-translation into German. One example is his translation of a poem from the cycle "The Caveman is Silent," which was published in the book *Gilgul* in 1970. There is no concrete evidence that Pagis completed the translations or that he intended to publish them. But the incomplete draft gives us a glimpse into the dynamics of Pagis's movements between the languages.[6] Under the handwritten Hebrew title, "Ba-ma'abada," we find Pagis's German version, "Im Laboratorium." The draft is unfinished, documenting the poet and self-translator's work process and giving us a glimpse of the decisions he makes, as well as some decisions he cannot make. The German version of "In the Laboratory" does not exist before the Hebrew one, nor is it a correction or annotation of it. In fact, it is not a known entity, but rather a series of crossroads that offer multiple possibilities, questions rather than answers. The document thus allows us to think of translation as a *process* rather than a *product*, highlighting the contingent nature of this pursuit.

The poem "In the Laboratory," which I quote here in a slightly amended version of Stephen Mitchell's translation, describes a curious and morbid experiment:

בַּמַּעְבָּדָה

הַנְּתוּנִים בִּכְלִי הַזְּכוּכִית: מִנְיָן עַקְרַבִּים
מִמִּשְׁפָּחוֹת שׁוֹנוֹת, חֶבְרָה אִטִּית, מִתְפַּשֶּׁרֶת,
רוֹחֶשֶׁת שִׁוְיוֹן. כָּל דּוֹרֵךְ גַּם נִדְרָךְ.
עַכְשָׁו הַנִּסּוּי: הַשְׁגָּחָה פְּרָטִית סַקְרָנִית נוֹפַחַת
אֶת אֲדֵי הָרַעַל פְּנִימָה
וּמִיָּד
כָּל אֶחָד וְאֶחָד יָחִיד בָּעוֹלָם,
זָקוּף עַל זְנָבוֹ, מְבַקֵּשׁ לוֹ
עוֹד רֶגַע מְקִיר הַזְּכוּכִית.
הָעֹקֶץ כְּבָר מְיֻתָּר,

---

6 This document is at the Dan Pagis archive at Gnazim Institute, Tel Aviv, 492:kaf-23456.

הַצְּבָתוֹת אֵינָן מְבִינוֹת,
גּוּף הַקַּשׁ הַיָּבֵשׁ נִצָּב לִשְׁעַת פְּקֻדָּתוֹ.
הַרְחֵק בֶּעָפָר נִבְהָלִים
מַלְאֲכֵי הַכָּרֵת.
רַק נִסּוּי, נִסּוּי. לֹא דִין
שֶׁל רַעַל תַּחַת רַעַל.

In the Laboratory
The data in the glass beaker: a dozen scorpions
of various species – a swarming, compromising
society of egalitarians. Trampling and trampled upon.
Now the experiment: an inquisitive providence blows
the poison gas inside
and immediately
each one is alone in the world,
raised on its tail, stiff, begging the glass wall
for one more moment.
The sting is already superfluous;
the pincers do not understand;
the straw body waits for the final shudder.
Far away, in the dust, the sinister angels
are startled.
It's only an experiment. An experiment. Not a judgment
of poison for poison. (Pagis 1989, 20)

The poem does not explain the nature of the laboratory in which this experiment takes place, nor does it describe what is ultimately learned from it. Instead, the stakes of the experiment are hinted at through a series of puns and multivalent expressions, and through biblical and rabbinical associations. This begins with the very first word of the poem, which refers to the scorpions as "netunim," which can be read as either a noun, meaning data, or as an adjective that describes the animals in the vial as passive creatures that are subjected to the experiment. The scorpions are also described as a "minyan" (a quorum of ten men required for traditional Jewish public worship), and the curious observer who poisons them as a divine intervener ("hashgakha pratit sakranit"), a contrast that casts the experiment as an encounter between God and the community who prays to him. But rather than blowing life into the creatures (Pagis uses the verb that appears in Genesis 2:7, "hefiakh"), this divine figure fills the vial with poisonous vapors, turning them all into straw and bringing them to their "final shudder." The Hebrew phrase is "she'at pekuda," which echoes Isaiah 10:3, a verse that also contains the word "Shoah": "What will you do on the day of punishment ("yom pekuda"), when the calamity ("shoah") comes from afar?" The reference to scorpions recalls another prophet, Ezekiel, who proclaims that God has told him not to fear rebuke "though thistles and thorns press against you and you sit upon scorpions" (Ezekiel 2:6). In Pagis's poem, the menacing scorpions have become passive objects of an experiment, but the reader is not informed of its purpose or of its results. The only response to it registered in the poem, apart from the death throes of the scorpions themselves, comes from an unexpected direction, through the "sinister angels." In Hebrew, they are described with a pun, not as "malakhei ha-sharet" (the traditional designation for the ministering angels), but rather as "malakhei ha-karet" (the angels of destruction). As if to balance this menacing figure, the poem ends with a reassurance: this is just an experiment, not an application of biblical retributive justice in the form of "an eye for an eye," or in this case, "poison for poison."

Vered Karti Shemtov has shown that, even though they are written in free verse, Pagis's poems employ rhythm and sound to substantial effect (Shemtov 2016). This is certainly the case here. Pagis uses these elements to draw attention to the immediate consequences of the infusion of gas into the vial. Firstly, he inserts a break. Following the insertion of the gas into the vial, comes the only short line of the poem, consisting of the single, tri-syllabic Hebrew word for "and immediately" ("u-miyad"). This change of pace is followed by a series of fricative *ḥet* sounds in the line that describes the isolation into which the scorpions fall in this tense moment. Before we attend to the weight of this moment, first a comment about the translation.

One detail of Pagis's German translation confirms Birkenhauer's argument that his poems are sometimes more explicit in his mother tongue, German, than in the language in which they were written, Hebrew. In Hebrew, Pagis chooses not to use the word "gaz" for the substance injected into the vial, but rather opts for the more neutral term "'ed" (vapor). In German he uses the term "Giftgas," which immediately brings to mind the gassing of the Jews by Nazis. In the German version of the poem, then, the mysterious experiment is likened to Nazi genocide. In this light, the theological and moral language invoked in the poem raises some powerful questions that are confronted in other poems by Pagis as well: if there is a divine intervener, how could such horror take place? How can one reconcile between the genocidal violence of the Nazis and the fact that they were seemingly rational, scientifically minded people? And, short of an impossible retributive retaliation to genocide, what is a viable moral response?

But if this translation decision seems to clarify or explicate an element of the poem, other parts of the draft emphasize the indeterminate relationship between the text and its translation. The draft, which is titled in both Hebrew and German, consists of several layers in pencil and in blue, green and black pens, suggesting several phases of revision and correction. Pagis considers various lexical alternatives, such as the Latinate "Experiment" as a replacement for the Germanic word "Versuch." By choosing the latter, Pagis seems to favor not only the scientific implications of the experiment, but also the possibility, through the association between "Versuch" (experiment) and "Versuchung" (temptation or seduction), that the poem describes a moral trial or test. Another dilemma documented in the draft is the choice between the different options for "immediately:" "sofort," "sogleich" and "im Nu." In these cases as in others, the decisions that the poet-translator is weighing also have prosodic and sonic implications. This seems to be an important motivation behind his dilemma between two slightly different options for describing the "inquisitive providence" behind the experiment: "eine neugierige Vorsehung" and "eine Vorsehung, neugierig." The two options are semantically identical, though they distribute the emphasis differently between the providential force that is filling the vial with gas and the curiosity that is fueling the experiment. But the reordering also has the effect of shortening the phrase by one syllable, an effect that must also have been on the poet-translator's mind. Another example is Pagis's consideration of "ist ein jeder allein" as an alternative for the lengthier "ist jeder Einzelne allein" in the line that describes the fateful moment in which the group of scorpions is broken down to isolated individuals, a choice between six and eight syllables.

It may be that Pagis was looking for the best equivalent for the rhythmic patterns that govern his Hebrew poem, seeking to replicate the break and its aftermath. But in his translation-experiment, one might read also an answer, or a complement, to the vision of the poem. Instead of asking what must inevitably happen in this one fateful moment of the experiment, the draft of the translation asks what are the multiple, contingent forms in which the moment might be described, highlighting the nature of translation itself as an open-ended experiment.

The confined space of the vial is thus opened up to a freedom of alternatives afforded by self-translation, a freedom that provides a much-needed relief from the strictures of history. To put it differently, rather than exposing a German subtext to the Hebrew poem, the draft of the translation exposes an abyss of uncertainty that accompanies it. In the laboratory of translation, Pagis glimpses this uncertainty and engages with it.

3 Conclusion

Pagis's missive to Jandl and his translation of "In the Laboratory" are two small German islands in the ocean of his Hebrew authorship. They are also instances of German creativity in an Israeli cultural context wherein Hebrew monolingualism was a widely held ideal and German was viewed as a language with a particularly problematic past. I read them not only as documentary evidence of the enduring relevance of the German language in Pagis's work and the Hebrew literary sphere more broadly but also as an invitation to reflect on the challenges and the potentials of reading him, and some of his contemporaries, as multilingual authors.

Works cited

Cordingley, Anthony. "Introduction: Self-translation, going global." *Self-Translation: Brokering Originality in Hybrid Culture*. Ed. Anthony Cordingley. London: Bloomsbury Academic, 2013. 1–10.
Eshel, Amir. *Zeit der Zäsur: Jüdische Dichter im Angesicht der Shoah*. Heidelberg: Universitätsverlag C. Winter, 1999.
Ezrahi, Sidra DeKoven. *Booking Passage: Exile and Homecoming in the Modern Jewish Imagination*. Berkeley and Los Angeles: University of California Press, 2000.
Hever, Hannan, ed. *Dan Pagis, mehkarim u-te'udot*. Jerusalem: Mosad Byalik, 2016.
Hokenson, Jan Walsh, and Marcella Munson. *The Bilingual Text: History and Theory of Literary Self-Translation*. London and New York: Routledge, 2014.
Jandl, Ernst. *Ernst Jandl: Werke in sechs Bänden*. Ed. Klaus Siblewski. München: Luchterhand Literaturverlag, 2016.
Pagis, Dan. *Variable Directions: Selected Poetry*. Trans. Stephen Mitchell. San Francisco: Northpoint, 1989.
Pagis, Dan. *Kol ha-shirim; "Aba" [pirke prozah]*. Tel Aviv: ha-Kibuts ha-meuhad and Jerusalem: Mosad Byalik, 1991.
Pagis, Dan. *An beiden Ufern der Zeit: Ausgewählte Gedichte und Prosa*. Trans. Anne Birkenhauer. Straelen: Straelener Manuskripte Verlag, 2003.
Shabat Nadir, Hadas. "Ha-eda ha-yehida le-yalduto shel Dan Pagis." *Haaretz*. http://www.haaretz.co.il/literature/study/.premium-1.3006597 (14 July 2016).
Shemtov, Vered Karti. "Shira sdura bli bayit: merhav ve-prosodia be-shirat Dan Pagis." *Dan Pagis, mehkarim u te'udot*. Ed. Hannan Hever. Jerusalem: Mosad Byalik, 2016. 240–249.
Stuckatz, Katja. *Ernst Jandl und die internationale Avantgarde. Über einen Beitrag zur modernen Weltdichtung*. Berlin and Boston: De Gruyter, 2016.

Rachel Seelig
Stuttering in Verse: Tuvia Rübner and the Art of Self-Translation

1 A dual identity

Tuvia Rübner bears a dual identity. Raised in Pressburg-Bratislava in an assimilated German-speaking Jewish family, he was given two names at birth: a secular one, Kurt Erich ("a name I can barely utter today," he notes), and a Jewish one after his paternal grandfather, Tuvia. Upon arriving in Palestine with a Zionist youth group in 1941, he set himself apart from his compatriots, who willingly replaced their "exilic" identities with Hebrew names that reflected a commitment to "build and be rebuilt" by the Land of Israel. Rübner, by contrast, refused to forego the name of the family he left behind in Slovakia. As the only family member to survive the Holocaust, he came to believe that his life had been spared so that he may represent those who perished (Rübner 2014, 38). The decision to preserve the family name posed certain challenges, however: Germans who do not recognize Tuvia as the equivalent of Tobias tend to mistake it for a woman's name, and since it is impossible to write Rübner phonetically in Hebrew, he has come to be known in Israel as Tuvia Rivner. Kurt Erich, Tuvia, Rübner, Rivner – the barrier to library searches is obvious. Yet such inconsistencies may be advantageous, the poet maintains, for they "confuse the angel of death" (Rübner 2006, 47). At ninety-three, Rübner still dwells in the ambiguous space between German and Hebrew, which for him is synonymous with the realm of the living.

Like his name, Rübner's oeuvre reflects a double life. During the 1990s, he began translating his Hebrew poetry into German, an ongoing project that has resulted in ten volumes of German verse to accompany twelve extant volumes in Hebrew. Since the translations are not labeled as such, Rübner is identified as either a German poet or a Hebrew poet depending on the readership. This point gestures at the challenge of analyzing his bilingual body of work. Although self-translation is the consummate expression of his bilingualism, it is as a practice rather difficult to pin down. The term "self-translation" denotes the transfer of a text from one language to another by its author. Yet few self-translators adhere to a strictly linear process, and they are less confined by the demand of "fidelity" (a primary tenet of translation theory since the nineteenth century).¹ Since self-translators are by definition beholden to no one but themselves, they are free to exercise creativity, to blend the process of translation with that of composition in order to produce not just two versions of a text but two "originals." The binary logic of source and target language, author and translator, original and adaptation is confounded. It is therefore not surprising that self-translators, with the exception of a canonical few (such as Samuel Beckett and Vladimir Nabokov), have remained "under the radar" even within the field of translation studies (Grutman 2013, 189).

There is another reason that self-translation remains a slippery and thus under-theorized concept: taken literally, the term points not to the act of translating one's texts but to a translation of the "self" that this act engenders. For Rübner, whose mother tongue is German but for whom Hebrew has long served as a primary spoken language, self-translation constitutes the ongoing renegotiation of subjectivity. When he translates finished Hebrew works into German, he effectively reverses a prior process of translation from German into Hebrew that was essential to his maturation as both a poet and a human being, thereby mediating between two halves of his identity. For Rübner this mediation is not secondary to but rather constitutive of creative expression. Translation, in short, is an essential component of his poetics.

Moreover, the relationship between composition and translation is for Rübner intimately linked with the negotiation of past and present, memory and lived experience, the permanence of childhood and the ephemerality of growing old. He has not abandoned one language for another, just as one does not forget one's childhood upon becoming an adult, but rather dwells with both languages simultaneously, allowing one to echo and inform the other. This mutual echoing of German and Hebrew in his work forms what I call "stuttering in verse." The motif of stuttering that runs through his poetry is key to understanding the bilingual tension upon which his writing process depends. The opposite of fluency, stuttering constitutes a hesitation between thought and speech. Yet Rübner is not a stutterer in speech but rather a "stutterer in language," as Gilles Deleuze describes the poet who effectuates a "perpetual disequilibrium or bifurcation" that causes language itself to "vibrate and stutter" (Deleuze 1997, 108–109). Manifesting itself in fractured verses, ellipses, tautologies, and befuddling repetition, Rübner's poetic stuttering poses a necessary

---

1 In contrast to eighteenth century translators such as John Dryden and Alexander Pope, who catered to the contemporary reader by adapting the "spirit" of the original to the aesthetic conventions of his own age, nineteenth century translators such as Matthew Arnold rejected the function of the translator and advocated for strict fidelity to the source text (Bassnett 1980, 70).

barrier to interpretation, challenging the reader to consider what lies beyond the words on the page. As both motif and technique, stuttering is a crucial aspect of his bilingual imagination, for what "lies beyond" is often located in another language.

This essay examines the function of self-translation both in Rübner's individual body of work, which remains underappreciated as a bilingual entity, and in the discourse on Hebrew literature, which until just one generation ago was produced primarily by non-native Hebrew speakers. Rübner's example also points to the need to carve out a more prominent place for self-translating writers in the discourse on world literature, in which the dissemination of translated texts plays a pivotal role. I proceed from the premise that self-translation is inherently subversive, not only because it obscures the conventional categories of translation, but also because its product cannot be labeled according to monolingual national literary borders (Cordingley 2013). Rübner's self-translation is shaped by a unique poetics that eschews hierarchical binaries of primary/secondary and original/translation in favor of doubling, dialogue, and contradiction. Indeed, contradiction, the poet himself has proclaimed, is the most important element in his work (Ofek 2004, 46).

2 "I am not who I am": becoming a bilingual poet in Israel

"It is among the paradoxes of my life," Rübner muses, "that the small amount of German literature I have internalized was acquired in Israel. I am like a tree whose roots reach into the air" (Rübner 2014, 55). Although Rübner was socialized in a German-speaking context, his formal education was cut short at the age of fifteen by an anti-Semitic policy calling for the expulsion of all Jewish students from local schools in the newly formed Slovak Republic.[2] It was only after immigrating to British Mandate Palestine that he acquired a proper literary education. Under the tutelage of two guides, fellow German-speaking émigrés Werner Kraft and Ludwig Strauss, he immersed himself in German literature. He was particularly inspired by Strauss's *Land Israel* (1935), a slim volume of Zionist poems in

---

[2] Under the influence of the Nazi regime, Slovakia passed its version of the Nuremburg Laws in 1939. Rübner, having just completed ninth grade, was banned from school together with all the Jews of the region. He began working clandestinely as an electrician's apprentice, although this too was forbidden, before leaving Slovakia for Palestine in April of 1941.

which the spirit of the German Romantic poet Friedrich Hölderlin merges with that of the medieval Hebrew bard Yehuda Halevi. As Rübner delved into German literature under Strauss's mentorship, the unfamiliar environment of Kibbutz Merhavia, a communal settlement in Israel's northern Jezreel Valley where he first settled and resides still today, became infused with the poetic universe of Goethe, Hölderlin, and Rilke.

The friendship that blossomed between Rübner and Strauss strengthened the former's motivation to write poetry in German, his sole language of composition for roughly twelve years. Yet Strauss continually urged his pupil to begin writing, as Rübner put it, "in the language I speak, which is Hebrew" (Rübner 2014, 59). Eventually, the young poet saw fit to make a shift. This decision marked a "caesura" that coincided with two pivotal life events: in August 1953 Strauss passed away, and in September Rübner married his second wife, Galila Jizreeli, who became a devoted reader of his Hebrew poems (she does not read German). A change of language, the poet recalls, now seemed inevitable:

> I wrote in a language that I now barely spoke. German was my home. In it, I continued to "speak" with my parents, sister, [and] grandparents [...] who possess no grave. But at some point I no longer wanted to live in my poems and remain in the past [...]. Not because I wanted to overcome the past but because I wanted *to live with it*. I started writing in Hebrew exclusively. [...] Hebrew is not a given for me. It is a learned language, but also a spoken language. (Rübner 2014, 66)

In this passage from his autobiography, Rübner presents German in characteristically contradictory terms as the language in which he "speaks" with the dead, that is, as the intimate yet *silent* language of memory. He characterizes Hebrew, by contrast, as a learned and hence artificial medium, but also as a language more accessible than his own mother tongue. Though technically a second language, Hebrew superseded German as a primary language of communication and expression, even if it could never hold the status of a native tongue. Only in Hebrew could the past be brought back to life in the present.

Notwithstanding the importance of the "caesura" that Rübner attaches to the year 1953, his Hebrew literary debut actually occurred several years earlier. In 1944, three years after his arrival in Palestine, he learned that his parents, grandparents, and twelve-year-old sister, Alice (Litzi), had perished in Auschwitz. Mired in grief, he sought solace in the company of a fellow Slovakian émigré, Ada Klein, who soon became his wife and the mother of his daughter, Miriam, born in 1949. Within a few months of the baby's arrival, the couple was in a bus accident that killed Ada and left Rübner severely burned. During his recovery he received a hospital visit from his friend Lea Goldberg,

already an established poet. He dictated his first Hebrew poem to her, which she later submitted to the newspaper *Davar*, where it appeared on 6 October 1950.

I am not who I was,	אֵינֶנִּי זֶה שֶׁהָיִיתִי.
I am not who I am.	אֵינֶנִּי זֶה שֶׁהִנְנִי.
I am neither here nor there.	אֵינֶנִּי לֹא כָּאן וְלֹא שָׁם.
Living between water and air.	חַי בֵּין אֲוִיר וּבֵין מַיִם.
Haltingly, I live in fire.	לְאִטִּי חַי בָּאֵשׁ.
My eyes are scorched.	עֵינַי שְׂרוּפוֹת.
My hands are scorched.	יָדַי שְׂרוּפוֹת.
My lips are scorched.	שְׂפָתַי שְׂרוּפוֹת.
Scorched are these words.	שְׂרוּפוֹת מִלִּים אֵלֶּה.
He who whispered them	זֶה שֶׁלְּחָשָׁן
lives in an open coffin.	חַי בָּאֲרוֹן-מֵת[ים], מִכְסֵהוּ פָּתוּחַ
Watching a square of sky	רוֹאֶה שָׁמַיִם מְרֻבָּעִים
drift by.	עוֹבְרִים.
(Translated by Rachel Tzvia Back)	(Freilich 2014)

At first glance, this sorrowful poem, replete with images of burning, seems a response to the injuries that Rübner sustained in the bus accident. Yet it takes on additional layers when read against the backdrop of his family history and his move toward Hebrew. The reference to scorched lips betrays an affinity with the prophet Moses, portrayed in the Bible as a reluctant messenger who initially resists God's summons, saying: "Please, O Lord, I have never been a man of words.... I am heavy of mouth and heavy of tongue" (Exodus 4:10). The rabbis of late antiquity interpreted this statement to mean that Moses was a stutterer, which the Midrash attributes to his having burned his tongue on hot coals as an infant. The poem's connection with Moses is bolstered by the words "I am not who I am," a variation on the biblical verse in which the prophet, having asked how he should introduce God to the Children of Israel, receives the following reply directly from the Lord: "I am that I am" (Exodus 3:13–14). Rübner's negation of this tautology calls into question not only the poet's identity but also the nature of the poem itself. The negation reaches its climax with the phrase "Burnt are these words," implying that the poem has consumed itself, leaving nothing but the faint stammering of a timid survivor forced to reckon with incalculable loss.

Stuttering, murmuring, and seemingly superfluous repetition emerge through Rübner's oeuvre to signal both the failure of speech in the face of loss and the struggle for self-expression in a new tongue. In "Hebrew, My Love" (*'Ivrit' ahuvati*), for instance, the poet's relationship to Hebrew is portrayed in terms of overcoming struggle: "I stuttered, became silent, I begged and whispered,/ and you, turning inward, saw nothing./ Until suddenly, you opened up wide like a field in the wind/ and your voice burst forth from my throat" (Back 2014, 279). Grappling with the foreign tongue often merges with the challenge of commemorating the dead, as in the following verses from "Oblivion" (*Shikheḥah*): "To these too many bones you sent me, Lord,/ me, the stutterer. Your spirit was within me." In this poem, which invokes Moses explicitly, the prophet laments his inability to speak on behalf of the dead in his new language: "My God, what am I to say? Oblivion/ veils your words ... Arise! ... As .../ In my mouth my foreign tongue flails about." (Back 2014, 10–11). The fractured, elliptical verses mimic the very act of stuttering.

If we read Rübner's first Hebrew poem in light of his fraught relationship with language, we discover the anxiety of a fledgling Hebrew poet who wishes "to live with" the past in his new language but can "commune" with the dead only in their language, German. The opening lines, "I am not who I was,/ I am not who I am./ I am neither here nor there," point to the threshold between the language of memory and the language of poetry, while the oscillation between past and present tense ("He who whispered [the scorched words]/ lives in an open coffin") suggests that the prior German-speaking self must be brought back to the realm of the living through the turn to a new mode of expression, indeed a new language. The tension between German and Hebrew is encapsulated in the very penname under which Rübner published the poem, T. Ben Moshe, or T. (for "Tuvia") Son of Moses, a double allusion to the biblical prophet and to Rübner's own father, Manfred-Moritz, whose Hebrew name was Moshe.

A recent archival discovery adds another layer to the story of Rübner's first Hebrew poem. Giddon Ticotsky came across an unpublished German version of the poem in Lea Goldberg's literary estate, along with a letter indicating that Rübner had begun, at Goldberg's encouragement, to translate some of his German poems into Hebrew months prior to the bus accident. Based on these documents, Ticotsky conjectures that Rübner's ostensible Hebrew literary debut may in fact have been a translation from German (Ticotsky 2016, 134–135). The existence of an unpublished German twin to Rübner's first Hebrew poem betrays the central role of self-translation in his transition from German to Hebrew (and suggests that the process was far messier than his "caesura" story implies).

It is therefore striking that Rübner later expressed reservations about the translation of his own work: "I was against the translation of my poems, not only because the transition was so difficult for me but also because I was a purist and a pupil of [Ludwig] Strauss [*Straussschüler*]" (Rübner 2014, 59). This resistance was undoubtedly shaped in part by the social and political climate of Israel in the early 1950s, when the taboo against German was especially strong.[3] And yet, notwithstanding Rübner's refusal to translate his own Hebrew poetry, he remained engaged in translation throughout his career. His seminal achievement in this arena was a translation of S.Y. Agnon's novella *Der Treuschwur* ("The Oath," 1965), commissioned by the Berlin publishing house Fischer Verlag at the recommendation of Gershom Scholem.[4] At a party hosted by President Zalman Shazar in honor of Agnon's reception of the Nobel Prize for literature in 1966, Scholem praised Rübner's translation and noted that his efforts "enabled this happy occasion by no small measure" (Ticotsky 2016, 139). Translation from Hebrew into German was seen as a necessary evil, a means of making the culture of the fledgling Jewish State accessible to the world, thereby garnering the international recognition it deserved. By the mid-1960s, Rübner had established himself as a notable translator of Hebrew literature into German.

Translation in the other direction, from German into Hebrew, was a different matter. The young State of Israel was focused on cultivating and expanding its own national literature; it was less interested in importing foreign works, especially those stemming from the land of the perpetrators, as Germany was commonly viewed. Attitudes toward German changed with the passage of time, however, and by the 1970s the taboo was gradually lifted. It was around this time that Rübner began to translate from German into Hebrew, focusing his efforts on prominent writers and thinkers such as Friedrich Schlegel, Johann Wolfgang von Goethe, Friedrich Schiller, and Walter Benjamin. He published German translations throughout the 1980s as part of a special series on aesthetics, which he himself edited for the publishing house Sifriyat Hapoalim (The Workers Library).

Viewed in the context of world literature, the two facets of Rübner's extensive translation project performed two distinct yet complementary functions. Translation from Hebrew into German played an integral role in the dissemination of Modern Hebrew literature worldwide, while translation of German texts into

---

[3] In her study of German language instruction at the Hebrew University of Jerusalem, Yfaat Weiss describes the intense opposition to German prior to and immediately following the establishment of the State of Israel. The ban against German instruction at the university that was instituted in 1934 in response to the rise of the Nazi regime went unchallenged until the late 1940s, when students and professors began to insist that German was a necessary component of scholarly training in the humanities. Despite their efforts, it was not until 1953, following the signing of the reparations agreement between Israel and West Germany, that German courses were finally reintroduced at the university (Weiss 2014). As Weiss's research illustrates, the animus toward German was particularly virulent during the period that Rübner was negotiating the shift from German to Hebrew.
[4] Scholem had himself translated several works by Agnon into German for the journal *Der Jude* while living in Berlin during the 1920s.

Hebrew was a means of feeding the incipient literary imagination of a society moving gradually toward a monolingual national paradigm. Rübner played a seminal role in both sides of this cultural project. By the same token, translation played a seminal role in his own literary oeuvre, setting the stage for his eventual turn to self-translation during the 1990s. How did he overcome the initial resistance to translating his own Hebrew poems? What did it mean to be translated *back* into German? Was such a "return" desirable or suspect? As we shall see, his change of heart was fueled not only by the social and political climate of the day but also by specific aesthetic concerns.

3 "Poetry is what is": writing between Hebrew and German

Although bilingualism has always been a key aspect of Rübner's writing process, he embarked on self-translation relatively late in life. He was sixty-six years old when the translators Efrat Gal Ed and Christoph Meckel approached him to request the publishing rights for *Wüstenginster* (Desert Broom, 1990), a collection of his poems that they had translated into German. Despite his initial opposition to any translation of his Hebrew writing, Rübner was pleased to discover upon reading Meckel and Gal Ed's work that "the poems were still poems" (Rübner 2014, 60). The happy realization inspired him to release a volume of as yet unpublished German poems, entitled *Granatapfel: Frühe Gedichte* (Pomegranate: Early Poems, 1995). The meeting with Gal Ed and Meckel was also the catalyst of his self-translation project, to which he devoted himself with great discipline for the next twenty years.

Underlying Rübner's self-translations are two key poetic principles adopted from his mentor, Ludwig Strauss. The first is the notion that poetry is inherently dialogical: "I learned from Strauss that the poem conducts a dialogue with its listener (reader), who, by virtue of his attentive eavesdropping... is made present by the poem, and the more he gives of himself, the richer [the dialogue becomes]." The second is the idea that "sound always takes precedence in a poem" (Rübner 2014, 53–54). At first glance, these two principles seem obstacles to translation, which implies a *mediated* dialogue between author and reader, as well as the necessary modification of sound. Yet Strauss, a bilingual poet and self-translator in his own right, maintained that translation provides an opportunity to foster exchange between source language and target language. Through translation, in other words, the unique sound of each language is preserved but also brought into contact with its counterpart. Strauss articulated this idea in the following verses from the poem "Dank des Übersetzers an die Dichterin" (The Translator's

Thank You to the Poet), dedicated to Lea Goldberg, whose poetry he translated into German:

> Und mir, in meinen beiden Sprachen lebend,
> Der einen aus der andern Echo gebend –
> Wie horchten beide auf bei deinem Tone!
>
> [For me, whose languages are two,
> The echo of one does the other imbue –
> How both attend to your sound!]
> (Strauss 2000, 543)

In a sense, Strauss's German rendering of Goldberg's Hebrew poetry allowed the original to reverberate more intensely for him; her writing became whole by virtue of being doubled.[5]

The influence of Strauss's cross-linguistic dialogue can be felt in Rübner's bilingual writing. Like his mentor, Rübner sought to honor the individual sound qualities of German and of Hebrew while bringing the two languages into contact with each other. A striking example of this seemingly contradictory impulse can be found in the differing titles of his German and his Hebrew volumes. At first glance, the German self-translations do not even appear to be self-translations, since the titles differ dramatically, as do the order and grouping of the content. Upon close inspection, however, certain thematic parallels emerge. For instance, many of the poems contained in the Hebrew volume *Shirim sotrim* (Contradictory Poems), published in 2011, appear in German translation in *Lichtschatten* (Light Shadows), released the same year. Although the titles differ, they convey the same sentiment, as the following artist's statement explains:

> My latest volume of Hebrew poems is entitled *Shirim sotrim* – contradictory poems, a poetics of the possible. The various poems often express disparate and opposing [sentiments], no less than the possibilities of life. In our confused, disbelieving, rapidly changing world… a closed statement is simply impossible, [for it is] imbued with both light and shadow. (Rübner 2011a, 80)

Taking advantage of the synthetic capacity of German to produce new words, Rübner offers the compound noun *Lichtschatten* as an imagistic equivalent of the phrase *Shirim sotrim* (contradictory poems). Thus, the two titles "echo" one

---

5 The paradox of unity through doubling played a central role in his ensuing bilingual writing. Although he claimed to master Hebrew only in his forties (he penned his first Hebrew poem, "To the Bay," at age forty-two), Strauss came to see himself as embodying two languages that inform and indeed "echo" one another (Seelig 2013).

another while preserving and highlighting the unique qualities of their respective languages.

The merging of light and shadow in a single word is just one example of the contradictory impulses that meld throughout Rübner's oeuvre to produce his "poetics of the possible," among them: living and aging, joy and suffering, and delight and pain. Perhaps the most important contradiction is an unspoken one, the sheer fact that the poems are both German and Hebrew. At times, the unique properties of each language blur the line between original and translation, making the distinction between original and translation practically indiscernible. If we compare the poem "What We Think Is Poetry" (*Mah shehoshvim shirah*) with its German translation, each version seems "original" based on the way in which it playfully engages with the language of composition. The Hebrew version reads:

WHAT WE THINK IS POETRY	מה שחושבים שירה
What we think is poetry isn't poetry it's what we think is poetry. Poetry isn't what we think thinking isn't poetry what we think we're not thinking is poetry.	מַה שֶׁחוֹשְׁבִים שִׁירָה זֶה לֹא מַה שֶּׁשִּׁירָה זֶה מַה שֶׁחוֹשְׁבִים שִׁירָה. שִׁירָה לֹא מַה שֶׁחוֹשְׁבִים מַחְשָׁבָה לֹא שִׁירָה מַה שֶׁחוֹשְׁבִים לֹא חוֹשְׁבִים שִׁירָה.
What we feel is poetry we feel as feeling. Not poetry. Feelings divided or disturbed perfumed praised or cursed are what we feel we love to feel what we love to feel we think we feel what we love to love we think is love not poetry.	מַה שֶׁמַּרְגִּישִׁים שִׁירָה מַרְגִּישִׁים הַרְגָּשָׁה. לֹא שִׁירָה. רְגָשׁוֹת מְפֻצָּלִים אוֹ מַבְהִילִים מְבֻשָּׂמִים מְהֻלָּלִים אוֹ מְקֻלָּלִים מַה שֶׁמַּרְגִּישִׁים אוֹהֲבִים לְהַרְגִּישׁ מַה שֶׁאוֹהֲבִים לְהַרְגִּישׁ חוֹשְׁבִים לְהַרְגִּישׁ מַה שֶׁאוֹהֲבִים לֶאֱהֹב חוֹשְׁבִים אַהֲבָה לֹא שִׁירָה.
What we sense is good or bad we sense. It's not good it's not bad it's sensing good and bad not poetry.	מַה שֶׁחָשִׁים זֶה טוֹב זֶה רַע חָשִׁים. זֶה לֹא טוֹב זֶה לֹא רַע זֶה חָשִׁים טוֹב וָרַע לֹא שִׁירָה.
Poetry is poetry is what is poetry (Translated by Rachel Seelig and Adam Seelig)	שִׁירָה הִיא שִׁירָה הִיא מַה הִיא שִׁירָה (Rübner 2002, 18)

The poem revolves around a basic lacuna in Hebrew grammar: the lack of a present tense form for the verb "to be." Due to this absence, Hebrew permits nominal sentences (i.e. sentences that lack a verb), such as *maḥshavah lo shirah* (thought [is] not poetry).[6] In light of the missing copular verb ("is"), the phrase *mah shehoshvim shirah*, or "What we think [is] poetry," is rendered ambiguous; it may either be understood as a statement of equation, i.e. "poetry is thought," or as a descriptive term, i.e. "what we think of as poetry" (which is promptly undercut by the words "isn't poetry"). The grammatical lacuna is crucial in the final three lines of the first stanza, which similarly may be read in two different ways. The first, more literal reading draws a clear distinction between the realm of thought and the realm of poetry: "thought and not poetry/ is what we think. We don't think/ poetry." A slight shift of emphasis produces a more positive yet puzzling reading: "thinking isn't poetry./ what we think we're not thinking / is poetry." According to the second reading, poetry is not separate from thought but rather constitutes the deepest form of subconscious thought. We the readers are clearly treading on shaky ground, for poetry is not what we think – and yet it also is.

The German version of the poem bears a very different title:

KLEINE POETIK	SMALL POETICS
Gedicht ist nicht, was man denkt, was man denkt	A poem is not what you think, what you think
ist gedacht, nicht Gedicht.	is thought, not poem.
Gedacht ist Gedanke, nicht Gedicht.	Thought is thought, not poem.
Gedicht ist	Poem is
Nichtgedanke	nothought
ist	is
nicht was man fühlt.	not what you feel.
Was man fühlt ist Gefühl nicht Gedicht.	What you feel is feeling not poem.
Was man fühlt liebt man fühlen	You love to feel what you feel
Liebt Gefühl, liebt Liebe fühlen	love feeling, love to feel love
Was man fühlen liebt wird gedacht, man fühlt	what you love to feel is thought, you feel
Gefühl ist	feeling is
Nichtgedicht	notpoem
Ist	is

---

6 A more precise and elegant way to say "thought is not poetry" would be: *maḥshavah 'eyna shirah*.

Was man meint es sei	what you consider
Gut oder schlecht	good or bad
Wird gemeint gut schlecht	is considered good bad
Was man meint wird gemeint	what you consider is considered
Nicht Gedicht.	not poem.
Gedicht ist – Gedicht ist –	Poem is – poem is –
Was ist ein Gedicht?	What is a poem?[7]
(Rübner 2007, 20)	

As in the Hebrew version, the German version is characterized by playful engagement with specific features of German grammar. Three come to the fore in the opening stanza. The first is repetition of the prefix "ge-," used to form both collective nouns and past participles, which produces assonance in the pairing of *Gedicht* (noun: "poem") and *gedacht* (past participle: "thought"). The second feature is the use of the contradictory compound constructions, *Nichtgedanke* and *Nichtgedicht*, comprised of a negation (*nicht*) and a noun (*Gedanke* means "thought" or "idea"), which reveal the proclivity of German for compound constructions. Bringing to mind Paul Celan's tendency to reify negations, as in the title of his volume *Die Niemandsrose* (the no-one's rose), Rübner's compound constructions preserve the negation (*nicht*) while simultaneously converting it into a substantive concept, a "thing." These concepts both do and do not exist, just as poetry both is and is not thought.

The third aspect relates to punctuation. German grammar marks a subordinate clause (*Nebensatz*) by setting it off with a comma, as in the following phrase: "Gedicht ist nicht, was man denkt" ("Poem is not what you think," with the words "was man denkt" serving as the subordinate clause). If we read this phrase as a complete statement, two possible readings emerge: first, "Poem is not that which is thought" (i.e. poetry surpasses thought); and second, "Poem is not what you think [it is]." Both readings are complicated by the fact that the subordinate clause is repeated twice, forming a "stutter": "Gedicht ist nicht, was man denkt, was man denkt." One way to make sense of the repetition is to read it as the start of a new sentence that flows directly into the following line: "Poem is not what you think. What you think/ is thought." Yet the latter reading overlooks the fact that the repetition is set off with a comma, and therefore, according to the rules

---

[7] Throughout the translation I have elected to translate the German indefinite pronoun "man" as "you" (used here as an unspecified pronoun rather than as the second person pronoun), rather than as "one," which sounds less colloquial than the German "man."

of German grammar, constitutes an additional subordinate clause. The result is a perplexing statement: "Poem is not what you think you're thinking" (Gedicht ist nicht, was man denkt, was man denkt). Doubling the subordinate clause exploits the precision of German grammar in order to create ambiguity and confusion.

The final stanzas of the two versions differ dramatically with respect to punctuation. In the German version, the first line contains dashes that produce a stammer: "Gedicht ist – Gedicht ist –" (Poem is – poem is –). This version concludes with a clear question: "Was ist ein Gedicht?" (What is a poem?). The Hebrew version, by contrast, is devoid of punctuation. Whereas the previous stanzas play with the absence of the verb "is," the final stanza employs the feminine third-person pronoun *hi* (pronounced *hee*), used in Hebrew either as the pronoun "it" or as an optional copula: *shirah hi shirah hi/ mah hi/ shira* (poetry is poetry is/ what is [it]/ poetry). The absence of a question mark suggests two different readings. The first, as in the German version, is a simple question: "What is/ poetry?" The second reading contains a question and an enigmatic answer: "What is it? It is poetry."[8] This reading produces a tautology, a statement whose negation is unsatisfiable. The implication is that poetry simply cannot be defined (so why bother asking?). Poetry is poetry is poetry.

In both languages, interpretation relies on the way in which the poem is spoken. It is therefore interesting to note that Rübner freely admits to reading Hebrew like "a six-year-old child who must sound out every word" (Rübner 2014, 86). Hebrew may have become a primary language in his daily life, but it remains an artificial medium. He reads German much more fluently and frequently, yet his spoken German has become ossified over the years. He also confesses that he required help translating his poems from Hebrew into German because he did not feel confident about his ability to write natural, idiomatic German, a language he spoke primarily as a child and during the early years of Israeli statehood. (It is for this reason, Rübner freely points out, that he sought the assistance of German poet and translator Frank Schablewski.) Rübner's remarks about both languages point to an implicit hesitation that lies between thought and speech. When read aloud, both versions of the poem capture the poet's inner stutter by forcing the reader to falter, stammer, and stumble. Reading aloud causes the tongue to become tied.

In light of this tongue-tying effect, it is perhaps no coincidence that the poem evokes a well-known German tongue twister: "Denke nie, gedacht zu haben, denn das Denken der Gedanken ist gedankenloses Denken" (Never think to have

---

[8] In public readings, Rübner prefers the latter interpretation, taking a noticeable pause at the line break between the penultimate and last lines of the poem.

thought, for the thinking of thoughts is thoughtless thinking). One wonders whether this playful aphorism was not the inspiration behind the poem, even if it was composed initially in Hebrew. Is it possible, in other words, that a specter of German underlies the Hebrew "original"? In private conversation with Rübner, I explained why I mistook the German for the "original." He cheerfully dispelled my error: "How lovely! I suppose such things can happen in translation," he replied. He went on to explain that the Hebrew versions of his poems are almost always "the original," and yet in the next breath described German unequivocally as "the source" (*hamakor*).[9] This paradoxical statement confirms Rainier Grutman's definition of self-translation as a kind of "cross-linguistic creation" in which the borders between source and target languages, poet and translator, creator and mediator are confounded – often deliberately.

4 "There are words from which writing recoils": poetry between life and death

The relationship between German and Hebrew, opposing languages paradoxically bound together, is connected in Rübner's imagination with the inextricability of life and death. In a sense, death has been the strongest and most constant presence in his life, a life marked not only by the loss of his family of origin in Slovakia but also by the sudden death of his first wife, Ada, and the inexplicable disappearance of his youngest son, Moran, during his travels through South America in the 1980s. Being and absence figure as inseparable phenomena in Rübner's writing, as the poem "My Father" articulates: "Today he gazes at me from the wall and asks with his eyes / if I know, do I really know, that one cannot separate / life from death, and that language is sometimes nothing more than / the mourning of lost tenderness" (Back 2014, 209). Just as life is often but a shadow of death, so too language bears witness to that which it cannot articulate. Read in these terms, the ontological negation contained in Rübner's first Hebrew poem, "I am not who I am," captures the anxiety of the bilingual poet who is suspended between linguistic, geographical, temporal and even spiritual realms.

Poetry's resistance to definition, the main theme of "What We Think is Poetry," may also be viewed from a negative angle; that is, poetry serves as a repository of suppressed thoughts and experiences, which, when transformed into words, threaten to crumble under their own weight. The poem "Ungedicht"

---

9 Rübner offered this paradoxical comment in one of our private conversations.

(which translates as "unpoem" or "anti-poem") offers an extreme counterpart to the neutral term *Nichtgedicht*. Like "What We Think is Poetry," this poem is metapoetic; yet, whereas the former inquisitively seeks a definition for poetry, the latter proceeds from the opposite angle to construct poetry's *via negativa*.

UNGEDICHT	UNPOEM
Nachdem ein Gedicht zuende ist, keine zu lauten, keine zu leisen Worte, und du fühlst: ein Druck hat dich nachgelassen, von einem Joch befreit atmest du auf.	After a poem has come to an end, No word too loud or too quiet, And you feel the pressure has left you, Freed of a burden you breathe freely.
Nicht immer. Bisweilen bäumen die Wörter sich, stoßen zurück in dich, gar nicht zart, bereiten dir Schmerz, den Schmerz, den du ihnen eingeimpft hast, drängen sich, pressen sich aneinander, fallen zusammen wie ein schwarzes Loch.	Not always. Sometimes the words rise up and thrust into you, not at all gently, causing pain, the pain with which you inoculated them, crowding together, pressing into each other and collapsing like a black hole.
Du schreibst: ersticken? Ersticken erwürgt ersticken. Du schreibst: Rauch? Rauch verdunkelt Rauch. Du schreibst: Asche? Asche häuft sich auf Asche. Du schreibst: Züge? Züge zertrümmern Züge, lautlos, in Totenstille.	You write: choke? Choking strangles choking. You write: smoke? Smoke expunges smoke. You write: ash? Ash piles onto ash. You write: trains? Trains crash into trains, silently, quiet as death.
Es gibt Dinge, die Schrift schrumpft unter ihnen zusammen. Es gibt Dinge, die Worte schrecken vor ihnen zurück.	There are things under which writing contracts. There are things from which words recoil.
Es gibt ein Gedicht, das ist ein Ungedicht. (Rübner 2007, 39)	There is a poem that is an unpoem.

The doubling of nouns in the third stanza points to a fundamental tension between events experienced and the poems they inspire. Can signifiers such as "smoke" or "ash" truly capture that which they purport to signify? Does the written word threaten to cover over or even "expunge" the poet's experience? Or is the opposite true, namely that the intensity of certain events has the capacity to incinerate the written word? A partial answer is supplied in the final stanza, which doubles as a definition of "Ungedicht": the poet who is compelled to relive certain events in the process of writing will necessarily fall prey to them, a victim of poetic post-traumatic stress.

In German, the inseparable prefix "un-" has a unique function that differs from negative prefixes in most other languages. When attached to a noun, it often denotes not just a reversal of the base noun's meaning but a perversion thereof, as in *Untat* (atrocity), *Unsinn* (nonsense), or *Unmensch* (barbarian; monster). The term "Ungedicht" therefore brings to mind a monstrous entity, a ghastly creature that vies with the poet as it comes into being, threatening to destroy and degrade poetry itself.[10] Echoing Theodor Adorno's oft-rehearsed adage, "poetry after Auschwitz is barbaric," Rübner implies that certain poems simply cannot be written, or at least cannot be counted as poetic. The *Ungedicht* is the *Unmensch* of poetry, the poem that rises up against its creator.

Whereas in German the conceptual kernel of the poem is contained in the title, the Hebrew version revolves around a double entendre that is absent from the German. The penultimate stanza and final line of the German version are reduced to two ambiguous lines in Hebrew:

יֵשׁ דְּבָרִים שֶׁהַכְּתָב מִתְכַּוֵּץ תַּחְתָּם.
יֵשׁ שִׁיר שֶׁאֵינֶנּוּ שִׁיר.

[There are words from which writing recoils.
There's a poem that's not a poem.] (Rübner 2002, 40)

The double meaning of the word *devarim*, which may be translated as either "words" or "things," captures the insoluble tension upon which the poem constructs itself, the tension between representations of words and events/experiences as they exist in the phenomenal world. According to Jewish mystical belief, which posits a link between the world of speech and the world of the spirit, the godhead represents "the original archetypal writer, who impresses his word deep into his

---

10 This struggle is amplified by the peculiar use of the phrase in line three, "ein Druck hat dich nachgelassen" (literally "a pressure has left you"), generally used in German only intransitively (i.e. "ein Druck hat nachgelassen," meaning "the pressure released"). The transitive use of this phrase personifies the poem and the pressure it produces within the poet.

created works" (Scholem 1972, 68). Rübner's poem, by contrast, presents words and the "things" they signify as a negative force that "unforms" the poem, producing "a poem that is not a poem" (*shir she'eyno shir*).

Since it is impossible to replicate this double entendre in another language, two additional lines are needed in the German version, which reinforce the word-thing duality through juxtaposition rather than wordplay: "Es gibt Dinge, / die Worte schrecken vor ihnen zurück" (There are things from which words recoil). This variation demonstrates an important strategy of self-translation: the substitution of a particular rhetorical structure or figure of speech in one language with another structure better suited to the other language. By the same token, the Hebrew version is unable to reproduce the evocative force of *Ungedicht*. Although the word '*Alshir* (literally "unpoem") is technically equivalent to *Ungedicht*, it sounds odd, since the Hebrew prefix '*al-* ("un-") is more often attached to adjectives than to nouns.[11] What the German version loses in one form of wordplay it gains in another, and vice versa.

The term *Ungedicht* can be seen as a microcosm of Rübner's poetic language, replete with paradox, negation, and contradiction. If we imagine the *Ungedicht* as an animate being, it might resemble Kafka's Odradek, that "extraordinarily nimble" creature made of "broken-off bits of thread, knotted and tangled together" (Kafka 1995, 428). The parallel is hardly incidental; Rübner pondered Kafka's work extensively and even claimed that Kafka "lives inside [him]" (Ofek 2004, 53). In a published in interview dedicated to Rübner's views on Kafka's writing, he argued that every aspect of "Kafka's world exists by virtue of self-negation" (Ofek 2004, 45–46). When asked to describe Kafka's impact on his writing, Rübner offered: "It is possible that an element exists in my poetry that may aggravate readers, lines that may be read this way or that way, an internal dynamic that causes them to become lost in the labyrinth of what is being said" (Ofek 2004, 46). If we consider Rübner's poetry in light of his affinity with Kafka, Odradek comes to life in the prevalence of tautologies and negations, forms of language that unravel as they come into being. Underlying this contradiction is not only the tension between signifier and signified, between word and world, but also a bilingual tension. Just as Odradek's name is either of Slavonic or of German origin, with neither interpretation providing "an intelligent meaning of the word," so too each of Rübner's Hebrew poems conceals a German counterpart that both completes and complicates it.

---

[11] There are a few exceptions, such as the noun '*almavet*, meaning "immortality" (literally: "non-death").

5 Unhomely homecoming: bilingualism, identity, and negation

The unraveling of language is amplified in the German translations, which sometimes seem less like translations from a Hebrew original than a reversion back into German that in turn expose a gap in the Hebrew "original." Self-translation from Hebrew into German performs an "uncanny" or "unhomely" (*unheimlich*) homecoming, exposing a familiar yet spectral German presence behind the Hebrew "original." At times this homecoming manifests itself in a direct "retranslation" of a German quote, as in the poem "Century," in which a phrase from Rilke's *Duino Elegies* ("Wie wenn ich schriee") returns to its source (Rübner 2007, 7). In other poems, the German translations introduce direct allusions that are at most subliminally present in Hebrew, such as the inclusion of quotations from Goethe's "Prometheus" and Kafka's parable *Der Aufbruch* (The Departure) in the German version of the poem "Anmerkungen zu einer Arbeit über Hiob" (Notes to an Essay on Job; Rübner 2007, 12–14).

At times the "reversion" back into German is even subtler, manifesting itself in a minor shift in translation. A clear example is the brief two-line poem "Postcard from Jerusalem," which in Hebrew reads as follows:

יְרוּשָׁלַיִם יָצְאָה מִירוּשָׁלַיִם וְהִסְתַּלְּקָה לָהּ.
זֶה שָׁם לְמַעְלָה בָּאֲוִיר, הֲלֹא לֹא יִתָּכֵן שֶׁזֹּאת יְרוּשָׁלַיִם?

[Jerusalem took leave of Jerusalem and made herself scarce.
That up there in the air, there's no way that's Jerusalem?]

The title of the German version, "Keine Ansichtskarte: Jerusalem," or "No Postcard: Jerusalem (Rübner 2000, 27), anticipates the very negation depicted in the poem:

Jerusalem hat sich aus Jerusalem aus dem Staub gemacht.
Das da oben in der Luft kann doch nicht Jerusalem sein?

[Jerusalem left Jerusalem in the dust.
That up high in the air couldn't be Jerusalem?]

The idiom "sich aus dem Staub machen" (meaning "to get lost," or, literally, "to make oneself out of the dust"), approximates the colloquial definition of *lehistalek* (to make oneself scarce), as well as the literal definition (to die), by invoking the biblical decree of mortality spoken by God to Adam and Eve: "For dust you are, and to dust you shall return" (Genesis 3:19). The two languages are almost equivalent here, yet German carries a biblical allusion that ironically is absent from the Hebrew. In a sense, the German version surpasses the Hebrew through its evocation of the stones and dust of "earthly Jerusalem" (*yerushalayim shel matah*), which is juxtaposed with the "heavenly Jerusalem" (*yerushalayim shel malah*) floating ephemerally in the air. Jerusalem is both earthbound and impermanent as dust, just as the language used to describe Jerusalem both concretizes and expunges it. Only by viewing the two versions of this poem alongside one another do the limitations and gaps of each language come into full view.

Like the relationship between the German and Hebrew "equivalents" (which, we have established, are never quite equal), Rübner's poems do not offer formulaic equations but rather gesture at the dissimilarity between words and things (*devarim*) and between past and present realities. The phrase "I am not who I am," an expression of the rift between former and existing selves, exemplifies this mode of signification through negation. This is not the language of a poet who has been reborn into a new language but rather that of a poet equally bound to and estranged from both of his languages. His identity exists only in bifurcation, differentiation, and mediation. In contrast to Gertrude Stein's famous quote, "Rose is a rose is a rose is a rose," Rübner's language may be described as the law of identity via negation, for no word can capture a definable essence, and the semiotic relationship between word and thing in one language often conceals an altogether different type of relationship in another language.

This negative law of identity is powerfully expressed in the poem *Te'udah*, translated as "Testimony," a word that may also denote a "certificate" or official "document" such as an identity card (*te'udat zehut*). In this poem, bearing witness doubles as a statement of identity and of purpose.

TESTIMONY	תעודה
I exist in order to say	אֲנִי קַיָּם כְּדֵי לוֹמַר
a house is no house	בַּיִת זֶה לֹא בַּיִת,
place of spread nets, bare rock, fear	מִשְׁטַח חֲרָמִים, צְחִיחַ סֶלַע, פַּחַד
there by the central square, did I say central square?	שָׁם לְיַד הַכִּכָּר, אָמַרְתִּי כִּכָּר?
Paved wilderness.	צִיָּה מְרֻצֶּפֶת.
I exist in order to say	אֲנִי קַיָּם כְּדֵי לוֹמַר
a path is no path,	דֶּרֶךְ זוֹ לֹא דֶּרֶךְ,
its caravans clinging, ascending in the rust of dreams	יַלְפְּתוּ אָרְחוֹתֶיהָ, יַעֲלוּ בַּחֲלֻדַּת חֲלוֹם
from the forest, the sand mountain	מִן הַיַּעַר, הַר הַחוֹל
I walk, there, who's walking? when I used to walk with childish steps, in the sun	אֲנִי הוֹלֵךְ, שָׁם, מִי הוֹלֵךְ? שֶׁהָיִיתִי הוֹלֵךְ בְּשַׁעֲלֵי יֶלֶד, בְּשֶׁמֶשׁ
of cessation, with outstretched arms, asking walking and asking after my father's face and my mother's	חִדָּלוֹן, בְּפֶשֶׂט יָדַיִם, שׁוֹאֵל, הוֹלֵךְ שׁוֹאֵל פְּנֵי אָבִי וְאִמִּי

I exist in order to say	אֲנִי קַיָּם כְּדֵי לוֹמַר
chronicles of my ancestors, coal, ash, wind	קוֹרוֹת אֲבוֹתַי, פֶּחָם, אֵפֶר, רוּחַ
of my sister in my hair blowing back and back, a night wind	אֲחוֹתִי בִּשְׂעָרִי הַנּוֹשֵׁב אָחוֹר, אָחוֹר, רוּחַ לֵילִית
in my day I exist in order to say	בְּיוֹמִי אֲנִי קַיָּם כְּדֵי לוֹמַר
to their nocturnal voices yes, yes to their weeping, yes to	לְקוֹלָם הַלֵּילִי כֵּן, כֵּן, לְבִכְיָם, כֵּן
the lost in the house of their absence, fallen from the	לָאוֹבֵד בְּבֵית אֵינוֹתָם, לַנּוֹפֵל מִצֵּל קְרוֹתָיו
shadow of its walls upon the fear of my voice saying yes	עַל פַּחַד קוֹלִי לוֹמַר כֵּן
in this vacant space.	בַּשֶּׁטַח הָרֵיק.
(Rübner 2005, 24).	

Negations such as "a house is no house" resemble mantras used by the poet to meditate on the painful experience of surviving his family. The house that once was the family home is twice purged, transformed in his memory into "the house of their absence" (*beyt 'eynotam*) and literally obliterated, reduced to "coal, ash and wind." The double-entendre of the word *korot*, meaning both "crossbeams" and "chronicles," suggests that his family's physical home has been reduced to memory. The "vacant space" where they once thrived is repeatedly juxtaposed with the poet's affirmation of his own survival – "I exist" (*'ani kayam*) – an ontological statement that doubles as a mission statement: "I exist in order to say…."

If we compare the Hebrew and German versions of the poem, we discover "gains" and "losses" in each. The Hebrew version contains biblical references that cannot be replicated in German, yet the German contains wordplay that is absent from the Hebrew. In the Hebrew version, the site where the family home once stood is described as "the top of a rock" (*tsiaḥ sela'*), a biblical phrase taken from Ezekiel's prophecy against Jerusalem following the Babylonian siege, and as "a place for spreading nets" (*mishtaḥ ḥeramim*), an allusion to Ezekiel's prophecy against the city of Tyre. In Modern Hebrew, the latter phrase takes on additional meanings, since the biblical word for "fishing net" (*ḥerem*) can be translated as either "excommunication" or "boycott," bringing to mind the boycott of Jewish businesses and the deportations of Jews during World War II. These biblical allusions are perforce lost in German translation, yet the translation to some extent compensates for these losses:

ZEUGNIS	TESTIMONY

Ich bin da um zu sagen	I am here to say
dieses Haus ist kein Haus dort neben dem Marktplatz, sagte ich Marktplatz? Gepflasterte Öde.	this house is no house, there next to the marketplace, did I say marketplace? Paved wasteland.
Ich bin da um zu sagen	I am here to say
dieser Weg ist kein Weg vom Wald, vom Sandberg her gehe ich, dort, wer geht? ging in der Sonne des Untergangs mit fragenden Händen Schritt für Schritt Nach dem Gesicht meines Vaters Nach dem Gesicht meiner Mutter.	this path is no path from the forest, from the sand mountain I walk, there, who walks? walked in the sun of destruction with hands asking step by step after my father's face after my mother's face.
Ich bin da um zu sagen	I am here to say
Die Balken meines Vaterhauses, Kohle Asche, Wind meiner Schwester in meinem Haar, es weht rückwärts, rückwärts, nächtlicher Wind	The beams of my father's house, coal ash, wind of my sister in my hair that blows backwards, backwards, nocturnal wind
in meinem Tag bin ich da um zu sagen Ja ihrer nächtlichen Stimme, Ja ihrer lautlosen, Ja Dem der verlorengeht im Haus ihrer Abwesenheit Dem das abfällt vom Schatten der Wände Auf die Furcht meiner Stimme zu sagen Ja Am wohnlosen Ort. (Rübner 1998, 66)	in my day I am here to say yes to her nocturnal, silent voice, yes to him losing his way in the house of her absence to that which falls off the shadows of walls at the fear in my voice to say yes in this home-less place.

An obvious "gain" in translation is the sinister-sounding *Sonne des Untergangs* (sun of perdition), which conceals the innocuous word *Sonnenuntergang* (sunset), symbolizing the end of an era. The path where the child once walked is not the same path upon which the adult now treads, for the sun has set, so to speak, on that former time and place. Another shift in translation is contained in the second line of the final stanza: "Ja ihrer nächtlichen Stimme, Ja ihrer lautlosen..." ("yes to her nocturnal voice, yes to her silent..."). Both adjectives modify the same noun, *Stimme* (voice), yet the unusual syntax allows for the omission of "voice" from the second clause, literally silencing it. In the final line, the term "wohnlosen Ort" (translated above as "home-less place") amplifies the absence of the speaker's former home. In contrast to the Hebrew version, which ends on the simple image of a "vacant space" (*shetaḥ reyk*), the German offers a neologism, "wohnlos," which denotes not just "empty" or "uninhabited" but "uninhabitable"; this is a place of non-domicile. Through the experimental engagement with German grammar, syntax, and vocabulary, Rübner effectively produces a second original that at once resembles and departs from the Hebrew original.

The tendency to express identity through negation often relies on subtle shifts in time, place, and language. In the poem "Postcard from Pressburg-Bratislava," for instance, a tautology is transformed into a trilingual enigma: "Bratislava is Pressburg is Pozsony" (Back 2014, 149). One city, three names, the subject of the poem is divided among the three nations – Slovak, German, and Hungarian – that competed to control it. The next line reads simply, "For me it is Pressburg," transporting the reader to the poet's childhood home in the German-speaking Jewish community of the Slovakian capital. Inspired by Rübner's travels through Europe several decades after emigrating, the poem reconstructs a conversation with a former teacher:

Bratislava is Pressburg is Pozsony.	בְּרַטִיסְלָוָה הִיא פְּרֶשְׁבּוּרג הִיא פּוֹזוֹנִי.
For me it is Pressburg.	בִּשְׁבִילִי הִיא פְּרֶשְׁבּוּרְג.
My teacher, Mr. Wurm from the elementary school	מוֹרִי, מַר וּוּרם מֵהָעֲמָמִי
drew a class photo from his drawer and pointed:	הוֹצִיא מִמְּגֵרָתוֹ אֶת תַּצְלוּם הַכִּתָּה וְהִצְבִּיעַ:
"This one was a Nazi, and this one and that one too. This one	זֶה הָיָה נָאצִי וְגַם זֶה וְזֶה. הַהוּא
was especially brutal. This one fell in Russia	הָיָה אַכְזָרִי בְּמְיֻחָד. הַלָּה נָפַל בְּרוּסְיָה
and that one was deported. Which of the Jewish pupils	וְאוֹתוֹ גֵּרְשׁוּ. מִי מֵהַתַּלְמִידִים הַיְהוּדִים
survived and lives – I don't know."	שָׂרַד וָחַי — אֵינִי יוֹדֵעַ.
Pressburg was a tri-lingual city. Its fourth language	פְּרֶשְׁבּוּרג הָיְתָה עִיר תְּלַת–לְשׁוֹנִית. הַלָּשׁוֹן
is silence.	הָרְבִיעִית הִיא הַשְּׁתִיקָה.

The last two lines of the passage, a response to the silence surrounding the fate of Pressburg's Jews, move fluidly between past and present tenses, as if to say that the history of this once trilingual city is now shrouded in silence. Oscillating between present and past, the poem weaves its way through layers of history. Although the Nazi-Slovak alliance lurks in the shadows ("Were there once borders to evil?"), it is obscured by older and more visible historical landmarks, from an ancient Celtic fortress to Roman ruins and strongholds built by medieval Moravian princes. As the poem comes to an end, the speaker bids farewell to the same city he had departed alone as a teenager in 1941, a city whose memory extends through the centuries but retains no monument to the poet's "happy childhood" there:

This is a very old city.	זֹאת עִיר בָּאָה–בַּיָּמִים.
So very old that I no longer know her.	כֹּה בָּאָה–בַּיָּמִים עַד שֶׁאֵינִי יוֹדְעָהּ עוֹד.
Until next time, my love, it's hard to imagine.	לְהִתְרָאוֹת אֲהוּבָה, קָשֶׁה לְשַׁעֵר.

The last two words of the poem – *kasheh lesha'er* (hard to imagine) – are puzzling. Do they refer to the past (i.e. it is hard to imagine what took place then) or to the future (i.e. it is hard to imagine that the poet will ever revisit his birthplace again)? The German translation contains a peculiar variation that in a sense answers this question without making the interpretation entirely transparent: "Auf Wiedersehen, Liebe, kaum," meaning, "Until next time, love, hardly" (Rübner 2000, 10). The German farewell, *Auf Wiedersehen*, like the Hebrew word *lehitraot*, literally means "see you again." Yet the future possibility implied in this leave-taking is undercut sardonically by the word *kaum*, meaning "hardly" or "rarely," which brings the poem to an inconclusive, seemingly interrupted ending. Yet when read alongside the Hebrew version, the German word *kaum* appears to be shorthand for *kaum zu glauben* (hard to believe), the equivalent of the Hebrew phrase *kasheh lesha'er*. Both endings break off into silence. Only when read in tandem does the sentiment behind the truncated ending emerge: the poet casually bids farewell to a city he doubts he will ever see again.

The sense of "homecoming" felt in Rübner's German self-translations betrays the limits of the cardinal binary categories of translation studies: original vs. translation, composition vs. interpretation, and poet vs. mediator. Only by brokering between German and Hebrew and their respective literary traditions is the bilingual poet able to explore the boundaries of self-expression while preserving ambiguity and opacity of meaning (the landmark of Kafka's writing that Rübner so admires). It is perhaps appropriately inconsistent – in light of Rübner's proclivity for contradiction – to describe the German and Hebrew halves of his bilingual oeuvre as simultaneously complimentary and antagonistic. Insofar as the German and Hebrew versions differ and yet "echo" one another, their pairing forms a vocal hesitation between languages and between thought and speech that is antithetical to conventional notions of fluency and mastery, notions for which Rübner has expressed disdain: "Why should the relationship to a language be one of mastery?" (Rübner 2014, 40). Relating to language less as master than as humble servant, he feels equally liberated and encumbered by German and Hebrew. The heavy-tongued prophet must retain both languages, even if this means submitting to paradox, contradiction, and stuttering as the only means of authentic expression.

6 Israeli or German? Rübner's reception and the limits of national literature

The deliberate confounding of borders between original and translation in Rübner's bilingual oeuvre presents a challenge not only to the conventional view of translation but also to the conventional conception of nationally demarcated literatures. Rübner's resistance to categorization along national lines comes into clear view when if we compare his reception in Israel versus his reception in Germany. In 2008, he came out of the shadows of the Israeli literary establishment with his receipt of the Israel Prize, the country's highest honor. The official "Judges' Decision" contains the following description of the poet: "Tuvia Rübner deals in his poetry with the major issues of Jewish history in modern times, chief among them World War II and the Holocaust of European Jewry" (Calderon et al. 2008). The essay makes no mention of German whatsoever; it is identified neither as his mother tongue, nor as his primary language of composition, nor as the language from and into which he has translated extensively for more than sixty years. Instead, Rübner is portrayed as an under-appreciated Holocaust poet who writes poetry about "Jewish history" exclusively in Hebrew.

Rübner's reception in Germany is quite different – yet equally problematic. In 2012, he was awarded the Konrad Adenauer Stiftung Literature Prize. In the essay about him that appears on the foundation's website his writing is described as "part of the corpus of modern exile literature" (Konrad Adenauer Stiftung 2012a). The implication is that Rübner is a German poet who living "in exile" in Israel. During the award ceremony in Weimar, however, Chairman Hans-Gert Pöttering remarked that the award was given to Rübner in recognition not only of his "autobiographical and extensive lyric work in German and Hebrew" but also of his "tremendous significance as a bridge-builder between cultures, languages and literatures" (Konrad Adenauer Stiftung 2012b). In contrast to the official Israeli context, where Rübner is identified primarily as a Hebrew poet and a Holocaust poet (thus furthering the Zionist narrative in which the Holocaust plays a central role), Pöttering presented Rübner as a proponent of German-Israeli rapprochement. Neither portrait properly captures the complexity of his bilingual identity.

During a conversation with Rübner, I asked how he responds to such attempts to categorize him, and how he would categorize himself. He stated emphatically that he regards himself as a bilingual poet, but "first and foremost as a poet." Yet he does not bristle at how critics categorize him. His indifference to the contrast between his reception in Israel and in Germany reveals both the complex self-image of the self-translator and the limits of nationalized literary cultures that invariably try based on the labels available to them to classify and thus flatten this image. Rübner's role as a self-translating poet allows him to rise above such designations, since he sees his Hebrew and German poems as twin expressions of a single voice. In either language, the poems are, as he puts it, "still poems," still *his* poems.

The failure of both German and Hebrew critics and award committees to account properly for Rübner's bilingual literary achievement can be attributed to the lack of attention given to the role of self-translation in his creative process. His achievement as a self-translating poet surpasses the constraints of national literary prizes. It is therefore more efficacious to explore his work through the lens of the contemporary discourse on world literature, which highlights unequal power relationships among languages and literatures on the global stage (Apter 2005; Casanova 2004; Lennon 2010). The question of linguistic hierarchy is particularly important for self-translation. As Rainier Grutman has shown, in contrast to the "symmetrical self-translation" of Samuel Beckett, who wrote in the world's two most established literary languages (French and English), an asymmetry is involved for self-translators working in languages of lesser diffusion. These include writers from established linguistic minorities who translate themselves into the language of the majority (such as Milan Kundera), postcolonial writers who alternate between native tongue and colonial European language (such as Rabindranath Tagore), and immigrant writers who move between native and adopted languages (this is especially prevalent in among Latino American writers like Rosario Ferré) (Grutman 2013, 195). In all three cases, self-translation is "centripetal," involving the transfer from a minor native language into a major language (Grutman 2013, 189).

The case of bilingual German-Hebrew writers like Rübner complicates Grutman's scheme somewhat. German, the poet's native language, is of course richer in literary capital than Hebrew, and can therefore be designated as the "major" language. Yet, within the Israeli context German represents, even today, a historical taboo. Although Hebrew is "minor" on the global scale with respect to literary capital and readership, it is nonetheless the dominant language within the multilingual Israeli state. For Rübner, German is a major language that became "minor" in Israel, whereas Hebrew is "minor" on the global stage yet endowed with power in its local context as the language of Israeli sovereignty. Self-translation, for Rübner, involves the crucial play between major and minor, between insider and outsider, and between global and local. Mixing German and Hebrew produces an ambiguous alternative in which each language deterritorializes the other.

Rübner's poetics cannot be fully appreciated without a careful examination of his self-translations. In contrast to Pöttering's bridge-builder metaphor, which implies mediation between two discrete camps, Rübner's self-translation project should be viewed as a "psychic dialogue" resounding within a "divided self." I borrow this psychological terminology from Naomi Seidman's work on German-Jewish translation, in which she recasts the German-Jewish "dialogue" as a "schizophrenic" rather than a "symbiotic" dynamic, "a form of talking to oneself" (Seidman 2006, 159). In keeping with Seidman's approach (which admittedly focuses exclusively on conventional source-target translation and not on self-translation), I argue that Rübner's self-translations must be seen not as a secondary phase in his writing process but rather as a foundational aspect of his poetics, an ongoing oscillation between German and Hebrew that precludes either language from being defined as "primary" or "secondary." The numerous gaps, slips, and variations that prevent the two versions of his poems from "lining up" form the heart of his "poetics of the possible," which is by the same token a poetics of the impossible. A masterful stutterer, Rübner has produced an unusual bilingual oeuvre borne of the hesitation between thought and expression, between youth and mortality, and above all between German and Hebrew.

Works cited

Apter, Emily E. *The Translation Zone: A New Comparative Literature.* Princeton: Princeton University Press, 2005.
Back, Rachel Tzvia, trans. *In the Illuminated Dark: Selected Poems of Tuvia Ruebner.* Cincinnati: Hebrew Union College Press, 2014.
Bassnett, Susan. *Translation Studies.* 3rd ed. New York: Routledge, 1980.
Calderon, Nissim, Dan Laor, Avidov Lipsker, and Chaya Shacham. "Judges' Decision." Recipients of the Israel Prize for the Year 2008. Israel Ministry of Education. http://cms.education.gov.il/EducationCMS/Units/PrasIsrael/Tashsch/TuviaRibner/NsTuviaRibner.htm (14 March 2017).
Casanova, Pascale. *The World Republic of Letters.* Cambridge, MA: Harvard University Press, 2004.
Cordingley, Anthony, ed. *Self-Translation: Brokering Originality in Hybrid Culture.* New York: Bloomsbury, 2013.

Deleuze, Gilles. "He Stuttered." *Essays Critical and Clinical*. Minneapolis: University of Minnesota Press, 1997. 107–114.
Freilich, Toby Perl. "Tuvia Ruebner Never Stops Mourning the Lost." *Tablet Magazine*. May 12, 2014. https://www.tabletmag.com/jewish-arts-and-culture/books/172169/tuvia-ruebner-never-stops-mourning-the-lost (14 March 2017).
Grutman, Rainier. "Becket and Beyond: Putting Self-Translation in Perspective." *Orbis Literarum* 68.3 (2013): 188–206.
Kafka, Franz. "The Cares of a Family Man." Trans. Willa and Edwin Muir. *Franz Kafka, The Complete Stories*. Ed. Nahum N. Glatzer. New York: Schocken Books, 1995. 428.
Konrad Adenauer Stiftung. "Zeitzeuge mit der Kraft zur Verständigung." Literaturpreis 2012a. http://www.kas.de/wf/de/71.11224/ (14 March 2017).
Konrad Adenauer Stiftung (Onlinekas). "Literaturpreis 2012: Verleihung an Tuvia Rübner." 2012b. https://www.youtube.com/watch?v=h6ggBIJPLYY (14 March 2017).
Lennon, Brian. *In Babel's Shadow: Multilingual Literatures, Monolingual States*. Minneapolis: University of Minnesota Press, 2010.
Ofek, Natan. "She-habilti nitfas bilti nitfas huh." *Siḥot 'al kafka ve'od*. Ed. Lea Tzivoni. Jerusalem: Tsivonim Publishing House, 2004. 43–57.
Rübner, Tuvia. *Rauchvögel: Ausgewählte Gedichte I, 1957–1959*. Aachen: Rimbaud Verlag, 1998.
Rübner, Tuvia. *Zypressenlicht: Ausgewählte Gedichte II, 1957–1999*. Aachen: Rimbaud Verlag, 2000.
Rübner, Tuvia. *Kim'at siḥa*. Tel Aviv: Keshev Leshirah, 2002.
Rübner, Tuvia. *'Ikvot yamim: mivḥar shirim, 1957–2005*. Tel Aviv: Keshev Leshirah, 2005.
Rübner, Tuvia. *Ḥayim arukim ketsarim*. Tel Aviv: Keshev Leshirah, 2006.
Rübner, Tuvia. *Wer hält diese Eile aus*. Aachen: Rimbaud Verlag, 2007.
Rübner, Tuvia. *Lichtschatten: Gedichte*. Aachen: Rimbaud Verlag, 2011a.
Rübner, Tuvia. *Shirim sotrim*. Tel Aviv: Even Hoshen, 2011b.
Rübner, Tuvia. *Ein langes kurzes Leben: Von Pressburg nach Merchavia. Erweitere und illustrierte Ausgabe*. Aachen: Rimbaud Verlag, 2014.
Scholem, Gershom. "The Name of God and the Linguistic Theory of the Kabbala." *Diogenes* 79 (1972): 159–180.
Seelig, Rachel. "The Middleman: Ludwig Strauss's German-Hebrew Bilingualism." *Prooftexts: A Journal of Jewish Literature History* 33.1 (Winter 2013): 76–104.
Seidman, Naomi. *Faithful Renderings: Jewish-Christian Difference and the Politics of Translation*. Chicago: The University of Chicago Press, 2006.
Strauss, Ludwig. *Gesammelte Werke in drei Bänden. Lyrik und Übertragungen*. Vol. 3. Ed. Hans-Otto Horch and Tuvia Rübner. Göttingen: Wallstein, 2000.
Ticotsky, Giddon. "A German Island in Israel: Lea Goldberg and Tuvia Rübner's Republic of Letters." *Naharaim: Zeitschrift für deutsch – jüdische Literatur und Kulturgeschichte* 10.1 (September 2016): 127–149.
Weiss, Yfaat. "Rückkehr in den Elfenbeinturm: Deutsch an der Hebräischen Universität." *Naharaim: Zeitschrift für deutsch – jüdische Literatur und Kulturgeschichte* 8.2 (2014): 227–245.

Giddon Ticotsky
Vera Europa vs. *Verus Israel*: Modern Jews' Encounter with Europe in Light of Lea Goldberg's *Encounter with a Poet*

I woke up one day and knew I was a European (Emmanuel Levinas)[1]

1 "Do we have the right to forget?"

On April 30, 1945, mere days after American and Soviet troops had met on the banks of the Elbe at the heart of Germany, and as Berlin's encirclement was being completed and concentration camps liberated one after the other – Buchenwald, Bergen-Belsen, and Dachau – the poet Lea Goldberg published an essay in the Hebrew socialist newspaper *Mishmar*. Titled "Your Europe" (*Eropa shelakhem*), this essay by the most European woman poet in modern Hebrew poetry was a poignant reckoning with Europe and its culture. Despite what the readers would surely have expected, the Holocaust, whose scale was starting to be widely acknowledged by this time, was not explicitly referenced in the essay. Instead, the essay opened with a discussion about the constant tension in European culture between adherence to and violation of form, and went on to lament the continent's spiritual destruction; it ended with a comment on the Jews' belonging to European culture.

Goldberg presented herself as a member of the generation that had grown up in the shadow of the Great War, a generation that, despite the terrible devastation it had experienced, still believed in the "'great and enlightened world'" (Goldberg 1945, 6). This was why, she explained, she and her contemporaries – "born in the semiconscious backwaters of Eastern Europe, captives of the Jewish *shtetls* in the broadest sense of the term" (Goldberg 1945, 6) – wandered to the "great centers, to gain erudition and knowledge," in the spirit of the pioneers of the Jewish Enlightenment (*Haskalah*) some one hundred and fifty years prior.

---

* I thank the editors of this volume, Rachel Seelig and Amir Eshel, for inspiring conversations – and later, fruitful comments – that have contributed so much to this article. Many thanks also to my colleagues Joshua Teplitsky, who helped me think through about the experience of East-European Jews in Central and Western Europe.
1 Malka 2006, 9. I thank Ofra Yeglin for bringing this quote to my attention and Karma Ben-Johanan who introduced me to the scholarly discourse about Verus Israel.

> What was Europe for us [at that time]? – Dante and Giotto, and Michelangelo, Goethe, and Flaubert, and Mozart, and Stendhal, and Verlaine, and Rilke and Rodin, Cezanne, and Stravinsky and James Joyce... Names, names, names, all with different meanings and values, that contradict one another [...] This was "the whole," that was the intellectual, spiritual atmosphere, that was the special scent of a world, the special light of that world, in whose forests stood ancient oak trees, in whose suburbs the parks autumn leaves would fall and cover the ground with gold, on whose mighty rivers unnamed architects have spent centuries building arched bridges of such beautiful balustrades... This was the first love despite it all, regardless of it all, regardless of the memories flowing in our Jewish blood, of slaughter, of burning at the stake, of pogroms.... (Goldberg 1945, 6)

Goldberg's essay opens with a debate between artists in which one lashes out at the other: "This is your Europe." It ends with the statement that implies that World War II (and maybe even the Holocaust) are nothing but another recurring episode in a long and tormented history of relations between Europe and its Jews:

> The snare is broken, and we have escaped.[2] Do we have the right to judge? Do we have the right to forget? [...] And we shall not forget thee, the wounds of the lover and the wounds of the hater we will not forget. Until the day we die we will carry it within us, this immense hurt whose name is Europe, "your Europe," "their Europe," but apparently... not "our Europe," even though we were hers, very much hers. (Goldberg 1945, 6)

In what follows I focus on the cultural-historical topos to which Goldberg's essay alludes: the sense of profound identification of Jews with the culture of Europe, despite or perhaps precisely because of their alienation from it, and despite or because of the historical events which had marked them as aliens and therefore as a target for repeated persecution. This topos, which has multiple representations, is thoroughly and beautifully elucidated in Jehuda Reinharz's and Yaacov Shavit's book *Glorious, Accursed Europe* (2010). Following their discussion, I would like to cast light on a specific trope of this topos which hasn't yet been explored, which I will call *Vera Europa*.

The *Vera Europa* trope, I argue, is modeled on the concept of *Verus Israel*. In the classical *Dialogue with Trypho*, St. Justin Martyr coined the term *Verus Israel* – "the true Israelites" – to refer to the Christian Church as having superseded the Jews as God's chosen people: "For the true spiritual Israel [...] are we who have been led to God through this crucified Christ."[3] This idea already appears in the New Testament, but it is Justin who imposed on this substitution the categorical

---
[2] See Psalms 124:7: "We have escaped like a bird from the snare of the fowlers; The snare is broken, and we have escaped" (all biblical quotes are from the English Standard Version, ESV).
[3] Justin Martyr, Dialogue With Trypho 11, in *Ante-Nicene Fathers* 1:200.

distinction between flesh and spirit. He thereby laid the groundwork for supersessionism or replacement theology, which lies at the heart of Christianity's self-definition vis-à-vis Judaism.[4] Beyond the theological significance of the church's supersession, Justin paved the way to a new paradigm: the authenticity of identity is no longer dependent on the flesh, but on the spirit. In other words, identification is more important than identity, and the substitute may be more authentic than the source, by virtue of sincerity.

Accordingly, the concept *of Vera Europa* – the true Europe – I claim, also encapsulates a fundamental substitution: the modern Jews who have arrived in Central and Western Europe from its provinces (be it geographical or cultural, real or imagined), often considered themselves the true Europeans, charged with safeguarding the continent's glorious humanistic legacy, especially the demise of this heritage (from World War I on). The idea of *Vera Europa* therefore extends beyond cultural or civic emancipation through education; it signifies not only the longing to belong (as in the case of many Germans Jews who tried to "out-German" their fellow Christian Germans) but also a passion to promote and advocate European values which had already been forgotten or disrespected.

Thus the idea of *Vera Europa* has certain spatial and temporal dimensions. It is useful to think through this concept about European Jews in times of crisis and especially after the Holocaust; and it may explain how Jews who lived on the margins of the German cultural circle (*Kulturkreis*) and adopted this culture as "outsiders," became passionate delegators for it even after that culture had been completely transformed and those Jews immigrated out of Europe. By that they could perceive themselves as "insiders" – in a culture that in many senses no longer existed.

In this article I explore the concept of *Vera Europa* through the writing of Lea Goldberg, specifically her book *Encounter with a Poet (Pgisha im meshorer)*. My choice of Goldberg (Königsberg, Prussia 1911 – Jerusalem 1970) is informed by her central position in modern Hebrew literature as a poet, cultural hero, and a kind of ambassador of European culture within pre- and post-statehood Israeli culture. As for the book, it is a memoir, published in 1952, that commemorates the poet Avraham Ben Yitzhak (Sonne; Przemyśl, Austro-Hungary 1883 – Ramatayim, Israel 1950) – one of the most European poets in Hebrew literature.[5] In the reading

---

4 For more on *Verus Israel* and its iterations, see Pelikan 1971, Vol. 1; Ruether 1974, Chapter 3; Simon 1986 [1948].
5 Avraham Ben Yitzhak was Sonne's nom de plume. In her book, Goldberg ascribed to him a decisive role in Hebrew literature: "He was the first Hebrew poet the hands of whose watch did not show just the specific Jewish time, but the hours and minutes of contemporary world literature" (Goldberg 2009, 73).

suggested here, the figure of the poet and the memoir as a whole become a metaphor for a simultaneous encounter with and departure from Europe.[6]

Ben Yitzhak and Goldberg both came from the periphery of the German *Kulturkreis*, from what may be even considered as "Halb-Asien."[7] Although Goldberg was born in Königsberg, she grew up, from her very early childhood on, in Kaunas (Kovno), then part of the Russian Empire and later a city in an independent Lithuania. She excelled in German and Russian and moved to Berlin when she was 19 years old, in 1930, to study philology and Semitic languages at Friedrich Wilhelm University (today The Humboldt University of Berlin). In 1935 she immigrated to Mandatory Palestine. Ben Yitzhak was born to a traditional Jewish family in Galicia. He arrived to Berlin and Vienna in his late twenties, in the late 1900s or early 1910s, and lived in Vienna for many years, until immigrating to Mandatory Palestine in 1938, due to the *Anschluss*.

2 Ben Yitzhak and *Encounter with a Poet*

Encounter with a Poet was written, Goldberg remarked, "with the modest hope that perhaps I would manage to convey some of the spiritual greatness" of Ben Yitzhak (2009, 5). Already as a boy, Ben Yitzhak wrote poems in German – the language used by the local educated class – as well as in Hebrew, which was emerging as a modern spoken language. By age twenty-five he had published his first Hebrew poems, which won him great acclaim in the emerging Hebrew literary republic, whose center at the time was Berlin. The poems offered an innovative and daring poetic alternative to those of the father of modern Hebrew poetry, Hayim Nahman Bialik. However, over the course of his life, Ben Yitzhak's oeuvre never exceeded a dozen poems and therefore remained unfulfilled.

Like many Galician Jews, Ben Yitzhak studied at universities in Berlin and Vienna. He did not graduate, perhaps because he was lured away by Zionist activism. After a short stay in Palestine in 1913, he moved to Vienna and soon became a prominent figure in the local Zionist community. After World War I he

---

[6] The book is divided into two parts, the first personal and the second scholarly. This article refers mostly to the former, which has been fully translated into German but not yet into English. See Goldberg 2013.

[7] The term "Half-Asia" or "demi-Orient" was applied by Karl Emil Franzos to refer to Galicia, which he described as "these lands placed between cultured Europe [*gebildete Europa*] and the barren steppe across which the Asiatic nomads move." Franzos located this region outside the borders of civilized society and European Enlightenment. See: Wolff 2010, 242–243.

was appointed to several positions in the Zionist leadership in London, and after a year was promoted to become Chaim Weizmann's political advisor. However, the two had ideological disagreements, which prompted Ben Yitzhak to return to Vienna and put an end to his public career. In Vienna he befriended several major artists and authors, including Arnold Schönberg, Robert Musil, Hugo von Hofmannsthal, Arthur Schnitzler, and Richard Beer-Hofmann. Many of them admired and even referred to him in their works, whether indirectly, for instance, as a character in Hermann Broch's *Der Tod des Vergil*, or directly, for example, in an extended episode in Elias Canetti's *Das Augenspiel*.

Ben Yitzhak's transition to Mandatory Palestine in 1938 represented the twilight of his life. The tuberculosis from which he had suffered in secret for years grew worse. He maintained very few social contacts; he met primarily with the German Jewish elite of Jerusalem, including Werner Kraft, Leopold Krakauer and Georg Landauer, and continued to be admired by his acquaintances. It was at this time that he became Goldberg's friend and mentor.

Due to the relative scarcity of information about Ben Yitzhak, and thanks to the extraordinary literary qualities of *Encounter with a Poet*, Goldberg's book became a key source in virtually every study about Ben Yitzhak, contributing immensely to the buildup of the mythical aura surrounding his name in Israeli culture. Her monograph became an invaluable resource, despite the fact that, like most memoirs, it deliberately emphasizes certain episodes in the protagonist's life (his years in Israel) at the expense of others (such as his adolescent years in Galicia) and is biased by the subjective perspective of its author. Nevertheless, *Encounter with a Poet* served as a biographical and historical source for Hannan Hever's comprehensive monograph on Ben Yitzhak published in the early 1990s (Ben Yitzhak 1992; Hever 1993), as well as for many of the articles in the special 2013 issue of *Naharaim* journal dedicated to the study of his life and works.[8]

Goldberg's book also attracted attention as an important piece of writing in its own right from almost all of her commentators. These include especially Tuvia Rübner (1980) and Ofra Yeglin (2002), who have emphasized Ben Yitzhak's unique contribution to Goldberg's development as a poet. Anat Weisman has interpreted the book not as a gesture of admiration but, on the contrary, as a subtle polemic between Goldberg and her erstwhile mentor, and as a text with which she sought to break free of Ben Yitzhak's powerful influence (2002, 2013).

Here I would like to shed a different light on *Encounter with a Poet*, and read it not merely against the backdrop of Ben Yitzhak's and Goldberg's lives and works

---

[8] The issue included articles by Anat Weisman, Natasha Gordinsky, Maya Berzilai and Paul Michael Lützeler.

but mainly as a forum for grappling with European heritage after the war in the newly established State of Israel. According to this reading, the book transcends the two poets' lives and times and may be reinterpreted as a text which reflects the feelings of many members of their generation regarding the encounter of young modern Jews with European culture in the first half of the twentieth century – and particularly the Jewish-German cultural encounter.

3 The Poet as Metaphor: Ben Yitzhak and Petrarch

Encounter with a Poet (hereafter, *Encounter*) is Goldberg's final prose work. In a certain sense, it is the twin to her first novel, published in Mandatory Palestine in 1937, *Letters from an Imaginary Journey (Mikhtavim minsiyah medumah*; hereafter *Letters)*; at the same time, *Encounter* is also its mirror image. In the two books, it seems Goldberg is parting with Europe – first on the eve of and then in the aftermath of World War II – with the allusion to the (future or past) catastrophe lurking in the background. The two books are based on a dialogue with an absent presence: in *Letters*, Ruth, Goldberg's alter ego, writes letters to her lover Immanuel, while in *Encounter*, Goldberg converses with the late Ben Yitzhak in a dialogue which, as in the former book, is actually a monologue. The novel's voyage through space has been substituted in *Encounter* by an imaginary voyage in time, to the "World of Yesterday," but while *Letters* depicted this dying world with a pinch of sarcasm, after its total collapse it was easier to reminisce it with nostalgia, particularly the heroic period of European modernism, which Goldberg had missed by a decade or two.[9]

It is therefore no coincidence that Goldberg includes among the reasons which motivated her to write *Encounter* the understanding that Ben Yitzhak personified "the essence of a generation, the essence of a period and its refinement in a single personality. [...] He had something in common with the generation the days of whose youth had been experienced in the previous century. That 'Europeanness' of broad horizons, of people who saw countries aplenty, for whom all borders were wide open" (Goldberg 2009, 10, 18). Thus, as much as it is dedicated to describing Ben Yitzhak as a real-life figure, the book also presents him as an icon (hence Goldberg's choice to call it *Encounter with a Poet* and not "Encounter with Avraham Ben Yitzhak").

---

9 For more on that delayed arrival, see Yeglin 2002, 15.

The book's almost metaphorical name could easily have been the title of another piece Goldberg was working on at the time: a brief scholarly monograph on Petrarch, a selection of whose poems she had previously translated into Hebrew.[10] In February and March of 1951, when she studied the oeuvre of the "father of the sonnet" at the Warburg Institute of the University of London, she was preoccupied with the same issues discussed in her writing about Ben Yitzhak, who, like Petrarch, had contributed to the development of culture as part of a nation-building enterprise.

In both works, Goldberg traced the poets' biographical-historical personae in order to gain insights into *the ideal* of the poet – one who heralded a golden age of European civilization and another who symbolized for her its demise. "Usually, the figure of a great poet, a poet whose style leaves a deep mark on his period and transcends the limits of a single generation, is that of a person profoundly involved in most contemporary issues," she wrote of Petrarch (Goldberg 1953, 50). Similarly, in *Encounter*, she emphasized Ben Yitzhak's deep involvement in the contemporary issues of his own people. Before her were a poet who struggled to decide between two languages – Latin and Italian – each representing a different cultural choice, and another who also moved between different languages and cultures – German and Hebrew:

> A poet or an author, who wrote in Latin, directed his writings to different peoples, to all *European scholars*, the language of Rome was their written language, while the one who wrote in Italian spoke directly to the masses in his country, and this two was not unappreciated by the intellectuals of that age. [...] Nowadays, we cannot fully understand the importance of that question, and the entire difficulty involved in deciding it. (Goldberg 1953, 67–68; emphasis in original)

Neither Petrarch nor Ben Yitzhak ever solved their bilingual (or multilingual, in Ben Yitzhak's case) dilemma, which actually defined their personal and professional identities. As Maya Barzilai points out, Ben Yitzhak self-translated his German poems into Hebrew and vice versa; moreover, in his notes he frequently mixed the two languages and sometimes used Yiddish as well (2014, 110). It is therefore interesting to read the footnote Goldberg added to the above

---

10 Goldberg began writing *Encounter* in September 1950, about three months after Ben Yitzhak's death (Goldberg 2005, 295). In December, major sections of the book appeared in print in the first issue of *Orlogin* literary journal, including most of the text subsequently incorporated in Chapters A, C and D and the end of the personal part. It seems that Goldberg delayed writing the scholarly part, as she waited to receive a copy of the poems from Ben Yitzhak's estate, which she obtained in October 1951 (Goldberg 2005, 308). In December 1951, the book was already set for print (based on the book's file in Sifriat Po'alim Publishing House's archive).

mentioned quote: "Nevertheless, it may be that some twenty years ago [in the 1930s] this vacillation between poetic language[s] would have been better understood by a Jewish poet faced with the choice of writing in either Hebrew or Yiddish" (Goldberg 1953, 67). With this comment, Goldberg actually compares the division between Latin and Italian in the fourteenth century to the one between Hebrew and Yiddish in the twentieth century; Latin and Hebrew are ancient, highly esteemed languages designated to the elites, while Italian and Yiddish, newer and seemingly deficient languages, belong to the masses. Choosing Italian over Latin, and Hebrew over German or Yiddish, was an ideological decision related to emerging nationalisms. Nevertheless, both Petrarch and Ben Yitzhak, even after composing poems in Italian and Hebrew, respectively, still believed they transcended nationality as *uomo universal*, a "universal man" who is familiar with all spheres of human knowledge.[11]

Finally, both Petrarch and Ben Yitzhak were proud poets who often paid a price for their pride, and both participated in the political lives of their nations until they retired from public life full of disappointments. (Petrarch supported Cola di Rienzo who sought to unify the Italian cities but became disillusioned after he had reneged on his ideals; Goldberg 1953, 125–147.) Goldberg concluded her monograph about Petrarch as follows:

> Francesco Petrarca, who died in his study at age seventy,[12] having lived life to the fullest, left a tilled and planted land behind him. The reapers came after him. His life's path was far from easy – the path of men of heart and character never is – but he knew how to walk through it, and that alone is an invaluable art of living. But he also knew more than that: to walk that path towards the future. (Goldberg 1953, 154)

The references to "a tilled and planted land" and "reapers" echo the lines of one of Ben Yitzhak's most famous poems: "Blessed are those who sow and do not reap – / they shall wander in extremity" (Ben Yitzhak 2003, 43). These lines reverse the biblical verse that promises to see the fruit of one's labors, "those who sow with tears will reap with songs of joy" (Psalms 126:5). In his poem, Ben Yitzhak wishes to be freed of the teleological order embedded in this biblical verse (and in Western rationalism in general). Instead, he suggests a different approach: rather

---

[11] Just as Goldberg wrote that "I could have expanded the discussion to refer to Petrarch the explorer, the archeologist, the paleographer, the geographer" (1953, 95), she emphasized the multifariousness of Ben Yitzhak's intellect in the context of his era: "His world was so broad, his knowledge areas so rich and diverse [...] He mastered botany, technology and economics in its various aspects, had surprisingly precise knowledge of all theories, characteristics, histories" (2009, 13).

[12] Approximately Ben Yitzhak's age at his death.

than privileging action and its future positive results, he renounces action, or at least acting with specific expectations. In this final paragraph, Goldberg defines Petrarch's endeavor with Ben Yitzhak's words and line of thought. She perceives the sowers who do not reap as a symbol of all poets, including Petrarch, Ben Yitzhak and maybe even herself; their deeds, which may seem futile – as poetry and literature seem to be – will be acknowledged only posthumously.

I have lingered on the parallels between Petrarch and Ben Yitzhak because I believe they were essential for Goldberg's attempt to portray the Austro-Hungarian Jewish poet Ben Yitzhak as *the* European poet of his time. In this way, she sought to establish a quasi-classical forebear for modern Hebrew poetry while simultaneously placing this Galician poet in the heart of a Central European literary tradition. She was not the only one who compared Ben Yitzhak to the Italian and Roman classicists. In one of his letters to Ben Yitzhak, Hermann Broch hinted that Ben Yitzhak had inspired him to write *Der Tod des Vergil*.[13] Wera Lewin (1910, Berlin – 1980, Tel Aviv), another acquaintance of Ben Yitzhak, wrote in her obituary of him: "People have often tried to guess why Avraham Ben Yitzhak had stopped writing poetry. When I read the conversation between Virgil and Augustus in *Der Tod des Vergil* by Hermann Broch – a close friend of Sonne – it seems as though the friend's image was before Broch's eyes when he wrote the novel" (Lewin 1955).

4 "Memory's not a historian, but a poet": memory and history in *Encounter with a Poet*

By virtue of its very genre, memoir, *Encounter* attaches central importance to memory. It seems, however, that it uniquely expands and refines that concept on two dimensions: horizontally and vertically. Horizontally, in that Goldberg seems to implant herself (and her readers) in the key junctures of Ben Yitzhak's life. His personal memories become her own – and that of her readers: "I remember many of the simple characters that he has depicted in his stories, *as if I have seen*

---

[13] "Recently, a critic attributed to me Dantesque aspirations in my Virgil [...] And after reading this I dreamt the following night of Dante: He was travelling in Vienna's textile trade center, that is in Gonzaga Street, cane in hand, looking like a businesslike and elegant Jew dressed in a caftan [...] Why am I writing you this? Simply because your image has accompanied and adjoined what I have just described here." Letter from Hermann Broch to Avraham Sonne, October 8, 1947; Quoted by Hever in Ben Yitzhak 1992, 108 and by Lützeler 2013, 167.

them face to face [...] The character of the soldier, the son-in-law of his mother's housemaid – *I remember him well*" (Goldberg 2009, 26; emphasis added).

Through Ben Yitzhak and his stories, Goldberg was able to experience herself as a citizen of the world, and especially as a *Westjude* ("West European Jew") who easily could converse with an Austrian cobbler (Goldberg 2009, 14), a guesthouse owner in the Tirol Mountains (11–12) or a Mother Superior (16–17). Goldberg, the East European Jew who appropriated a West-Central European identity – just like Ben Yitzhak – clings passionately to the shining example of the Galician Jew who has earned the respect of Vienna's literary café patrons. Perhaps this is also the secret of *Encounter*'s enduring magic in the eyes of generations of Hebrew readers, to the point that it has become part of the *biographia literaria* of Israel's intellectual elite: it enabled Hebrew readers to feel part of the wider world, to feel at home in enlightened Europe, whose image had not yet been desecrated by the calamities of the twentieth century. This Europe was completely different from the Europe introduced to Israeli youngsters by the national education system and their familiar environment: a Holocaust-free Europe. Aharon Shabtai (Tel Aviv, 1939), one of Israel's leading poets and translators, once mentioned that it was reading *Encounter* that led him to study German in his youth, quite an unusual move at the time, when German culture was taboo in Israeli society, and that to this day, as he moves from one apartment to the next, he makes sure a copy of the book accompanies him (2009).

The memoir also refines the concept of memory vertically, in depth, by employing the memory-of-a-memory technique. This means that the book includes not only Goldberg's or Ben Yitzhak's personal anecdotes but also those of people acquainted with the latter. Such for example is the story of the elderly Swiss sisters in whose house Ben Yitzhak lived before World War I, who recall how, in the café they used to frequent with their father at a young age (i.e. in the mid-nineteenth century), "a small man used so sit and have tea, he was small and hunched and would always, always sit on his own, a tired and wan face was his. And he used to wear an old jacket, and never look at anyone, and nobody ever approached him. And our father told us, this is Professor Nietzsche" (Goldberg 2009, 39). Published in 1952, Goldberg's book is thus a treasure trove of reflections by people who lived a hundred years prior. These reflections are presented as lived experience, since the author does not conceal the fact that these are second- or even third-hand experiences (the sisters had told Ben Yitzhak, who told Goldberg, who tells the readers). In that sense, *Encounter* may be read as a relay station, able to receive radio waves from distant station that have already ceased transmitting, and to pass them on to the readers' present.

Beyond her expansion of the dimensions of memory as described, Goldberg made a conscious choice to write *Encounter* as a poet rather than a historian.

She therefore preferred to describe moods and impressions rather than dwell on factual details. As a disciple of the neo-symbolist school of poetry, Goldberg warmly adopted the following recommendation by French poet Paul Géraldy regarding photography: "Memory is a poet / don't make him a historian."[14] She repeated this message elsewhere (Goldberg 1939, 1944, 1958), including in a newspaper essay she published in January 1939:

> The common aphorism, that our memory is a poet rather than a historian – does it truly allow us in this day and age to remember everything, as much as we wish? Does the title "poet" not charge us with heavier responsibility? The historian, the chronicler, may write as he will, as objectivity as his gifts allow him, and his texts – will be eternally debatable. Whereas the poet – it is he who sets the mood of his time, its background, that medieval golden set which "holds" the picture, the zeitgeist. But the poet does not create that mood, but also bound thereby. Poetry's unique logic usually justifies its little caprices and oversights. (Goldberg 1939: 5)

This conceptualization of literature's unique ability to capture the tenor of the times even better than history – perhaps in the spirit of Schopenhauerian idealism – is a cornerstone of Goldberg's poetics, also articulated in *Encounter*. The book's avowed subjectivity – foregoing in advance any pretense of providing a comprehensive description of its subject – is what ensures its precision and "artistic objectivity,"[15] as paradoxical as this turn of phrase may sound.

Precisely because *Encounter* is a book by a poet rather than a historian, it describes a different (but not necessarily alternative) history of European modernism, one in which "we belonged to her [to Europe], very much so," as Goldberg wrote in "Your Europe" – a history that describes the canon from the margins, from the point of view of the Jewish immigrant and later on refugee. In its subtle approach, the book seeks to establish Ben Yitzhak's (and through him, many other Jews') substantial belongingness to Central and Western European culture by glimpsing behind the scenes of modernity. Like the contemporary film hero Forrest Gump, Ben Yitzhak appears in various milestones of modern German and Austrian history as an absent presence—present enough to witness, but absent from official historiography.[16] A silent witness of various scenes, he rescues

---

14 In the poem "Stéréoscope": "Le souvenir est un poète / N'en fais pas un historien" (Géraldy 1939, 55).
15 The expression is borrowed from Ezra Zusman (Odessa, 1900 – Nahlat Yehuda, Israel, 1973; Zusman 1952).
16 Such for example is the story about the birthday present Ben Yitzhak arranged to Jewish inventor and scholar Josef Popper-Lynkeus (Goldberg 2009, 49).

valuable memories from oblivion, whose value lies precisely in being anecdotal, which is often at least as important as being "historical." For example:

> Sonne met Joyce in person only once. It was in Switzerland. The three of them were sitting on the porch of some house – Joyce's German publisher, Joyce and Sonne. Joyce remained silent throughout. This was in his final years, his illness having overcome him and his eyes almost sightless. Soon enough they were joined by a young writer who had previously probably read out some of his writing to Joyce. He wanted to hear what the author of *Ulysses* had to say about those texts, but he could not bring Joyce to say a word. Then – most probably to curry favor with the great author – this young wordmonger began saying that in order to write a novel today, one must be a cosmopolitan and be well aware of all that goes on in the entire world. And to be very familiar with the lives of all nations and lands and so on and so forth... Until Joyce's lost his patience and snapped: "To write a novel these days, one must be well aware, especially of all that goes on in his little hometown." (Goldberg 2009, 32–33)

Through the retelling of these ostensibly true anecdotes, a triple alliance is formed: Ben Yitzhak, Goldberg and the reader all share secrets to which no other, not even the non-Hebrew reader, is privy. In a way, this alliance builds up the sense of belonging, albeit belatedly, to a different Europe, historical and imagined at one and the same time—a humanistic civilization that provided Jews with modern identity and a feeling of being accepted, a culture that let Galician Jew (like Ben Yitzhak) or Lithuanian Jews (such as Goldberg or Emmanuel Levinas, who studied at the same gymnasium as she did) the aspirations to participate actively in that culture.

5 *Verus Israel* vs. *Vera Europa*

According to the reading proposed above, *Encounter* represents a site of conflict between individual and collective memories, between official historiography and anecdotes that seem as important as history itself, and between "historical" and "literary" memories. Moreover, it is the arena within which to grapple with the appropriation of memory as a way of establishing belongingness and identity. In the background of all these negotiations lies the idea of the Jews, and specifically those from the provinces of Central Europe, as *Vera Europa*.

While the Christian narrative of *Verus Israel* is basically optimistic (the supersession redresses the flawed past and almost enables its erasure), the *Vera Europa* narrative is more pessimistic because the flawed past – meaning mainly World War II and the Holocaust – is constantly in the background, persistently projecting itself on the narrative. To illustrate this point I offer a close reading of an allegorical anecdote retold by Goldberg on Ben Yitzhak's behalf. As in other episodes in *Encounter* that relate stories from the distant past, this one reflects on the time of Goldberg's writing and illustrates a principle larger than the anecdote. Indeed, as much as this is Ben Yitzhak's story, its artistic design, steeped in Jewish scriptures, is completely Goldberg's:

> I remember full well, how in a single day I saw the fulfillment of my complete happiness and its entire collapse. And I was only five years old at the time.
>
> We were at a village summer house, and I used to see peasant children coming out of the woods, carrying a basket full of red berries: wild mulberries. And I too wanted to go out to the forest and pick berries like them. But I knew I could only do it very early in the morning, when everyone is still asleep, before those who pick berries for sale have left for the woods. I remember that in the evening they [maybe his parents, GT] washed me well and shampooed my hair, and on the chair next to the bed they placed a clean white shirt. And before I fell asleep I made up my mind to go out to the woods at morning by morning [בבוקר-בבוקר].
>
> I woke up at the crack of dawn and wore my clean clothes, and even had a handkerchief, big and white. I took it, and left the house through the window, so as not to be noticed; the forest was nigh and I walked through it, first in a path I knew, and then ever further, where the trees were very tall and dense. At first I found nothing, but it felt good to walk the woods on a summer morning, when all the scents were still fresh, and the dew covered everything. And I was not the least bit afraid and did not feel alone and did not fear that I may lose my way and was only anxious that I may not find many berries. But then I arrived at this place, where there were fewer trees and the grass was green and soft, and I began finding berries, first few and not many, but then later I suddenly came upon this glade, almost all red with mulberries. I made four knots in my kerchief, as the peasant children would, to turn it into a basket. And I began picking and filling up the kerchief, until it was overflowing with ripe and juicy red berries, which gave off an excellent smell, and the forest was already fully awoken, and teeming with life. And in my hand was this treasure, only a short while ago the object of my fantasy, and now right there at hand.
>
> So happy was I that I didn't notice how the sky became clouded, and the trees began bustling and rustling, and suddenly a great wind blew, followed by a terrible silence, and the first big drops fell on my head. Within seconds, it was raining with vengeance, and I felt lost and alone in the woods. And the rain waxed stronger, and before long all the berries in my kerchief became an ugly red mess. I stood under a big tree, trying to salvage whatever I could still salvage, and in my fear I pressed the kerchief and the berries to my heart, and my clean white shirt was all covered with red stains. I started running and I ran without knowing where.
>
> When finally I came out of the woods, my family members approached me, having looked for me everywhere. But I was not at all glad to see them. I was wet and dirty, and in my hand was a stained kerchief, with a bit of that red sticky porridge still in it. And it was as though I had seen a big, beautiful and happy world that had collapsed into rubble and ruin before my very eyes. (Goldberg 2009, 28–29)

Is this not an allegory of Ben Yitzhak's path – and perhaps that of many modern Jews in general – through European culture? The Jewish Ben Yitzhak envies the Christian peasant children and wants to pick the coveted fruit, which is akin to the fruit of the tree of knowledge "morning by morning [בבוקר-בבוקר]." Here, Goldberg uses the biblical Hebrew expression that appears in the description of the Children of Israel gathering manna in the desert "morning by morning."[17] The allusion gestures at what comes next: just as manna melts in the heat of the sun in the desert, so is this fruit bound to rot by noon, destroyed by the rain in the European woods. "Morning by morning" (or in other translation, "early in the morning") was also the time when Abraham took Isaac to Mount Moriah, to be slain (Genesis 22:3), and it is at this time that Avraham Ben Yitzhak (literally, Abraham son of Isaac, a reversal of the biblical dynastic order) goes out to the woods.[18]

Moreover, Goldberg emphasizes the child's cleanliness, as if he were purified in preparation for some terrible ordeal, as well as the clean shirt, which for Hebrew readers readily evokes Joseph's robe (or coat) of many colors (Goldberg's "shirt" and the biblical "robe" are both the same word in Hebrew, כותונת), given to him by his father, Jacob son if Isaac, also called Israel, as a token of being the favorite, chosen son. Before his envious brothers threw him into the pit, they had stripped him off his robe, and then dipped it in goat's blood so that they could show it to their father as evidence that "a fierce animal has devoured him" (Genesis 37:33). And here: "my clean white shirt was all covered in red stains." Finally, the great wind that passes through the woods is also a biblical reference: God hurled such a wind at Jonah's ship to prevent him from escaping to Tarshish.[19] It is also a great wind that destroys Job's house and kills his sons.[20]

Reading this allegorical tale illustrates the sophisticated artistic design of *Encounter* and highlights the storyteller's meticulous styling, as opposed to this memoir's seemingly associative structure, which is inherent to the genre to begin

---

17 "Morning by morning they gathered it, each as much as he could eat; but when the sun grew hot, it melted" (Exodus 16:21). This phrase recurs in the Hebrew Bible in reference to the time of sacrifice (Leviticus 6:5; Ezekiel 46:13–14), and elsewhere.

18 Tuvia Rübner commented to me on the reversal inherent in Avraham Sonne's nom de plume (personal conversation in Kibbutz Merchavia, March 2013). This name had been used by at least three Hebrew poets in various periods prior to Ben Yitzhak (see Ben-Yishai 1950, 21).

19 "But the Lord hurled a great wind upon the sea, and there was a mighty tempest on the sea, so that the ship threatened to break up" (Jonah 1:4).

20 "And behold, a great wind came across the wilderness and struck the four corners of the house, and it fell upon the young people, and they are dead, and I alone have escaped to tell you" (Job 1:19).

with. Goldberg wove into the fabric of her story both European motifs (Little Red Riding Hood) and Jewish motifs (such as the biblical stories of Eden and Joseph, and the Talmudic story about the four rabbis who entered the *pardes*, or orchard, only one of whom survived).[21] These allusions portray the young Ben Yitzhak as a prophet on the run, a modern-day Job, as Joseph who nearly died but would later attain greatness, or an Isaac spared from slaughter. His personal story can therefore be interpreted as an allegory of the Jew saved from destruction by the skin of his teeth, and in Goldberg's modern context – the destruction of the Europe with which he was so enamored and which nearly executed him by executing itself: "And it was as though I had seen a big, beautiful and happy world that had collapsed into rubble and ruin before my very eyes."[22]

Preferring allegories and allusions to direct representation, and offering the *Vera Europa* narrative instead that of *Verus Israel*, Lea Goldberg addressed the open wound of the war and the Holocaust in *Encounter with a Poet*. She sheltered the world created in this book (as in all her writing), to prevent it from being destroyed by external events – by "history" – as well. Next to the traditional Jewish vow, spoken in the first person singular – "*If I forget you*, O Jerusalem, let my right hand forget its skill!" (Psalms 137:5) – she placed her own, in the first person plural, "*and we shall not forget thee*," Europe – which, in spite of everything, did belong to her, to them.

Works cited

Barzilai, Maya. "Translation on the Margins: Avraham Ben Yitzhak and Yoel Hoffmann." *The Journal of Jewish Identities* 7.1 (2014): 109–128.
Ben-Yishai, Aharon Ze'ev. "Avraham Ben Yitzhak." *Orlogin* I (December 1950): 21–24 (Hebrew).
Ben Yitzhak, Avraham. *Collected Poems*. Edited and with an afterword by Hannan Hever. Tel Aviv: Hakibbutz Hameuchad / Sifrey Siman Kri'ah, 1992 (Hebrew).
Ben Yitzhak, Avraham. *Collected Poems*. Edited and with an afterword by Hannan Hever, trans. Peter Cole. Jerusalem: Ibis, 2003.
Géraldy, Paul. *Toi et moi*. Paris: Stock, 1939.

---

21 Four men entered pardes – Ben Azzai, Ben Zoma, Acher (אחר, Elisha ben Abuyah), and Akiba. Ben Azzai looked and died; Ben Zoma looked and went mad; Acher destroyed the plants (became a heretic); Akiba entered in peace and departed in peace (Babylonian Talmud, Chagigah 14b: 1).
22 A poem published by Goldberg in September 1944 uses the same expression, "rubble and ruin," to allude to the war and the Holocaust: "Rubble and ruin, blood and ashes, / years, years like void they weigh / 'tween lightheaded school fancies / and my heavy adulthood today" ("First Love," Goldberg 1986, Vol. 2, 82).

Goldberg, Lea. "Where the Person Stands." *Turim* 2.39 (11 January 1939): 5 (Hebrew).
Goldberg, Lea. "Literary Diary: Memories, Memories..." *Mishmar* (9 June 1944): 4 (Hebrew).
Goldberg, Lea. "Your Europe." *Mishmar* (30 April 1945): 6 (Hebrew).
Goldberg, Lea. *Francesco Petrarca: His Life and Time*. Merchavia: Sifriat Po'alim, 1953 (Hebrew).
Goldberg, Lea. "Distant and Recent Memories: For Fifty Year-Old Zalman Lebiush."
    Al HaMishmar (14 March 1958): 5 (Hebrew).
Goldberg, Lea. *Collected Poems*. Ed. Tuvia Rübner. Tel Aviv: Sifriat Po'alim, 1986 (Hebrew).
Goldberg, Lea. *The Diaries of Lea Goldberg*. Eds. Arieh and Rachel Aharony. Bnei Brak: Sifriat
    Po'alim, 2005 (Hebrew).
Goldberg, Lea. *Encounter with a Poet*. Bnei Brak: Sifirat Po'alim, 2009 [1952] (Hebrew).
Goldberg, Lea. "Begegnung mit einem Dichter." Aus dem Hebräischen von Markus Lemke.
    Naharaim 7.1–2 (2013): 1–50.
Hever, Hannan. *The Flowering of Silence: The Poetry of Avraham Ben Yitzhak*. Tel Aviv:
    Hakibbutz Hameuchad, 1993 (Hebrew).
Lewin, Wera. "Avraham Ben Yitzhak: Fifth Anniversary of his Death." *Ha'aretz*, Culture &
    Literature suppl. (10 June 1955): 1 (Hebrew).
Lützeler, Paul Michael. "'Mir verging die Srapche vor den Dingen, die ich kommen sah' –
    Hermann Broch und Abraham Sonne in ihren Briefen," *Naharaim* 7.1–2 (2013): 131–170.
Malka, Salomon. *Emmanuel Levinas: His Life and Legacy*. Foreword by Philippe Nemo, trans.
    Michael Kigel and Sonja M. Embree. Pittsburgh: Duquesne University Press, 2006.
Pelikan, Jaroslav. *The Christian Tradition: A History of the Development of Doctrine*. Chicago:
    University of Chicago Press, 1971.
Reinharz, Jehuda, and Yaacov Shavit. *Glorious, Accursed Europe: Essay on Jewish Ambivalence*.
    Trans. Michelle Engel. Waltham, MA: Brandeis University Press; Hanover: University Press
    of New England, 2010.
Rübner, Tuvia. *Lea Goldberg: Monograph*. Tel Aviv: Sifirat Po'alim, Hakibbutz Hameuchad &
    Tel Aviv University, 1980 (Hebrew).
Ruether, Rosemary Radford. *Faith and Fratricide: The Theological Roots of Anti-Semitism*.
    New York: Seabury Press, 1974.
Shabtai, Aharon. "'The Stars are Very Beautiful' (Upon Receiving the Lea Goldberg Prize.")
    Yedi'ot Aharonot (3 July 2009): 25 (Hebrew).
Simon, Marcel. *Verus Israel: A Study of the Relations between Christians and Jews in the Roman
    Empire, 135–425*. New York: Oxford University Press, 1986 [1948].
Weisman, Anat. "The Memoir as Polemics." *Encounters with a Woman-Poet: Studies and
    Essays on the Work of Lea Goldberg*. Eds. Ruth Kartun-Blum und Anat Weisman. Tel Aviv &
    Jerusalem: Sifriat Po'alim & the Hebrew University of Jerusalem, 2000. 74–97 (Hebrew).
Weisman, Anat. "Hommage mit doppeltem Boden: Die Gestalt Lea Goldbergs in *Begegnung mit
    einem Dichter*." Aus dem Hebräischen von Markus Lemke. *Naharaim* 7.1–2 (2013): 51–74.
Wolff, Larry. *The Idea of Galicia: History and Fantasy in Habsburg Political Culture*. Stanford, CA:
    Stanford University Press, 2010.
Yeglin, Ofra. *Perhaps with Different Eyes: Modern Classicism and Classical Modernism in Lea
    Goldberg's Poetry*. Tel Aviv: Hakibbutz Hameuchad & Tel Aviv University, 2002 (Hebrew).
Zusman, Ezra. "*Encounter with a Poet*." *Davar* (18 July 1952): 3. Also in his book: *Nightfall and
    Separation*. Nahlat Yehuda: Eliah, 1987. 52–54 (Hebrew).

Stefanie Mahrer
Texts and Objects: The Books of the Schocken Publishing House in the Context of their Time

1 Introduction

> Books are not absolutely dead things but doe contain a potencie of life in them to be as active as the soule whose progeny they are; nay they do preserve as in a violl the purest efficacie and extraction of that living intellect that bred them. (Milton 1644)[1]

John Milton argued in this 1644 speech that books have an existence independent of their authors. According to the English poet, books turn into living creatures beyond the text they contain. Following this line of thought, this article addresses the topic of German-Jewish literature in times when German-Jewish life and culture were being suppressed, ostracized, persecuted and annihilated. Its focus is the production of the Berlin Schocken publishing house, which was founded in 1931 by Salman Schocken, a wealthy owner of a chain of department stores in Germany and an important cultural Zionist. Only seven years later, at the end of 1938, the publishing house was closed down by the National Socialist regime. The Schocken *Verlag* Berlin is a consummate symbol of German-Jewish literary culture during the first half of the Nazi dictatorship. Salman Schocken, together with his managing director Lambert Schneider, chief editor Moritz (later Moshe) Spitzer and freelance editor and consultant Martin Buber, published just under 200 titles, including bilingual editions of traditional Jewish religious texts, folklore, reproductions of rare prints, Hebrew poetry and books by contemporary writers such as Samuel Joseph Agnon, Ludwig Strauss, and Karl Wolfskehl.[2]

In this paper I focus on German-Jewish literary culture as presented in the program of the Schocken *Verlag*. This perspective allows us to study the role of literature as an actor in the social and cultural history of a specific period. The field of book history has demonstrated that books have a social function beyond the texts they contain. Robert Darnton, one of the theoretical founders of the field, defined the book as an active force in human history (1982). For him,

---
[1] Here quoted from Hales (1904, 5).
[2] The complete bibliography of books published by Schocken Verlag Berlin can be found in Dahm (1979, 473–501).

DOI 10.1515/9783110473384-007

the history of the book is first and foremost a "cultural history of communication by print" (Howsam 2006, 28f.). In this circuit of communication, the book is the mediator of relationships between people: "The circuit runs full cycle. It transmits messages, transforming them en route, as they pass from thought to writing to printed characters and back to thought again..." (Darnton 1982, 67). While Darnton's idea to study the communication circuit to understand the role of the book in society is fertile, the complete averting from the text, the content of the book, seems problematic. Understanding the book as an abstract mediator in a structure of communication opens up new approaches and leads to new insights that are of the utmost relevance for the study of societies, but the complete suppression of the book as a carrier of culture and discourse neglects an important factor in the studies of individuals and communities.

Leslie Howsam defines the book as "simultaneously a written text, a material object, and a cultural transaction" (2006, vii). Not without reason, Benedict Anderson states in *Imagined Communities* that people who read texts in approximately the same time constitute a community without knowing each other personally. The book trade was a "silent bazaar," which linked producers and consumers likewise to a community with its own identity (Anderson 2006, 77). The study of the book calls for an integrated approach that includes historical perspective as well as insights from literary studies. Textuality and history need to be studied inclusively to understand the role of books in societies. For the subject of this paper, this approach seems promising. It not only combines cultural and social history but also helps to understand the importance that the book – both as physical object and as text – carried for German Jewry between 1933 and 1945. This paper aims to understand the production of these books as well as their cultural and social context.

Books are means of encounter and exchange: In the case of the Schocken publishing house during the Nazi era, they had three key roles. First, they built a bridge between Jews and non-Jews through the collaboration between the publisher and skilled artisans, despite the National Socialist policy to exclude Jews from social and cultural interactions with non-Jews. Studying the production process of Schocken books allows us to address the encounter of two otherwise forcibly separated social groups. Second, Schocken books unified the German-Jewish community and made assimilated Jews more culturally and traditionally literate by providing traditional texts in translation and editions with accessible explanations. By understanding books as an important factor in community building, we can trace their importance for persecuted German Jews. Third, a significant number of publications from the Schocken *Verlag* voiced resistance to the National Socialist regime by applying a method deeply enrooted in the Jewish theological tradition and contextualised exegesis of religious texts. These three aspects will be dealt with in detail through analysis of several exemplary publications.

2 Books as mediators of relationships: producing Jewish books in Nazi Germany

Despite the harsh anti-Jewish policies that the National Socialist state implemented immediately after Adolf Hitler rose to power in end of January 1933, it remained possible to publish Jewish content books in Germany until the end of 1938. However, the conditions for publishing were, to put it mildly, not simple. On 10 May 1933, books viewed as opposing Nazism were burnt in twenty-two university cities across Germany. The book-burning was organized as a nationwide "Campaign against the Un-German Spirit" (*Aktion wider den undeutschen Geist*) by the Main Office for Press and Propaganda of the German Student Union and was supported by leading Nazis such as Joseph Goebbels, who delivered a speech on the occasion of the *auto-da-fé* in Berlin, where some 40,000 people gathered to witness the burning of the books (Sauder 1983; Sauder 1985). Even though the *Aktion* was not organized by the party or the government (Barbian 1995, 139f.; Dahm 1986, 58), the separation of undesired literature was considered an important factor in the *völkisch* revival of the German people. Already on 5 April 1933, Hans Hinkel, an SS officer and member of the Blood Order and Reich Organization Leader of the Militant League for German Culture (*Kampfbund für deutsche Kultur*), organized an evening under the motto "Book and Spirit" (*Buch und Geist*). The subject of this gathering was how to achieve the national revolution in the fields of literature and book trade (Sauder 1983, 105).

Books by Jewish authors were indexed and burned together with texts of communist, Marxist, liberal, democratic and exiled authors, to name just a few relevant categories. The "Campaign against Un-German Spirit" was perceived as a serious threat within the Schocken publishing house. On 23 May Lambert Schneider wrote to the important German-Jewish scholar of *Kabbalah* Gershom Scholem, who had lived in Jerusalem since the early 1920s, "that all plans in the publishing house were suspended as long as it was uncertain if the publishing house will be able to continue its work." Nevertheless, he told Scholem that the Schocken publishing house was very much interested in working with him and asked how fast Scholem would be able to finish "the single volumes."[3] Schneider was referring to a conversation between Salman Schocken and Gershom Scholem in which the two men agreed that Schocken would publish a five-volume study on *Kabbalah* by Scholem.[4] Just a few days earlier, Schneider also contacted Samuel Joseph Agnon because he heard from Gustav (later Gershom) Schocken, Salman's eldest son, that Agnon had recently finished a new story. The publishing house was very much interested in publishing this story amongst other texts and invited Agnon to send "all German material."[5]

The two letters to the authors, written only a few days after the book burnings, show that the Berlin Schocken publishing house did not plan to surrender to the anti-Semitic literature politics of the National Socialist regime. On the contrary, Schocken and Schneider were planning into the future. When in June 1933 the works of Martin Buber were taken over from the Lambert Schneider *Verlag*, it became notable that the initial shock was overcome. In the summer of 1933 Schocken and Schneider, together with Martin Buber and Moritz Spitzer, decided on the expansion of the publishing house. Whereas in the first two years of its existence the Schocken *Verlag* mainly published finished material by S.J. Agnon and Martin Buber, most of it was taken over from the Lambert Schneider *Verlag* when Schocken assumed the Buber/Rosenzweig Bible translation (Schneider 1969), the year 1933 was a turning point (Schneider 1965).

In the autumn of 1933 the publishing house introduced two new series that instantly became very popular: *Schocken Bücherei* (Schocken library series), a collection of small volumes similar to the *Insel Bücherei*; and the yearly Schocken *Almanach*, which presented the program and new books to its readership. The *Bücherei* quickly became the most successful series within the publishing house. The 92 issues published in 82 volumes reflect the rich tradition of Jewish literary culture. The house published contemporary German authors such as Karl Wolfskehl, Franz Kafka and Ludwig Strauss, and the Hebrew writer S.Y. Agnon in German translation, works by Martin Buber, Gershom Scholem and Herman Cohen, traditional Jewish texts such as *Midrashim* and works by ben Maimon in translation, biblical texts in bilingual editions, folkloristic texts such as songs for Shabbat and Eastern European tales, as well as historical works and biographies of important Jewish figures.

---

[3] Letter Lambert Schneider to Gershom Scholem, 23 May 1933, in: National Library of Israel Archive (henceforth NLA) Arc. 4 1599 (folder 1).
[4] Letter Lambert Schneider to Gershom Scholem, 21 January 1933 and letter from Gershom Scholem zu Lambert Schneider, 6 April, both in: NLA Arc. 4 1599 (folder 1).
[5] Letter Lambert Schneider to S.J. Agnon, 13 May 1933, in: NLA Arc 4 1270.

Schocken was able to develop his program and to expand the publishing house without any major restrictions from the government. Ironically, the self-implemented restriction to only publish texts from Jewish authors (there are a few famous exceptions, like the later banned book *Die Judenbuche* by the non-Jewish author Annette von Droste-Hülshoff) protected the publishing house from interference from the Nazis. The Reich Chamber of Letters (*Reichsschrifttumskammer*), of which Schocken was a member until summer 1937, did not interfere with the publisher's work. Most publishing houses that exclusively published books of Jewish content could do so without much difficulty. In July 1937 the Schocken *Verlag* was excluded from the Reich Chamber of Letters but received a permit to continue publishing Jewish books under the condition that it would imprint the addition "Jewish Publishing House" *(Jüdischer Buchverlag)* in all its publications. Only a number of Jewish publishers, among them Schocken, were henceforth allowed to publish books. Until 1937 economic reasons led to the permission of Jewish publishing houses – the president of the Reich Bank stressed the negative consequences for the national economy – the loss of jobs and foreign currency – if Jews were banned from the trade. After the summer of 1937 and the ghettoization, the Nazis believed that Jewish books would only be read by Jews and therefore did not pose an immediate danger to the desired *völkisch* culture (Barbian 2010, 224, 230f.).

Publishing houses that specialized in Jewish literature, including the *Jüdische Verlag*, the *Jüdische Rundschau*, the Hebrew publishing house *Menorah*, and the publishing houses J. Kaufmann and M. Lehrberger, were in fact much freer in their choice of what to publish than so-called Arian publishers. The historian Jan-Pieter Barbian has shown that authors and publishers were subject to fierce oppression when they published works by unwanted authors. By means of brutal intimidation the NS-state contained deviant behaviour. Strategies to avoid reprisals included self-censorship, political restraint, and exclusion of undesired authors. Only a very small minority of authors and publishers exercised resistance or even open protest (Barbian 1995, 405–409). Schocken not only continued producing Jewish books but also published texts that openly criticized the NS-state and its fascist and anti-Semitic politics (Mahrer 2016). I will refer to the oppositional aspect of Schocken's publishing program in the following section.

Work conditions for exmployees of the Schocken publishing house were very challenging. The production of Jewish books during the early years of the NS-regime was not a simple task, and the production of books that met Salman Schocken's high standards was even more difficult. Salman Schocken strove in all his endeavours for the highest quality possible. Indeed, the nexus between functionality and aesthetics was the hallmark of his public persona (Mahrer

2015b). The first-ever book he published more than a decade before he founded the publishing house set the example for his future work. In 1914 he gave all convention delegates at the Zionist Federation of Germany's annual meeting a volume of Theodor Herzl's Zionist Congress speeches. Schocken had the volume printed at the Offizin Drugulin in Leipzig. "It was," wrote Kurt Blumenfeld, "the first Zionist book that fulfilled the highest artistic standards of modern printing technique" (1962, 93). Blumenfeld, secretary of the World Zionist Organization, recalled an even earlier meeting when Schocken showed him a well-designed advertisement for his department store. Schocken said, "Here you see my position and opinion regarding print. In principle, no more than a quarter of a page. Not much text, the empty spaces redesigned, and the most important element: typefaces whose clarity is impressed on the mind" (Blumenfeld 1962, 93).

Schocken maintained that the setting and content of books must complement each other. This becomes visible in the Schocken *Bücherei* series. Despite the unified external design, 11x19cm size and jackets in a single color, the width of the pages in the series varied, as did the typography used. Thus, for example, Martin Buber's book on the Baal-Shem Tov and Ludwig Strauss' book of stories were printed in old-fashioned lettering – the former in Dutch lettering dating from 1670 and the latter with red capitals at the head of each chapter, giving it an old appearance – while Heinrich Heine's *Der Rabbi von Bacherach* (The Rabbi of Bacharach) was given a modern look, accentuated by black-and-white illustrations. Another special book whose richness and complexity were not belied by the monochrome cover common to the series was *Joseph und seine Brüder* (Joseph and His Brothers). The pages of the text were not bound by the cover; rather, they were inserted as a booklet in an envelope attached to the cover, as were illustrations by an unknown Russian artist. The Passover *Haggadah* was a model of bilingual typographical design. Hebrew and Latin characters were juxtaposed in the notes, and despite the stylistic difference between them and the difference in the direction of reading, the notes appear fluent and coherent.[6] This book was the only one in the series that opened from right to left in keeping with the direction of Hebrew script (Mahrer 2015a).

Although the books were produced in a short period of time, Salman Schocken took pains to produce each one; was careful about appearance and supervised pagination. For Spitzer and Schneider, who were responsible for all the organizational tasks such as communication with authors, authorities, printers and suppliers, as well as reviewing and translating manuscripts, book

---

[6] The book was put together by Spitzer with the help of the professional compositor Max Malte Müller.

production was not a simple undertaking. Even in 1938, under immense pressure from the National Socialist regime, they managed to publish twenty-five books. In August of that same year, Schneider was forced to leave the publishing house because he was considered "Aryan" and was therefore no longer allowed to work for a Jewish patron and publishing house.

The history of the Schocken *Verlag* not only shows that producing Jewish books in the first half of the Nazi dictatorship was feasible but is also a testament to the fact that business contacts between Jews and non-Jews remained still possible. Lambert Schneider, managing director of the publishing house, was a German non-Jew. His collaboration with Jewish authors such as Franz Rosenzweig and Martin Buber extended over many years, and his expertise in Jewish literary culture was widely acknowledged.[7] The books produced between 1933 and 1938 were therefore also a means of cross-cultural communication. They built a bridge over the abyss that the NS-state created between Jews and non-Jews.

The cooperation between the publishing house and the printers is a strong example of this type of bridge-building.[8] Schocken worked first and foremost with the Leipzig-based printing houses Haag-Drugulin, Poesche & Trepte, and Oswald Schmid. None of the owners of these houses were Jewish, yet they continued working with Schocken. Schocken not only printed books in German but also created a full section in Hebrew, which included books addressed to an academic readership. These works were almost exclusively set at Haag-Drugulin, which had a special division for foreign-language prints (Schneider 1969, 192–202). Schneider remembered that Ernst Keller, owner of Haag-Drugulin, was proud to be able to produce "beautiful Hebrew prints" and that he was happy to try out new things together with the Schocken *Verlag* (Schneider 1969, 189–202).

A major challenge was posed by bilingual editions, which, on the one hand, made the work of the publisher's staff and the printing presses more difficult, yet, on the other hand, encouraged them to think in new, experimental ways (Tamari 1994, 327–346). Particularly complex projects required the expertise of Max Malte Müller, who was instrumental in achieving the much-admired typography of Schocken Verlag. Müller, a religious socialist and friend of Gustav Landauer, for

---

[7] Despite Schneider's fascinating life story and his many achievements in the German (Jewish) publishing history, no biography of Lambert Schneider has been written. He did, however, publish an autobiography that gives some insight into his public and private life. See Schneider (1965).

[8] Unfortunately, a large part of the correspondence between the publishers and printers was lost. It is not clear whether the documents were left behind in Germany when the publishing house was forced to close down or whether they were lost when sent to Schocken's offices in Jerusalem.

whom he produced the socialist-cum-anarchist publication *Der Sozialist* (The Socialist), was a highly skilled and talented typesetter.[9] After World War One he worked for Jakob Hegner in Hellerau, Dresden, and after Hegner's bankruptcy for Heinrich Mercy Son in Prague, where amongst other titles volumes five and six of Schocken's Kafka editions were printed (Dahm 1979, 394).

The difficulty of printing Hebrew books was a recurring theme at staff meetings, and the proposed solutions were creative. One idea was to set up a Hebrew printing press in Germany; Müller had already collected materials with this aim in mind,[10] but failed to realize it due to the overly high cost.[11] Another plan was to move the printing operations to Poland. It is unclear why this plan did not go through. Another idea, thoroughly considered but likewise never realized, was the establishment of a printing press in Palestine.[12] The plan was for Müller to prepare a disposition and for Henri Friedlaender, who had worked as a typesetter with Müller at the Hegner publishing house, to serve as the technical director of the new printing press.[13] Yet the collaboration between Schocken and Friedlaender never materialized, and steps toward the realization of the idea are not mentioned in existing documents. In any case, all of these ideas reveal that tension in Germany was growing, pushing the Schocken *Verlag* to search for printing venues outside the country.

Despite harsh conditions, book production brought together people with a shared passion. Schocken's bibliophilic ideas were picked up by his staff. For example, Moritz Spitzer designed a number of books himself and later became an important figure in the printing scene in Palestine/Israel (Wardi 2015). The Schocken publishing house together with the presses and the typesetters constituted an island of professionalism during stormy times. They became, as Howsam has stated, mediators of relationships between people who, according to the prevailing ideology, should no longer have been in contact.

---

9 There is not much information on Müller's work and life other than the few pieces which can be found in Lambert Schneider's autobiography. See Schneider (1965, 51–55). Schneider and Müller had their refusal to serve in Hitler's army in common. Whereas Schneider deserted Müller chose a more tragic solution: when drafted for the army he committed suicide.
10 Correspondence from 1935, SchA 851/822; see also Grundlegende Bearbeitung für eine Druckerei von Herrn M. Müller, 1936, ibid.
11 Report for Mr. Schocken from Dr. Schneider, 16 January 1936, ibid.
12 SchA 351/821 (Pläne Druckerei Palästina).
13 This was the outcome of the staff meeting in Zurich between Salman Schocken and Lambert Schneider on 5–6 March 1936, SchA 331/12.

3 Giving German Jewry a voice: Selected texts from the Schocken *Verlag*, Berlin

Die Bücherei des Schocken Verlages will in allmählichem Aufbau aus dem fast unübersehbaren und häufig unzulänglichen Schrifttum aller Länder und Zeiten in sorgfältiger Auswahl dasjenige darbieten, was den suchenden Leser unserer Tage unmittelbar anzusprechen vermag.

[The Schocken Library aims to present, gradually, a careful selection from the immense and often inaccessible literature of all countries and epochs that will appeal directly to the searching reader of our day.] (Translated by Rachel Seelig)

This quote from an advertisement for the newly introduced 1933 *Schocken Bücherei* series stands, so Salman Schocken said in an introduction to a never-published history of his publishing endeavours, for the work of the Berlin Schocken publishing house in general.[14] Schocken's objective was to bring "assimilated German Jewry" back to its roots. He was not a religious man, and hence did not view religious traditions as the core aspects of Judaism. For him, rather, culture was the essence of Judaism. He portrayed himself as a man who returned to his Jewish roots by reading Jewish books, gaining access to his own tradition through literary culture. As a man who struggled until the end of his life to master the Hebrew language, he understood that he had to offer translations of the Hebrew writings if he wanted German Jews to read traditional texts; German Jewry perceived his efforts in a positive manner. Although no sales figures survive, the high distribution rate and the fact that a fair number of the Schocken *Bücherei* volumes appeared in more than one edition demonstrate the popularity of these small books.

Schocken sought to offer his readers "carefully selected Jewish literature from all countries." In order to fulfil this promise, Schocken called upon his editor, Moritz Spitzer, to prepare two volumes every month, a request that was almost impossible to meet. Despite his employee's complaints, Schocken insisted on this high volume of production, even when the strict policies of the National Socialists made work in the publishing house more difficult. As onerous and anxiety-inducing as it must have been for Spitzer and Schneider, Schocken's high standards and persistence were no doubt responsible for producing the *Bücherei* as we know it today.

---

14 SchA 30 (Vorwort).

Books and texts are not only transmitters of culture but also vehicles for community-building. According to Benedict Anderson, people who read the same books around the same time constitute a community (Anderson 2006, 64f.). Such a community was formed by the publications of the Schocken *Verlag*. It was Salman Schocken's expressed goal to offer assimilated German Jews access to their cultural roots by providing them with accessible Jewish texts. Looking at these texts, which include prose and poetry, songs and folk tales, as well as biblical and *midrashic* texts, it is clear that he succeeded in making Jewish literary culture available to a broad readership. But close reading of the texts in their historical contexts of publication demonstrates another important factor: some, mainly those of religious origin, represented an outright criticism of the National Socialist regime and its inhuman stance against the Jewish people in Germany.

No written records exist that might indicated when and why Schocken, Schneider, Spitzer and Buber decided to criticise Nazi politics, but the first examples appear as early as fall 1933. When launching the new series of the *Almanach*, the editor, Moritz Spitzer, decided to open it with a text by Martin Buber, quoted here in full:

> Der jüdische Mensch von heute ist der innerlich ausgesetzteste Mensch unserer Welt. Die Spannungen des Zeitalters haben sich diesen Punkt ersehen, um an ihm ihre Kraft zu messen. Sie wollen erfahren, ob der Mensch ihnen noch zu widerstehen vermag, und erproben sich am Juden. Wird er standhalten? Wird er in Stücke gehen? Sie wollen durch sein Schicksal erfahren, was um den Menschen ist. Sie machen Versuche mit dem Juden, sie versuchen ihn. Besteht ers? ... Etwas ist geschehen. Statt des einen Wesens, an dem die Spannungen des Zeitalters sich auslassen wollten, sind zwei zu schauen, – ein zerfallendes und ein unbezwingliches. Eins, das Licht ausgibt wie ein phosphoreszierender Sumpf, und eins, das Licht ausgibt wie der Orion. Aber dieses steht für jenes ein. Dieses sagt von jenem: Das bin ich. Es streckt sich über es hin, es deckt es, es duldet, was zu dulden ist. Und wenn eure Probe bestanden sein wird, Spannungen des Zeitalters, werden nicht mehr zwei dasein, sondern einer, der Überwinder. (Buber 1933/34, 5)[15]

> [The Jewish person of today is he most exposed person in our world. The tensions of the era have chosen this moment to measure their strength on him. They want to know whether man can still resist them, and test themselves against the Jew. Will he withstand? Will he fall to pieces? Through his fate they to seek to learn the state of humanity. Will he survive? ... Something has happened. Instead of one being, against which the tensions of the era wished to rail, two appear: one decaying and the other invincible. One that emits light like a phosphorescent swamp, and one that emits light like the Orion. But this represents that one. It says about the other: this is me. It stretches over it, covers it, tolerates what is to be tolerated. And once your test has been overcome, tensions of the era, there will no longer be two, but one, the one who overcomes.] (My translation)

---

[15] In 1936 the same text was published a second time by the Schocken *Verlag* (Buber 1936b).

This short text was the opening of the first *Almanach*, published on the occasion of *Rosh Hashana* in 1933. Even though Buber refrains from naming the ones responsible for the "tensions of the time" (*die Spannungen des Zeitalters*), the text could hardly be more specific. It was bold of Schocken, Schneider, Spitzer and Buber to publish this text in the fall of 1933, for it not only offered German Jews comfort but also warned non-Jews not to be seduced by the "phosphorescent swamp" (*phosphoreszierender Sumpf*) of National Socialism. Indeed, the text is addressed to Jewish and non-Jewish readers alike. Just as the sirens sought to seduce Odysseus with their beautiful song, only to destroy him, Buber's proverbial marsh radiates a seductive light that attracts the masses, but will ultimately lead them to ruin. While its offers consolation to the Jews, it expresses a stark warning to all others. Despite this apparent perspicuity of the text, it was neither objected nor banned by the Nazi authorities.

The 1934 published text *Zwiesprache* (Dialogue) (Buber 1934) was a reissue of *Ich und Du* (*I and Thou*, 1929, 201–222), which was published in 1923 in *Die Kreatur* (The Creature). *Die Kreatur*, an important cultural magazine in the Weimar Republic, was published by Martin Buber, Joseph Wittig and Viktor von Weizsäcker. The quarterly laid its focus on the dialogue between Judaism and Christianity on the basis of mutual tolerance an absolute equality. In 1934, the decision to republish as an independent publication a text with such provenance, a text that stemmed from a journal which promoted the equality of Jews and Christians, was a clear affront to the ruling power, which strove to disrupt any form of dialogue between Jews and non-Jews. Buber, however, did not only republish his 1923 text, which emphasized the deep connection between adherents of the two religions, but also added some thoughts on the current political situation. In both versions of the essay he explored the concepts of dialogue and companionship on different levels. In the 1934 version he added an analysis of the present times:

> Die Männer des Kollektivums blicken mit überlegner Gebärde auf die ‚Sentimentalität' der nächstvergangenen Generation, des Geschlechts jener ‚Jugendbewegung' nieder. Damals befasste man sich weitläufig und tiefsinnig mit der Problematik aller Lebensbeziehungen, man intendierte ‚Gemeinschaft' und problematisierte sie zugleich, man kreiste in Kreisen und kam nicht vom Fleck. Jetzt aber wird kommandiert und marschiert, denn jetzt gibt es die ‚Sache'. Man ist aus den Irrgängen der Subjektivität auf die zielgerichtete Strasse des Objektivismus gelangt. Doch wie dort eine Pseudo-Subjektivität, da es an der elementaren Kraft des Subjektseins fehlte, so besteht hier ein Pseudo-Objektivismus, da man nicht einer Welt sondern einer weltlosen Parteiung eingefügt ist. Wie dort alle Loblieder auf die Freiheit ins Leere gesungen wurden, weil man nur die Freimachung von den Bindungen, nicht aber die Befreiung zur Verantwortung kannte, so sind auch hier die edelsten Hymnen auf die Autorität ein Missverstand, weil sie faktisch nur die erredete, erschriene Scheinautorität stärken, hinter der sich eine in die mächtigen Faltenwürfe der Haltung gewandte Haltlosigkeit birgt, die echte Autorität aber, die jene Hymnen feiern, die des echten Charismatikers in seiner steten Verantwortung zum Herrn der Charis, dem politischen Raum der Gegenwart unbekannt geblieben ist. (Buber 1934, 64f.)

[The men of the collective look down on the "sentimentality" of the last generation, the generation of the "youth movement," with a gesture of superiority. Back then one dealt extensively and in depth with the challenge of all human relations; one sought "community" and simultaneously problematized it, going in circles and remaining fixed in one spot. Now, however, we have commands and marching, for now there is the "cause." One has emerged from the meanderings of subjectivity and arrived at the goal-oriented street of objectivity. Yet, just as there was a pseudo-subjectivity, since an elementary force of the subject-being was lacking, so we find here a pseudo-objectivity, since one is integrated not into the world but rather into a worldless faction. Just as the hymns of freedom were sung into the void because one only knew freedom from bonds and not freedom with responsibility, so too the noblest hymns to authority are misunderstandings, for they only strengthen the pseudo-authority, behind the mighty drapery of which hides a stance of instability. However, the true authority that those hymns celebrate, that of the real charismatic in his constant responsibility to the Lord of the Charis, remains unknown within the present political sphere.] (Translated by Rachel Seelig)

Buber and the publishing house took a considerable risk by publishing these lines. In no other publication of the Schocken Verlag was the National Socialist regime attacked in a similar manner. Buber not only denounces the faulty ideology and the misdirection of the marching masses but also calls the authorities an "authority phantom" (*erredete, erschriene Scheinautorität*), which lacks any substance whatsoever.

Who is the audience of this text? Unlike the previous passage, no words of solace can be found in this essay. The text and the initial context of publication do, of course, allude to the possibility of equal coexistence between Jews and Christians; this is not so of the 1934 edition quoted above. One cannot help but think that it is indeed written for a non-Jewish audience. Buber's text opened, one can argue, room for dialogue between two societies that were no longer allowed to speak with each other.

The memoirs of Lambert Schneider indicate that the Schocken publications were extremely popular with certain groups of non-Jewish readers. Although so-called Aryan bookstores were officially prohibited from selling Jewish publications, many still did so illegally (Schneider 1965, 42). Furthermore, Jewish bookstores were freely accessible, and all the books of the Schocken publishing house could be ordered directly by mail.

The self-chosen limitation to publish Jewish books exclusively made it possible for the Schocken *Verlag* to print such texts. According to Schneider's memoirs, the National Socialist regime attempted to banish the publishing house into a metaphorical ghetto and thereby enabled them to publish critical and oppositional texts. Another text by Buber, on the occasion of *Rosh Hashana 5696* (1935), entitled *Erkenntnis tut not* (knowledge is necessary), reveals that the publishers targeted a non-Jewish audience. In this three-page essay Buber dwells on the space of dialogue. He writes:

> Es gibt den Raum nicht mehr, in dem wir zu den anderen sprechen und von ihm vernommen werden können. Es gibt den Dialog nicht mehr. ... Der Raum ist taub geworden. Und doch auch wieder nicht. Denn was wir im ertaubten Raum der Öffentlichkeit zu uns selber, nur noch zu uns selber sagen, kann ja doch von jedem Beliebigen, dem es gar nicht zugedacht war, gehört werden. Wohl, so werde es gehört. (Buber 1935/36, 11–14)
>
> [The space no longer exists where we can talk to and be heard by others. Dialogue no longer exists. ... The space has become deaf. And yet, it has not. For what we say in the deafened space to ourselves, and only to ourselves, can be heard by everyone, by those it was not meant for at all. Surely, so it can be heard.] (My translation)

In these few lines, Buber makes clear that in autumn 1935 the room for dialogue no longer existed. State-organized terror against Jews reached a new level. In March of that year the president of the Reich Chamber of Letters (*Reichsschrifttumskammer*) issued a ban on Jews working as writers in Germany; by September, the so-called Nuremberg Laws were introduced. With these laws the National Socialists institutionalized their anti-Semitic ideology just two weeks before the Jewish New Year. For Buber, who wrote the essay *Erkenntnis tut not* for the Schocken almanac, the events of 1935 had a deep impact; in his view, the new racial laws put an end to the German-Jewish dialogue. And yet, as Buber noted, everyone can eavesdrop on the inner-Jewish soliloquy. The self-talk, the thoughts that can henceforth only be uttered to oneself, as Buber notes, were in the case of the Schocken publishing house so pronounced and belligerent that they had to be heard beyond the inner-Jewish sphere. Buber alludes to the fact that, by law, texts of Jewish origin or authorship could only be published by Jewish publishing houses. The literature politics of Nazi Germany tried to confine Jewish literary culture to a Jewish readership, making it an inner-Jewish matter only – or as Buber puts it, reducing it to Jewish self-talk. However, Buber also states that this self-talk, texts written by Jews, did find a readership beyond Jewish circles.

Despite Buber's notion that the window for dialogue between Jews and non-Jews had closed, it is clear that the Schocken *Verlag* publications were bearers of communication between the two groups. In times when direct communication and open criticism put people at risk, the published word took over the task of accusing and explicating. Books and periodicals served as mediators and as the space within which where dialogue continued to unfold. They provided German Jewry with a safe space of self-assurance while also opening a channel of communication between two groups who had been separated by racial policies and laws.

Thus far, I have highlighted three essays by Martin Buber, which exemplify the manner in which the Schocken *Verlag* openly criticized the National Socialist regime and its ideology. However, if we analyse the whole corpus of the Schocken publishing house, it becomes clear that the regime was accused and criticized primarily in another genre: biblical and religious texts served as the main sources of political critique. Old Hebrew script translated into German provided German Jewry with a powerful voice.

The very first volume of the Schocken *Bücherei* opened with a biblical quote taken from Isaiah 40.1: "Tröstest tröstest mein Volk / spricht euer Gott" (Comfort, comfort my people / says your God) (Buber 1933, 4). In 1933 the Jews of Germany were in need of solace, and the ancient biblical text in the translation of Martin Buber and Franz Rosenzweig fulfilled this need.

> Du aber,
> Jissrael, mein Knecht,
> Jaakob, den ich wählte,
> du Samen Abrahams, meines Liebenden!
> du den ich erfasste von den Rändern der Erde her,
> von ihren Achseln her habe dich ich gerufen
> und sprach zu dir:
> Mein Knecht bist du!
> Gewählt habe ich dich einst
> und habe dich nie verworfen, –
> fürchte dich nimmer,
> denn ich bin bei dir,
> starre nimmer umher,
> denn ich bin dein Gott,
> ich stärke dich,
> ich helfe dir auch,
> ich halte dich auch
> mit der Rechten meiner Wahrhaftigkeit. (Buber 1933, 8)

[But you, Israel, my servant, Jacob, whom I have chosen, the offspring of Abraham, my friend; you whom I took from the ends of the earth, and called from its farthest corners, saying to you, "You are my servant, I have chosen you and not cast you off"; fear not, for I am with you; be not dismayed, for I am your God; I will strengthen you, I will help you, I will uphold you with my righteous right hand.] (Isaiah 41:8–10)[16]

---

16 English translations of biblical quotations are taken from the English Standard Version.

The book of Isaiah constitutes the first of three large collections of prophetic books: Isaiah, Jeremiah, and Ezekiel. The first part, chapters 1–39, date the prophecies of Isaiah ben Amoz in the mid-eighth century B.C.E. The abrupt shift from oracles of doom (chapters 1–9) to prophecies of consolation, which refer to the historical reality of the return from exile, has led commentators to believe that their origins date two centuries later (Fishbane 2002, 409). Buber chose for the first volume of the Schocken *Bücherei* verses 40–55, a "collection of prophecies of comfort emphasizing imminent redemption" in verses 40–48, as well as prophecies emphasizing reconciliation with God and physical restoration (verses 49–55) (Fishbane 2002, 410). The book of Isaiah is full of metaphors and rich in symbols that lend it "to being understood as an open text." (Gray 2006, 7f.) Jewish tradition is characterized by the emphasis on the need for constant interpretation of the Bible. According to rabbinic sources, human interpretation started at the moment of the revelation at Mount Sinai and is thus part of the revelatory itself (Zetterhom 2013).

What Buber offered his readers was not an interpretation of the Biblical text per se, but, by choosing these exact verses – prophesies of consolations, promises of redemption, reconciliation with God and physical restoration – he provided them with a text that speaks directly to them. "Fear not, for I am with you; be not dismayed, for I am your God; I will strengthen you, I will help you, I will uphold you with my righteous right hand" (Isaiah 41, 10–11). In the fall of 1933 these words gained an imminent significance for Jewish readers, for they promised the despair of destruction would be reversed. The feeling of being at the mercy of the Nazi persecutors is juxtaposed by the eternal promise of God to stand by his people.

As stated in a prospect from 1935, the Schocken Library series aimed to provide "the searching reader of today" with carefully selected Jewish texts from all countries and all times that address their imminent needs. By publishing noted editions of biblical or other religious texts translated into German the publishers honored their promise.

Promising imminent fulfilment of prophecies of restoration through repeated references to God was only one aspect of this and other publications in the Schocken *Verlag*. In verse 41:11 the Biblical text promises revenge: "Behold, all who are incensed against you shall be put to shame and confounded; those who strive against you shall be as nothing and shall perish." Whereas the previous lines are directed to the despairing Jewish people, this verse was intended to invoke the wrongdoing of the Nazis. The openness of the text, as Gray stated, as well as the tradition of constant interpretation of the biblical text, allows the contemporary reader to make a connection between the ancient religious text and their own world. It also allowed the authors and the publishers of the Schocken *Verlag* to level criticism at the Nazi regime.

One last and rather peculiar example from the publications of the Schocken *Verlag* is volume 51 of the Schocken *Bücherei* (1936), which contains twenty-three psalms of thanksgiving and lamentation translated into German, with an introduction by Martin Buber. What makes the publication stand out from other editions of the psalms is Martin Buber's choice to rearrange the sequence. He ordered them in a manner that created a direct link between the biblical text and the presence of the reader (Buber 1936a, 7). Starting with Psalm 130, which begins, "Lord, I call to you from the depths," a psalm that refers to the direct dialogue between man and God, Buber focused on the living deity rather than on the demand for the cessation of misery. The lamentation reads, "Why have you forgotten me?" rather than, "Why must I suffer?" After a short revolt provoked by the almost unbearable torment expressed by the question, "How much longer?" man submits to the divine plan. The hope of liberation and redemption awakens towards the end of the text when, finally, the weak triumphs over the perpetrator.

Buber's rearrangement of the psalms creates a new text in its own right. The biblical text of thanksgiving and lamentation is transformed into a passionate and belligerent version, as the following excerpt from Psalm 74 illustrates:

> Ist doch Gott mein König
> von ureinst her,
> der Befreiung wirkt
> im Innern des Erdlands!
> Du,
> du zerbrocktest mit deiner Macht das Meer,
> du zerbrachst Drachenhäupter überm Wasser,
> du,
> du zerstücktest die Häupter des Lindwurms,
> du gabst ihn als Frass dem Wüstenspuk-Volk,
> du,
> du erspaltetest Quell und Bachtal,
> du,
> du vertrocknetest urständige Ströme.
> Dein ist der Tag,
> dein auch die Nacht,
> du,
> du errichtest Geleucht und Sonne,
> du,
> du stelltest alle Marken des Erdballs auf, –
> Sommer und Winter,
> du, du bildest sie.

Gedenke dies:
der Feind höhnt DICH!
schändlich Volk schmähn deinen Namen!
Nimmer gib dem Wildlebenden
die Seele deiner Turtel!
das Leben deiner Gebeugten,
nimmer vergiss es in die Dauer!
Blick auf den Bund!
denn gefüllt haben sich die finstern Plätze des Erdlands
mit Triften der Unbill.
Nimmer möge sich abkehren müssen
der Geduckte beschimpft!
der Gebeugte, der Dürftige
sollen deinen Namen preisen!
Steh auf, Gott!
streite deinen Streit!
gedenke deiner Verhöhnung
durch den Schändlichen all den Tag!
Vergiss nimmer
die Stimme deiner Bedränger,
das Toben der gegen dich Aufständischen,
das stetig hinansteigt! (Buber 1936a, 27–29)

[Yet God my King is from of old, working salvation in the midst of the earth. You divided the sea by your might; you broke the heads of the sea monsters on the waters. You crushed the heads of Leviathan; you gave him as food for the creatures of the wilderness. You split open springs and brooks; you dried up ever-flowing streams. Yours is the day, yours also the night; you have established the heavenly lights and the sun. You have fixed all the boundaries of the earth; you have made summer and winter. Remember this, O LORD, how the enemy scoffs, and a foolish people reviles your name. Do not deliver the soul of your dove to the wild beasts; do not forget the life of your poor forever. Have regard for the covenant, for the dark places of the land are full of the habitations of violence. Let not the downtrodden turn back in shame; let the poor and needy praise your name. Arise, O God, defend your cause; remember how the foolish scoff at you all the day! Do not forget the clamor of your foes, the uproar of those who rise against you, which goes up continually!] (Psalm 74: 12–24)

Psalm 74 deals with the destruction of the first temple in 587 BCE and has an immense potential for biblical and post-biblical interpretation (Cordes, Hansberger and Zenger 2002). The readers of the Schocken *Bücherei* were generally neither educated in Biblical exegesis nor in rabbinical literature, but even without a background in traditional Jewish exegetic texts, a Jewish reader in 1936 could make a connection between the Psalm and his own situation.

The first part of the psalm, which is not quoted here, speaks of a deep rupture in the relationship between the Jewish people and its God. Verses one and eleven each start with a why-question: The first ("Why do you cast us off forever?") laments the fact that God has turned away from its people, but already the second ("Why do you hold back your hand?") is in fact a plea to punish Israel's enemies. The second part of the psalm (verses 12–17), which stand out with the stylistic rhythmical repetition of the personal pronoun "you" at the beginning of each verse, proclaims the omnipotence of the Jewish God as the savior ("You divided the sea by your might; you broke the heads of the sea monsters on the waters. You crushed the heads of Leviathan; you gave him as food for the creatures of the wilderness.") and as the creator ("Yours is the day, yours also the night; you have established the heavenly lights and the sun. You have fixed all the boundaries of the earth; you have made summer and winter.")

The text is characterized by a steady increase and culminates in the plea to God to use his omnipotence to destroy his and his people's enemies. "Arise, O God, defend your cause; remember how the foolish scoff at you all the day! Do not forget the clamour of your foes, the uproar of those who rise against you, which goes up continually."

The initial lamentation of the rupture between God and the Jewish people in the first verses turns toward the end of the psalm into a forceful appeal to God to take revenge. In Buber's edition psalm 74 is followed by psalm 64, which relates thematically to the previous text. The psalmist pledges for protection from the enemies, who are here described in some detail: "Hide me from the secret plots of the wicked, from the throng of evildoers, who whet their tongues like swords, who aim bitter words like arrows, shooting from ambush at the blameless, shooting at him suddenly and without fear. They hold fast to their evil purpose; they talk of laying snares secretly, thinking: 'Who can see them?'" The enemy is described as a force ambushing the innocent trying to hide its evilness. When reading this text in the context of the year 1936 one cannot help but see allusions to the 1936 Summer Olympics taking place in Berlin. The Nazi government saw the games as an opportunity to camouflage its racist policies and present itself to the world as a peaceful and tolerant country. Most anti-Jewish signs were removed – temporarily – and the newspapers toned down their racist and anti-Semitic rhetoric.

Texts like these resonated strongly with their German-Jewish readers, who could see parallels between their own world and that of the biblical texts. Their fears of being abandoned are addressed and countered with a promise of an omnipotent and revenging power. The millennia-old Hebrew text gained in Buber's translation and arrangement new meaning in the context of 1930s Germany. It spoke to a secular and assimilated population that, under other circumstances, might not have looked for solace and support from biblical sources. In so doing the text turns into a dialogical space of support for the ill-fated and tormented Jews of Germany.

The few lines from psalm 64 show yet another function of Biblical texts published in the Schocken *Verlag*: an open but at the same time hidden critique of the Nazis. By means of the psalm Buber warns his readers of the threat the Nazis and their policies pose. On the surface, the Schocken *Verlag* did nothing other than publish biblical texts in a special edition, when in fact the selection of the verses read in the context of Nazi oppression took on a new meaning: it is no longer the demolition of the temple that is being lamented but the destruction of German-Jewish life, not the Babylonians who should be punished by a vengeful God but the Nazis, the enemies of the present. The biblical text served to camouflage an angry critique.

4 Material objects and written text – a conclusion

The books of the Schocken *Verlag* Berlin gained great importance during the early years of the National Socialist dictatorship. In the contemporary Jewish press their significance for German Jewry was praised in book reviews and editorial articles alike (Schreuder 1994). As objects, as printed books, they served as visible and touchable reminders of the rich Jewish culture that was being destroyed by Nazism while also bearing witness to the persistence of Jewish life in Germany, to the fact that German Jews were still part of a larger society. The processes of typesetting, printing, and binding included the Jewish publishers in the circle of book production that was not organized by religious affiliations and racial denomination, but by the common interest in the book as an object of material culture.[17] Typesetting has its own rich history and is a culture in its own right. The high demands Salman Schocken placed on the aesthetics of his books led to close cooperation between his staff and the typesetters and printers they worked with. This places the Schocken books in the general history of book design and typesetting but also in the circle of communication between likeminded professionals. The bilingual German-Hebrew editions were the most challenging to set. Even for experienced typesetters, combining the Latin and Hebrew letters in a balanced manner was a difficult task. Some of the bilingual

---

[17] I owe my knowledge about typesetting and book design to Ada Wardi, with whom I had the pleasure of working in an exhibition project on three German-Jewish graphic designers who learned their profession in Germany and became important for Modern Hebrew type and book design in the State of Israel.

editions were particularly successful in this regard. For example, in volume 54, the *Passover Haggada*, edited and commented on by E. D. Goldschmidt, the proportion between the Hebrew Drugulin typeface and the Latin Bodoni-Antiqua is well balanced.

On the textual level, the German translation of biblical and post-biblical texts opened up a possibility to speak up and be heard. By translating the Hebrew of religious tradition into contemporary German, the texts were transformed into a means of camouflaged resistance. The old texts had previously not played an important role for many of their assimilated and secular readers, but became accessible and relevant again. By this, they lent their voice to the brutally silenced Jews of Germany. The books of the Schocken *Verlag* indeed became "living creatures," as Milton stated in the mid-seventeenth century. They played an active role not only in transmitting ideas but also in unifying human beings.

Works cited

Anderson, Benedict. *Imagined Communities. Reflections on the Origin and Spread of Nationalism*. London: Verso, 2006 [1983].

Barbian, Jan-Pieter. *Literaturpolitik im "Dritten Reich". Institutionen, Kompetenzen, Betätigungsfelder*. Überarb. und aktualisierte ed. München: Deutscher Taschenbuch Verlag, 1995.

Barbian, Jan-Pieter. *Literaturpolitik im NS-Staat. Von der "Gleichschaltung" bis zum Ruin*. Überarb. Ausgabe. Frankfurt a.M.: Fischer Taschenbuchverlag, 2010.

Blumenfeld, Kurt. *Erlebte Judenfrage. Ein Vierteljahrhundert deutscher Zionismus*. Hg. und mit einer Einführung versehen von Hans Tramer. Veröffentlichung des Leo Baeck Instituts. Stuttgart: Deutsche Verlagsanstalt, 1962.

Buber, Martin. "Ich und Du." *Die Kreatur* 3.2 (1929): 201–222.

Buber, Martin. *Die Tröstung Israels mit der Verdeutschung von Martin Buber und Franz Rosenzweig*. Bücherei des Schocken Verlages Vol. 1. Berlin: 1933.

Buber, Martin. "Der jüdische Mensch von heute." *Almanach des Schocken Verlags auf das Jahr 5694*. Ed. Schocken Verlag Berlin: Schocken Verlag, 1933/34. 5.

Buber, Martin. *Zwiesprache*. Bücherei des Schocken Verlages Vol. 16. Berlin: Schocken Verlag, 1934.

Buber, Martin. "Erkenntnis tut not." *Almanach auf das Jahr 5696*. Ed. Schocken Verlag Berlin: Schocken Verlag, 1935/36. 11–14.

Buber, Martin. *Aus den Tiefen Rufe ich dich. 23 Psalmen in der Urschrift mit der Verdeutschung von Martin Buber*. Bücherei des Schocken Verlages Vol. 51. Berlin: Schocken-Verlag, 1936a.

Buber, Martin. *Die Stunde und die Erkenntnis. Reden und Aufsätze 1933–1935*. Berlin: Schocken Verlag, 1936b.

Cordes, Ariane, Therese Hansberger, and Erich Zenger. "Die Verwüstung des Tempels – Krise der Religion? Beobachtungen zum Volkslkagepsalm 74 und seiner Rezeption in der Septuaginta und im Midrasch Tehillim." *Zerstörung des Jerusalemer Tempels. Geschehen-Wahrnehmung-Bewältigung*. Ed. Johannes Hahn. Wissenschaftliche Untersuchungen zum Neuen Testament. Tübingen: Mohr Siebeck, 2002. 61–91.

Dahm, Volker. *Das jüdische Buch im Dritten Reich*. Frankfurt a.M.: Buchhändler-Vereinigung, 1979.
Dahm, Volker. "Anfänge und Ideologie der Reichskulturkammer. Die "Berufsgemeinschaft" als Instrument kulturpolitischer Steuerung und sozialer Reglementierung." *Vierteljahreszeitschrift für Zeitgeschichte* 34.1 (1986): 53–84.
Darnton, Robert. "What Is the History of Books." *Deadalus* 111.3 (1982): 65–83.
Fishbane, Michael A. *The JPS Bible Commentatory: Haftarot*. Philadelphia: Jewish Publication Society, 2002.
Gray, Mark. *Rhetoric and Social Justice in Isiah*. London, Oxford, New York, New Delhi & Sydney: Bloomsbury Publishing, 2006.
Hales, John. M. *Milton. Areopagitica. Edited with Introduction and Notes*. Clarendon Press Series. Oxford: Clarendon Press, 1904.
Howsam, Leslie. *Old Books and New Histories: An Orientation to Studies in Book and Print Culture*. Toronto: University of Toronto Press, 2006.
Mahrer, Stefanie. "A Microcosmos of Jewish Culture. The 'Schocken Library Series'." *The Graphic Design of Moshe Spitzer, Franzisca Baruch and Henri Friedlaender*. Ed. Ada Wardi. Jerusalem: Israel Museum, 2015a. 88–105.
Mahrer, Stefanie. "Tradition and Modernity – Salman Schocken and the Aestheticisation of everyday life." *The Graphic Design of Moshe Spitzer, Franzisca Baruch and Henri Friedlaender*. Ed. Ada Wardi. Jerusalem: Israel Museum, 2015b. 58–71.
Mahrer, Stefanie. "Schreiben aus den Katakomben. Bücher als Widerstand. Der Schocken Verlag Berlin in den Jahren 1933 bis 1938." *Jüdischer Widerstand in Europa (1933–1945). Formen und Facetten*. Eds. Julius H. Schoeps, Dieter Bingen and Gideon Botsch. Berlin: De Gruyter, 2016. 222–239.
Milton, John. *Areopagitica. A Speech of Mr. John Milton for the Liberty of Unlicenc'd Printong. To the Parliament of England*. London: 1644.
Sauder, Gerhard. "Der Germanist Goebbels als Redner bei der Berliner Büchervebrennung." *"Das war ein Vorspiel nur..." Berliner Colloquium zur Literaturpolitik im 'Dritten Reich'*. Eds. Horst Denkler and Eberhard Lämmert. Schriftenreihe der Akademie der Künste. Berlin: Akademie der Künste, 1985. 56–81.
Sauder, Gerhard, ed. *Die Büchervebrennung. Zum 10. Mai 1933*. München: Carl Hanser Verlag, 1983.
Schneider, Lambert. *Rechenschaft über vierzig Jahre Verlagsarbeit 1925–1965. Ein Almanach*. Heidelberg: Lambert Schneider, 1965.
Schneider, Lambert. "Salman Schocken." *Imprimatur. Ein Jahrbuch für Bücherfreunde* 6 (1969): 189–202.
Schreuder, Saskia. "'Inmitten aller Not und aller Angriffe'. Der Schocken Verlag im Spiegel der jüdischen Kritik." *Der Schocken Verlag/ Berlin. Jüdische Selbstbehauptung in Deutschland 1931–1938*. Eds. Saskia Schreuder and Claude Weber. Berlin: Akademie Verlag, 1994. 377–395.
Tamari, Ittai Jospeh. "Hebräische Typographie des Schocken Verlags." *Der Schocken Verlag Berlin. Jüdische Selbstbehauptung in Deutschland, 1931–1938. Essayband zur Ausstellung 'Dem suchenden Leser unserer Tage' der Nationalbibliothek Luxemburg*. Eds. Saskia Schreuder and Claude Weber. Berlin: Akademie Verlag, 1994. 327–346.
Wardi, Ada. "Moshe (Moritz) Spitzer." *The Graphic Design of Moshe Spitzer, Franzisca Baruch and Henri Friedlaender*. Ed. Ada Wardi. Jerusalem: Israel Museum, 2015. 75–79.
Zetterhom, Karin. "Jewish Interpretation of the Bible. Ancient and Contemporary." *The Bible and Interpretation* (2013). Web. http://www.bibleinterp.com/articles/2013/zet378014.shtml [last access: 17.03.2017].

Galili Shahar
איכה/Ach: Lament and Being in Hebrew and German

1

The Hebrew word *Eicha* implies a *question*, the question "how?" This word that appears at the beginning of the biblical Lamentations is read, however, as a cry: *Eicha* is a liturgical expression of sorrow and anger, an articulation of anxiety, a question that repeats itself in verses and rhymes of lament. *Eicha* is not only a word, a name, a question, but also a sound – a foundational lamenting voice. In the Hebrew liturgical tradition it expresses the mourning of destruction (the destruction of the First Temple in Jerusalem), also transformed into a sad reflection of language itself, echoing its own (in)ability to articulate the meaning of loss. The word, the question, the cry, *Eicha*, is how Hebrew laments the disasters of being, exile and death, and also the downfall of the liturgical language itself. The word *Eicha* laments not only the ruin of Zion, but also the destruction of the holy tongue, failing to fulfill its own liturgical tasks by finding no answer and comfort in prayer. *Eicha*, following this line of thought, is how the liturgical poem reflects its own distortions and puts into question its own future. Something else, however, "another thing" is left out and heard in this word, in the syllable *cha*, a voice that is a sigh, a cry, a groan, a sound of lament and of relief. It is the breath itself, a sound of life – air and living, that appears before and after all words, as a pure (yet unmusical) sound of being. This sound also recalls the last breath, since there is death in life.

Eicha, the question of the Hebrew prayer ("how"), the liturgical opening of language, is based on a voice which itself says "life and death." In its ebbing and emptying, as the word of lament loses its meaning, being deprived of its semantic values, transformed into an opening of language – into an empty sign, it becomes a pure voice, a sound of beginning and end, the breath of a creature – all which was created.

This voice, however, the sound of creaturely being (the breath, the voice of a creature – the sound of a body, human, animal), resonates and finds a strange, unfamiliar echo in the call, the cry *ach*, the German word that is also a voice of beginning and of end: a call, a sigh that recalls both birth and death. The association of the Hebrew *Eicha* with the German *Ach* is not based thus on comparative semantic values, or on original affinities of meaning, but rather on sounds and vocal effects. Our study is based on this minor difference – on the echo, the breath *ch*. What we offer here is a reading based on vocal textures: The subject matter of our discussion is not a notion regarding the historical and cultural possibilities of a dialogue between German and Hebrew but rather an encounter which itself is based on recalling the remnants of language itself – short syllables, creaturely voices and the sounds of the body. We present an attempt to bring Hebrew and German into an encounter, based on the leftovers (the beginnings and ends of languages themselves). We return to listen to the *fugue*, the double call – of call of escape, the cry of rupture and binding of languages – the counterpoint, the dissonance of Hebrew and German, the sound *ach/cha*.

This is the path of listening: the Hebrew word *Eicha*, the name given to the poetry of lamenting, the cry of mourning, is echoed in the German call *ach*. This is not to argue about sameness or similarities of meaning in or between both words, but rather to hint at an encounter which itself becomes possible only when language is emptied of meaning. Hebrew and German thus meet at a place of lingual poverty. Where language expresses its end (but also its point of departure), when it arrives at its limits, at the abyss of semantic order itself in lamenting a great disaster, a shortage, and a crucial loss of being and meaning, it turns into a pure sound. In these crucial moments language reveals its foundational vocal textures – the sigh, the cry, the scream.

We offer a reading that begins in listening, in a move from semantic values (names, words and symbols) to vocal textures (cries and moaning), a reading that invites Hebrew and German to an encounter which reflects the in-ability of both languages to mourn, for lamenting depends on the fall of language itself – its semantic collapse. Yet, in its moments of destruction and emptying language reflects and gives a voice to the experience of mourning. The work of mourning begins with the collapse of symbolic layers in language. This is the resonance (the inverted sound, the echo) being heard in the lamenting syllable *cha* and the German cry *ach*.

We thus ask: could such a reading establish an exegesis, a mode of interpretation? What can we learn from an echo alone, from sounds which are pure reflections, a return of an empty sign?

2

We recall: the Hebrew cry, *Eicha*, is known from the Hebrew poems of Lamentations, the ancient liturgical poems, which tradition attributes to the prophet Jeremiah, lamenting the destruction of the First Temple, the fall of Zion and the devastation of Jerusalem. The poems mourn the death of the people and the exile of Israel. The call *Eicha*, however, mourns not only the temple and the city but also being itself. The cry *Eicha* expresses astonishment, confusion, and misunderstanding regarding the facts of life and their meaning (or: meaninglessness). *Eicha* is an expression of a deep sorrow that turns into an act of doubt and accusation. It is a question, "how?" – "how could it be?" that is doomed to find no answer.

One of the major Rabbinical commentaries on Lamentations, *Midrash Eicha Rabba*, asks about the meaning of this word, *Eicha*, which appears in the beginning of the first poem, calling:

How doth the city sit solitary   אֵיכָה יָשְׁבָה בָדָד

It is agreed among commentators that the word *Eicha* expresses קינה ותוכחה, the call of "lament and accusation," *Klage und Anklage* (Midrash Eicha Rabba, 63). The cry *Eicha*, the question "how," is an articulation of doubt and disagreement, an expression of sadness and of complaint, an act of protest. A critical notion (perhaps: the notion of critique) is embedded in this word repeated in the Hebrew Lamentations. Yet, it is not the word alone, the name *Eicha*, but also the sound that accompanies it, which is crucial for establishing the language of lament. In the lamenting poems the voice that is heard is the voice of a sigh, אנחה, the sound *cha*, which is repeated in the poems:

"שָׁמְעוּ כִּי נֶאֱנָחָה אָנִי" (They have heard that I sigh); "כִּי-רַבּוֹת אַנְחֹתַי" (for my sighs are many), "כֹּהֲנֶיהָ נֶאֱנָחִים" (her priests sigh), "כָּל-עַמָּהּ נֶאֱנָחִים" (All her people sigh).

The sighing sound, the moaning voice, the syllable *cha*, is the foundational vocal texture of the lamenting poem. This is the material condition, the substance of the lament: all that is recounted in the Lamentations, the sorrow of destruction, the suffering of exile, hunger and poverty, orphanhood, sin and its regret, accusations and hopes of salvation, are expressed in a language that is itself based on the vocalization of sighing and mourning.

The language of mourning in the Hebrew Lamentations is rich and has many different speakers, protagonists and performers. Here a mother speaks and women cry in collective lamentation; the old men of Jerusalem relate prophecies and a poet sings his final lament. In the last poem of the Lamentations recited in the synagogue, the whole community joins the cantor, singing and praying for salvation. The poetry of *Eicha* thus has a heterogeneous, performative character: it is written in different vocal registers and encompasses a diversity of speech-acts, rhetorical questions and performative stages. The language of lament is filled with symbols; its words and names are heavily charged with rich and varied implications and meanings, both literal and allegorical. However, it is precisely the richness of the Lamentations and the heavy symbolic load it carries, which also cause the fall and destruction of language. The lament cannot hold the symbolic weight of its verses. The opening question of the lament (איכה, how) thus refers to its own conditions. Language questions its own possibilities of praying, turning into a discourse of doubt: *Eicha* also implies: *how can I?* This becomes apparent in the series of questions in the second poem of Lamentations:

מָה־אֲעִידֵךְ מָה אֲדַמֶּה־לָּךְ הַבַּת יְרוּשָׁלַם מָה אַשְׁוֶה־לָּךְ וַאֲנַחֲמֵךְ בְּתוּלַת בַּת־צִיּוֹן

> What thing shall I take to witness for thee? What thing shall I liken to thee, O daughter of Jerusalem? What shall I equal to thee, that I may comfort thee, O virgin daughter of Zion?

These lamenting questions signify one of the essential procedures of the lament – questioning its own possibilities of expression and of testimony. But these questions (the questions or "the questioning" of language, namely its critical reflections) are articulated in the same vocal texture of sighing and mourning: all of these verses end with the syllable *cha*. This implies that in the language of lament which is rich in symbols, words and names, and produces a narrative about the fall and destruction of Zion, a dreadful process of semantic deprivation takes place. The essence of lament is signified in the collapse of the names into vocal textures of lamenting. Lament begins where the sign (the word) ends, in collapsing into a sigh (a vocal). What is left in this poetry is a noise of friction, a sound of breath, *cha*.

This is the paradoxical experience of the lamenting poem: it tells of the end of all things, yet in so doing collapses into initial, creative vocals, revealing also the beginnings of language, its foundational, concrete substance. *Eicha*, one could argue, is thus the first and the last word of Hebrew.

3

The cry, the moan and the groan, the sigh and the sounds of lament which constitute the poems of Hebrew Lamentations are foundational voices. Reading the Hebrew poems of Lamentations, therefore, demands first a listening: hearing a noise, a breath. Such a listening is also necessary when one returns to read the laments of Greek tragedy. The tragic poem, itself a poetic adaption of the liturgical songs of the Dionysian chorus, is being challenged by the return of creaturely voices which invade and occupy the semantic registers of the Greek language. This is the case in Aeschylus' tragedy *The Persians*, which recounts the defeat of the Persian army in the battle of Salamis. The tragic verses first tell about the anxieties of the Persians, the women and the old men who are left in the city, while the army, the great fleet go to the Greek sea. The drama, however, turns into a poem of lamentation when word spreads about defeat in battle, until finally, with the return of the beaten king Xerces to his homeland, the language of the tragedy collapses in cries and screams, becoming a cantata of sorrow consisting of moans and sighs alone. The Greek play (the first European tragedy known to us) ends with the cry "oi."

This is how the lamenting body of the Greek tragedy is born – as a foreign body returning from the East, crying and moaning its defeat with "barbarian" (non-Greek, unfamiliar) vocal gestures. When we discuss the implications of the lamenting poem and its sounds, we should thus recall its dual role in the history of Western literature, being a reminder of the rupture and the binding of West and East.

4

The discussion on the poetical implications of the sound *cha*, a voice of a moan, a sigh, a breath embedded in the name *Eicha*, should now lead us to the vocal commentaries (the vocal reading) in the chapters of the Zohar that are dedicated to *Eicha*. This what the Midrash says about God responding to the destruction of the temple and the exile of his beloved:

| He Asked about his temple and this was destroyed. He went and asked for the mistress of the temple, his beloved – and she was expelled and fled, and her house was destroyed. Then he began to cry, cry after cry. He growled as a rooster on his female. It is written: breaking down the walls. The roar of the rooster *Kir* is the voice of the sovereign, the ruler. Crying to the mountains, where she fled. Crying, calling with a growl, crying *Eicha*. | שָׁאַל עַל מִשְׁכָּנֵיהּ, וְהָא אִתְחָרַב. עָאל וְאַשְׁגַּח עַל מָארֵי דְמַשְׁכְּנָא, מַטְרוּנִיתָא רְחִימְתָא דְּנַפְשֵׁיהּ, וְהִיא אִתְּתָּרְכַת וְעָרְקַת, וְכָל בְּנְיָינָהּ סָתִיר. כְּדֵין שָׁארֵי לְמִגְעֵי, גּוֹעָא בָּתַר גּוֹעָא, כִּנְהֵימוּ דְּתַרְנְגוֹלָא עַל נוּקְבֵיהּ. הֲדָא הוּא דִכְתִיב מְקַרְקַר קִר, נְהֵימוּ כְּתַרְנְגוֹלָא. קִיר, רִבּוֹן שַׁלִּיטָא. שׁוֹעַ אֶל הָהָר, עָבִיד שׁוֹעָה וְצָוַוח לְגַבֵּי טוּרָא, דְּעָרְקַת תַּמָּן מַטְרוּנִיתָא. עָבִיד שׁוֹעַ צָוַוח וְקָרֵי בִּנְהֵימוּ דִּבְכִיָּה אֵיכָה. |

The Zohar's portrayal of God crying like a rooster is based on a vocal interpretation of verse 5 from chapter 22 in the Book of Isaiah, telling about the occurrences in Jerusalem on the day of destruction, as it says:

מְקַרְקַר קִר וְשׁוֹעַ אֶל־הָהָר

Breaking down the walls, and crying to the mountains.

This verse was commonly read in the Talmudic Midrash as recounting the breaking of the city's wall by its conquerors, leading to its fall. Some commentaries read it as if it tells about walls being used for protecting Jerusalem from invasion during the siege. The Zohar commentary thus transforms the Rabbinic, semantic interpretation into a semiotic one, stressing the sound of repetition that is echoed in the syllables *kar, kar* (קר קר) as hinting at the voice of a creature, the cry of a rooster. The commentary on *Eicha* becomes a *listening*, citing and echoing the cries and sighs of Lamentations. The Midrash itself becomes now a "noise of a great rushing" (רעש גדול). This turning point of the exegesis into a vocal interpretation, however, is also gendered; the lamenting body is considered female – a female singular body or a female chorus. The cry is the voice of a mother and the sigh is the sound of her lament. The Zohar tells in this context about Rachel, the mother who was left to cry before God and to lament the catastrophe brought upon her children:

Only Rachel stayed there and raised her voice with great bitter cries. The Holy one asked her: "Rachel, what are you crying about?"	אִשְׁתָּאֲרַת תַּמָּן רָחֵל, וַאֲרֵימַת קָל בְּכִיָה בִּמְרִירוּ דְתַמְרוּרִים, אָמַר לָהּ קוּדְשָׁא בְּרִיךְ הוּא, רָחֵל, מָה אַתְּ מְבַכָּה.
She answered him: "Why shouldn't I cry?! Where are my sons, and what were their sins?" God answered: "They brought troubles into my house", she replied immediately: "Didn't I do more when I allowed my trouble to come into my house."	אָמְרָה קַמֵּיהּ, וְלָא אֶבְכֶּה, בְּנַי אָן אִינוּן, וּמָה חָטָאן לְגַבָּךְ. אָמַר לָהּ עָאֲלוּ צָרְתִי לְקָמַי, וְאָעֵילוּ לָהּ בְּבֵיתִי. מִיָּד אָמְרָה, וְכִי לָא עֲבָדִית אֲנָא יַתִּיר, דְּאָעֵילְנָא צָרְתִי בְּבֵיתִי.

The voice of Rachel, the call of a mother lamenting the death of her sons, turns into the call of *Shekhinah* – a feminine manifestation God's body (Hasan-Rokem 2014, 33–63). This is how one cries and prays in the Hebrew Lamentations: One cries in a *mother tongue* (the language of lamenting woman). Yet this language, we are hearing, is not only the language of Hebrew proper names, but rather that of sounds and vocals – cries and signs – emptied of meaning.

5

The Hebrew call *Eicha* is not only a question that turns into a cry of lament and accusation, an expression of depression, doubt and shame, a liturgical articulation of destruction; it also echoes a pure sound of a creaturely being bemoaning the work of creation itself.

With a similar cry, with a sigh, modern German drama begins. This is the voice of Faust, an old, weary scholar, a desperate astrologer who, in the beginning of Goethe's tragedy, we recall, mourns all faculties of knowledge:

Habe nun, ach! Philosophie,	Well, that's Philosophy I've read,
Juristerei und Medizin,	And Law and Medicine, and I fear
Und leider auch Theologie	Theology too, from A to Z,
Durchaus studiert, mit heißem Bemühn.	Hard studied all, that have cost me dear.
Da steh ich nun, ich armer Tor!	And so I sit, poor silly man,
Und bin so klug als wie zuvor.	No wiser now than when I began.
(Goethe 2002, 20)	

German poetry opens with this voice, the cry of a "poor silly man" who sighs *ach*. In this cry, in this word, itself emerging in German in the 10th century, in a sound of weariness (the cry itself is so old), we hear a German scholar who bemoans the major faculties of knowledge – the major disciplines of the German university in early modern times. In this call we hear the end of experience (*Erfahrung*), the final consequence of his studies, embodied in the appearance of a new tragic figure, an intellectual of the best kind, who, like Hamlet and other protagonists of modern European drama, articulated the melancholic gesture of Western thought, as documented also in Dürer's *Melancholia I*: the new hero is a scholar, a wise man, a good reader, a person of great visions, yet weary and despaired.

What is heard, however, in this opening scene of modern German drama is also the call, a prayer for a radical transformation in the conditions of being. The cry *ach*, with all of its ironies and sad affirmations – as a melancholic gesture, serves as a caesura in Faust's verses. The sigh of Goethe's protagonist prefigures the demonic return (of Mephistopheles), the contract with the devil, the travels to come, the erotic temptations and the (false) promises – the great experience of time and space and of beauty too, all that is called "life." Faust, in crying *ach*, does not merely lament the knowledge of high faculties, but rather mourns the fall of all creatures – all that had been created, and cry for renewal of being. He calls for a "deed." Possibly this *ach* is the real "word" (*das Wort*) that he searches for (in vain) in the later scene of translation in his study, looking for the right German word for the Greek *logos*. For language itself, the word, begins and ends with this breath.

More despairing, yet more vivid, is this sigh, *ach*, as it appears in the works of Heinrich von Kleist. *Ach* is the cry, the word that opens the final lament in Kleist's play *Penthesilea*, being called after the death of Penthesilea (who was committing suicide), the priest of the Amazons mourns the fate of human beings as being so *gebrechlich*, fragile:

Ach! Wie gebrechlich ist der Mensch, Ihr Götter!	Oh gods! How fragile is this humankind!
Wie stolz, die hier geknickt liegt, noch vor kurzem,	How proudly she, who now lies snapped, stood tooted/
Hoch auf des Lebens Gipfeln, rauschte sie!	High on the peaks of life just hours ago!

This lament gives voice to the tragic experience of (wo)man. The sound of being, life itself (*Rausch*, the last breath) is heard in these verses. The cry *ach* is the wording of a non-word, an expression of inexpressible experience, a way of language lamenting its own crisis in recounting the fall of man. This is how one listens to Penthesilea's own lament, as she bemoans the death of her beloved:

Ach, diese blut'gen Rosen!	Oh gods, these bloody roses!
Ach, dieser Kranz von Wunden um sein Haupt!	Oh gods, this wreath of wounds around his head!
Ach, wie die Knopen, frischen Grabduft streuend,	These buds, all drifting of downward with the scent
Zum Fest für die Gewürme, niedergehn! (Kleist 1987b, 256)	Of Fresh-turned graves, to make to worms of feast!

With these cries, the *ach*, the cries of Penthesilea, mourning the fall of Achilles, the hero, her beloved, who was killed by her own hands (and by her mouth, in kissing and baiting), the misfortune of the human body is being lamented: wounded, beaten, fallen. When we listen to this cry – the *ach*, the lamenting syllable of German drama, we hear the voice of language itself – the breakdown, the *Niedergehn*, of the semantic order, collapsing into its vocal textures, the sounds of all that was created – the call of the creatures. One can also hear the violence being expressed in these vocal gestures. The sounds are violent, not only because of imminent aggression, but also because being itself is a form of *Gewalt* (force, power, violence) – a meaningless form of existence, a movement that creates and destroys.

This is the expression, the cry *ach* that returns also at the end of Kleist's *Amphitryon*, in the final scene of the third act of his play. In no other place in the history of modern German drama does this lamenting syllable become so full and so empty, meaningful and absurd. It is when Alkmene answers with a sigh, with the cry *ach* to the call of her man (Kleist 1987a, 461), Amphitryon, who comes back to his homeland with *so vieler Ruhm*, "so much fame," after a great victory, yet to find that in his absence the God Jupiter appeared before his wife as if he were Amphitryon himself, replacing him, taking his place in his home. Because of Jupiter's trickery two Amphitryons now enter the stage. And when the confusion is solved and the "real" Amphitryon finally calls his wife, Alkmene responds with this voice: her *ach* is both lament and relief, an expression of having too much and too little.

This cry, which implies the dual possibilities of Kleist's play (is it a tragedy? is it a comedy? is this a beginning or rather the end?), at once a lament and a joke, gives voice to the ambiguous element of the German literary tradition itself.

This call, the word that is a sigh, a lamenting yet ironic expression of language itself, returns also in the third scene of the second act of Georg Büchner's play *Dantons Tod*, in "a room," when Danton and Camille, hour before their arrest by the revolutionary cabinet of Paris, still discuss the question of art, *Kunst*. For was there anything better to do? But art, we read, everywhere takes the form of a creature, or better – that of a marionette dressed up with a coat and trousers, bemoaning and agonizing its short life, until "at last it has either married or shot itself dead." Is this the nature of art? This is *ein Ideal*, Camille says, the idea of art itself, a work of creation (or creative work) that turns today so artificial, mechanical, and strange. This is the essence of a work of art that turns into a dance of puppets, moving on stage in "iambic line," singing with odd voices. Indeed, *ach die Kunst!* (Büchner 2006, 45)

What Camille laments in his ironic remarks on the work of art is not only the tradition of art and poetry, especially the degeneration of the lyric poem in its traditional iambic structure that has governed German poetry since the *Goethezeit*. What he is mourning in crying *ach* is rather the disorder of creation itself and the fall of the creatures, the human beings. And at the end of that day, Camille and Danton will be brought to this stage of terror, now as protagonists in political play of the guillotine.

The cry "*ach die Kunst*" thus turns into a sentence that laments being, a call that re-calls human life from its own historical/esthetic alienation. In the name of art (*ach die Kunst*) Camille names the crimes against humanity – the political terror and the dictatorship, and the great wars to come. But this is also the way of language itself, as Paul Celan refers to it in his *Meridian Rede*: Camille's sentence, Celan's reminds us, although it was left in Büchner's play as an aside on the essence of art, invites us to rethink the (dialogical) essence of language and the forgotten elements of poetry and their possible return to the liturgical realm, transforming themselves into a "form of a prayer."

An *ach* as a prayer? We learned: the language of prayer is associated with the question mark of the lament, the question "how?" For poetry, once it recalls its origins, returns to pray for the sake of the creatures, and cries and mourns in the name of creation and asks thus "how?" This is how the first poem of the *Duineser Elegien* by Reiner Maria Rilke opens: with a question that finds no answer and no reply, yet it cries:

> Wer, wenn ich schriee, hörte mich denn aus der Engel/Ordnungen?
> (Rilke 1996, 201)

> Who, if I cried out, would hear me among the angels'/ hierarchies?
> (Rilke 2009, 3)

In Rilke's lamenting poem the question itself is a scream, a cry ("wenn ich schriee"). What is being summoned in this verse is the "call" itself, namely the quest for an angel, a God, a man, to hear the call, the prayer of the poem. For the poem (the elegy) is this voice, the sounds of being (*es rauscht*). These are the voices, the sounds which are the air itself, the breath that is heard in the world. This *die erste Musik*, "the first music," emerges from the open space that was left by the dead, the one who dies too early and vanishes. This is the essence of language (in the elegiac worldview): the initial voices of language are still to be heard before, between and after the words. These are the lamenting voices, the sound of a breath, the air.

The cry of the poem, the *Lockruf*, is thus "dark," but remains unheard, and ends with this voice, with a sigh:

> Und so verhalt ich mich denn und verschlucke den
>   Lockruf
> dunkelen Schluchzens. Ach, wen vermögen
> wir denn zu brauchen? (Rilke 1996, 201)

> And so I hold myself back and swallow the
>   Cry
> Of a darkened sobbing. Ah, who then can
> We make use of?

One word, a call, the cry *ach*, begins and ruptures the elegiac line in Rilke's poem. The lament that opens with a question, with a dark cry, finds no answer in this world, not even in love. What remains for the poem is the empty space, the opening of the world, *das Offene*, the space being created by the dead himself, who by his absence, in the nothingness of his being, evokes this voice, the breath, the sigh of the universe lamenting a young man:

> Ist die Sage umsonst, daß einst in der Klage um Linos
> wagende erste Musik dürre Erstarrung durchgang;
> daß erst im erschrockenen Raum, dem ein beinah
> göttlicher Jüngling

Plötzlich für immer enttrat, das Leere in jene
Schwingung geriet, die uns jetzt hinreißt und tröstet
und hilft. (Rilke 1996, 204)

Is it a meaningless story how once, in the grieving for Linos,
first music ventured to penetrate arid rigidity,
so that, in startled space, which an almost godlike youth
suddenly left forever, the emptiness first felt
the quivering that now enraptures us, and comforts, and helps.

What is lament? It is the poetry of the dead. It begins with a sound, arising from the opening, the beginning, the emptiness of the world. The call, the cry, *ach*, is another sound of the empty space, the last breath left by the dead. But this sound – the sound of the air itself, is a breath, the sound of life and death. The dead, like Linus, the son of Apollo, the musician who left this world too early, as we are told in Rilke's *Elegie*, left his traces in the air, in a sigh that turns into a "first melody." These are voices (*Stimmen, Stimmen*) – the initial vocal textures of the lamenting poem. In Rilke's elegiac version the lament is finally transformed into a lyric expression of solitude that recalls the prayer and its eternal question, "how?"

6

The experience of Hebrew as a liturgical language is encapsulated in the cry *Eicha*. This cry, we argue, is associated (as an echo) with the German sigh, the cry *ach*. The two languages enter into an encounter at a place of semantic deprivation. Where language says no more but expresses its deficiency, where language withdraws from its symbolic layers, it also re-turns, transforming itself into a vocal texture, a pure voice, yet one that is weary and drained. Is this the "secret of an encounter"? Do Hebrew and German meet in the open space, in this emptiness? Is this the path, the method of languages, to lament together? Is this an opening, namely the future itself, where languages re-turn into a breath?

These are valid questions. Once we argue about the possibility of an encounter taking place in which language is brought to a standstill, we still have to ask about the complications of such a silent meeting, which, perhaps, is the noisiness of all, for in this symbolic silence Hebrew and German return to mourn together. Another hint at the nature of this encounter, based on the echo of the lamenting syllable, can be traced in the remarks by Gershom Scholem and Franz Rosenzweig regarding their translation enterprises. Both Scholem and Rosenzweig translated poems from the Hebrew tradition of mourning and lament into German, understanding their own deed as the first and the final steps of German-Jewry, as a point of departure and a farewell.

In one of his unpublished essays, titled "Über die Klage und das Klagelied," accompanying his German translation of the Hebrew Lamentations that he undertook in the winter of 1917, Scholem addresses also the vocal aspects of the Hebrew lament (Ferber 2013; Witte 2014; and Weigel 2014). The lament is silent, Scholem argues, not only because it expresses the essential experience of destruction, exile and death, and thus articulates the experience of nothingness – the void of this world, but also because it expresses the "how," the inexpressible of being. The lamenting silence is thus the highest register of language – an essential moment in the life of every language – a terminal moment which also prefigured its new beginning. This is what the Hebrew word *Eicha* conveys as a name. This *Leere*, the emptiness of language trapped in endless repetitions, is the only *Lehre*, the law, the theory of the Hebrew lamentations, Scholem writes. The question, the cry of the lamenting poem thus reflects a borderline – the line between two essential realms of language – the revealed (*das Offenbarte*), the spoken word, and the silenced (*das Verschwiegene*). This is core of the Hebrew prayer, itself is based on the possibility of an endless question, the question "how" – a question doomed to find no answer. The Hebrew Lamentations that carries the cry of destruction, lament first and foremost the destruction of language, and "how"! For in the repetitive questions ("how"), which are to find no reply, Hebrew poetry destroys its own symbolic means. In adopting this path, Scholem argues, lamentation, despite its absurdity and oddness, purifies language and signifies a condition for a radical correction, the hope for redemption. This is how the lament, the poet of the last-day, turns into a new beginning.

However, this odd principle of the Hebrew Lamentations to destroy and to recreate its own possibilities as a language of correction, as we have learned, is based on vocal texture, the rhyme (X)*aijch*, the sound that echoes the cry *Eicha* itself and that turns into the most significant rhyme in the Hebrew lamenting tradition. This rhyme, Scholem writes in his remarks on a medieval lamenting poem, is a symbol of endlessness – the poetical power of repetition (Scholem 2000b, 607). An echo, a remnant of this sound is found in the traditional laments on Zion, a tradition founded by the Jewish-Arabic poet of Spain, Yehuda Halevi (Scholem 2000b, 378). The rhyme *aijch*, so essential to the Hebrew Lamentations does not, however, have an appropriate translation in German. Scholem writes:

> Die Übertragung verzichtet schon deswegen prinzipiell auf den Reim, weil dessen Wesen in den Zioniden durchaus auf der Klangbeziehung des genannten Suffixreims zu dem für die ursprüngliche Kinah kanonischen Klagelaut ejcha („wie") beruht, zu

welchem Verhältnis es innerhalb des Deutschen keine Parallele geben *kann*. (Scholem 2000b, 607)

In his own translation of the Hebrew liturgical poetry of *Eicha*, Scholem does not suggest any German vocal equivalences to the lamenting rhymes of Hebrew. The symbolic power of the *Klagelaut*, the lamenting voice *Eicha*, is articulated in the question *wie*/how. The question itself now carries the most disturbing, yet silent and hopeful sound.

The work of translation thus reveals the impossibility of the Hebrew *Eicha* to be heard in translation. For we learn: what is significant is not the question alone ("how?"), but also its sound – the cry itself, the sigh and the breath. In his translation of Yehuda Halevi's liturgical poetry, a project he completed in 1927, Franz Rosenzweig faced a similar challenge – how to translate the Hebrew lamenting rhyme, the syllable *aijch*, into German. This is the closing rhyme of Halvei's great poem "Zion, Won't you Ask," a lamentation Rosenzweig translated into German and on which he commented:

> [Der Dichter] gab diesem Versmaß durch den gewählten Reim, obwohl er ihn auch sonst angewandt hatte, etwa in Liebesgedichten – es ist das weibliche besitzandzeigende Fürwort der zweiten Person, - vielleicht also unbewußt, einen Anklang an das *Ach*, mit dem die an jenem Tage verlesenen Klagelieder des Jeremia beginnen, einen Anklang, der, wie man sicher richtig bemerkt hat, dazu beigetragen hat, diesen Reim zum klassischen Reim der Klagelieder des Tages zu machen. (Rosenzweig 1927, 258)

> [By the rhyme he chose here, but which he had also used elsewhere, for instance in some love poems – it is the feminine possessive pronoun in the second person,- [the poet] gave, maybe unconsciously, to that meter a sound reminiscent of the "Alas!" [*Ach*] at the beginning of the Lamentations of Jeremiah, which are read on that day. That sound, as has been noted, and probably correctly, may have contributed to making this rhyme the classical one for that day's Lamentations.]

This is how Rosenzweig hears the echo of the Hebrew lamenting syllable, the rhyme (X)*aijch* in German, he hears it as *ach*. Although he notices the nature of the Hebrew suffix rhyme as a combination of vocal and a consonant, arguing thus that the actual Hebrew rhyme in Halevi's poem is not *aijch* but rather *rajich*, namely a tonal arrangement of consonant and the vocal that ends with the sigh *ch*, Rosenzweig accepts however the vocal interpretation of the lamenting poet, that is a sound, a voice alone – a rhyme (Rosenzweig 1927, 158). This, we argue, is the secret of the encounter between Hebrew and German: Only when both languages fail, deprived of their symbolic layers, despairing enough, almost silent (or perhaps: already in silence), do they revert to their origins as lamenting languages, crying and praying for the correction of being.

7

The lamenting sound, the syllable *cha/ach* is not only a voice for telling (nonverbally) on the historical encounter between Germans and Jews, an encounter whose complexities and discontinuation, its ending and its futures no other word can perhaps express. Rather, when language laments its own failures it gives a voice, a sound for the experience of being. Yet, by the same token, this empty sign, a sound which is a breath, the voice of being, signifies the opening of being itself. The Hebrew word חלל perhaps expresses both: an "empty space" (an opening) and a "fallen person" (the dead). This word with all its ambiguities expresses also the essence of what we call the "future."

Works cited

Büchner, Georg. *Dantons Tod. Dichtungen*. Frankfurt am Main: Deutscher Klassiker Verlag, 2006.
Ferber, Ilit. "A Language of the Border: On Scholem's Theory of Lament." *Journal of Jewish Thought and Philosophy* 21 (2013): 161–186.
Goethe, Wolfgang Johann, *Faust*, München: Verlag C.H. Beck, 2002.
Hasan-Rokem, "Bodies Performing in Ruins: The Lamenting Mother in Ancient Hebrew Texts." *Lament in Jewish Thought: Philosophical, Theological and Literary Perspectives*. Ed. Ilit Ferber and Paula Schwebel. Berlin: De Gruyter, 2014. 33–63.
Rilke, Rainer Maria. "Die erste Elegie." *Werke*. Vol. II. Frankfurt am Main: Insel Verlag, 1996. 199–204.
Rilke, Rainer Maria. *Duino Elegies and the Sonnets to Orpheus*. Trans. Stephen Mitchell. New York: Vintage International, 2009.
Rosenzweig, Franz. *Jehuda Halevi, Zweiundneunzig Hymen und Gedichte*. Berlin: Verlag Lambert Schneider, 1927.
Scholem, Gershom. "Über die Klage und das Klagelied." *Tagebücher*. Vol. I: 1913-1917; Vol. II: 1917–1923. Frankfurt am Main: Jüdischer Verlag, 2000a.
Scholem, Gershom. "Ein mittelalterisches Klagelied" *Tagebücher*. Vol. II: 1917–1923. Frankfurt am Main: Jüdischer Verlag, 2000b.
von Kleist, Heinrich. *Amphitryon. Sämtliche Werke*. Vol. 1. Frankfurt am Main: Deutscher Klassiker Verlag, 1987a.
von Kleist, Heinrich. *Penthesilea. Sämtliche Werke*. Vol. 2. Frankfurt am Main: Deutscher Klassiker Verlag, 1987b.
Weigel, Sigrid. "The Role of Lamentation for Scholem's Theory of Poetry and Language." *Lament in Jewish Thought: Philosophical, Theological and Literary Perspectives*. Ed. Ilit Ferber and Paula Schwebel. Berlin: De Gruyter, 2014. 185–203.
Witte, Bernd. "Silence, Solitude, and Suicide: Gershom Scholem's Paradoxical Theory of Lamentation." *Lament in Jewish Thought: Philosophical, Theological and Literary Perspectives*. Ed. Ilit Ferber and Paula Schwebel. Berlin: De Gruyter, 2014. 173–181.

Part Two: **German-Hebrew Encounters in the Arts Today**

Ruth Ginsburg
"I write bilingual poetry/in Hebrew and in silence"

"Moving beyond," they say; fifty years have passed.

How many people are left who won't listen to Wagner, who refuse – on principle – to buy a Volkswagen or speak German? The editors' abstract for this volume invited us to move beyond "concepts of rupture and collective memory," to redefine the hyphen connecting-separating German-Jewish, "this fraught relationship," and to move beyond German-Jewish studies to German-Hebrew studies. Although not explicitly stated, the subtext of this call invites us to alleviate, perhaps work through, traumatic memory with the help of "concepts like migration, bilingualism, dialogue, and translation" as we seek to redefine disciplinary boundaries. It is easier, or perhaps just more useful and timely, to conceptualize unspeakable history as a relationship between linguistic cultures rather than perceive it as a relationship between people, human beings, as if the one were not implicated in the other?

The project proposed by the editors of this volume follows such initiatives as expressed in Amir Eshel and Na'ama Rokem's programmatic essay "Berlin and Jerusalem: Toward German-Hebrew Studies" (2015), in which the new hyphenated discipline is portrayed as follows:

> The field encompasses the study of German-Jewish culture, literature, and thought; modern Hebrew literature; and contemporary Israeli culture. It also includes the broad sphere of intellectual exchange between contemporary Germany and Israel; the extensive work of Israeli artists in Germany; the nascent Hebrew culture in Germany; the extensive translation and reception of Hebrew literature in Germany; the role Israel plays in the German literary and cultural imagination and vice versa; and the role Germany and its past play in contemporary Israeli cultural, literary and political discourse. (Eshel and Rokem 2015, 265)

The formulation of this wide-ranging description is interesting for what it includes and for what it excludes, or covers up. "Jewish" is mentioned once, at the beginning, to be completely covered up by "Hebrew," "Germany" and "Israel," sounding almost like lip-service to the long list following, from which "Jewish" is excluded. "History" (which does not appear in this paragraph even once) is elided in favor of "contemporary." "Jewish" seems to belong to a past to be overcome. "Shoah" is out. In what follows, it is euphemized by terms like "crisis" and "upheaval." Referring to history, the writers continue: "accounting for this history without ignoring its moments of crisis but not reducing everything to them. The radical upheaval at the heart of the twentieth century casts a difficult shadow on any talk of German-Hebrew bilingualism and eclipses the perception of a fruitful engagement of Hebrew authors with the German cultural realm" (Eshel and Rokem 2015, 266). There seems to be a tone of impatience with both "Jewish" and the over-shadowing past.

Yet, is there a going beyond before all those who have a personal, not a collective, memory have died, except in the abstract, in scholarly, academic discourse, or in actual migration? Is it a question of the impatient young for whom it is history, as opposed to the tired, remembering, hyphenated old for whom it is a never-ending life story? Is there a difference between German-Hebrew and Hebrew-German; that is, between those whose mother tongue is/was German and their acquired language Hebrew and those whose mother tongue is Hebrew and who for many different reasons adopt German as their first, second, or other language? Which language haunts which in the fruitful exchange? Might there be a difference between a mother tongue and a father tongue?

From the moment of its emergence around the middle of the nineteenth century as a revived, modern language, Hebrew has been a site of struggle. The struggle can be described as having two facets: horizontal and vertical. Horizontally, it was a struggle against other Jewish languages (or languages used by Jews); vertically, it was a struggle with its own layered history as an ancient, holy tongue. "Was" a struggle is historically incorrect; "has been" is more appropriate. A battle that seemed to have been decided some time in the fifties of the last century turned out to be an ongoing challenge.

The following is an attempt to describe "migration, bilingualism, dialogue, and translation" as guiding principles underlying Israeli poet, writer, publicist and scholar, Almog Behar's particular version of multilingual Hebrew; to suggest that it is precisely *collective linguistic memory* and acknowledged rupture that may enable translation and dialogue and facilitate the creation of a Hebrew language open to its past and to its rival Jewish languages. This essay explores the role of the dual struggle, horizontal and vertical, in the shaping of Behar's silenced/silencing-multilingual-Hebrew in which he writes – as the title of one of his poems and of this essay suggests.

***

Two parallel cultural-historical phenomena are in the background of this discussion: first, the burgeoning struggle between suppressed ethnic languages and the hegemonic status of Hebrew in present-day Israel, and second, the historical reversal of the direction of e/immigration between Germany and Palestine-Israel. Efforts to conceptualize both (in academic conferences and journals) in terms of post-colonial, post-modern terminology seem to be challenged by poetry, at least in the case under review. The memory of poetic language differs from that of intellectual-academic discourse.[1]

When discussing the "fraught relationship" between German and Hebrew, common sense psychology tends to resort to psychiatric terminology, in particular to the language of trauma based on notions of memory and rupture. This is also the case when referring to the relationship between hegemonic Hebrew and other ethnic languages (Arabic, Jewish-Arabic, Yemenite, Ladino, Amharic, Yiddish, etc.) within contemporary Israel. We still hear, perhaps more than ever, terms like "repression," the "return of the repressed," or linguistic "schizophrenia." Even when we try to evade these labels and rather use *post*-labels instead, and speak of suppression, revolt and mimicry, we still use the concepts of trauma and psychological mourning to describe the effects of the loss of language, and of forced loss in particular. In our everyday discourse we have not untied the language-identity knot that for so long has been impressed upon and internalized by us. It is this knot that propels us to use medical-psychiatric terminology whenever there arises the in/ability to know in which language I can properly, persuasively say "I"; when I do not know what my or a mother tongue is, whether I have one at all, and by what language, or accent, I am identified. The notion of language as id is still prevalent.

It is this prevalence, oscillation and inability that lead Almog Behar to hide under a cloak of a contagious language sickness and to scream voicelessly, *Ana Min Al Yahud* ("I am of the Jews"), in a story that bears that phrase as its title (2008a, 55–61). The title suggests a link between linguistic deprivation and insecurity with (mental) disease. What does it mean to say, "I am of the Jews," rather than, "I am Jewish," in a language that is not Hebrew, when your looks, accent and the very language you are using seem to contradict what you are saying, when your life depends on your being identified with the language you are *not* using, Hebrew? The protagonist of the short story, an ostensibly monolingual Israeli who awakes one morning to discover that he now speaks Hebrew with the heavy Arabic accent of his grandfather, mutely stutters Arabic, inwardly, in Hebrew characters, because, as Behar says in one of his poems: "My Arabic is afraid/ silently disguises itself as Hebrew," a poem that ends with the verse: "And my Hebrew is deaf/ Sometimes very deaf indeed" (2008b, 15–16).[2] Is Arabic written in Hebrew characters a frightened disguise, a strategy of defiant bilingualism, or, perhaps, a symptom of a disease?

---

[1] I am well aware of the irony of the fact that I cannot refrain from using that kind of discourse myself, while censuring it.
[2] All citations of Almog Behar's poetry and prose and of other Hebrew writings are my own translations from the Hebrew, unless otherwise noted.

Behar's 2010 novel, *Rachel and Ezekiel*, reflects an effort to overcome fear, cast off the disguise, and adopt Jewish-Arabic as part of an identity that openly speaks itself bilingually. If throughout the novel each Arabic sentence or phrase is given in vocalized Hebrew characters and immediately followed by a Hebrew translation, translation is dispensed with (and only thematized) towards the end where Arabic characters are openly introduced (Behar 2010, 242–243).[3] Psychiatric or psychologistic terminology may therefore refer not only to trauma and the return of repressed material in the abstract but also to their symptomatic effects: the breakdown of linguistic boundaries, loss of voice and linguistic disorientation.

Israeli poet Roni Somek has characterized Behar's poetry as schizophrenic. In a critique of Behar's first poetry collection he writes: "This is perhaps the poetics of this book of poems. An Arabic hand groping towards a German hand. In psychology you call it schizophrenia, and in poetry it is the law of connected vessels. In Behar's poetry these are the stamps in his birth certificate" (Somek 2008). An Arabic hand groping towards a German hand in a Hebrew in dire need of an audiometry. In contrast to Somek's allusion to Behar's German, critics of Behar's work have mainly concentrated on the inclusion of Arabic in his Hebrew poems and stories, and on the problematic Mizrahi identity presented in his writing.[4] Behar himself has written about his Arabic-speaking Mizrahi roots in poetry, prose and academic and popular-academic articles. It seems indeed to be his main concern. Yet there is also a German side to Behar's work (and life), on which I wish to concentrate here.[5]

But first let me quote Behar's own skeptical words about the use of postcolonial theory and terminology regarding the Mizrahi problem and, by extension, hyphenated identity in general:

> A wholesale acceptance of postcolonial critique as a major component of the new Mizrahi identity in the country [...] can bring about consequences contrary to the ones hoped for. True, reading Mizrahiness through this critique has immense political force [...], but it sterilizes the past Mizrahi world of its specific content and continues, in a new way, to cause us to forget its particularities and its uniqueness. Homi K. Bhabha's theoretical talk about

---

[3] The role of women as representatives of mother tongue and as agents of its retrieval and restoration is most important in the novel.

[4] An exception is Ariel Levinson who writes: "But what can you do, Behar's identity is divided in two. Not only between Hebrew and Arabic or between Eretz Yisrael and Babel, but also between his Spanish grandfather and his German grandfather. [...] So that beside the Mizrahi poems of protest in the book we can meet poems of stunning power about Germany and the Holocaust. Behar succeeds in burning the Israeli candle at both ends, and takes part in the discourse on the holocaust, in which most Mizrahi Jews could not participate" (Lewinson, 2008).

[5] Apart from the Arabic and the German, there is also a Ladino component in this complicated linguistic-identity complex.

> hybridity leads to too much concentration on the hyphen of Jewish-Arab rather than on [...] its two sides [...] and instead of on a new study of the Jewish-Arab cultural space, with all its complexity and languages. (Behar 2008c, 241)

In other words: beware of a conceptualization (mainly in the English language) stemming from a world outside the one under discussion.[6] The world under discussion must produce its own terminology. In Behar's view the question of traditions, cultural and linguistic, is the key to any critically and creatively fruitful discussion of the problem.

***

Almog Behar is indeed the realization of a Jewish hyphenated identity, the offspring of western and eastern diaspora. At the beginning of the twentieth century, his paternal great-grandfather left Istanbul for Germany, then during World War I left for Denmark and returned to Germany after the war, where the family settled and where the poet's father was born to a mother of German-Jewish descent. Eventually the family immigrated to Israel, where Almog Behar was born. The poet's mother stems from a Jewish Iraqi Family. Behar has repeatedly spoken of this complex but not unusual Jewish family history in verse and prose. In his prose-poem "Another Country" (*Eretz 'aḥeret*) he writes:

> Hebrew was my father's third language after Danish and German, and in the same way that he lost Ladino, his father's mother's tongue, I – under the authority of Zionist positive command – was left with Hebrew alone, and with the encouragement to study English. My father, in the official forms of the Israeli school that asked for the parents' origin, was dishonest and wrote: Denmark. I learned to be precise in his stead: the Holocaust. (Behar 2008b, 73)

Behar was brought up by a father who spoke to him in a language that was not his mother tongue, and a mother whose language is absent from this text, to become a monolingual Hebrew speaker and writer. In his retrospective musings, he depicts his language as a "monolanguage" in the Derridean sense, a language that "bears the ineradicable trace of a far-removed mother tongue. It is marked by a feeling of alienation, unease, or uncanniness" (Gellen 2015, 300). In Behar's case, though, it is not a mother tongue but rather mother tongues, in the plural, and they are not that far-removed. They hover right there at home, yet he is deprived of them. A mixture of irony, suppressed anger and deep-seated mourning is the affective tone of the piece, mourning for something that he never

---

[6] Bakhtin might have said here: "think chronotopically!"

had and felt was his due. As a result of this parental decision, he grew up with "many mute languages in me and I am much deaf," as he says in "Dreams in Spain" [Castles in the Air] (2005).

The languages of the entire Diaspora lie suppressed under the weight of Behar's Hebrew, which makes him feel that he must "learn the language of the exiled till I can finally write/ all my poems in the language of the exiles, the language of silence./ [...] till my body supplicates (implores) to return to my Exile,/ into my body, into my language and the language of my parents [...]." These lines are taken from a poem entitled "The Exacerbation of Exile" (*Haḥrafat galut*), whose motto is taken from a poem by Moise Ben Harosh: "I am an exilic Moroccan poet [...] in exile from my Exile" (Behar 2008b, 88). *Haḥrafah* means aggravation, literally, "increasing bitterness." Hebrew and its territory have become a bitter site of exile rather than a land of sweet homecoming. In contrast to the generation-long diasporic experience of home-in-exile, the new exilic experience of exile-at-home undermines the poet's sense of belonging. Exile from Diaspora, which was a linguistic home, and the suppression-repression of all these language-homes under or away from Israeli Hebrew, turn Hebrew into an unhomely mother tongue haunted by repressed ghosts who speak a foreign tongue mutely. Like elsewhere in Behar's poetry, here too, language, both mute and vocalized, is part of the body. It is not something of abstract intellectual identity but rather visceral. It is not externally visible, like clothing, but rather resembles skin and that which lies under it. Poem, language and body are one. Thus, the pain of body-language is felt as physical pain, as Behar writes elsewhere: "There came the knife of Hebrew and cut us in two pieces" (Behar 2006).

Of all the mute, suppressed languages, the one which Behar refuses to confront and revive is his inherited German. In an interview with Omri Herzog, in response to a question about his relation to Arabic and German, Behar says:

> At home there was a presence of Arabic and German. Two languages of which one felt to be ashamed outside home. I read Kafka at the end of high school and was practically absorbed into it, because he too – as a Jew living in Prague – has a problematic relationship with German. Like Arabic, German too is a language of Jews and a language of the enemy of the Jews at the same time. The bridge with Germany was quickly reconstructed, with exaggerated swiftness even. When the talk is of Arabic, the bridge was not reconstructed, because politics destroys it again and again. (Herzog 2008)

This different attitude of Israeli society, both official and unofficial, towards his father and mother tongues haunts Behar's writing. While acknowledging his attraction to German culture he admits his inability to approach it unmediated.

> Many mute languages in me and I am much deaf.
>
> And now, after many years in which those languages were silent in me, they begin and try to have a voice [...] Arabic [...] Ladino [...]; and German, with which too I am partly familiar

through the art of translation, to whose lonely and sad margins I have been drawn for years mainly through the writing and life story of Franz Kafka, is still an unsolved story/problem for me, and I cannot see myself approach and study that deathbringing speech, as Celan called it. (Behar 2005)

Despite the insight, or the wishful thinking expressed in what follows, that Hebrew has reached the stage where it is ready "to open up to the languages of the lands of the Diaspora that are the languages of the greater part of Jewish existence," Behar still cannot make peace with German for both personal and historical reasons; he still feels bound by his grandfather's testament that forbade the re-building of that bridge. Although he is drawn to Celan's poetry, he cannot follow Celan and remains unable to acknowledge, as Celan did, that

> [i]t, the language [German], remained not lost, indeed in spite of everything. But it had to pass through its own answerlessness, pass through frightful muting, pass through the thousand darkness of deathbringing speech. It passed through and gave back no words for that which happened; yet it passed through this happening. Passed through and could come to light again, "enriched" by all this. (Celan 2001, 395)

***

Yet, despite himself, Behar allows German to infiltrate his poetry "through the art of translation." In his first collection of poetry, *Thirst of Wells* (*Tsim'on be'erot*, 2008), which includes poems written between 2000 and 2006, there is a whole section in which German is spoken, usually indirectly. A number of these poems are dedicated to Behar's paternal grandfather, whose death marked a critical moment in Behar's life, as a result of which he has undergone a process of "sobering up" regarding his "place in Israeli society" (Behar 2005).

If Behar needed assurance of this shaky "place" and a sobering prod, he received it from at least one prominent critic.[7] The hegemonic critical institution, as represented by renowned critic Dan Miron, scornfully rejected him. In a vitriolic comment Miron remarks:

> There is a poet hanging around in the role of a kind of a new Amichai. His name is Almog Behar and I read many words of highly exaggerated praise bestowed on him in critical write-ups. And I say to myself, for Heaven's sake, what is happening here? This is a poet who constantly compensates for the weakness of his verse and for the fact that his poetical line lacks power and strength by writing more and more senseless lines. (Miron 2010)

---

[7] Behar's inaugural poetry collection received, on the whole, very favorable write-ups, in particular from the younger generation of critics. Not so his second collection, *A Thread Drawing from the Tongue* (2009), which includes poems written between 1996–2008.

One can hardly imagine contempt more patronizing and condescending published in a mainstream literary supplement. No wonder Behar turned his back on the comparison with Amichai; it is the Arabic language and a Mizrahi identity that he openly and defiantly embraces, whereas German, to which, ironically, Miron inadvertently refers by mentioning the German-speaking Amichai, remains an unsolved problem.

Behar's loved, adored, and lamented Danish-German grandfather symbolizes for the poet the language of death. "The German language reminds me of a home/ and death," he writes in "My Death Tongue" (*Sfat hamavet sheli*), and continues: "And sometimes even from home/ I wish to distance myself. When I hear German/ It is grandfather's voice speaking to father, [...]." German is heard at home, inside; it is the haunting "un" of the unhomely. The poet writes lamentations commemorating his grandfather who "knew that no encounter will draw a bridge over the abysses of the twentieth century, / and therefore commanded us not to be bridge-crossers" (Behar 2008b, 70–71). Behar's grandfather is the treasurer who holds the keys to lost languages: "In what language passed through grandfather's mind/ the pain of his emptying body/ In Ladino? German? Danish? Hebrew? English?" (Behar 2008b, 75). In the mourning imagination of the poet-grandchild, the grandfather's identity is split between languages, not only during his life but also in death. In the dedication to his Lamentations, the German-of-death is tolled in the names of the dead, German names that stand out defiantly against the Hebrew family names and will never be absorbed into Hebrew:

> Dedicated to the holy memory of my grandfather Yitzhak Behar, blessed be his memory, and to the memory of the members of his family who perished in the Holocaust and were not given a Jewish burial: to his parents Eliyahu and Rachel, his sister Simḥa, his brother Ya'akov, and his brother Leo/ (Yehuda) who was murdered by the fascists while escaping from the Nazis. And in memory of the family members of my grandmother *Lisl (Annalise)* Behar, blessed be her memory, who too perished in the Holocaust, her parents *Adolf* and *Frieda Jordan* and her brother *Gerd*. (Behar 2008b, 74; emphasis mine)

The language of death screams in the blatantly vocalized non-Jewish names of the victims, distinguished from the traditional Hebrew names of the others; all victims of the Shoah that never distinguished between Ashkenazi or Mizrahi names.[8]

Silenced languages, even death-languages, infiltrate life. At this point a technical comment is in order. In contrast to present-day German-Turkish authors, such as those discussed in Yasemin Yildiz's *Beyond The Mother Tongue: The*

---

[8] Ironically, in the English translation, it is the Hebrew names that do not integrate harmonically into the text.

Postmonolingual Condition (2012), whose attempt to create a hybrid German-Turkish language is not obstructed by different scripts and different directions of writing (Hebrew is written from right to left, German from left to right), a Hebrew poet who wishes to absorb German, to interlace it with Hebrew and create smooth hybridity, has a much more difficult task. In spite of the widespread use of American English in Hebrew characters in the language of technology and advertising, and the long history of foreign-language terminology (written in Hebrew characters) in scientific and discursive Hebrew prose, no extensive attempt has been made so far to write German in Hebrew in modern Hebrew poetic language.[9] It is perhaps easier for Behar to cope with his "German-problem" in this other way – in the language of poetry – mediated by poets and translators, rather than to confront it directly. It is easier to listen to translated German, to turn a deaf ear to it in translation, rather than listen to the familiar, opaque German at home.[10] Thus Behar not only speaks about German in his poems but also absorbs translated German into his poetry. He concretizes that which Lital Levy calls "creating a monolingual text with a bilingual consciousness" (2014, 271). In Behar's case, I would rather say, "with a multi-lingual consciousness." German, as a suppressed non-activated language, even if hardly ever used in Behar's text, "re-articulates the mother-tongue as uncanny rather than familiar" (Levy 2014, 271).

Although Behar repeatedly refers to Kafka as a major influence on his German consciousness, it is clearly Paul Celan who dominates some of his "German" poems. His poetry collection of 2008 contains a number of poems that openly refer to Celan, amongst them: "The Sky Opened like an Abyss," a variation, as he says, on Celan's "Conversation in the Mountains"; "Four Comments on the Nakedness of the Inception of the Poem," a prose-poem on Derrida, Celan and the languages; and "That Deadening Speech," a speech-grille through which Celan's "Psalm," "Death Fugue," "There was Earth Inside" and other poems are knitted into Behar's own speech. Behar, who does not read German, uses translation, and the Hebrew of these poems clearly points to Shimon Sandbank's translation of Celan's German. Behar is silent in German but at the same time speaks it through Sandbank's Hebrew and through his own. The reader of Behar's poem can hear Sandbank-Behar speak Celan's silenced German in Hebrew.

---

9 In this respect it would be interesting to follow the consequences of the growing Israeli Hebrew speaking community in Berlin. Prose literature has seen such attempts as Joel Hoffmann's stories ("Kätzchen", for instance) or Yehudit Katzir's *Schlafstunde*. Shoa literature did use German in Hebrew characters for Nazi command language like, "Halt!" or epithets like "Jude."
10 Of course, all Behar's muted languages are also the languages of parental secrets and therefore the languages of desire and anxiety.

אותו דיבור ממית

לפאול צלאן

סֵרַבְתָּ לְהַלֵּל אֶל אֲשֶׁר סֵרַב
לְהַלֵּל אוֹתְךָ. סֵרַבְתָּ לַחְפֹּר בְּאַדְמָתוֹ
שֶׁל מִי שֶׁבִּקֵּשׁ לַחְפֹּר בְּאַדְמָתְךָ
אֶת מוֹתוֹ. לָקַחַת בְּיָדְךָ שׁוֹשַׁנָּה
שֶׁל אַיִן, שֶׁל שׁוּם-אִישׁ,
כְּדֵי לְדַבֵּר עַל קְמִילָתְךָ.
כָּתַבְתָּ פֶּרֶק-תְּהִלִּים חָדָשׁ,
קָצָר מְפוּגַּת-מָוֶת, כְּדֵי לְהָעִיד
עַל אַבְקָן שׁוֹמֵם-שָׁמַיִם
וְעַל מִלִּים שֶׁל אַרְגָּמָן
בֵּין הַחוֹחִים. וְתָמִיד עִגּוּל עֵינַיִם,
תָּמִיד אֲבַק פְּרָחִים.

כָּתַבְתָּ גֶּרְמָנִית, אוֹתוֹ דִּבּוּר מֵמִית,
דֶּרֶךְ סוֹרֵג-שָׂפָה
אֲשֶׁר סָגַר עָלֶיךָ וְיָצַר לְךָ צֹהַר
עַד שֶׁפִּיךָ נִמְלָא
עַד שֶׁצָּעַקְתָּ שְׁתִיקוֹת מְלֹא-הַפֶּה
וְלֹא דָרַשְׁתָּ שֶׁיֵּאָמַר דָּבָר
אוֹ יַסְבִּיר אֶת צֵל-הֶעָבָר.
אֱלֹהֵי הַכַּדִּים הַמְלֵאִים חָלָב שָׁחֹר
הַשּׁוֹתִים אֶת עֵינֵי הָעֲוֵרִים הָרֵיקוֹת
שֶׁשּׁוּב אֵינָן מְצַפּוֹת
לַבְּקָרִים. אֱלֹהֵי שַׁקֵּי הַשְּׁקֵדִים הַמָּרִים,
אֱלֹהִים הָאִלֵּם, תְּהוֹם מְעָרְטָל-מְחוֹרָר.
וְתָמִיד אֶבֶן קַלָּה, תָּמִיד לַיְלָה כָּבֵד.

שָׂרַפְתָּ לְגַרְזֶן פּוֹרֵחַ, לְקֶבֶר
שֶׁנִּתַּן לָנוּ בָּרוּחַ. וְעַיִן-שֶׁל-אַיִן
נִפְקְחָה מֵעַל רַעַשׁ שֶׁל רֶגַע בִּנְהַר הַסֵּיְּנָה
וְשׁוּב נֶעֶצְמָה. וְתָמִיד הַמִּלִּים שְׁבוּרוֹת
בְּהֶעְדֵּר תְּשׁוּבָה, תָּמִיד הַגּוּף שׁוֹקֵעַ
בַּמַּיִם. וְהַמָּוֶת, אָמָּן מִגֶּרְמַנְיָה,
מִלֵּא פִּיךָ שְׁתִיקוֹת-יָם.

That Deadening Speech
To Paul Celan

You refused to praise a god who refused
To praise you. You refused to dig in the earth

Of him who wished to dig his death
In your earth. You took in your hand a rose
Of nothing, a no-one's rose,
To speak of your withering.
You wrote a new psalm-chapter,
Shorter than a deathfuge, to testify
Of a heaven-waste stamen
And of purplewords
Among the thorns and always a circle of eyes,
Always flower dust.

You wrote German, that deadening speech,
Through a speech-grille
That closed on you to create a chink of light for you
Till your mouth filled
Till you screamed a mouthful of silences
And never demanded he should say anything
Or explain the shadow of the past.
God of the jars full of black milk
That drink the empty eyes of the blind
That no more expect
The mornings. God of the bitter almond sacks,
Mute god, naked-punctured abyss.
And always a light stone, always a heavy night.

You sang to a flowering axe, to a grave
Given us in the wind. And the eye-of-nothingness
Opened over the noise of a moment in the Seine
And closed again. And always the broken words
With no answer, always the sinking body
In the water. And death, a Master aus Deutschland,
Filled your mouth with sea-silences.
(Behar 2008b, 66–67)

In my translation of Behar's poem above, I borrow from John Felstiner's English translation of Celan's poetry wherever a Celan phrase or idiom is incorporated, sometimes subversively. Thus, the first lines clearly refer to Celan's 1963 poem "There was earth inside them":

They dug and dug, and so
Their day went past, their night. And they did not praise God,
Who they heard, wanted all this,
Who, so they heard witnessed all this. (Celan 1980, 135)

Like all translation, the English translation is of course also an interpretation. Michael Hamburger rightly translates the last line here, "who, they heard, knew all this," since Celan uses *wußte;* "knew" and not "witnessed" (Hamburger 1980, 131). Between the three languages – German, English and Hebrew – interpretative transmission is inevitable.

Additional obvious references in the poem are to Celan's "Psalm," to "no-one's rose," to "nothing," to "stamen heaven-waste" and the "thorn." And then there are the references to the "Deathfugue" whose title is explicitly cited, to its "black milk" and "death the master aus Deutschland." One could go on and mention the "speech-grille," the "flowering axe," "a mouthful of silence" and so forth. Behar's poem is imprinted with Celan's unique language. And yet it is not. It is Sandbank's rendering of Celan that dominates Behar's language. Indeed, all of the above references are taken from that translation. The rose, the axe, the heaven-waste stamen and the purplewords are all given in Sandbank's Hebrew. Even "Psalm-chapter" (*Perek tehilim*) is Sandbank's variation (Celan says simply "Psalm"). Behar absorbs Sandbank's language into his poem and willy-nilly absorbs Sandbank's inevitable interpretation of Celan. Most obvious is his incorporation of the Hebrew *shum-ish* (for the German *Niemand*), a word central to the understanding of the poem. Sandbank's use of the negation *shum*, probably preferred for poetic-musical reasons to *af-lo*, turns Celan's *No*-body of the "Psalm" into *Some*-body, and the absolute Nothingness of god into an ever so flimsy "somethingness" of God. Behar, unknowingly perhaps, adopts here an interpretation that suits his own beliefs and poetics, which would not annihilate God, in spite of it all. In his own poem there is no absolute negation; there is a "chink of light."

Behar's attraction-repulsion to and from German and his coping, via Celan and Sandbank, with that "deathbringing" language (the one Celan embraced and molded, kneaded, deconstructed, to find a new language that would scream mutely) is expressed very differently in a poem that on the surface has nothing to do with German.

באותו לילה כתבתי על קירות הספרייה

בְּאוֹתוֹ לַיְלָה כָּתַבְתִּי עַל קִירוֹת הַסִּפְרִיָּה מִבִּפְנִים
מִלִּים שֶׁל פְּרוֹפֶסּוֹר זָקֵן לְקַבָּלָה: "אֱלֹקִים לֹא
יִוָּתֵר אִלֵּם בַּשָּׂפָה שֶׁבָּהּ הִשְׁבִּיעוּ אוֹתוֹ אַלְפֵי
פְּעָמִים לָשׁוּב וְלַחֲזוֹר אֶל חַיֵּינוּ". הַסְּפָרִים פָּעֲרוּ
פִּיּוֹת וְאִיְּמוּ לְהוֹצִיא מִתּוֹכָם מִלִּים אֲיֻמּוֹת וּלְחָשִׁים
קָשִׁים, וַאֲנִי הִבְטַחְתִּי לָהֶם שֶׁאֱלֹהִים לֹא יִשְׁתֹּק
בַּשָּׂפָה שֶׁבָּהּ יָשְׁבוּ אַלְפֵי דּוֹרוֹת שֶׁל חֲכָמִים
וּגְאוֹנִים וּמְקֻבָּלִים וְסוֹפְרֵי סְתָ"ם לִכְתֹּב לְפָנָיו. הַדְּלָתוֹת

נֶעֶלוּ עַצְמָן בֵּין הַחֲדָרִים וּבִקְשׁוּ לִכְלֹא אוֹתִי,
וַאֲנִי הִבְטַחְתִּי לָהֶן שֶׁאֱלֹהִים לֹא יִשְׁתֹּק בַּשָּׂפָה
שֶׁבָּהּ דִּבְּרוּ נְבִיאָיו אֶל הָעָם עַד שֶׁפָּתְחוּ
פְּתָחִים מִבַּעַד לְעָרְלַת לִבּוֹ. רָאשֵׁי נִרְדַּם עַל
הַסְּפָרִים שֶׁשָּׁאַלְתִּי בַּבֹּקֶר וְנִסָּה לִישֹׁן גַּם אוֹתִי,
וַאֲנִי הִבְטַחְתִּי לוֹ שֶׁאֱלֹהִים לֹא יִשְׁתֹּק בַּשָּׂפָה
שֶׁבָּהּ דִּבֵּר הַלֵּב הֶעָר אֶל הַגּוּף הַיָּשֵׁן
אַלְפַּיִם חֲמֵשׁ מֵאוֹת שָׁנָה. בְּאוֹתוֹ לַיְלָה כָּתְבוּ
קִירוֹת הַסִּפְרִיָּה בְּתוֹךְ הַסְּפָרִים אַלְפֵי מִשְׁפָּטִים מְבֻלְבָּלִים
עַל אֱלֹהִים, בְּאוֹתוֹ לַיְלָה מָחֲקוּ הַסְּפָרִים בְּמִחָאָה
אֶת הַמִּשְׁפָּט שֶׁכָּתַבְתִּי עַל קִירוֹת הַסִּפְרִיָּה, בְּאוֹתוֹ
לַיְלָה יָשַׁנְתִּי כְּפִי שֶׁלֹּא יָשַׁנְתִּי בְּחַיַּי. וְאִם
הִתְעוֹרַרְתִּי וְלֹא שָׁמַעְתִּי אֶת אֱלֹהִים שׁוֹתֵק, הָיָה
זֶה לְבִּי שֶׁדָּרַשׁ שֶׁאֶצְטָרֵף לְצַעֲקוֹת הַסְּפָרִים שֶׁבִּקְּשׁוּ
לְהַחֲרִישׁ אֶת קוֹלִי. בְּאוֹתוֹ בֹּקֶר מָחַקְתִּי מִמַּחְבְּרוֹתַי
אַלְפֵי מִלִּים שֶׁלֹּא זָכַרְתִּי אֶת מַשְׁמָעוּתָן, וּכְשֶׁנִּכְנְסוּ
הַסַּפְרָנִים הֵם מָצְאוּ אוֹתִי מֻכֶּה עַל הַקִּירוֹת
שֶׁמָּחֲקוּ מֵהֶם הַסְּפָרִים מִלִּים שֶׁלֹּא הִצְלַחְתִּי לִשְׁכֹּחַ,
וְנִסִּיתִי לְהַבְטִיחַ לָהֶם שֶׁאֱלֹהִים לֹא יִשְׁתֹּק אֲבָל
כָּל מַה שֶּׁהִצְלַחְתִּי לוֹמַר הָיָה שֶׁאֲנִי לֹא
אֶשְׁתֹּק עַד שֶׁהֵם לֹא יָנוּסוּ, עַד שֶׁאֲנַחְנוּ
לֹא נְנֻסֶּה, לְהַשְׁבִּיעַ אֶת אֱלֹהִים לַחֲזֹר לְחַיֵּינוּ.

גרשום שלום במכתב לפרנץ רוזנצווייג
מז' בטבת תרפ"ז, 26.12.1926:
"אלוקים לא יוותר אילם בשפה
שֶׁבָּהּ השביעו אותו אלפי פעמים
לשוב ולחזור אל חיינו" (במקור בגרמנית).

That Night I Wrote on the Library Walls

That night I wrote on the library walls, inside,
Words of an old Kabbala professor: "God will not
Stay mute in the language in which he was adjured
A thousand times to return and come back into our lives." The books
Opened their mouths wide and threatened to emit terrible words and spells,
And I promised them that god will not keep silent
In the language in which a thousand generations of sages
And learned Rabbis, Cabbalists and scribes
Sat to write before him. The doors
Locked themselves between the rooms and wished to lock me in,

And I promised them that god will not keep silent in the language
In which his prophets spoke to the people till they opened
Gates through the obtuseness of its heart. My head fell asleep on
The books I had loaned in the morning and tried to put me to sleep too,
And I promised it that god will not keep silent in the language,
In which the wakeful heart had been speaking to the sleeping body
For two thousand and five hundred years. That night
The walls of the library wrote inside the books thousands of confused sentences
About god, that night the books erased in protest
The sentence I had written on the library walls, that
Night I slept as never before. And if
I woke up and never heard god silent, it was
My heart that demanded I join the screams of the books that beseeched
To deafen his voice. That morning I erased from my notebooks
Thousands of words whose meaning I did not remember, and when
The librarians entered they found me banging on the walls
Off which the books had erased words I never managed to forget,
And I tried to promise them that god will not be silent but
All I managed to say was that I shall not
Be silent till they not try, till we
Not try, to adjure god to return to our lives.

Gershom Scholem in a letter to Franz Rosenzweig
Of 7 Teveth 5687, 26.12.1926
"God will not stay mute in the language
In which he was adjured a thousand times
To return and come back into our lives" (German in the original).
(Behar 2008b, 129–130)

Behar's poem is about language, the Hebrew language, in which it is written. It was inspired by Gershom Scholem's note to Franz Rosenzweig about Hebrew, written in German. Once again, translation enables Behar to weave a whole poem around erased German, in a repetitive technique that does not let us/him forget the original that is its source. The trigger-sentence appears and re-appears in the poem in its so-called *original* and in slight variations, in a way that leaves no way out of its word-net, sending us, with the poetic-I, back into its snare until, exhausted, we swear to do what is demanded of us. In German-Hebrew. It is also a particular Hebrew translation that enables Behar to incorporate that sentence in a way that would conveniently serve his poetics and beliefs. Translation erects the bridge to Scholem's German-in-Hebrew on a slightly distorted foundation.

Although the Scholem text has recently become well known, a few words about it are nonetheless in order.[11] The 1926 note, *Bekenntnis über unsere Sprache,* known as "the (famous) letter," of which two "originals" exist, is apparently a reworking of an earlier note entitled *Sprache* (1925). Scholem contributed it to a collection presented to Rosenzweig on his fortieth birthday, never to mention it again in writing or in conversation. Its rediscovery after Scholem's death and its translation by Stéphane Mosès into French (1985) and by Avraham Broide into Hebrew the same year brought it to the attention of scholars, notably Jacques Derrida, who quickly turned it into a key text about Scholem, Hebrew, Zionism and language in general. The note is an exasperated, ambivalent outcry against the inevitable results of the unavoidable secularization of the Hebrew language by those who revive it. It contains a warning against the outburst of catastrophic religious forces enshrined in the holy language and inadvertently reawakened and debased by its modern users. Towards the end of the text Scholem writes the sentence that serves as the catalyst of Behar's poem. The German original says (in my literal, somewhat clumsy, translation): "In a language, in which he has been invoked/adjured a thousand times to [rise and] return to our lives, God will not stay mute." The Hebrew translation used in the poem says (again my literal translation): "God will not stay mute in the language in which [people] adjured him a thousand times to return and come back into our lives." The difference may be slight, yet it is meaningful. It is *a* language that the original invokes and not *the* language. More importantly, in the original German version God is invoked (in the passive voice) by language; in the Hebrew translation, by contrast, the users of language actively invoke him. Behar's quote should thus be translated literally as follows: "God will not stay mute in the language in which [they] adjured him a thousand times to return and come back into our lives." Passive and active voices are of course norm-dependent and are differently employed in German, English and Hebrew. Yet with that difference the accent falls differently. If the Celan poems point to Behar's inadvertent opening of Hebrew on the horizontal line, as it were, his Scholem poem grapples with the vertical re-opening of the language. This grappling leads him, surprisingly perhaps, to a complete subversion of the original.

Scholem was deeply concerned about the direction Modern Hebrew was taking, and not only because he feared the inevitable future outbreak of divine wrath. He abhorred the secularized flattening of the language, its impoverishment,

---

[11] The bibliography about this text is too vast to enumerate. For a recent discussion of its reception in Hebrew critical writing – which is the pertinent question here – see my forthcoming "A text and Its Metamorphosis: Gershom Scholem between Confession and Credo" (Hebrew).

and lamented the abandonment of its ancient treasures. In an undated note, found in the Scholem archive of the National Library, he writes:

> With the wandering of the language from the book into life its "soul" was lost. That of which we boast, is by no means praiseworthy, since we have not revived Hebrew, only a Golem of it, an Esperanto, that is, we have just achieved something negative. Yet such a language can by no means bear the competition with Arabic and English, and it is not true that it deserves to withstand it.

Behar appears to join Scholem in bewailing the poverty of contemporary Hebrew usage. He might have other fears about the competition between languages. He writes from the perspective of a victorious Hebrew, which does not only contain the potential to provoke divine violence but has also manifested practical violence against other languages, Arabic in particular.[12]

At first glance, the poem seems to be a concretization of the threatening metaphors used in the Scholem text, of the actual outbreak of Hebrew's hidden destructive forces that drive its users mad. Yet Behar transfers Scholem's metaphors of an impending volcanic outburst and a menacing abyss from cosmic nature into the closed four walls of an academic library, where old authoritative professors confront young, confused students in search of a God. On the surface, the only way to overcome insanity caused by the fury of the holy tongue and prevent catastrophe is to invite God openly to come back into our lives. And the invitation is extended in a poem using the kind of Hebrew against which Scholem was warning us, and which he hardly ever used it in his own writing. Yet, what seems at first to be a following in Scholem's footsteps is in fact a provocative challenge. Just as Hebrew should open itself and listen to all Jewish languages, it should also open itself to its past and listen to the voice of God that echoes inside it. It should learn how to absorb all the layers of its past in the new secular language. A language is dead when cut off from its past linguistic life sources. Yet there is no life in it if it shuts its ears to the voices of the present. Behar's poetic language points to the past as well as to colloquial Hebrew, even to popular songs. Hebrew is an ongoing process, as should be, in both directions, horizontal and vertical.

An exhaustive analysis of both Scholem's note and Behar's poem are far beyond the scope of this essay. Suffice it to say that both Scholem and Behar produced a monolingual text with a bilingual consciousness, yet from opposite directions. Scholem wrote German with Hebrew in mind, whereas Behar writes Hebrew while trying, in vain, not to have German in mind. Scholem could bewail the wrath of Hebrew and its grotesque modern offshoots, and hide in a German shelter. Behar

---

[12] Nor should one forget Hebrew's violence against Yiddish.

is tied to his Hebrew and it drives him mad. But he does not give up Hebrew. On the contrary; the Hebrew of his poem includes all that Scholem hoped for and all that he feared. It opens up both vertically and horizontally to include its ancient treasures, its present-day dialects and the diverse suppressed *other* languages.

In Behar's 2010 novel, *Rachel and Ezekiel,* Behar repeatedly declares that the narrator "wishes to show his face since he does not believe in those hiding-places in which authors pretend to be like ghosts in their books, and he wishes to come out of his hide-out, as he knows that in spite of the author his face can never be completely hidden" (Behar 2010, 130). And in one of his "outings" he tells of his unfulfilled desire to make his hero

> go to Mea She'arim and meet a young *Yeshiva* boy, Ezekiel, [who] will speak to him in Jewish-Baghdadi-Arabic and the young man will answer him in Yiddish, and he [the narrator] will write everything in Aramaic square letters without explaining, and he who reads and understands will read and understand, and he who reads and doesn't understand will read and understand that he doesn't understand. But he doesn't know Yiddish and doesn't know Judeo-Arabic, and neither does Ezekiel, so how will he do it? (Behar 2010, 132)

This indeed is Behar's enterprise: to retrieve his lost languages, quench his thirst, drink of all the wells in his *Thirst of Wells,* to open Hebrew to its past and present for all its users so that it will be deaf no more.

Works cited

Behar, Almog. "Castles in Spain" https://almogbehar.wordpress.com/%d7%97%d7% 2005 (23 March 2017) (Hebrew).
Behar, Almog. "There came the knife of Hebrew and cut us in two pieces" *Ha'aretz.* www.haaretz.co.il/literature/1.1107888 (23 March 2017) (Hebrew).
Behar, Almog. *Ana Min Al-Yahud.* Tel Aviv: Babel Press, 2008a (Hebrew).
Behar, Almog. *Thirst of Wells.* Tel Aviv: Am Oved Publishers, 2008b (Hebrew).
Behar, Almog. "The Hegemonic Remains, the 'Others' Change." *Teoria Uvikoret* 33 (2008c): 238–254 (Hebrew).
Behar, Almog. *A Thread Drawing from the Tongue.* Tel Aviv: Am Oved Publishers, 2009 (Hebrew).
Behar, Almog. *Rachel and Ezekiel.* Jerusalem: Keter Books, 2010 (Hebrew).
Celan, Paul. *Poems: A Bilingual Edition.* Selected, translated and introduced by Michael Hamburger. Manchester: Carcanet, 1980.
Celan, Paul. "Speech on the Occasion of Receiving the Literature Prize of the Free Hanseatic City of Bremen." *Selected Poems and Prose.* Trans. John Felstiner. New York and London: W. W. Norton, 2001. 297–321.
Eshel, Amir and Na'ama Rokem. "Berlin and Jerusalem: Toward German-Hebrew Studies." *The German-Hewish Experience Revisited.* Eds. Steven Aschheim and Vivian Liska. Berlin and Boston: De Gruyter, 2015. 265–272.

Gellen, Kata. "'Ein spanischer Dichter in deutscher Sprache.' Monolanguage and *mame-loshn* in Canetti, Kafka, and Derrida." *Sprache, Erkenntnis und Bedeutung – Deutsch in der Jüdischen Wissenskultur.* Eds. Arndt Engelhardt and Susanne Zepp. Leipzig: Leipziger Universitätsverlag, 2015; 297–321.

Herzog, Omri. "The Enemy Within." *Y-Net* 2 February 2008. http://www.ynet.co.il/articles/0,7340,L-3512485,00.html (23 March 2017) (Hebrew).

Levy, Lital. *Poetic Trespass, Writing between Hebrew and Arabic in Israel/Palestine.* Princeton: Princeton University Press, 2014.

Lewinson, Ariel. "The Song of the Last Man." https://almogbehar.wordpress.com/2008/06/27/ (23 March 2017) (Hebrew).

Miron, Dan. "Professor Dan Miron Reads Contemporary Literature and Longs for Sholem Aleichem." *Ha'aretz.* July 30, 2010. http://www.haaretz.co.il/misc/1.1214686 (23 March 2017) (Hebrew).

Scholem, Gershom. National Library, Jerusalem, Gershom Scholem Archive, Arc 4, 1599/277-I/56.

Somek, Roni. "Almog Behar's *Thirst of Wells:* Closes Eyes and Opens Heart." *Ha'aretz.* 24 December 2008. http://www.haaretz.co.il/literature/1.1369362 (23 March 2017) (Hebrew).

Yildiz, Yasemin. *Beyond the Mother Tongue. The Postmonolingual Condition.* New York: Fordham University Press, 2012.

Freddie Rokem
Before the Hebrew Notebook: Kafka's Words and Gestures in Translation[1]

Verstecke sind unzählige, Rettung nur eine, aber Möglichkeiten der Rettung wieder so viele wie Verstecke. Es gibt ein Ziel, aber keinen Weg; was wir Weg nennen, ist Zögern. (Kafka 1970, #26)

["There are innumerable hiding places and only one salvation, but the possibilities of salvation are as numerous as the hiding places. There is a destination but no way there; what we refer to as way, is hesitation."] (Kafka 2006, 26)

Dann erst wird man mit Sicherheit erkennen, daß Kafkas ganzes Werk einen Kodex von Gesten darstellt, die keineswegs von Hause aus für den Verfasser eine sichere symbolische Bedeutung haben, vielmehr in immer wieder anderen Zusammenhängen und Versuchsanordnungen um eine solche angegangen werden. Das Theater ist der gegebene Ort solcher Versuchsanordnungen. (Benjamin 1977, 418)

["... Kafka's entire work constitutes a code of gestures which surely had no definite symbolic meaning for the author from the outset; rather, the author tried to derive such a meaning from them in ever-changing contexts and experimental groupings. The theatre is the logical place for such groupings."] (Benjamin 1999, 801)

The Hebrew Notebook – And Other Stories by Franz Kafka[2] is a performance of the Ruth Kanner Theatre Group that was inspired by the notebook that Kafka used for studying Hebrew, housed in the archives of the National Library of Israel in Jerusalem.[3] The performance was initially commissioned for the 120th anniversary of the library, for which twelve Israeli artists had been invited to create a work of art connected to the library or based on any of its holdings and it premiered in November 2013. It is a performance about the mechanisms and procedures of

---

1 Without the long and ongoing exchange of ideas with Ruth Kanner it would not have been possible for me to write this article. I want to thank her for inspiring my research as well as from a more practical perspective, for providing me with her own sources of inspiration as well as giving me crucial keys to the Kafka performance. My warm thanks also go to the marvelous actors of the group.
2 In the original Hebrew: מחברת העברית - וסיפורים אחרים מאת פרנץ קפקא; referred to hereafter as *The Hebrew Notebook*.
3 According to Dr. Stefan Litt, the notebook was deposited in the National Library of Israel (Kafka, "Hebrew Notebook") by the Schocken family in the early 1990s. There are five additional Hebrew notebooks in the Bodleian Library in Oxford (MSS. Kafka 24; 26, fols. 28v–29v; 46, fols. 5–8; 47, fols. 4–15). I thank Dr. Litt from the National Library of Israel in Jerusalem and Margaret Czepiel from the Bodleian Library in Oxford for making them available.

DOI 10.1515/9783110473384-010

"translation" between languages and cultural contexts. Besides presenting the Hebrew studies that Kafka pursued intermittently during the last seven years of his life, the piece includes several prose texts and aphorisms that Kafka wrote during these years, but it also reflects and comments on contemporary Israeli society and culture. It is still occasionally performed, mainly at the Tel Aviv Museum of Art, as well as at other venues in Israel.[4]

According to its website, the Ruth Kanner Theatre Group "has been engaged since 1998 in exploring its own surroundings by searching for a local theatrical language, interweaving storytelling, physical theater and visual imagery. The group's re-examination of Israeli narratives is performed through literary and documentary texts, creating Storytelling Theater" (Ruth Kanner Theatre Group). The group has an avant-garde agenda in terms of both the form and the content of their productions. The actors collectively tell a story, with each either appearing as her- or him-self, or presenting several "figures," swiftly shifting the focus through an assemblage of short "sketches" or momentary flashes, rather than staging dramatic situations in which the actors impersonate (or represent) fully "visible" characters within a coherent fictional context. For the actors of the Ruth Kanner Theatre Group it is the performance itself which serves as its all-embracing context.[5]

The Hebrew Notebook consists of two main sections with a short transition between them. The first part reveals how the director first learned about Kafka's Hebrew notebook, and presents short fragments related to Kafka, serving as "documentation" of preparations for the performance. It takes place in a "white box" gallery space where the spectators are invited to observe different "exhibits" presented by the individual actors as well as pictures or texts mounted on the walls. During a short ritual transition, the spectators are led through a door to the second section of the performance, which takes place in a more traditional performance space that features a small, elevated stage with five chairs and a few rows of identical chairs for the spectators. This section consists of two parts, beginning

---

[4] The performance was also invited to participate in the symposium on "Kafka and the Theatre" at the Goethe University in Frankfurt am Main, in December 2014 and was shown twice at the *Künstlerhaus Mousonturm* in Frankfurt for an audience, most of which did not have any knowledge of Hebrew. In the version shown for the predominantly German speaking audience, the German language (together with English, because the actors are not German speakers) was much more prominent than in the 'original' Israeli/Hebrew version of the performance. This essay was completed in November 2016.

[5] The actors have studied in the Department of Theatre Arts at Tel Aviv University, where the director of the group, Ruth Kanner holds a position as professor in acting and "scenic expression" (Ruth Kanner). Together with Daphna Ben-Shaul, we organized a "shift" presenting the work of the Ruth Kanner Theatre Group at the Psi #15-conference in Zagreb in 2009, which was later summarized and discussed in Ben-Shaul et al 2010. See also Ben-Shaul 2004; 2009.

with the actors reciting the words in the notebook, mostly in Hebrew but also in German.[6] In the second part they tell a few of Kafka's stories (in their own form of collective story-telling), showing how some of the words from the notebook relate to Kafka's writing from the period when he studied Hebrew, including fragments from his notebooks and the short stories "An Old Document" (*Ein altes Blatt*) and "Jackals and Arabs" (*Schakale und Araber*). As these fragments and stories are told, some of the words from the notebook are screened on the wall behind the actors, serving as repressed echoes as well as ongoing commentary.

Although the performance ostensibly tells the story of Kafka's Hebrew studies, it implicitly tells the larger story of the revival of Hebrew as a vernacular language, an important aspect of the Zionist project that began during the last decade of the 19th century. Three key events of this early revival period connected to the performance are the first Hebrew theatre performance at the Lemmel School in Jerusalem in 1889; the establishment of the Hebrew Language Committee in Jerusalem in 1890; and the founding in 1892 of the B'nai Brith Library in Jerusalem, the first Jewish public library in Ottoman Palestine, considered the forerunner of the National Library of Israel. Kafka, who wrote exclusively in German, began studying Hebrew in 1917, after he was diagnosed with tuberculosis, and continued these studies with interruptions and with three different teachers up until a few months before his death in June 1924.[7] At this time, following the British conquest of Palestine and the Balfour Declaration of 1917, the utopian dream of a Jewish homeland where Hebrew would be spoken had become more real and urgent.

The Hebrew Notebook implies that the Zionist utopian dream – in which Kafka to some extent participated by studying Hebrew (and by playfully considering making Mandatory Palestine his home, even if he knew this was an unrealizable fantasy) – has been transformed into the dystopian "nightmares" depicted in Kafka's writings. The performance even suggests that Kafka was able to write these nightmarish stories because he intuited that there was something inherently threatening in a national project that promoted Hebrew while marginalizing and even oppressing the language and culture of other national groups in the region, especially that of the Arabs, as depicted in "Jackals and Arabs" (see Butler 2011; Hannsen 2012).

---

[6] In the Frankfurt performances many more German words were recited than in the original Israeli performance.

[7] Kafka's Hebrew studies have been discussed in many contexts: See for example (Binder 1967; Alter 1991; Bodenheimer 2004; and Suchoff 2011). See also (Menczel-Ben-Tovim 1995.) Kafka used Moshe Rath's Hebrew textbook (1918), for his studies. This textbook, which is featured in the performance, was the source of many words in Kafka's notebook.

Kafka was not the only one who had such early premonitions. Gershom Scholem, who had been living in Jerusalem since 1923, begins his December 1926 letter about the Hebrew language (written in German!) to the ailing Franz Rosenzweig by directly connecting the Arab issue with the revival of the Hebrew language. It is worth quoting this letter at length because of the figurative manner in which Scholem identifies the profound ambivalence with which he, also an admirer of Kafka, expressed his fears concerning the consequences he argued this national linguistic revival would have:

> This country is a volcano! It harbors the language! One speaks here of many matters that may make us fail. More than of anything else we are concerned today about the Arab. But much more sinister than the Arab problem is another threat, a threat which the Zionist enterprise unavoidably has had to face: the "actualization" [*Aktualisierung*] of Hebrew.
>
> Must not the conundrum of a holy language break open again now, when the language is to be handed down to our children? Granted, one does not know how it will all turn out. Many believe that the language has been secularized, and the apocalyptic thorn has been pulled out. But this is not true at all. The secularization of the language is only a *façon de parler*, a phrase! It is impossible to empty out words which are filled to the breaking point with specific meanings – lest it be done at the sacrifice of the language itself! The ghastly gibberish which we hear spoken in the streets is exactly the faceless lingo that "secularization" of the language will bring about; of this there cannot be any doubt! /.../ Is it not true that almost all of us live with this language over a volcano with the false security of the blind? Must not we or those who came after us stumble into the abyss when we fail to see again? And nobody can know whether the sacrifice of those who perish will suffice to close the hole and avoid the plunge into the abyss. (Cutter 1990, 431)

The Hebrew Notebook, can be seen as a scenic realization of Scholem's dystopian vision of the "volcano" and the "abyss", his chosen metaphors for the catastrophe of the revival of Hebrew.

The performance was created and shown at a time when the legal disputes over the ownership of the Kafka manuscripts were frequently reported in the media. Kafka's manuscripts had been brought to Mandatory Palestine by his close friend Max Brod, who refused to burn them, as Kafka had requested. Brod fled to Tel Aviv from Prague in 1939 with these manuscripts in a suitcase after most of Kafka's writings had already been published posthumously. Following Brod's death, the manuscripts were passed on to Brod's secretary, Esther Hoffe, who later sold many of them to libraries and archives. After her death in 2007, the National Library of Israel began a legal battle over the ownership of the Kafka manuscripts that had not yet been sold. In 2012, the court decided that these manuscripts belong to the State of Israel, which it deemed the representative of the Jewish people, to which Kafka's writings, the court concluded, therefore 'rightly' belong. In 2015, the Israeli Supreme Court upheld this position. I will not go into the details of this legal conflict between the daughters of Esther Hoffe and the State of Israel, except to note that the transformation of the Kafka manuscripts into a fetish with an extremely high market value no doubt added to the magic of the notebook itself, albeit in facsimile copies, as a prop in the performance.⁸

Kafka's notebook is the private Hebrew-German dictionary in which he recorded Hebrew vocabulary words and their German equivalents. Each page of the notebook is a kind of "stage" in its own right where isolated words in both languages are written down with pencil in large lettering, with much more space around the individual words than in most of Kafka's preserved letters, diaries or literary manuscripts. This most likely reflects Kafka's position as a pupil studying the Hebrew words, literally making room for them, enabling him to reflect on each individual word separately. The German words, written from left to right in Kafka's unique handwriting, and the Hebrew words, carved out with a much less trained hand from right to left, approach each other from the respective margins of the two columns on each page.⁹

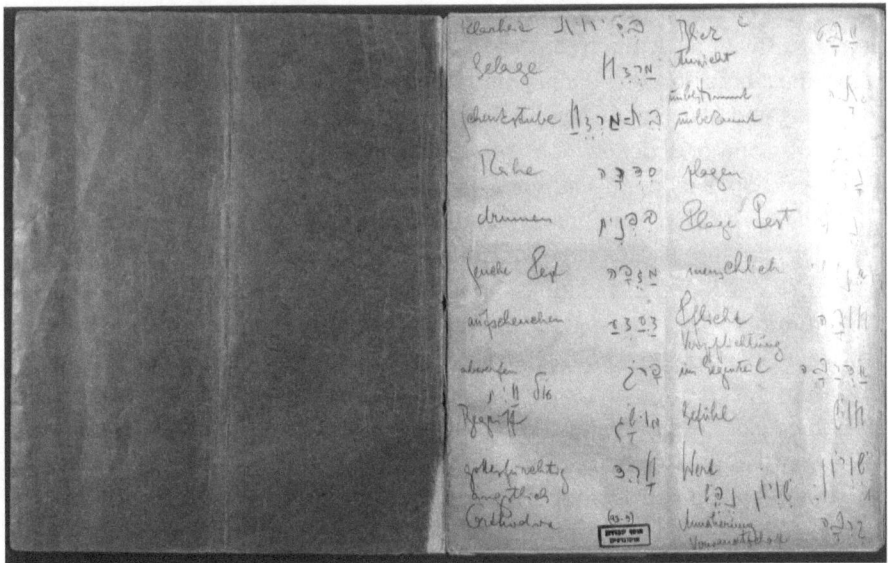

Fig. 1: The first page of the Hebrew Notebook, beginning (in the upper right hand corner) with the Hebrew word מבט (*Mabat*), translated as *Blick* (meaning "gaze" or "glance") and *Ansicht* (meaning "view" "outlook," "notion," or "judgment"). This is the first word the actors read from the notebook in the second part of the performance.

---

8 Because of the fragile condition of the original notebooks researchers are today only allowed to see the electronic copies. For a critical analysis of this legal dispute and its implications for the understanding of Kafka's view of Zionism, see Butler 2011b.
9 For a fascinating discussion of the "meeting" between German and Hebrew words on the page of a Yehuda Amichai manuscript see N. Rokem 2010.

Although the notebook opens from right to left like a German book, the second part of the performance gives precedence to the Hebrew portion of the page, beginning with the word in the upper right-hand corner. The reading of the notebook in the second part begins with the actor Tali Kark somewhat hesitantly pronouncing the word מבט (*mabat*; reading it *ma...bat*), initiating the spectators into the innermost secrets of the notebook by establishing a "gaze" that transforms the word on the page (which is simultaneously projected on the wall behind the actors) into the performance towards which the spectators turn their gaze. This initiation is followed by the Hebrew word *stam* (סתם), the second word in the right column on the page, which Kafka translated as *unbestimmt*, meaning "indecisive" or "undefined." In today's Hebrew, the slang word *stam* refers to something that occurs or exists for no particular reason or purpose, something ordinary or even meaningless. It is also significant to note that the acronym סת"ם, also pronounced *stam*, denotes "Torah scrolls and *mezuzot*," the doorpost amulet of a Jewish home containing a small parchment with a section from the Torah. A *sofer stam* (סופר סת"ם) is the scribe who writes these holy texts, someone who passes on the foundations of the Jewish traditions and learning through writing. In Modern Hebrew, the word *sofer* also refers to an author of fiction. The use of this word in the performance suggests that Kafka was both a modernist author as well as an amateur Hebrew "scribe."

The Hebrew Notebook presents a broad range of associative strategies, creating a labyrinthine "word-scape" and offering suggestions as to how many of these words have "invaded" his writings, appearing in the performance as echoes emerging from his texts. The suggestive evocations of the individual words open up new venues for understanding Kafka's texts but do not offer any definitive interpretations. Instead of trying to decipher Kafka's enigmas, the spectators are merely made aware of them by being allowed to peep below the surface. Their *mabat* and what they can grasp remains limited. As is always the case with enigmatic texts that present a "riddle," the belief that the correct interpretation has been found is immediately deflated by the realization that it is only temporary, thus compelling the search for new answers which will inevitably also be provisional. Through this process, however, the contours of the enigma become more clearly visible.

In this respect, Ruth Kanner's performance has either intentionally or subliminally been modelled after one of Kafka's most renowned texts, "Before the Law" (*Vor dem Gesetz*), which was published during Kafka's life in the collection called *A Country Doctor*, where it was situated between the two short stories concluding the performance, "An Old Document" and "Jackals and Arabs."[10] "Before the Law"

---

[10] These stories were published, though not for the first time, in the collection of stories *A Country Doctor* (*Ein Landarzt*), published by the *Kurt Wolff Verlag* in Leipzig in 1918.

first appeared in the 1915 New Year's edition of the independent Jewish weekly *Selbstwehr*, edited by Martin Buber, and became the penultimate chapter of *The Trial* (*Der Prozess*), published posthumously a year after Kafka's death. "Before the Law" relates the lifelong wish of "a man from the country who asks to gain entry into the law," who is told by the gatekeeper "that he cannot grant him entry at the moment." After the man from the country has spent many years – in fact, his whole life – waiting to be let through the gate to "the law" (which has been left open the whole time), he "gathers in his head all his experiences of the entire time up into one question which he has not yet put to the gatekeeper." On the verge of death, he finally asks the gatekeeper why, after "these many years, no one except me has requested entry?" The gatekeeper answers: "Here no one else can gain entry, since this entrance was assigned only to you. I'm going to close it now" (Kafka, "Before the Law"). This story was not included in the performance itself, but it is constantly present, as a subtext representing the abyss and the volcano Scholem describes in his letter to Rosenzweig. It can also be read as a text about the theatre, where the law is an almost invisible performance, which can be seen as a weak illumination as the life of the man from the country comes to an end.

The performance of *Kafka's Hebrew Notebook* also shows that Kafka's texts, as Benjamin suggested in his essay published on the tenth anniversary of Kafka's death (quoted as the second epigraph above and presented as an exhibit on the wall in the first part of the performance), constitute a "code of gestures which surely had no definite symbolic meaning for the author from the outset; rather, the author tried to derive such a meaning from them in ever-changing contexts and experimental groupings" (Benjamin 1999, 801). Following Benjamin's suggestion, the Ruth Kanner Theatre Group continues Kafka's own efforts to derive the meaning from these gestures (here represented by the Hebrew words), creating new and constantly evolving performative contexts. They present their performance as the "*gegebene Ort solcher Versuchsanordnungen*," i.e. the given site or place (*Ort*) for such experimental arrangements. The performance invites the audience to participate in a laboratory experiment in which the lexical and gestural components of Kafka's texts are carefully examined, empowering the spectators to continue with their own reading "experiments" of Kafka's writings. The Hebrew words are the true protagonists of the performance, while the performers – five actors and a visual artist – are their vehicles for what they term "speech theatre."

1 The gallery installations

The first part of *The Hebrew Notebook* takes place in an open gallery space where each of the six participants presents a relatively short individual piece, consisting of a monologue or an installation. The spectators are encouraged to move around freely, exploring the different "exhibits" individually or in small groups. The two male participants, the visual artist Guy Sagi (who is responsible for the projections of the Hebrew and German "word images" in Kafka's handwriting on the wall in the second part of the performance) and the actor Ronen Babluki present mute installations; while three of the female actors, Shirley Gal, Tali Kark and Adi Meirovitch recite short texts by Kafka to one or a small group of listeners. The fourth female actor, Yael Mutsafi, impersonates Ruth Kanner, telling us how the performance came about when Ruth Kanner was invited to participate in the National Library anniversary celebration. There are also some short texts by Kafka glued onto the gallery-walls, quotes from the Walter Benjamin essay discussed earlier, as well as a well-known photograph of Kafka wearing a straw hat, seated with two men and a woman in a mock *papier-mâché* airplane taken in the Viennese Prater in September 1913. In this photograph, as opposed to most existing photographs of Kafka, he is smiling, apparently enjoying himself, while posing for the camera.

Yael Mutsafi's impersonation of Ruth Kanner offers a somewhat parodic sense of the director's intonations and gestures of hesitation, as well as her idiosyncrasies as a contemporary Hebrew speaker (quoted here in English translation):

> Did you know that The National Library in Jerusalem celebrated its 120th anniversary? And towards these celebrations they made a special project – they invited 12 artists, to choose, each, an archival item from the library and to do some work with it. I went to the library. I was looking for something that would be of interest to me, but didn't find anything. I was on the verge of giving up ... and then – just like that – without any real expectations I asked the archivist – perhaps, by any chance – you do have there something hidden on... of...probably not... 'cause everything has been published and said but... perhaps... yet... you have by any chance something in the archives of... Franz Kafka???
>
> And he said: yes... and went underground – that is where they hide all of their special treasures in safes – and came back with a thin, blue notebook and put it in my hands!!! I am holding in my hands a notebook that Franz Kafka himself wrote! His own handwriting! I didn't know what to do with it – I smelled it! I wanted to eat it!!! And then, I opened it and saw a list of words in Hebrew! This was the notebook from which Franz Kafka had studied Hebrew.[11]

Smelling the notebook causes the director to want to devour the words. Her performance originates from and explores the materiality of the words, each with its

---

[11] Document sent to the author by Ruth Kanner.

unique qualities and taste as well as the infinite potentials for combinations with other words, creating the basis for the speech acts which gradually developed into complex stories. The notebook is an unexplored linguistic territory that has been hidden in the archives of the National Library, now revived as the point of departure for the performance that is about to commence.

After this prologue about the "birth" of the performance, Adi Meirovitch presents a short passage from Kafka's diary that provides a sharp contrast with the kind of appetite the notebook triggered for the director. After removing a small piece of red candy from her mouth and holding it in her hand, she begins to recite the following passage:

Fig. 2: Adi Meirovitch's presentation of a short passage from Kafka's diaries during a performance in Frankfurt. Photo: Kineret Kisch.

> This craving that I almost always have, when for once I feel my stomach is healthy, to heap up in me notions of terrible deeds of daring with food. I especially satisfy this craving in front of pork butchers. I see a sausage that is labeled as an old, hard sausage; I bite into it in my imagination with all my teeth and swallow quickly, regularly, and thoughtlessly, like a machine. The despair that this act, even in the imagination, has as its immediate result increases my haste. I shove the long slabs of rib meat unbitten into my mouth, and then pull them out again from behind, tearing through stomach and intestines. I eat dirty delicatessen stores completely empty. Cram myself with herrings, pickles, and all the bad, old sharp foods. Bonbons are poured into me like hail from their tin boxes, I enjoy this way not only my healthy condition but also a suffering that is without pain and can pass at once. (Kafka 1976, 96)

As opposed to Yael Mutsafi's tongue-in-cheek impersonation of the director, this is a recital of a text in which the speaker establishes a critical distance from the first-person voice of the narrator. Instead of showing the different dishes that Kafka mentions, Adi puts the candy back into her mouth for a short while, then takes it out again, ending the presentation by offering a piece of candy from the jar to her listeners.

In one of the corners of the room, while playing with a little human shaped figure, Shirley Gal recites a section from the *First Octavo Notebook* about a Chinese visitor who does not speak German but insists on coming to see the narrator of the story-fragment. She ends her presentation when she – as if breaking some secret taboo – suddenly takes a small bite from the figure, demonstrating an additional form of eating. In another corner of the space it is possible to hear Tali Kark whispering some of Kafka's so-called "Zurau Aphorisms" from *The Blue Octavo Notebooks*, including part of the one quoted as the first epigraph: "*Es gibt ein Ziel, aber keinen Weg; was wir Weg nennen, ist Zögern* [There is a goal/destination but no way there; what we call way is hesitation]." Tali Kark is a fortune-teller who reveals a terrible secret about ourselves.

The two male participants invite the audience to enter the world of Kafka's Hebrew Notebook without uttering a single word. Guy Sagi – who is responsible for the projections of the words on the wall in the second part of the performance – sits on a chair with a sketch block on his knees and draws concentric circles with a pencil. He gradually fills the page with the circular pencil movements, fulfilling the endless cyclical patterns of history by returning to the Hebrew language, or perhaps just creating a "black hole." During his introductory installation, Ronen Babluki stands in front of a gallery wall holding a paint brush while watching a video showing him photographed from behind while painting a white wall with a big brush and with a bucket of paint just behind him. When the figure on the screen kneels down to dip the brush in the bucket the actor in the gallery space also kneels, with his back turned to the spectators. Since this is not a regular mirror, we are watching the same figure twice, from behind. When the figure on the wall resumes the act of painting, the live actor in front of us comes to a standstill, watching himself painting like before.

Fig. 3: Ronen Babluki dipping the paintbrush/es in the bucket(s). Photo: Noa Elran.

This is a demonstration of the creative process whereby the "ever-changing contexts and experimental groupings" of Kafka's gestures – as Benjamin suggests in his Kafka essay – are explored in a performative context. At the beginning of the video installation there is a short quote in Hebrew from the opening section of Benjamin's Kafka essay: "Weltalter hat der Mann beim Tünchen zu bewegen" (Benjamin 1977, 410).[12] Benjamin likens the man who is painting to Georg Lukács, who thinks in terms of historical ages, while Kafka thinks in terms of "cosmic epochs" (*Weltaltern*). Lukács, according to Benjamin, is the historical materialist, while Kafka, as Benjamin's essay gradually claims (but without using this term) should probably in the suitable oxymoronic fashion be termed a metaphysical materialist.

2 The *Kabbalat Mila* ceremony

Even before the introductory section outlined above begins, one of the actors explains that the spectators will be able to see all of these introductory installations if they follow certain rules of time-keeping. At a given sign, however these preparatory introductions will end enabling the audience to participate in the *kabbalat mila* ceremony to enter the space where the "performance itself will take place."

---

12 In Hebrew: נצחים חייב האיש להניע כשהוא מסייד. The English translation reads, "The man who whitewashes has epochs to move" (Benjamin 1999, 795).

This very simple *rite-de-passage* – giving the performance a mock-educational dimension – will involve each and every one of the approximately 30–35 spectators and it only takes a few minutes; with one of the actors presenting a little grey card with a word from the notebook in Kafka's handwriting – in Hebrew on one side and in German on the other – to each individual spectator as she or he passes through the door leading to the more traditional performance space.

The term *kabbalat mila* literally means "Receiving the Word," an invented Hebrew collocation that evokes an ambivalent tension between two existing ceremonies. The first is *kabbalat shabbat*, the ceremony for greeting the day of rest on Friday evenings. The word *Kabbalah*, besides meaning "greeting," "receiving" or "acceptance," also refers to the mystical teachings of Judaism, where letters and words have numerical values holding hidden secrets about a person's life or about the Godhead. The second ceremony evoked by the pairing of *Kabbalah* and *mila* is the *brit mila*, or circumcision, through which the Jewish male child is brought into the covenant between God and Abraham (Genesis 17:10–14) when he is eight days old. But the word *mila*, though from another lexical root, also means "word." Thus the ceremony is playing on the double meanings of *mila*, the Hebrew words for "word" and "circumcision," symbolizing the covenant between man and God. Studying the words in Kafka's Hebrew notebook with the actors is an initiation into the work of Kafka through the art of storytelling.

Fig. 4: Ronen Babluki gives a word-card to a spectator in the *kabbalat mila* ceremony. Photo: Kineret Kisch.

3 Inside the performance space: the classroom

After the spectators have entered the performance space and are seated facing a small elevated stage, on which there are five chairs and a small table, the actors enter one by one, showing their hesitation and formality while collecting the blue notebooks from the table as they find their way to their designated chairs on the elevated stage. Behaving like pupils entering a classroom on the first day of school, they refrain from looking at each other. Once they are seated on the stage, they begin to recite the words in the notebook, finally finding the courage to utter the word *mabat*, and then *stam*. They have already acted out a whole event without looking at anyone of their fellow actors, as they are watched by the spectators establishing their gaze. The connection between the gaze (*mabat*) and what is illogical and meaningless (*stam*) is never fully clarified or elaborated. However, this collocation (*mabat-stam*) establishes a dialectic based on Kafka's "Before the Law," which begins with the gaze of "the man from the country" (*ein Mann vom Lande*).[13] through the open gate of the law; as "the gatekeeper walks to the side... the man bends over in order to see through the gate into the inside" (Kafka, "Before the Law"). Since nothing comes from his request and he spends the rest of his life in front of this gate, through which he never entered and which will soon be closed, the entire event, i.e. his whole life, turns out to be *stam*, merely meaningless nonsense.

Fig. 5: The actors are reciting (or: the pupils are learning) the word "stam" (*unbestimmt*, the second word in the notebook). Photo: Daniel Tchetchik.

---

13 Eli Schonfeld shows that the man from the country is an *am-ha'aretz* (literally "the people from the earth"), the Hebrew expression in the Talmud for someone who is ignorant. This is one of the rare Hebrew expressions Kafka used in his Diaries (Schonfeld 2016).

Another word from the notebook on one of the cards handed out in during the *kabbalat mila* ceremony is *shachefet* (שחפת), meaning "tuberculosis," which Kafka translates as *Schwindsucht*. The Hebrew word appears twice in the Bible (in Leviticus 26:16 and Deuteronomy 28:22). The King James Bible translates the word as "consumption," while Kafka's German translation is a dated term for pulmonary tuberculosis. *Schwindsucht* is a compound of two words: *Schwind*, meaning "wasting" or "dwindling" (as in *verschwinden*, to "disappear," which is precisely what the man from the country does while waiting a lifetime opposite the open gate) and *Sucht*, meaning "search" or "addiction," as in *Sehnsucht* ("longing," "desire" or "nostalgia"). Instead of investigating the causes of the "infection" or impersonating the patient, the performance develops a meta-theatrical dimension whereby the words appearing on the page in two opposing columns perform their meanings.

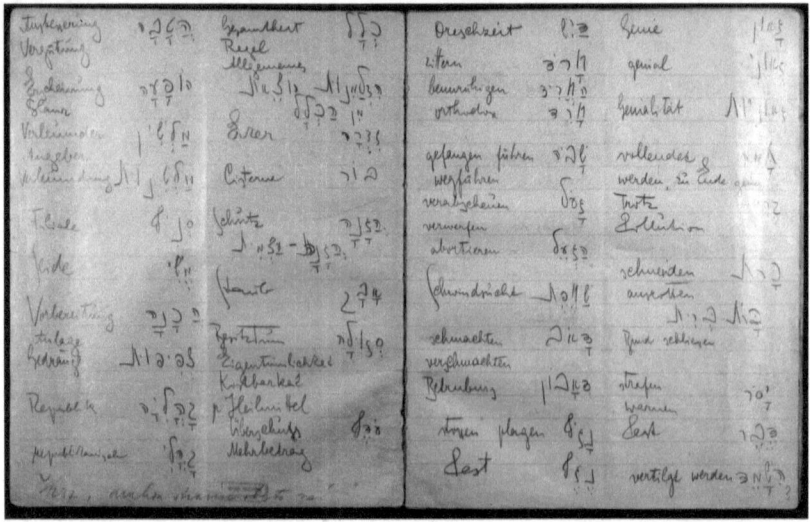

Fig. 6: *Schwindsucht* שחפת appears on the right-hand page, left column, fifth word from the bottom in Kafka's Hebrew notebook.

According to Susan Sontag,

> The fantasies inspired by TB in the last century, by cancer now, are responses to a disease thought to be intractable and capricious – that is, a disease not understood – in an era in which medicine's central premise is that all diseases can be cured. Such a disease is, by definition, mysterious. For, as long as its cause was not understood and the ministrations of doctors remained so ineffective, TB was thought to be an insidious, implacable theft of a life. (Sontag 1978, 5)

Sontag's description of terminal disease as a mysterious language that invades and infects the human body resembles Scholem's description of the threat of "the language" for the body politic. Kafka, meanwhile, experienced his illness as a "symbol." In his first diary entry about a month after the diagnosis, dated 15 September 1917, Kafka gives expression to a euphoric state considered typical of the illness:

> You have the chance, as far as it is at all possible, to make a new beginning. Don't throw it away. If you insist on digging deep into yourself, you won't be able to avoid the muck that will well up. But don't wallow in it. If the infection in your lungs is only a symbol, as you say, a symbol of the infection whose inflammation is called F. and whose depth is its deep justification; if this is so then the medical advice (light, air, sun, rest) is also a symbol. Lay hold of this symbol. (Kafka 1976, 383)

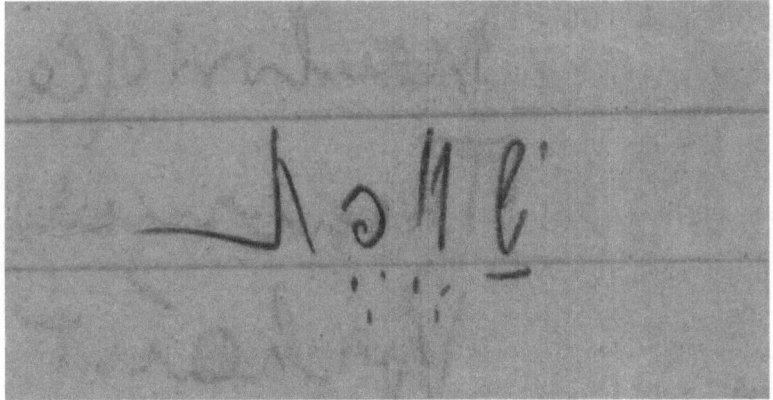

Fig. 7: The flashcard with the Hebrew word for tuberculosis.

Fig. 8: Guy Sagi projecting *Schwindsucht* on the wall as the word is recited in Hebrew.

After a long sequence of reading, reciting, and even singing words from the notebook, individually and in unison, Adi Meirovitch begins to lead the recital of a fragment from the "Third Octavo Notebook," which begins, "There was once a community of scoundrels...." This quote is followed by a fragment from the "Second Octavo Notebook," beginning, "At last our troops succeeded in breaking into the city through the southern gate...." The recitation is led by Ronen Babluki, while the other actors accompany with strange sounds and noises. Then they all resume the recital of words from the notebook in order to restore the order or the discipline it has come to represent.

Following the readings, Shirley Gal collects the notebooks and begins to recite the conjugations of the Hebrew verb *radaf*, meaning "chase" or "pursue," quickly and with obsessive intensity, using Moshe Rath's textbook as her source. After finishing this exercise she begins telling the story "An Old Manuscript," followed by Tali Kark's recitation of "Jackals and Arabs." Throughout, words in Kafka's handwriting are projected on the wall behind them. During this final section of the performance, the spectators gradually realize that the strategies of spectator attention have changed. The audience is transported from the world of individual words and their associative potentials to the disturbing narratives of conflict where the words now serve the development of the story. The power of the individual words can still be felt, like in the repetitions of words the spectators have become used to. But the disturbing, even uncanny characteristics of the situations, with the performers, still situated on the same "classroom" platform as earlier, begin to take over. The previously more or less disciplined pupils become increasingly unruly, offering an eerie glance into Kafka's stories, as they gradually become overwhelmed by their narratives.

Fig. 9: Photo: Daniel Tchetchik.

Both "An Old Manuscript" and "Jackals and Arabs," like many of Kafka's stories, begin with the sudden entrance of an unknown stranger (F. Rokem 2015). Yet, in the performance of "An Old Manuscript" the intruder is not an individual but rather an unidentified collective or a tribe, and the situation resembles a military invasion. The invaders strip a town's inhabitants of their possessions and force two local women to remove all their clothing save their underwear. Each of the women then takes out a long blond braid hidden inside her remaining garments and attaches it to her much darker hair – an image reminiscent of Paul Celan's poem *"Todesfuge"* ("Death Fugue"), which repeatedly refers to the "golden" hair of Margerete and the "ashen" hair of Sulamit. The women hesitantly recite two words that reach the spectators like echoes from a more confident, now threatened past: *moladeteynu* (our homeland) and *leshoneynu* (our language).

"Jackals and Arabs," the final story recited and portrayed in the performance, also depicts an invasion, but here the narrator is the invader. The jackals, who are the newcomers to this place, say they have been waiting for him in order to help them – the animals living in this desert, apparently the Zionists – to curb the Arabs with whom the stranger is travelling and with whom they, the jackals have an ancient conflict: "We want cleanliness, nothing but cleanliness" they howl before asking the stranger to cut the "throats [of the Arabs] with a pair of scissors" (Kafka 2015, 37). The performance ends with the harsh description of the jackals the Arab leader of the caravan communicates to the storyteller as they are about to leave their resting place in the oasis: "You've seen them. Marvelous creatures, aren't they? And how the despise us!" (Kafka, 2015, 39). This pronouncement, which has been interpreted as an expression of Kafka's profound skepticism towards Zionism, refers in the context of the performance to the ongoing and gradually increasing racism of Israeli Jews towards the Palestinians, those who are Israeli citizens as well as those in the occupied territories.

After the recital of "Jackals and Arabs," silence and emptiness hover over the stage. The performance returns once more to Kafka's notebook, creating an uncanny closure with the recital of the words *hashrasha* (השרשה, rooting) and *geza* (גזע, race), ending with *hofa'a* (הופעה) meaning "appearance" or "performance" and *tsafo* (צפה) which is translated in the notebook as "Überziehen" (overcoat, cover) in Kafka's handwriting, but is actually the Hebrew root for "watching." It is possible that Kafka made a mistake. With the penultimate word of the performance – *hofa'a* (הופעה) – Kafka is also incorrect, at least literally, translating it as *Erscheinung* (meaning "apparition") and *Glanz* (meaning "gloss," "shine," or even "glamour"), rather than simply "performance." Yet, every performance is an apparition, at least if we take Shakespeare's *Hamlet* as the measure for what a performance is. In the opening scene of *Hamlet*, Horatio (or Marcellus, depending on which edition we follow) asks, "What, has this thing appeared again tonight?" (Shakespeare I,1,21). The question refers not only to the ghost of

Fig. 10: Photo: Daniel Tchetchik.

Hamlet's father but also to the performance ("this thing") in which he will appear that evening. *Glanz* is the term Kafka used in "Before the Law" to describe the light which the man from the country sees breaking out "*unverlöschlich aus der Türe des Gesetzes*" (Kafka, "Vor dem Gestetz"), where *unverlöschlich* can be translated as "enduringly," "ineradicably," "unforgettably" and "hauntingly," indirectly returning us to the understanding of Kafka's short story as a life-long, haunted/haunting spectacle. It feels as if something has been disrupted, remaining unresolved and impossible to decipher.

Works cited

Alter, Robert. *Necessary Angels: Tradition and Modernity in Kafka, Benjamin and Scholem*. Cambridge, MA: Harvard University Press, 1991.
Ben-Shaul, Daphna. "Her Role as a Storyteller: On Theatre Creator Ruth Kanner." *Motar* 12 (2004): 107–118 (Hebrew).
Ben-Shaul Daphna. "Ideology of Form in Storytelling Theater: The Politics of Inter-medial Adaptation in *Discovering Elijah, A Play about War*." *Gramma, Journal of Theory and Criticism* 17 (2009): 165–182 (Hebrew).
Ben-Shaul, Daphna, Ruth Kanner, Janelle Reinelt and Freddie Rokem. "Capturing Moments of Misperformance: 'Local Tales.'" *Performance Research* 15.2 (2010): 66–73.
Benjamin, Walter. "Franz Kafka: Zur zehnten Wiederkehr seines Todestages." *Gesammelte Schriften*. Frankfurt am Main: Suhrkamp Verlag, II.1 (1977), 409–438.
Benjamin, Walter. "Franz Kafka: On the Tenth Anniversary of His Death." *Selected Writings*. Vol. 2. Ed. Michael W. Jennings. Cambridge, MA: Harvard University Press, 1999. 794–818.
Binder, Hartmut. "Kafkas Hebräischstudien: ein biographisch-interpretatorischer Versuch." *Jahrbuch der deutschen Schillergesellschaft*, 11 (1967): 530–533.
Bodenheimer, Alfred. "A Sign of Sickness and a Symbol of Health: Kafka's Hebrew Notebooks." *Kafka, Zionism, and Beyond*. Ed. Mark H. Gelber. Tubingen: Max Niemeyer Verlag, 2004. 259–270.

Butler, Judith. "Who Owns Kafka?" http://www.lrb.co.uk/v33/n05/judith-butler/who-owns-kafka. *London Review of Books*. March 3, 2011 (24 March 2017).
Cutter, William. "Ghostly Hebrew, Ghastly Speech: Scholem to Rosenzweig, 1926." *Prooftexts: A Journal of Jewish Literary History* 10.3 (1990): 413–33.
Hannsen, Jens. "Kafka and Arabs." *Critical Inquiry* 39 (Autumn 2012): 167–197.
Kafka, Franz. "Hebrew Notebook." The National Library of Israel, Schwadron Collection, Schwad 01 19 268.
Kafka, Franz. "Before the Law." http://www.kafka-online.info/before-the-law.html. Trans. Ian Johnston (12 October 2016).
Kafka, Franz. *Diaries 1910–1923*. Ed. Max Brod. New York: Schocken Books, 1976.
Kafka, Franz. "Jackals and Arabs." *A Country Doctor*. Trans. Siegfried Mortkowitz. Prague: Vitalis Verlag, 2015.
Kafka, Franz. "Schakale und Araber." http://gutenberg.spiegel.de/buch/franz-kafka-erz-161/19 (9 October 2016).
Kafka, Franz. "Vor dem Gestetz." http://gutenberg.spiegel.de/buch/franz-kafka-erz-161/5 (22 March 2017).
Kafka, Franz. *Aphorismen: Betrachtungen über Sünde, Leid, Hoffnung und den wahren Weg*. http://gutenberg.spiegel.de/buch/franz-kafka-aphorismen-166/1. Frankfurt a.M.: Suhrkamp Verlag 1970 (7 October 2016).
Kafka, Franz. *The Zurau Aphorisms*. Trans. Geoffrey Brock & Michael Hofmann. New York: Schocken, 2006.
Ruth Kanner Theatre Group Website, http://www.ruthkanner.com/en/Content. aspx?t=10&p=3&iid=14&eof (17 March 2017).
Menczel-Ben-Tovim, Puah. "Ich war Kafkas Hebräischlehrerin." *"Als Kafka mir entgegenkam ..." Erinnerungen an Franz Kafka*. Ed. Hans-Gerd Koch. Berlin: Wagenbach, 1995.165–167
Rath, Moshe. *Lehrbuch der Hebräischen Sprache für Schul- und Selbstunterricht: Mit Schlüssel und Selbstunterrricht*. 3rd ed. Vienna: Selbstverlag des Autors, 1918.
Rokem, Freddie. "'Suddenly a stranger comes into the room': Interruptions in Brecht, Benjamin and Kafka." *Studies in Theatre and Performance* 36.1 (2015): 21–26.
Rokem, Na'ama. "German–Hebrew Encounters in the Poetry and Correspondence of Yehuda Amichai and Paul Celan." *Prooftexts: A Journal of Jewish Literary History* 30.1 (2010): 97–127.
Schonfeld, Eli. "*Am-ha'aretz*: The Law of the Singular. Kafka's Hidden Knowledge." *Kafka and the Universal*. Eds. Arthur Cools and Vivian Liska. Berlin and Boston: De Gruyter, 2016. 107–129.
Sontag, Susan. *Illness as Metaphor*. New York: Farrar, Straus and Giroux, 1978.
Shakespeare, William. *Hamlet: Prince of Denmark*. Cambridge: Cambridge University Press, 1985.
Suchoff, David. *Kafka's Jewish Languages: The Hidden Openness of Tradition*. Philadelphia: University of Pennsylvania Press, 2011.

Yael Almog
Europe Will Be Stunned: Visualization of a Jewish Return

In recent years, Jewish migration to Germany has drawn wide attention in both Germany and elsewhere; the phenomenon has been described as a movement of "return" to Europe. It is the wave of Israeli migration in particular that seems to signal a new image of Germany that dissolves its grim reputation as the land of perpetrators.[1] Under the influence of Zionist discourse, Israel has long been presented as a safe haven for European Jews, who are portrayed as individuals disinherited of their cultural capital on the continent, and, consequently, of the option of portraying it as their home.[2] The choice of Germany as a desirable destination for Israeli migrants thus depends on the warm acceptance of Jews in contemporary Germany, i.e. on an image of the country which attests to the "normalization" of German society. If Germany embraces the Israeli presence in Berlin as marking a linear "recovery," in Israel migration to Germany's capital has at times been described as a momentary *crisis* in Israel's political and cultural agenda.[3]

This article seeks to trace how visions of a "Jewish return to Europe" inform contemporary cultural production. I am particularly interested in asking how the presence of Israeli émigrés in Germany, a dramatic instance of such a "return," challenges the country's memorial culture due to the "exportation" of dispositions relating to the Holocaust construed in Israel. I view this dislocation of memorial practices, a new instance of Hebrew-German exchange, as embedded in a broader discourse on migration, integration and xenophobic violence. At the core

---

1 In her 2001 monograph, arguably the first work that traced a wave of Israeli migration to Germany's capital, Fania Oz-Salzberger suggests that Berlin demonstrates "Israelis' longing for Europe through an unequaled lens" (Oz-Salzberger 2001). This citation is taken from the book cover to the monograph's Hebrew translation. All translations from the Hebrew are my own.
2 As Diana Pinto writes, "After the near extermination of European Jewry, most Jews in the world were convinced that Europe had become, after Auschwitz, the equivalent of post-1492 Spain: a place with a spent Jewish past no longer harboring significant Jewish life. On this count, ideology seemed to back history. Zionism, well before Nazism and the creation of the state of Israel, delegitimized a Jewish presence in incurably anti-Semitic Europe and produced the return of all Jews to their historic homeland, Eretz Israel" (Pinto 2002, 240).
3 Such an attitude toward Israeli migrants to Berlin characterizes, for instance, former Minister of Finance Yair Lapid's attack of Israeli migrants to Berlin as diffident, since their act cancels out the Zionist achievement of establishing an autonomous Jewish state. In his critique, Lapid recounts the experiences of his own family members during the Holocaust (*TheMarker* 2013).

of my argument is the 2007–2011 film trilogy *And Europe Will Be Stunned*, directed by Israeli artist Yael Bartana, who is based in Berlin and Amsterdam. The trilogy presents a fictional national movement that advocates the return of 3,300,000 Jews to Poland, with the claim that Poland's ethnic and religious homogeneity is a deficiency that could be corrected with the renewal of Jewish life in the country. Wearing the form of an enthusiastic political manifesto, the trilogy mirrors early Zionist images and motifs in articulating the vision of the return to the homeland. The trilogy's end reveals this endeavor as a failure, to which the assassination of the movement's leader, Slawek, attests.

Strategic displacement of national norms, narratives and rituals is central to Bartana's work (Bell 2015, 2). Observing the trilogy's cogent portrayal of an alternative history, several scholars have situated the trilogy in relation to contemporary Polish culture and art which display so-called reminiscences of the Jewish past in Poland (see Underhill 2011; Lehrer and Waligórska 2013; Blacker 2014). My alternative contextualization of the trilogy presents its engagement with Jewish history in relation to two other memory cultures: of Israel and of Germany. I argue that by evoking an affinity between Zionism and European nationalism the trilogy unearths and problematizes presumptions that are at the core of Israeli and German hegemonic norms of commemorating the Holocaust. Among these presuppositions are the view of Jews as necessarily *absent* from European society and the perception of Israel as the center of Jewish life after the Holocaust.[4] A possible Jewish return to Europe is thus exposed as jeopardizing institutionalized memory norms that presume an irreversible breach between European societies and Jewish life.

1 Emulating the Zionist vision

Bartana's Polish trilogy has garnered wide interest among art critics and in the European press due to its supposedly inflammatory statements that could be interpreted as commentaries about contemporary politics. The agenda of the

---

[4] Bartana was not the only Israeli artist in recent years to visualize a national project of a Jewish "return" to Europe, nor was she the only artist residing in Germany while conceptualizing such a project. In 2013 Ronen Eidelman declared the founding of "Medinat Weimar" (the State of Weimar), calling for the establishment of a Jewish state in the German federal state of Thuringia. The preference of Weimar over Erfurt, Thuringia's actual capital, enables the use of eminent tokens of German history: the institutions of the new Jewish state neighbor the Goethe and Schiller houses. The project thus presents an image of Goethe and Schiller's sculptures that are "guarded" by an army car of the Israel Border Police, a section of Israeli military that is often criticized for excessive aggression in the occupied territories.

fictional movement could be claimed to echo the migration of young Jews to Europe in recent years, a historical phenomenon that resonates with the artist's residency in Europe. The remarkable fact that Bartana presented the trilogy at the Venice Biennale as a representative of Poland adds to the impression that her biographical stance as a Jew who resides in Europe merges with the trilogy's images and statements.

Jacqueline Rose is one among several critics who view the Polish trilogy as grounded in political dispositions and claim that the artist bases her political intervention on her own biography as an Israeli émigrée.[5] Rose contends that Bartana's biography evinces a stance of "partial homecoming" and notes that Bartana "describes herself as an 'ongoing returnee'" through her repeated moves between Israel and other countries (Rose 2012, 140). This description turns the artist herself into a marker of constant transition between countries. Bartana emerges as a wandering Jew of sorts, with the historically new fact that the continual detachment from (and attraction to) one's place of birth is now tied to Israel. The ostensible endpoint of Jewish wandering, a Jewish state, is revealed to be only one of many coordinates for this nomadic existence.

Bartana's description of a national movement of "return to the homeland" generates tensions pertaining to the use of this concept in Zionism. Israel's "Law of Return" plays a major role in the country's long-term policies and particularly in the institutional attempt to integrate all immigrants of Jewish origins (Peled and Shafir 2002, 16–18). The notion that Jewish migration to Israel embodies a return to the homeland is constitutive of Israel's national ethos; this vision permeates Israel's recruitment of Jews worldwide by granting them equal national status (Segal, Elliott and Mayadas 2010, 231). By the same token, emigration from Israel can be seen not as an act of protest against the country's national agenda but as a paradoxical act of regression: having already "returned" to the Land of Israel, Israeli emigrants undo this process by "returning" to the Diaspora. Adding another layer of paradox, these emigrants do not simply oppose the Israeli ethos of return but in a sense also perpetuate it, for if the Diaspora continues to exist, the possibility to encourage the return to the "holy land" remains. The emigration of Israeli Jews thus implies an endless cycle of "Diaspora" and "return."

---

5 Rose further notes that, "Born in Jezreel Valley, south of lower Galilee, Bartana lived in New York and then Amsterdam for several years before returning briefly to Israel in 2006. Since 2000, Israel-Palestine has become the focus of her work" (Rose 2012, 140). Rose's essay was originally published in *And Europe Will Be Stunned: Exhibition Catalogue*, Australian Center for Contemporary Art, Melbourne, 2011. See also Waner 2012 and Sclodnick 2014.

This notion of oscillating migration can be traced in Bartana's Polish trilogy, a work that builds on famous Zionist narratives of nation building. The artwork emulates familiar images and tropes from early Zionism, particularly from the first settlements in Palestine, while situating these figures "back" in Europe. With this dislocation, the Polish trilogy *reiterates* and reinforces the status of early Zionism as a climactic historical moment. Yet, ironically, it is exactly the mimicry of these scenes and the depiction of a second Jewish settlement movement that blurs the perception of *one* climactic conclusion of Jewish history.

Alluding to Bartana's biography, Rose argues that the artist dismantles some eminent Zionist concepts by rendering them relative:

> [S]he has mounted the fiercest challenge and rebellion to the concept of return as a final, redemptive destination [...] We cannot talk here about ascent — *aliyah* — the word already indicating the elevated status accorded the Jewish daughter who "returns" to the land of her ancestors; nor precisely can we talk of descent — *yeridah* — the word used to describe those who fall, decline, betray the nation by choosing to live elsewhere. (Rose 2012, 140)

What appears provocative in *And Europe Will Be Stunned* is not the encouragement of Israelis to emigrate from their country but the disrupting of the notion of migration – be it to Israel or to Europe – as a deterministic act. The artwork thus reiterates the meaning of "return" to the holy land while transgressing, in the same gesture, the poles that define this concept in Zionist discourse.

Building on these tensions, Bartana's use of the figure of return reproduces the raison d'être of the Zionist project of settling in Israel while "displacing" it in Europe. In this sense, Bartana's project could be seen as a conceptual suggestion to displace the contemporary hegemonic vision of this ideology from its current center in Israel. This attempt is evocative of the roots of Zionist ideology, including the affinity of early Zionism to socialist and communist ideologies. As Boris Groys argues, the universal character of Bartana's fictional movement is epitomized in the amalgamation of two diverging national visions of 1920s–1930s Zionism and Eastern-European ideologies:

> [T]he small settlement looks a bit like a Stalinist labor camp, and seems to be lost in the middle of nowhere. This nowhere is symbolized at the end of the film by another reference to Poland's past — the anonymous-looking mass architecture of late socialism, examples of which can be seen behind the fragile structure of the settlement. The Jewish builders of the new future are depicted by Bartana as vital men and women, full of energy and hope. But the way in which they work is deeply anachronistic, belonging to a period of early industrialization, such as the Jewish collectivist agricultural projects in Palestine in the 1920s and 1930s. These young Jewish enthusiasts with their socialist work ethics and primitive technology seem to be lost not only in space but also in time. They build something resembling a cross between an Israeli kibbutz and a Soviet kolkhoz in the middle of post-communist, post-industrial, postmodern Europe. (Groys 2012, 135)

By transferring the concept of Zionist "return" to Europe, Zionist ideology itself returns to its roots in the European Diaspora, where it developed alongside other national ideologies. The alert to this proximity challenges the image of animosity between the settlement project in Palestine/Israel and European nationalism.

Thus, the films feature group activities of Zionist activists in Eastern Europe who are preparing for life in an autonomous Jewish country, such as agricultural training. The choice of Poland as a new site for Jewish settlers is provocative because it enacts a "return" not only of Jews to a land of their ancestors (against the focus of Zionist ideology on Israel) but also, in a sense, of Zionist ideology to its place of its conception, an act that transgresses the fatal image of Europe's treatment of the Jews that culminated in the Holocaust. The members of the imaginary Jewish Renaissance movement emulate early Zionist settlements in Israel through their "return" to Poland. While the longing for a national movement of Jewish "return" appears to wear familiar forms, the coordinates of Jewish migration have shifted.

The second part of the trilogy is entitled "Mur i wieża" (Wall and tower). In this film, the Jewish settlers in Poland perform famous scenes from the first settlements in Palestine, such as the quick construction of temporary buildings. The images of the wooden buildings in Poland are similar in form to the "Wall and tower" system used in Palestine in 1936–1939 to erect new establishments rapidly – sometimes in the course of only one day – and fortify them (the Ottoman law determined that settlements with a wall and tower could not be destroyed).

Fig. 1: Yael Bartana, *Mur i wieża (Wall and Tower)*, 2009, video still, courtesy of Annet Gelink Gallery, Amsterdam and Sommer Contemporary Art, Tel Aviv.

Fig. 2: Yael Bartana, *Mary Koszmary (Nightmares)*, 2007, video still, courtesy of Annet Gelink Gallery, Amsterdam and FoksalGallery Foundation, Warsaw.

Another expression of the movement's "Zionist" character is its internationalism. Its members appear to be citizens of countries with starkly diverging economic and cultural conditions such as Poland, Israel, the United States and England; their "cultural differences" and language barriers are overcome as they are united in their common goal. The movement's agenda of assimilation is manifested in the multilingual nature of its activity and ceremonies (monologues, speeches and slogans are presented in English, Polish, Hebrew and German). This linguistic plurality does not harm the activists' communication with each other; rather, it stresses their ability to transcend national boundaries. The "melting pot" appears effective for a national agenda. Similarly to the "original" image behind the movement, that of Zionist migration to Israel/Palestine, it is expected that the migrants to Poland will gradually master its vernacular.

The Zionist endorsement of Hebrew as Israel's dominant vernacular similarly renders diverging languages inferior, a peculiarly rapid historical transition considering the well-established European cultures with which it had to contend.[6]

---

[6] According to Liora Halperin, this insistence was aimed at distinguishing the Zionists from both the Europeans and the locals: "The norm of monolingualism not only protested the importation of a European Babel but also resisted full integration with the Middle Eastern context, a context that in any case did not welcome Hebrew's linguistic intrusion any more than it welcomed Zionist settlement. Few Arabs took it upon themselves to learn Hebrew" (Halperin 2015, 180).

Bartana's trilogy plays on the manner in which Zionist multilingualism has been subsumed by Hebrew in Israel by depicting a parallel shift from multilingualism to monolingualism in the European context. A clear example of this shift occurs in a scene that depicts Jewish migrants to Poland (who appear to be Israeli) in a Polish language class, which takes place in a pastoral setting. The teacher translates into Polish Hebrew words that are especially pertinent to the movement's vision: "earth," "freedom" and "peace." The presentation of the settlers as united in their enthusiasm reaches a climax as one of the group members comments, "Polish is a pretty language," in Hebrew, with a heavy Eastern European accent. This accented proclamation reiterates a familiar image in Israeli collective memory: the Eastern European migrant to Israel declaring, "*Hebrew* is a pretty language" (*ivrit safa yafa*). The mass migration from the former Soviet Union to Israel throughout the 1990s made such a scene constitutive to the Israeli melting pot vision in its contemporary formulation. Ironically, fulfilling her part in a "national movement" of Israelis, the Eastern European migrant has already accomplished the Israeli melting pot ideal. In light of this presumption, the scene features optimistic atmosphere in its affirmation of Zionism's "previous" success.[7]

As Erica Lehrer and Magdalena Waligórska write in their analysis of the trilogy, "The idea of the Jewish return to Poland serves here as a catalyst to 'overcome history,' imagine political change, and trigger new processes of group identification in a globalized world shaped by mass migrations" (Lehrer and Waligórska 2013, 531). Depicting a former Eastern European migrant to Israel who is now "returning" to the European continent represents a globalized world of volatile migration. Offered in accented Hebrew, the utterance validates the Zionist ideal of a unified collective of idealist migrants while at the same time transferring this vision in a location that reverses the historical circumstances which led to its constitution. The trilogy thus presents a reversal of the historical circumstances involving the rise of Nazism, the extermination of European Jews and the consequent mass migration from Europe concurrently. In so doing, it does not ignore the status of the commemoration of the Holocaust as a moral imperative but explores how this disposition depends on the view that history has led to the inevitable and fatal absence of Jewish life from Europe.

---

[7] This impression stems not only from the integration of Eastern European migrants in Israeli society but also from the general cultural view of their overall successful assimilation in the West. As Steven J. Gold writes, "Jewish migrants from Eastern Europe have been the paradigmatic case of successful assimilators in many Western countries. They have actively identified with the nationality and culture in points of settlements, had little propensity to return to the country of origin, and overcame discrimination to attain levels of educational, economic, and cultural prominence exceeding those of the native-born elite" (Gold 2004, 331).

2 The cultivation of memory

In 2013 Bartana held a performance in Cologne that explored the displacement of Israel's and Germany's respective norms of commemorating the Holocaust. She asked a group of citizens, students and pedestrians, to stand still on for two minutes on June 28 at 11:00,[8] an act, which, as she has notified them in advance, mimics the Israeli custom conducted every "Holocaust Remembrance Day." Roughly four hundred people took part in the performance, titled "Two Minutes of Standstill." Bartana chose to hold the performance on Keupstraße in the Mülheim district. Located in the midst of an area populated with Turkish migrants, this street saw in 2004 the explosion of a pipe bomb that resulted in the injury of twenty-two people. The bombing has since been connected to the activity of the Neo-Nazi group National Socialist Underground, which targets immigrants. Connecting different generations of victims of Nazi (and Neo-Nazi) ideology, Bartana aimed to attract members of Germany's current minority groups and newcomers to this memorial ceremony; she also wished to include families who were the target of Neo-Nazi terrorism in the recent past (Malzacher and Wenner 2013, 8–14). In keeping with her intentions, the majority of participants were students from a nearby school with a large population of students with a migration background.

Andreas Huyssen has emphasized the analogy between Turkish immigrants, who in a sense sought to leave a mark on Germany's hegemonic memorial culture in order to establish their own place in the nation, and that of Jews in Germany, who construe their identity vis-à-vis a charged relationship to Germans (Huyssen 2013, 15–8).[9] Based on fieldwork at the memorial (conducted in 2005–2006 and in 2010–2011), sociologist Irit Dekel has demonstrated that visitors are led by the memorial's guides to cultivate their social capital throughout their visit, honing their belonging to the hegemonic German culture or to groups that are expected to relate to the Holocaust differently than the German majority: tours of the memorial serve to reinforce inherited national myths and identities (Dekel 2013, 2–5). Bartana's work with students of migratory background approaches a group that is left out of the dominant German memory culture. The performance's gesture of selecting individuals with migratory background as a target audience has thus

---

[8] Bartana chose deliberately a date that had not been dedicated to any preexisting memorial day as a "gesture of inclusion" of potential participants (Malzacher and Wenner 2013, 8).
[9] Central to Huyssen's analysis is the literary work of the German author of Turkish origin, Zafer Şenocak, who has described Turkish emigrants as driven to place themselves in Germany's past in reaction to their absence from Germany's hegemonic memorial culture.

the potential of rendering them apt memory agents. Yet, the performance intentionally circumvented this expectation by adhering to the "wrong" cultural norm: the ceremony at its center pertains to a different country's memory culture improperly exported to the German context.

The performance thus puts at its center the amalgamation of two nonconventional strategies of relating to the Holocaust: the "exporting" of an Israeli ritual to the German public sphere, and the linking of the victims of the Holocaust to present-day victims of Neo-Nazism, hate crimes and racism. In an interview concerning the performance, Bartana has reflected on her position as an Israeli who resides in Germany as the driving force behind this endeavor, noting that her own presence in Germany makes her come to terms with the past while being attuned to "the tragedies still taking place today."[10]

According to Bartana's statements, not only do Israeli migrants to Germany have the potential of relating to the past in new, pertinent ways, but they also *embody* the transition from one memory culture to another, and thus create in their migration between Israel and Germany new perceptions of memory. In other words, by means of their physical presence in Europe, Jews and Israelis who live in Germany are agents of innovative memory practices as much as they are a new case study for the memory cultures to which they belong. Israelis' relocation to Germany generates, according to Bartana, a first-hand experience of the fatal Jewish history in Europe:

> Something has changed, this is obvious by the fact that so many Israelis, and many other Jews, are now living in Berlin.... This cannot only be due to economic reasons. It is also related to wanting to deal with the past in a more present way. Since I moved to Europe I realized that what makes me myself is the very fact that I am hover[ing] between two countries, two or three languages, in several cultural traditions, and in an ongoing reflection, questions, and inner conflict. We are talking about second and third generation, a generation that did perhaps encounter the Holocaust through their grandparents' testimonies or learned about it in school, but did not experience it personally. We grew up in Israel, in the Middle East, devoting ourselves to the past by obeying the Zionist narratives, which have only been put into doubt in recent years. (Malzacher and Wenner 2013, 17)

"Two Minutes of Standstill" provoked heated reactions in Germany, which attacked the artist's alleged critique of Israel. Journalist Alan Posener has described Bartana's plans for the performance as revoking some of Israel's eminent symbols and rituals pertaining to the Holocaust, calling such critique of Israel "porn for

---

10 The conversation with Florian Malzacher is including in Malzacher and Wenner 2013, 12–23 (here 14).

intellectuals."[11] Such critiques fail to acknowledge the complexity of the artist's position regarding Israeli memory culture. According to Bartana, it is not the case that Israelis who move to Berlin put the Holocaust behind them, belittle Jewish history or forget it. Against such accusations, the artist describes Israeli migrants as incessantly concerned with the memory of the Holocaust; their presence in Germany causes them to experience this history "personally." Insofar as the commemoration of the Holocaust is at the epicenter of Israeli education and upbringing, the migrants are in fact further honing their education. Nevertheless, the Israeli presence in Germany also transgresses that "devotion," since it entails an experience of history "here and now," that is opposed, according to Bartana, to Zionist narratives focused on the past.

The ongoing shift between Israel and Europe is an essential component of this existence; the experience of the Holocaust as a migrant to Europe is informed by Israeli identity with its memory practices. One never leaves Israel entirely. The so-called return to Europe is motivated by striving for a point of origins, one which can only be construed in the context of the Israeli collective: "The two minutes of silence in Israel are very locally rooted, they have their tradition, they belong to the Israeli national identity. So we brought something to Germany that is very much connected to the, let's say, victims. We migrated this form of collective commemoration to the 'primal scene'" (Malzacher and Wenner 2013, 15).

3 Mourning and return

In the Polish trilogy, a main characteristic of Zionism rendered uncanny when transferred to a European context is the promise of a safe haven from persecution. The trilogy repeatedly presents the Jewish renaissance in Poland as a corrective of historical injustice. The viewers are reminded of the "real" historical fate of European Jewry through the appearance of a Jewish woman known as Rivke. Wearing grim black clothing, her hair covered, skin pale, Rivke is the antithesis of the movement's virile men and women (and thus, by way of comparison, of Zionist settlers in Israel). The figure makes a significant appearance at the end of the trilogy as one of the people who pass by Slawek's coffin to bid him a final

---

[11] The article was published on 06.05.2013 under the title "Israelkritik als Porno für Intellektuelle." https://www.welt.de/kultur/kunst-und-architektur/article115893945/Israelkritik-als-Porno-fuer-Intellektuelle.html (12 November 2016). Bartana notes that her work was approached offensively by German political activists during the performance and after it (in Malzacher and Wenner 2013, 14).

farewell. In that moment, Rivke's monologue explicates her own role in modern politics:[12]

> I am Rivke who was murdered and buried anew, who was disinherited, who was moved, breathless, from the mass graves of Auschwitz, Babi Yar, Treblinka, Majdanek, Sobibor, to the shrine of memory to the mausoleum of architecture of the sublime in Jerusalem. I can be found everywhere. I am the ghost of return, the return returning to herself. Sunken in the crypt of grief that cannot be expressed in words, my dead tongue hides something that was buried alive. I am here to reveal the destruction of the understood through the tongue. I am here to weave the torture of identity from the threads of forgetfulness. I am condemned to exist in a frozen crystal, saved from healing, removed from the present.[13]

Rivke's appearance upon the assassination of the movement's leader creates a few strata of irony. The assassination signifies that the renewal of Jewish life in Europe led also to the renewal of anti-Semitism. Instead of commemorating the victims of the Holocaust through settlement in Europe, we are now facing the commemoration of the individual who initiated this enterprise. The assassination brings about the memory of the victims of both forms of fatal violence, against the Jews or their local supporters. Yet, at the same time, Rivke is recognized not as an ally of the national movement but as its other. Whereas the movement calls for a Jewish renaissance, Rivke's eerie existence personifies the repeated destruction of Jewish life. Her monologue commemorates not the repeated renewal of Jewish life – in Europe, Israel or elsewhere – but its continual destruction. She embodies the conflict between the Jew's role as an active agent in a memorial culture – a disposition which is at the core of Israeli identity – and the figural standing of the Jew in European culture as the signifier of a tragic lack. It is a conflict between the role of a subject and an object in collective memory, a dissonance which exposes the inconsistencies between different nations' accounts of the Holocaust and of its pertinence to Jewish and European history. A Jewish return to Europe is impossible, since such a vision echoes competing national and collective memories whose divergence from one another is brought to the fore through the migrant's move between countries.

Bartana's *And Europe Will Be Stunned* emphasizes this conflict by reconfiguring the "return to the Holy land" through familiar scenes of early Zionism to illustrate a "renewal" of Jewish life in Europe. The trilogy thus references expectations concerning the present and future presence of Jews in the continent

---

[12] In this scene translation of the English monologue into German which follows creates a dramatic echo effect.
[13] The monologue is featured in the final part of the Polish trilogy *Zamach* (Assassination) released in 2011.

following Jewish migration to Germany as well as other processes of global demographic shifts. "Return" is shown in the Polish trilogy both as a messianic trope, which maintains its usage in diverse political movements, and as a motion which may fluctuate, reverse itself or accommodate conflicting ideologies. *And Europe Will Be Stunned* hints at Bartana's exploration of new forms of relating to history in her later work, which shows migration to Europe as a catalyst for new practices of memory. The physical Jewish presence in Europe – both fictional and real – cancels out institutional norms grounded in unwavering national belonging. The trilogy thus presents the Jewish presence in Europe as both the accomplishment of memory cultures which dictate the safety of Jews in Europe as their goal and as a lacuna that contradicts basic presumptions that are at their core.

Works cited

Bartana, Yael. Mary Koszmary (Nightmares). Video still. Annet Gelink Gallery, Amsterdam and Foksal Gallery Foundation, Warsaw, 2007.
Bartana, Yael. Mur i wieża (Wall and Tower). Video still. Annet Gelink Gallery, Amsterdam and Sommer Contemporary Art, Tel Aviv, 2009.
Bell, Kirsty. "Yael Bartana." *Art Agenda* (catalogue), 25 February 2015.
Dekel, Irit. *Mediation at the Holocaust Memorial in Berlin*. New York: Palgrave Macmillan, 2013.
Gold, Steven. "From Nationality to Peoplehood: Adaptation and Identity Formation in the Israeli Diaspora." *Diaspora* 13.2/3 (2004): 331–358.
Groys, Boris. "Answering a Call." *And Europe Will Be Stunned – The Polish Trilogy*. Eds. James Lingwood and Eleanor Nairne. Artangel, Ikon, Birmingham, Louisiana Museum of Modern Art, Humblebaek, Museum of Modern Art in Warsaw, Van Abbemuseum, Eindhoven, 2012. 134–139.
Halperin, Liora. *Babel in Zion: Jews, Nationalism, and Language Diversity in Palestine, 1920–1948*. New Haven: Yale University Press, 2015.
Huyssen, Andreas. "Diaspora and Nation: Migration into Other Pasts." *New German Critique* 88 (2003): 147–164.
Lehrer, Erica and Magdalena Waligórska. "Cur(at)ing History: New Genre Art Interventions and the Polish-Jewish Past." *East European Politics and Societies and Cultures* 27. 3 (2013): 510–544.
Malzacher, Florian, and Stefanie Wenner, eds. *Two Minutes of Stand-Still*. An Edition by Impulse Theater Biennale. Berlin: Sternberg Press, 2013.
Oz-Salzberger, Fania. *Israelis, Berlin*. Jerusalem: Keter, 2001 (Hebrew).
Peled, Yoav, and Gershon Shafir, eds. *Being Israeli: The Dynamics of Multiple Citizenship*. Cambridge: Cambridge University Press, 2002.
Pinto, Diana. "Jewish Challenges in the New Europe." *Challenging Ethnic Citizenship: German and Israeli Perspectives on Immigration*. Eds. Daniel Levy and Yfaat Weiss. New York: Berghahn Books. 239–252.
Posener, Alan. "Israelkritik als Porno für Intellektuelle."
https://www.welt.de/kultur/kunst-und-architektur/article115893945/Israelkritik-als-Porno fuer-Intellektuelle.html (12 November 2016).

Rose, Jacqueline. "History is a Nightmare." *And Europe Will Be Stunned – The Polish Trilogy*. Eds. James Lingwood and Eleanor Nairne. Artangel, Ikon, Birmingham, Louisiana Museum of Modern Art, Humblebaek, Museum of Modern Art in Warsaw, Van Abbemuseum, Eindhoven, 2012. 140–145.

Sclodnick, Hilary. "Yael Bartana and Post-traumatic Culture: Utopian Reversibility and the Case of Polish National Melancholia." *International Journal of Applied Psychoanalytic Studies* 11.1 (2014): 60–74.

Segal, Uma A., Doreen Elliott, and Nazneen S. Mayadas, eds. *Immigration Worldwide: Policies, Practices, and Trends*. Oxford: Oxford University Press, 2010.

TheMarker. "Don't Scrap Home Because 'It's Easier to Live in Berlin,'" Lapid Tells Israelis. *Haaretz*, 1 October 2013. http://www.haaretz.com/news/national/premium-1.549942 (12 November 2016).

Underhill, Karen C. "Next Year in Drohobych: On the Uses of Jewish Absence." *Eastern European Politics and Societies* 23.3 (2011): 581–596.

Waren, Kate. "Rites of Return: Yael Bartana." *Metro Magazine: Media & Education Magazine* 171 (2012): 98–101.

Amir Eshel
"In His Image": On Dani Karavan's Artwork in Germany

1 Walking *The Way of Human Rights*

Fig. 1: Dani Karavan, *The Way of Human Rights* 1988–1993, Nürenberg © Roman Mensing.

In 1993, the city of Nürnberg inaugurated Dani Karavan's artwork *Die Straße der Menschenrechte – The Way of Human Rights*, which showcases the 30 articles of the Universal Declaration of Human Rights (UDHR), in 30 different languages, on 29 white concrete columns and on a building wall adjacent to an oak tree. The work was erected in the Kartäusergasse to create a meaningful artistic link between the old and new wings of the Germanisches Nationalmuseum, the Germanic National Museum. The artwork thus enacts a metaphoric connection between a past in which "Germanic" served to emphasize the superiority of race and culture and a yet to be determined future. In a speech he delivered at the inauguration, the artist reflected on his decision to situate the work in this specific location and expressed the hope that his work, and the ideals and values of the UDHR expressed therein, might open up new possibilities for Nürnberg, a city so often seen through the lens of its troubled recent history as the site of "the Nürnberg Laws [...] the Nürnberg of Hitler" (Karavan 1993).

> I walk this street with my grandmother who was barbarically murdered by the Nazis and has no grave, and I read the first article of the Universal Declaration of Human Rights, which is inscribed on the first columns [...] [in Yiddish] 'all people are born free and equal in dignity and respect.' She was murdered in 1941 on an open road, in Lwów (Lviv). And I walk this street with my uncles and aunts and cousins who vanished into smoke while I was growing up in Israel, by the dunes of Tel Aviv. (Karavan 1993)

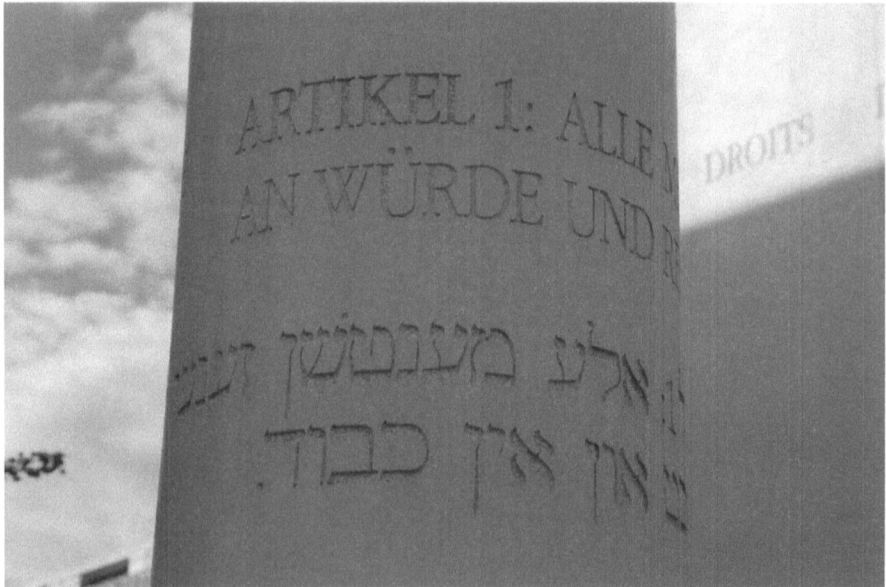

Fig. 2: Dani Karavan, *The Way of Human Rights* 1988–1993, Nürenberg © Amir Eshel.

This imagined walk with his grandmother through *The Way of Human Rights* leads the artist to recall the crimes committed by the Nazi regime – the outcome of the racial ideology and politics which were codified in 1935 by the so-called Nürnberg Race Laws. The artist's attention is not restricted, however, to the memory of discrimination and persecution, to the remembrance of the Holocaust as a catastrophic event in Jewish history. Walking this street means also experiencing the artwork and the declaration as a contemporaneous opportunity for personal and communal orientation: reading and considering statements such as "all people *are* born free and equal in dignity and respect," evokes at one and the same time Nürnberg's history during the Nazi era, the present moment as inscribed in the verb "are," and the hope for a better future, thereby drawing past, present and future together in a provocative gesture. As they face the engraved articles in the columns, visitors are invited to reflect on their impressions and on how their experience at *The Way of Human Rights* might alter their own course of action.

Karavan reiterates this fusion of past, present, and future by turning in his address to Anne Frank, saying:

> I take you by the hand, little Anne Frank – at that time, I was younger than you – and we go together this very street to the third column and the third article of the Universal Declaration of Human Rights, and we read the Dutch inscription [...] "Everyone has the right to life, liberty and security of person". And I see children, many children, whose right to life has not been observed. (Karavan 1993)

By addressing Anne Frank in the present tense ("I *take* you;" "Everyone *has* the right;" "and I *see*") Karavan ties her experience in the past, as a child victim of the Holocaust, directly to present-day children whose rights are being brutally trampled upon. Rather than passively admiring the stately circular shape of the white cement columns or the words inscribed onto them, those who walk *The Way of Human Rights* are confronted with the meaning-laden words of the UDHR. Combining the imposing visual elements of the columns and the historic text to form an aesthetic whole, Karavan's work encourages the viewer to reflect, and possibly act on all aspects of what they experience here: their thoughts and emotions, the questions and debates the artwork engenders, or the reactions of other visitors to this site.

The memory of the past and the experiences of the present finally lead Karavan to shift the register of his short speech to a general question: "Is there still a God, in spite of what had happened? Are we, humans, made in his image?" (Karavan 1993). Karavan's questions offer a fruitful perspective on *The Way of Human Rights*, as well as on some of his other major works in Germany and elsewhere. Taken together, the works I discuss in this essay are modes of poetic thinking. What they offer is not a statement based on logical certainty, a declaration backed by methodical argumentation, but rather a creative meditation on the biblical notion that humans are created "in his image" (Karavan 1993).

Karavan's reference to the Book of Genesis 1, 26–28 – "Then God said, 'Let Us make man in Our image, according to Our likeness...'" is remarkable. Raised in the Zionist-Socialist youth movement Hashomer Hatzair, Karavan is a secular Jew and his invocation of the notion that humans are created in God's image should not be read as an affirmation of a divine presence in human life. Rather, his use of this theological trope should be understood as a figure of speech that affirms the life and dignity of each and every human being as an ultimate, uncontested value that must be protected at all costs. Karavan's poetic thinking is manifested in works such as *The Way of Human Rights* through the fusion of a specific locality with material and verbal components. Together, these form a comprehensive aesthetic experience central to which are ethical and political considerations.[1] Many of Karavan's works in Germany and elsewhere draw on the history and current utility of the particular site, while also incorporating external material and verbal elements (such as biblical texts) in order to engage, whether directly or implicitly, with the notion of the human as created "in his image."

Karavan's creative engagement with the question, "Are we, humans, made in his image?" is reflected in his choice of materials, in the symbolism of the artistic arrangements, and in his careful consideration of the artworks' location.[2] It is furthermore evident in the use of language – often of Hebrew – in titles, textual elements, interviews, and public statements. His art touches on ethics and politics without prescribing conclusive judgments or choices. To be created "in his image," to envision an ethics based on human dignity today means, in Karavan's work, to question the stance of idle observation: rather than passively consume the artwork, we are encouraged to walk through the pathway created by the work of art; to engage in the kind of creative thinking that is inscribed in the artwork as well as in the UDHR; and possibly to act by caring for those who can't speak for themselves, and by encouraging others to join the walk.

---

[1] Many critics have commented on the ethical dimension of Karavan's work. Marc Scheps, for example, has suggested that Karavan's systematic approach to the location and material elements of his work represent more than an artistic method, incorporating "an ethical position" (עמדה מוסרית) (Scheps 1990, 8). In her general discussion of the ethical and political dimension of Karavan's work, Idith Zertal views his aesthetics in light of the Judaic notion of *tikkun olam*, mending the world (Zertal 2008, 356–361).

[2] On numerous occasions, Karavan underlines that his artwork emerges from the specific place or space chosen for the work by those who invite him to create. See, for example, Jacobi 2008, 364.

2 The artwork as a passage

Fig. 3: Dani Karavan, *Monument to the Negev Brigade* 1963–1968, Beer Sheva, Israel © Amir Eshel.

Fig. 4: Dani Karavan, *Monument to the Negev Brigade* 1963–1968 [detail], Beer Sheva, Israel © Amir Eshel.

Fig. 5: Dani Karavan, *Environment Made of Natural Materials and Memories*, 1977, Kassel, Germany © Studio Dani Karavan.

Like many Israeli writers and artists of his generation, Dani Karavan initially refused to travel to Germany to present his work there. Following the Second World War, Germany was seen as the home of the murderers and their descendants. It was only after his encounter with the German artist Joseph Beuys at the 1976 Venice Biennale and, later, with Manfred Schnekenburger, a German art historian and curator, that Karavan finally agreed to come to Germany. In 1977 Schnekenburger invited Karavan to present at the *Document 6* in Kassel – the epicenter of the international contemporary art scene – and Karavan accepted.[3] Karavan began working on his Kassel project, "Environment Made of Natural Materials and Memories," soon after completing his 1963–68 "Monument to the Negev Brigade," which was situated on a small hill near the southern Israeli city of Beer Sheva, and with which he had established his notion of "environmental art." *Monument to the Negev Brigade* is a work in which the material artwork itself – the cement geometrical figures and the trees Karvan planted – is but one facet of an artistic totality, which also includes the hilltop views, the soil, the natural light of the Negev desert, the wind blowing between and through the white fortress-like shapes, and – crucially – the visitors' active engagement with the

---

[3] On Karavan's encounter with Beuys, see "Biografie," in Jacobi 2008, 372.

work. Walking through the elements of this "monument," reading the different inscriptions poems, historical records of the 1948 War – the viewers become a part of the work itself. More than a shrine for fallen soldiers or yet another war memorial, this work constitutes a space of and for individual and communal experience, personal and shared reflection, conversation, and debate (a notion I will further address below).

Like *Monument to the Negev Brigade*, *Environment Made of Natural Materials and Memories* is a *Gesamtkunstwerk*, a total work of art that includes – besides the physical creation – the surrounding scenery, the visitors' engagement with the site, their experiences there, memories they bring along as they step up the stairs, and those they will take with them once they have left Kassel behind. Taken together, these early works are manifestations of a modern מקום (*makom*) – a richly connoted Hebrew noun which in biblical antiquity denoted God himself as well as a sanctified place, and which, in the wake of secularism and modernist art, gained meaning as a transformative, spiritual space where the artist and the beholder step out of the realm of habitus and ordinariness to gain an existential or an ethical perspective on their lives.[4]

Karavan's concept of public artwork as creating an environment stands in close proximity to the phenomenological philosophical tradition, especially to Martin Heidegger's ideas in "The Origin of the Work of Art" and to Hannah Arendt's notions of "plurality," "natality" and "insertion" (to which I will turn later in this essay). For Heidegger, meaningful artworks transcend the realm of mimesis – the attempt to represent a world outside the work itself. Heidegger rejects any separation of "objective" work and "subjective" viewer, artistic artifact and passive beholder. Rather than giving those who engage the artwork an external image of what is, the artwork first emerges *through* our active encounter and engagement with it. For Heidegger, the artwork "opens up" a space (Heidegger 2001, 40). A work of art is never external to its creator, location, materials, and the audience's experience in the encounter. As poiesis, that is, as a verbal, visual, or material assemblage, the artwork is not an image *of* what *is*, but rather constitutes the transformation of that which is. Thus, the artwork reshapes the material and metaphorical worlds we inhabit and ultimately transforms us.

Heidegger offers as examples Van Gogh's 1886 "A Pair of Shoes" and – more relevant to our discussion of Dani Karavan – an edifice, a Greek temple. The

---

[4] On Karavan's notion of his artwork as *makom*, see Jacobi 2008, 10–11. See also Pierre Restany 1992, 76–80; Mordechai Omer 2008, 13. On the notion of *makom* in Judaic thought and Jewish literature, see Eshel 2003.

temple, Heidegger notes, "portrays nothing" (2001, 40). It stands in the middle of a rock-cleft valley. Upon completion of its construction, the temple gave the space it now inhabits its specific, new shape. "Standing there (*dastehend*)," the temple "gives to things their look and to men *their outlook on themselves*" (Heidegger 2001, 42). The artwork thus "set[s] up" a world and "[…] holds open the Open of the world" (Heidegger 2001, 44). The work of art is an event: "In the midst of being as a whole an open place occurs. There is a clearing, a lighting…." This clearing, in turn, gives those among us who choose to engage actively with the work of art the opportunity to fashion ourselves anew. In Heidegger's own words, it "grants and guarantees to us humans *a passage to those beings that we ourselves are not*, and access to the being that we ourselves are" (Heidegger 2001, 51).

The critic and art historian Pierre Restany places Dani Karavan's work in close proximity to Heidegger's view of art when he states that, for Karavan, "Art is not something to be 'applied,' but must be an integral part of the site in every respect, from the materials to the forms and the lighting" (Restany 1992, 26). He thus echoes Heidegger's phenomenological notion of the artwork as never separated from its totality, which includes artist, materials, location, and audience. Restany rightly notes that Dani Karavan's oeuvre "precludes all dualistic oppositions or binary models: body/soul, emotion/intellect, signifier/signified" (1992, 16). Karavan's aesthetics, Restany concludes, is "generalized ontology: the self is the world, man is god, the Messiah is in each and every one of us" (Restany 1992, 16).

Karavan's *Environment Made of Natural Materials and Memories* in Kassel, for example, draws together the existing material and visual elements of its specific location, such as the trees and meadows in the surrounding parks, with new, carefully selected inserted elements. Among these new elements are abstract vertical walls and a staircase made of white cement blocks. The title's reference to "Memories" suggests that the work draws not only on the memories of the artist, but also on those of its potential audience, which play a crucial role in shaping the artwork. In Heidegger's terms, the work transforms the site itself, giving the park a new "look". Moreover, it offers visitors, who might utilize the space in order to sit, relax, and think or converse with others, a new "outlook on themselves." It opens to them "the Open of the world," and – as an artistic event that includes them as full participants – it also provides them "a passage to those beings" who they "are not" yet, access to that which they themselves may choose to become.

3 The sign of plurality

Fig. 6: Dani Karavan, *Ma'alot* 1982–1986, Köln [view from the bank of the Rhine] © Amir Eshel.

In Karavan's subsequent artwork in Germany, the idea of the transformative capacity of the artwork is often tied to its place in the public realm, and thus to politics and ethics. Beginning with *Ma'alot* in Köln (1980–1986), some of the artist's most significant works develop the idea of the artwork as "a passage to those beings" we are not yet but can become by engaging language, specifically Hebrew. The Hebrew name of the artwork shapes a prominent German public space anew, bringing Hebrew, with its linguistic and cultural inheritance, into an urban space which has thus far been marked only by German street names and buildings (such as the cathedral), and by Christian theology and history. Entering this space and encountering its Hebrew name, the linguistic and potential experiential vocabulary of visitors and passersby grows, even if only by uttering what may seem to be a strange, "foreign" name. Using a warm carpet of red bricks which encompasses the large terrain from the Rheine to the Köln cathedral, *Ma'alot* brings together into one visual-topographic frame, one spatial context, the 13th century gothic Kölner Dom (the Cologne Cathedral), the Heinrich-Böll-Platz (named after the famous post Second World War writer), the contemporary *Ludwig Museum*, the Rhine with its rich, troubled history, and the Köln train station. The work blends the lively red of bricks with serpentine white concrete borderlines. It enriches what used to be a mere transitory space with elegant circular shapes and striking straight lines. Drawing on a variety of sourced materials including iron and marble, the work also makes use of natural local elements such as the water of the Rhine or the falling rain as it accumulates in little ponds.

Ma'alot is a public "makom," a cohesive, communal place which invites those who enter it to dwell therein. It summons them to inhabit this place for a while, to observe the sculpture made of six giant granite and iron blocks set along the path, to reflect, to interact with others. Dwelling is closely associated in *Ma'alot* with memory and history. Visually uniting the Cathedral and the *Ludwig Museum*, the Rhine and the train station, the work draws together past, present, and future: Köln's Roman and Christian heritage as inscribed in the Cathedral is just as contemporaneous here as the destruction of the city through massive air raids during the Second World War, or the deportation of the city's Jewish population to Lodz, to Theresienstadt, and from there to the extermination camps in Poland. The straight lines running from the six-cube granite structure toward the Cathedral and through the rounded staircase toward a circular pond at the bottom of the stairs, for example, are made of old train tracks similar to those which were used to deport Jews from Cologne and other cities to their deaths.

Fig. 7: Dani Karavan, *Ma'alot* 1982–1986, Köln [view of the sculpture] © Amir Eshel.

Fig. 8: Dani Karavan, *Ma'alot* 1982–1986, Köln [view of circular pond, bottom of the stairs]
© Amir Eshel.

Karavan has rejected suggestions that the train tracks and the six granite and iron blocks that comprise the abstract, gigantic staircase at the center of *Ma'alot* represent the six million Jewish victims of the Holocaust, and that *Ma'alot* as a whole is an "illustration of history" (1986, 32).[5] Yet, he also acknowledged that his work does not prescribe the viewer's experience. Like his later works in Germany, *Ma'alot* is an ongoing, multifaceted, and polyphonic creation in which the artist's intentions are but one voice in a rich choir in which a broad array of voices participate equally. Included in this choir are Karavan's collaborators in Köln's city hall, urban architects, visitors to the site, passersby, and others who, together, create *Ma'alot* as an aesthetic experience (Karavan 1986, 31). Karavan tellingly emphasized that *Ma'alot* does not exist "without the people for whom it was made" – that is, it depends upon the voices of others, and what they bring to the work of art, with their multiple, at times conflicting memories, experiences,

---

5 The multivalence of the number six in conjunction with the noun *maalot* is reflected, for example in the description of King Solomon's grandeur and wisdom in Kings I, 10. There we read that King Solomon made a great throne covered with ivory and overlaid with fine gold and that the throne had "six steps" and that on both sides of the seat were armrests, with a lion standing beside each of them and thus that twelve lions stood on the six steps, one at either end of each step. "Nothing like it had ever been made for any other kingdom."

fantasies, thoughts, and reactions (1986, 34). Neither didactic nor prescriptive, *Ma'alot*, much like Karavan's other works, respects what Heidegger called the "Open of the world," and as such remains committed to the ideals of the avant-garde and the conceptual art movement.

Ma'alot's capacity to serve as an open space for personal and communal reflection and experience is inscribed in its title, which inserts into a German public space a Hebrew word rich with historical and cultural associations. *Ma'alot* originates in Psalms, 120–134 – the so-called Songs of Ascents (שירי המעלות) – songs that may have been sung by the priests of the Jewish temple as they ascended the steps leading to the holy sanctuary (Liebreich 1995). These psalms address the themes of exile and homecoming, despair and hope, and personal and communal ethics. With its steps leading from the Rhine to the city and the biblical allusions contained in its name, *Ma'alot* creates an invisible line – a meridian, one may say – linking Köln and Jerusalem, where the Song of Ascents were once sung. *Ma'alot* is thus not only a reconfiguration of a particular urban space but also the creation of a metaphorical "makom," a new space altogether – in which German and Jewish/Hebrew culture can co-exist.

The Hebrew noun מעלה (*ma'ala*) and its plural form מעלות (*ma'alot*) both point to the ethical and political dimension of Karavan's work in Köln. *Ma'ala* denotes merit, value, and virtue (Karavan 1986, 36). Inhabiting this environment may involve rethinking one's own values, principles, and ideals. Yet *Ma'alot* also serves as a space to consider and reflect on communal ethics. The communal has been inscribed in this work from the beginning; ever since its inauguration, *Ma'alot* has encouraged public experience and interaction as the site of concerts, performances, commemorative events, group walks and meditation.[6] When the artwork suffered physical erosion, a grass-roots group of citizens came together to demand that the city of Köln ensure its preservation and integrity.[7] Like so many of Karavan's works, *Ma'alot*, too, fuses aesthetic experience with the realms of ethics and politics.

By "politics" I do not mean the overt political meaning inscribed in some of Karavan's works, but rather the philosophical dimension of the political as outlined by Hannah Arendt. For Arendt, the human condition is predicated on "natality," and "plurality." "Natality" marks for Arendt our "ontologically rooted" capacity – as creatures born into life – to begin, to set off, to take meaningful political actions (Arendt 1958, 247). Patricia Bowen-Moore rightly ties Arendt's "natality" to futurity: to the human capacity to relate actively to the future with its promises and threats alike through such actions (Bowen-Moore, 1989, 18–19).

---

[6] See http://maalot25.de/wordpress/maalot-das-kunstwerk-als-kolner-raum-fur-kulturelle-gestaltung/ (26 February 2017).

[7] See http://maalot25.de/wordpress/titelseite/beispiel-seite/ (14 October 2015).

"Plurality" denotes in Arendt's vocabulary the fact that humans are born into an already existing communal sphere, and "the human condition of plurality" is "*the conditio per quam* [Condition by means] – of all political life" (Arendt 1958, 7). Politics is thus the range of actions in which human beings engage as they gradually become a fully integrated part of the civic fabric they entered upon birth. While Arendt's definition of meaningful human action is often confined to the realm of politics, there are clear indications in her work that action is hardly divorced from aesthetics. The link between politics and the arts lies in Arendt's notion of "insertion." In *The Human Condition* she famously states: "With word and deed we insert ourselves into the human world, and this insertion is like a second birth, in which we confirm and take upon ourselves the naked fact of our original physical appearance" (Arendt 1958, 176–177). Arendt's notion of insertion "with word and deed" is primarily related to political speech or action.

Karavan's public artworks suggest additional possibilities for the kinds of words and actions that can move between and thus link the realm of art and that of politics.[8] The environments that Karavan creates are thoroughly public and thus always already in the realm of plurality, of the political: they are spaces that emerge from a lengthy process of planning, deliberation, and decision-making.[9] Once completed, the works themselves open up spaces in which humans experience what Arendt calls plurality; they present themselves to and interact with others in a variety of ways. Long after works such as *Ma'alot* are set in place, they continue to challenge those involved in their creation – city officials, citizens, and visitors to the site. Connoting in its title human merit and virtue, *Ma'alot* captures the process by which a community examines its values, for example, the importance it attaches to its public spaces where citizens come together to encounter each other and to present themselves in the public sphere.

There is a clear affinity between Arendt's notion of insertion and Karavan's "environments," as he often calls his public artworks. Karavan's creations and his stated belief in art's ability to actively engage viewers echoes Arendt's assertion that: "Every birth marks the possibility of 'mending' the world [*eine Garantie des Heilens in der Welt*], the possibility of salvation [*Erlösung*] for those who are no longer a beginning – the living" (Arendt 2002, 1:208). Arendt's "possibility" points to the potentiality Karavan's works *conceptually* reflect: his constellations of found materials, such as train-tracks; evocative titles, like *Ma'alot;* and provocation of public debates all model our capacity as humans to shape and reshape – for good or for bad – our physical and communal environments. With "possibility" Arendt

---

8 I present my reading of Hannah Arendt's notion of "insertion" in detail in Amir Eshel, "Hannah Arendts Politik und Poetik der Einfügung" (Eshel 2014, 151–182).
9 See Zertal 2008.

underscores the fact that we are offered no guarantees. Nothing ensures that we will, in fact, give a new form to our natural and human circumstances and that we can, finally, "mend the world". However, "possibility" also indicates, as do Karavan's works, that if we choose to exercise our capacity to act as agents of our history, for example by bringing about "mending," we may in fact succeed. Like Karavan, Arendt is fully aware of humanity's capacity for evil; at the same time, like Karavan, she offers us a reason to hope. Her work expresses philosophically what Karavan seeks to communicate through his art: the notion that we humans may opt for more reflective, more ethically aware modes of being in the world.

4 Encounter: the artwork, politics and ethics

The image of human beings coming together to experience plurality and engage with each other also marks Karavan's "Mifgash–Herrenabend" (2005; Encounter – A Gentlemen's Evening) in the Garden of Villa Lemm, the Piepenbrock family's residence in Berlin. The work is ensconced in a large estate located on the banks of the river Havel, which was designed and built between 1907 and 1913 by the famous Berlin architect Max Werner (1877–1933) for the manufacturer Otto Lemm.

Fig. 9: Dani Karavan, *Mifgash–Herrenabend* 2004–2006, Villa Lemm, Berlin © Studio Dani Karavan.

In the course of its rich history, the majestic Villa Lemm has served as the home of several prominent owners, including the renowned Jewish-Hungarian physician János Plesh (1878–1957), who regularly hosted his good friend Albert Einstein on the premises.

"Mifgash–Herrenabend" consists of a flat circle of Carrara marble, approximately fifteen feet in diameter, atop which stands a circular set of nine marble chairs. As the title suggests, the work invokes a מפגש, the Hebrew word for an encounter, a gathering. On the backs of the chairs, Karavan engraved the names of the nine men who gathered here in February 1927 at the behest of János Plesh for an evening of personal and intellectual exchange: the composers Arthur Schnabel (1882–1951) and Fritz Kreisler (1875–1962); the painters Max Slevogt (1868–1932) and Emil Orlik (1870–1932); the chemist Fritz Haber (1868–1934); the legal scholar and politician Ulrich Graf Brockendorff-Rantzau (who was the first Foreign Minister of the Weimar Republic, 1869–1929); Josef Grünberg (a fried of János Plesh); and Albert Einstein (Jacobi 2008, 345). The work thus evokes a moment in history when Germans and Jews could still engage as equals in conversations about culture, politics, and the natural sciences. That distant gathering reflected the cultural and scientific renaissance of the interwar period at its best. "Mifgash–Herrenabend" is hardly confined, however, to a remembrance of things past. The ring of marble chairs is intended for use by visitors who, when seated, are surrounded by the large, round marble disc, and thus form a human circle. The circle is a global symbol denoting a benevolent, celestial order. Karavan's circle should not, however, be read as an affirmation of a religious or metaphysical moral system. Rather, his circle of uniformly sized chairs captures what Arendt calls the condition of plurality.[10]

Visitors to this site may choose to inhabit the space and to take up as a topic for conversation the words of Albert Einstein that appear here, in both German and English, etched into the circular marble plate which serves as the foundation of the artwork: "Only actions can give beauty and dignity to life" (1981, 95). The words are taken from Einstein's famous "Letter to a Minister," in which he writes:

> The most important human endeavor is the striving for morality in our actions. Our inner balance and even our very existence depend on it. Only morality in our actions can give beauty and dignity to life. To make this a living force and bring it to clear consciousness is perhaps the foremost task of education. The foundation of morality should not be made dependent on myth nor tied to any authority lest doubt about the myth or about the legitimacy of the authority imperil the foundation of sound judgment and action. (1981, 95)

---

10 See Chevalier 1994.

An assemblage of physical, spatial, and textual components, "Mifgash–Herrenabend" illustrates and expands Einstein's words: the human circle can only endure when ethics and politics are intertwined, when there is, to quote Einstein, "morality in our actions." Karavan's chairs physically rest on this idea. Ensuring "dignity," that is, the notion of humanity as created "in his image," requires both an ethical stance and the will to act in the political realm.

The consequences of failing to safeguard the fabric of moral politics are inscribed in another artwork Karavan began realizing in 2005 in Berlin – "The Memorial to the Sinti and Roma Victims of National Socialism."

The round pool in the middle of this space resembles a bottomless, dark pit. A black triangular block in the pond evokes the black or brown triangles the Sinti and Roma were forced to wear during the Nazi era. This symbol of persecution is accompanied by a sign of renewal: a flower. When the flower atop the triangular stone withers it is replaced by a fresh one. At the edge of the pond visitors can read the words of the poem "Auschwitz" by Rom Santino Spinelli: "Sunken in face / extinguished eyes / cold lips / silence / a torn heart / without breath / without words /

Fig. 10: Dani Karavan, *Memorial to the Sinti and Roma Victims of National Socialism* 2012, Berlin © Amir Eshel.

no tears."[11] The pond is surrounded by flat stepping stones, some of which bear the names of the concentration camps in which Sinti and Roma were murdered.

This is a quiet space of remembrance and contemplation. In Karavan's words: "Only tears, only water, surrounded by the survivors, by those who remember what happened, by those who know the horror as well as those who never experienced it. They are reflected, upside down, in the water of the deep, black pit, covered by the sky – the water, the tears" (Endlich 2013, 24–25). As in *The Way of Human Rights* and *Ma'alot*, remembrance of the Nazi past is accompanied by decisive futural elements. The dark circle anticipates a reestablishing of the human circle through individual human beings standing around the pond and partially filling the void with their reflections. Plurality and politics are inseparable in this artwork: the memorial is located at Simsonweg in Berlin's Tiergarten, steps away from the German parliament, the Reichstag. An image of the Reichstag is reflected in the pond at various vantage points, thus evoking the realm of politics, which is, of course, implicated in the crimes and in the remembrance of them. The murder of the Sinti and Roma resulted from the political will and deeds of a few, and the unwillingness of many others to act. More recently, politics has played a role in the commemoration of these crimes. Indeed, it was only after lengthy and heated debates that the German government decided, in 1992, to commission the memorial, which was finally inaugurated in 2012.

The challenge of "sound judgment and action" that Einstein invoked and that Karavan's works in Berlin take on, is similarly reflected in *Tzaphon*, located at the entrance to the parliament of the German state of North Rhine-Westphalia in Düsseldorf.

The material choice and the shape of *Tzaphon* are telling. The work consists of a gigantic fifty-foot cast iron circle through which runs a shaft, a straight line, from north to south, from bottom to top, generating motion and energy. The cast iron relates to the tradition and place of the heavy metal industry in North Rhine-Westphalia while the circular form of the plate merges seamlessly with the rounded architectonic shape of the parliament building itself. Karavan placed in the shaft what has by now become a hallmark of his artwork in Germany: a set of train tracks. The dynamism of the artwork and the liveliness of the political process inside the building are thus informed by the traces of history.

Karavan has noted on multiple occasions that he is a politically involved citizen, yet insists that his work should not be mistaken for political art

---

[11] See http://www.stiftung-denkmal.de/en/memorials/sinti-and-roma-memorial/poem-by-santino-spinelli.html (26 February 2017).

Fig. 11: Dani Karavan, *Tzaphon* 1990, Düsseldorf © Studio Dani Karavan.

(Karavan 2008, 11). Avoiding didactic or political message, the Hebrew name of the work, *Tzaphon* צפון ("north") invokes Polaris (in Hebrew כוכב הצפון, literally 'the north star') and thus points metaphorically to personal and communal orientation – the very foundation of politics. Karavan's title echoes Hannah Arendt's understanding of politics as the personal and communal activity by which we acknowledge our plurality by negotiating our needs and concerns with others. This complex process takes into consideration that all humans are indeed different, and thus that we need to navigate, align, and realign our positions in view of the common cause – the thriving of the polity – as seamen once related to Polaris. The round sculpture and the line which runs through it point the visitors to the building's entrance, and invite them to cross the threshold between the realm of the personal and what Arendt calls plurality, that is, the public space of the parliament as the incarnation of a meaningful communal life.

Politics and ethics inhere in the very title of this work: the semantic field of *Tzaphon* includes "matspen" (compass) and "matspoon" (conscience). The title opens up a space of and for reflection on the proposition that politics as practiced in the parliament should involve a communal path that is oriented around conscience and ethics.

While *Tzaphon* frames the task of personal and communal orientation through the word "north," Karavan's work *Mizrach*, meaning "east" (1997–2005), in Regensburg turns to the east and touches on questions of memory, history,

"In His Image": On Dani Karavan's Artwork in Germany — 229

Fig. 12: Dani Karavan, *Mizrach* 1997–2005, Regensburg © Uwe Moosburger.

and public engagement at the intersection of east and west, "Morgen-" and "Abendland," that is, orient and occident.

Mizrach is located at the Neupfarrplatz, right by the Lutheran church Neupfarrkirche. It stands at the center of the large area that served as the Jewish quarter in Regensburg beginning with the arrival of Jews in the city in the 10th century up until their expulsion in 1519. Marking the exact location of the old Regensburg synagogue, *Mizrach* commemorates the structure that was once the spiritual center of Regensburg's vibrant Jewish community until (following the death of Emperor Maximilian I, 1458–1519) that community was deemed undesirable and forcibly expelled. The work thus also evokes a political act: the decree passed by Regensburg's city council on 12 January 1519 to expel all Jews from the city within two weeks.

Using white cement blocks, Karavan's work traces the precise foundations of the old synagogue. Marking the location of the holy ark where the Torah was housed, at the eastern perimeter of the site, the point closest to Jerusalem, is a single, elevated block that bears the Hebrew inscription מזרח. The multivalency of the title evokes the memory of Jerusalem, the city where the Jewish temple stood until its destruction in 70 CE. It also invites visitors to reflect on the city's Jewish past, and on the obliteration of that past. As in the works previously discussed, Karavan's *Mizrach* is not restricted to memorializing a traumatic past. Rather, as a public signpost at the site states, in three languages, the work is intended as an "Ort der Begegnung," a "Place of Encounter," "מקום מפגש" in which "people of all religions come together ... a sign and food for thought for their children and children's children."

Like *Ma'alot* and *Tzaphon*, *Mizrach* is multilingual: the Latin letters display a Hebrew word, thus symbolically reversing the political act of expulsion by bringing back into the German public space the Hebrew used in prayer by Regensburg's Jewish community.

In addition to its literal meaning (east), and the fact that it points towards Jerusalem, the name מזרח also marks symbolically the beginning of the day's cycle – the rising of the sun – and denotes through the Latin "orient" (also referring to the east) the possibility of personal and communal orientation. Karavan has also pointed to the modes in which this orientation may take place. In the inauguration ceremony for *Mizrach* in 2005 he said:

> This place [*Mizrach*] can serve as a stage where people perform, read poetry, and play music or theatre. It is a cultural space in the middle of the city. A part of everyday life and not a place which should remind of the hate and the destruction [*Teil des Alltags, nicht ein Ort an dem man sich an Hass und Zerstörung erinnern soll*]. (*Misrach* 2005)

Karavan's insistence that this is "not a place in which one should only remember hate and destruction" is crucial to understanding the futural dimension of Karavan's work in Regensburg and elsewhere. The past is remembered in Regensburg since *Mizrach* displays the outline of the shattered synagogue. Yet, remembrance is

Fig. 13: Dani Karavan, *Mizrach* 1997–2005, Regensburg © Amir Eshel.

placed here in clear and provocative conversation with the present and the future, since the work invites visitors to utilize the white concrete blocks as a space in which to rest, gather, and engage in conversation and debate. Remembering the expulsion of Jews who used to pray facing the east, toward *Mizrach*, those who dwell today in Karavan's public space may choose to reflect on present day cases of religiously and ethnically motivated discrimination or even expulsion. In other words, *Mizrach* offers visitors the opportunity to reflect on their point of departure as citizens of a polity and on how they may choose to evolve while considering the history of this very space.

5 The artwork and futurity

To elaborate on what I view as the "futural" element of *Mizrach,* as well as many of Karavan's public artworks in Germany and elsewhere, I would like to return now to *The Way of Human Rights*. Karavan began working on this project in 1989, while completing *Mizrach*. The challenge he faced in Nürnberg was to establish a meaningful architectural bridge between the old and the new wing of the city's prestigious Germanisches Nationalmuseum. Founded in 1852, the museum houses the largest collection of Germanic cultural history in the world. It was initiated by the Franconian nobleman Hans Freiherr von und zu Aufseß with the romantic-national vision of establishing "a well-ordered general repertory of the entire source material for German history, literature and art."[12] This emphasis on Germanic cultural history could not have been retained in light of Nürnberg's role during National Socialism. The museum proclaims today that it does not wish merely to present a regimented roadmap through Germanic cultural history, but also "to investigate[s] art and culture in German-speaking areas in an internationally integrated and innovative way, offering educational experiences in dialogue form."[13] Created by the internationally renowned Karavan, *The Way of Human Rights*, with its engraved white columns and displays in multiple languages, is thus in dialogue with the museum's new

---

12 See http://www.gnm.de/en/museum/about-us/ (26 February 2017).
13 The museum's mission statement goes on to revise the institution's original romantic-national scheme with a linguistic one, by stating: "The word 'germanisch' in the museum's name refers to the "Germanic cultural area," i.e. those areas in which German was spoken at one time. The founding of the museum intended to document the unity of the German-speaking cultural regions, specifically in view of the failed political unification of German states in 1848 – a politically and culturally forward-looking vision." See http://www.gnm.de/en/museum/about-us/ (26 February 2017).

vision, and with a broad array of aesthetic-structural ideas that span from ancient Egyptian architecture to post-Second World War modernism.[14] Columns were often used in antiquity to support the roofs or crests of large public structures such as palaces and temples. Resembling an erect human body and often made of costly materials such as marble, they were seen as giving expression to the ability to carry a substantial weight, and thus projecting spiritual, religious, or political potency. Often adorned with elaborate capitals and other ornaments, columns reflected the capacity of the mighty to bring to fruition grand architectonic and political visions. Echoing this tradition, yet leaving its elitist legacy behind, Karavan's imposing columns set their content, the engraved articles, at a respectful distance from viewers while still ensuring that they are readable, thus making the articles of the declaration effortlessly accessible for all.

If Franz Kafka's famous parable "Before the Law" points to the perils of a detached juridical system deprived of any relation to humans and their concerns, *The Way of Human Rights* presents in form and content an innovative, global legal discourse that is eminently reachable. The columns project at one and the same time the festive, spiritual dimension associated with ancient columns, and, in their lack of adornment and ornamentation, a modern, minimalist aesthetic which suggests practical use. Like the Greek temple Heidegger describes, they "portray nothing" (cf. 2001, 40). Instead, the inscription of the Universal Declaration of Human Rights the foundation of a metaphorical edifice that has yet to be realized – a legal and political structure that places all human beings, irrespective of age, origin and personal circumstances at its center. We visitors and beholders are invited to consider what we would want to place atop the columns, how we would utilize the foundation in our own construction of an ethical and political framework for the future. With Heidegger, we may say that the columns wish to give Nürnberg's citizens and visitors a new "outlook on themselves" (Heidegger 2001, 42); that they grant and guarantee to them "*a passage to those beings that we ourselves are not, and access to the being that we ourselves are*" (Heidegger 2001, 51).

And yet, the futurity of Karavan's artwork remains hardly as abstract as Heidegger's notion of a "passage." Rather, it is overtly non-nationalist as it calls on viewers and visitors to consider, with Hannah Arendt's words, how they may insert themselves, in word and deed, into the human world. The font size of each inscription is identical across all languages. Thus, while German nationalism (which is, of course remembered in the adjacent Germanisches Nationalmuseum)

---

[14] On the history of columns, see Rykwert 1996.

"In His Image": On Dani Karavan's Artwork in Germany — **233**

Fig. 14: Dani Karavan, *The Way of Human Rights* 1988–1993, Nürnberg © Amir Eshel.

viewed the German language as the superior expression of Germans as an advanced "Sprachnation" (an exceptional nation based in an exalted language), *The Way of Human Rights* sets German as one language among others, all of them equally valuable means for connection and communication.[15] The very notion of a single, coherent, stable Germanic culture based in a cohesive language is confronted by the idea driving The Universal Declaration of Human Rights: the notion of a meta-language across histories, cultures, and locations, a language that protects the integrity and lives of all humans.

Emerging from the experiences of totalitarianism and genocide, the Declaration represents the attempt to develop a global framework of rights to which all humans are inherently entitled. Its articles lay the foundation for subsequent international treaties, regional human rights instruments, national constitutions, and other laws. Karavan's work inscribes through its multilingualism the thrust of this very idea. The thirty columns illustrate how the experiences of German and European nationalism, specifically the ideology of a superior race, are confronted in the Declaration by the idea of a diverse humanity in which the rights of all are protected.

The futurity of *The Way of Human Rights* is further reflected in its open structure: the path visitors choose to take through the street is not predetermined, and neither, of course, are their associations, conversations, or reactions to the inscription on the columns. Instead, they are encouraged to navigate freely through the terrain, to orient themselves as they wish. Indeed, nothing in Karavan's work indicates that the Universal Declaration of Human Rights itself wields an ultimate path one has to take, a finite ethical authority. Rather, the work suggests that the Declaration is malleable and can be debated with others, rearranged, extended, even rewritten. The suggested discourse of the Declaration is a critical attempt, one conceivable point of departure for ethical and political orientation. This openness is displayed in another inscription engraved in Hebrew at the arc of one of the entrances: the sixth of the Ten Commandments, "Thou shalt not kill":

לא תרצח.

This engraving stands in dialogue with the inscriptions on the columns and suggests that we have at our disposal multiple codes of ethical and political conduct, and that it is ultimately up to us to form our own personal and communal ethical codes and to orient our life's path accordingly.

This aesthetic approach to public spaces as they may present legal documents and thus engender political and ethical discourse underlies also Karavan's *Grundgesetz 49* (Basic Law 49). Located on the Spree promenade in Berlin, within short walking distance of the German parliament, *Basic Law 49* features nineteen

---

15 On the notion of "Spachnation" in German nationalism, see Koselleck 1992.

Fig. 15: Dani Karavan, *The Way of Human Rights* 1988–1993, Nürnberg © Amir Eshel.

transparent glass plates, each about three meters high, and each presenting the articles of the German Basic Law, the German constitution, starting with the first article, which begins with the words "Human dignity shall be uninfringeable. To respect and protect it shall be the duty of all state authority."

These words can be easily read both by those who enjoy the promenade and by those who inhabit the house behind the glass plates – the Jakob-Kaiser-Haus. Named for Jakob Kaiser, a Christian member of the trade unions and an active member of the German anti-Hitler resistance, the building houses some sixty percent of the German parliament members. Karavan's *Basic Law 49* enjoins the parliamentarians to reflect on the foundational moral values of postwar Germany as they engage in the daily business of politics. From the other side, passersby look at the offices of their representatives through the prism of the constitution. They are invited to stop for a while; to take measure of the work done on the other side of the glass wall; to read, to reflect, to converse with others on the meaning of human dignity and on what it would take to protect it. The subtle yet distinct glass plates clearly display in the form of what Karavan calls an "environment" what Arendt called human "natality" our "ontologically rooted" capacity – as creatures born into life – to begin, to set off, to take a meaningful political action (Arendt 1958, 247), such as the adoption of a constitution which places human dignity, the notion of the sacredness of human life as its core principle.

Fig. 16: Dani Karavan, *Basic Law 49*, Berlin © Amir Eshel.

Both the members of the parliament and those who are merely strolling along the promenade may decide to continue their walk in the direction of the German Reichstag. It is there by the southern section of the Reichstag that they may encounter Karavan's earlier mentioned *Memorial to the Sinti and Roma Victims of National Socialism*. This work would remind them of what transpired at a time when human dignity was not protected. Both *The Way of Human Rights* and *Basic Law 49* are a momentous reminder of what is liable to happen when, as in Kafka's *The Trial*, the law is invisible, impenetrable. Both works remind visitors and beholders of Germany's recent past, yet they are also future-oriented meditations on communal values and political responsibilities in Germany and around the world. They invite us to consider which path we may choose as individuals and as a political community, or, in Arendt's words, how we may choose to insert ourselves into the world.

In 2013, Karavan indicated what such a personal and communal orientation could look like when he delivered a speech on the twentieth anniversary of the inauguration of *The Way of Human Rights*. In this speech, he specifically referred to the fifteenth column and its Hebrew inscription (here, in translation into English): "Everyone has the right to a nationality. No one shall be arbitrarily deprived of his nationality nor denied the right to change his nationality" (Karavan 2013). The article evokes the statelessness of Jews over the millennia, and especially during the Holocaust.

As Karavan underlined in his address, statelessness is hardly unique to Jews. Indeed, the state of Israel, as he noted, still needs to recognize the rights of Palestinians to their own state: "We, Israelis, have also signed this article. Maybe it's time to realize this signature by recognizing the right of Palestinians for their own homeland and to recognize their state. For a life in freedom and dignity" (Karavan 2013). Karavan concluded his address by noting the power of art to change the perception of a city such as Nürnberg in the eyes of the world, to turn a curse into a hope.

Karavan's concluding remarks may also shed light on his 1993 Nürnberg speech referred to earlier, in which he metaphorically addressed his grandmother and Anne Frank. Karavan points to what he sees as the capacity of the arts to transform viewers from passive observers and consumers into active participants in the act of creation. The article on the fifteenth column is not a mere object of aesthetic pleasure or consumption. Rather, it is an invitation to relate actively to what is in front of us and in this way to become involved participants in our respective political circumstances. This expansive notion of the artistic experience has been particularly effective in Nürnberg, which has undergone a series of transformations since the 1993 inauguration of *The Way of Human Rights*. Inspired by Karavan's work, the mayor of Nürnberg, Dr. Peter Schönlein, established an International Nuremberg Human Rights Award in 1993. Two years later, a municipal Human Rights Office was instituted. And, since 1999, Nürnberg has hosted the biennial Nuremberg International Human Rights Film Festival. Alongside the municipal activities, an independent Human Right Center was established to support the defense of human rights throughout the world (http://www.menschenrechte.org/lang/en/ueber-uns).

Dani Karavan's work consists of the insertion of words and artistic deeds into the public sphere in the vein of what I see as Hannah Arendt's "poetics and politics of insertion" (Eshel 2014, 151–61). In works such as *The Way of Human Rights* and others considered in this essay, Karavan asks, "are we created in his image?" His work implicitly answers this question by suggesting that if we humans are indeed to hold on to the idea of being "created in his image," to the inviolability of human life and dignity, then we must engage with our own words and deeds in the worlds we inhabit. His artistic insertions model and encourage such a turn from idle observation to active participation. Karavan himself does this through his artwork, but also through his political activism. A member of the board of בצלם *B'TSELEM* – The Israeli Information Center for Human Rights in the Occupied Territories – his words and deeds are attempts to realize the promise of "in his image," the ethical demands of the ancient biblical conception of human life and dignity as fundamentally sacred, always calling on us to protect it through our actions.

Works cited

Arendt, Hannah. *The Human Condition*. Chicago: University of Chicago Press, 1958.
Arendt, Hannah. *Denktagebuch: 1950–1973*. Eds. Ursula Ludz and Ingeborg Nordmann. 2 vols. Munich: Piper Verlag, 2002.
Bowen-Moore, Patricia. *Hannah Arendt's Philosophy of Natality*. Basingstoke, Hampshire: Macmillan, 1989.
Chevalier, Jean. "Circle." in Jean Chevalier, Alain Gheerbrant, *The Penguin Dictionary of Symbols*. Trans. John Buchanan-Brown. London et al: Penguin, 1994. 195–200.
Einstein, Albert. *The Human Side*. Eds. Helen Dukas and Banesh Hoffman. Princeton, NJ: Princeton University Press, 1981, 95.
Endlich, Stefanie. "'Homage to the Sinti and Roma.'" Kunststadt Stadtkunst, Nr. 60, 2013, 24–25. Available also at http://www.bbk-kulturwerk.de/con/kulturwerk/upload/kioer/kssk/skks_60_web.pdf (26 February, 2017).
Eshel, Amir. "Between Cosmos and Makom. Inhabiting the World and Searching for the Sacred Space in Jewish Literature." *Jewish Social Studies* 9.3 (2003): 121–138.
Eshel, Amir. "Hannah Arendts Politik und Poetik der Einfügung." *Hannah Arendt zwischen den Disziplinen*. Eds. Ulrich Baer and Amir Eshel. Göttingen: Wallstein Verlag, 2014. 151–182.
Heidegger, Martin. "The Origin of the Work of Art." *Poetry, Language, Thought*. Trans. Albert Hofstadter. Perennial Classics ed. New York: Perennial Classics, 2001. 15–87.
Jacobi, Fritz. "Das Grundgesetz 49 und Mifgash – Herrenabend – Zwei Berliner Werke von Dani Karavan," in Karavan, Dani., Jacobi, Fritz., Omer, Mordechai., Reuter, Jule., and Karavan Cohen, Noa. *Dani Karavan: Retrospektive*. Berlin: Wasmuth, 2008. 344–347.
Karavan, Dani. "20 Jahre Strasse der Menschenrechte" (24 October 2013). https://www.nuernberg.de/imperia/md/menschenrechte/dokumente/rede_karavan_festakt_20_jahre_24okt_2013-2-de.pdf (21 October 2015).
Karavan, Dani. "Gedanken über einen Weg." in in Karavan, Dani., Jacobi, Fritz., Omer, Mordechai., Reuter, Jule., and Karavan Cohen, Noa. *Dani Karavan: Retrospektive*. Berlin: Wasmuth, 2008, 10–11.
Karavan, Dani. "Ma'a lot." Brockhaus, Christoph. *Ma'alot, Museumsplatz Köln, 1979–1986*. Köln: Museen der Stadt Köln, 1986. 31–36.
Karavan, Dani. "Rede zur Eröffnung der Straße der Menschenrechte" (24 October 1993). https://www.nuernberg.de/imperia/md/menschenrechte/dokumente/karavan-rede-1993_neu.pdf (26 February 2017).
Koselleck, Reinhart, Gschnitzer, Fritz., Werner, Karl Ferdinand., Schönemann, Bernd. "Volk, Nation, Nationalismus, Masse." *Geschichtliche Grundbegriffe. Historisches Lexikon zur politisch-sozialen Sprache in Deutschland*. Vol. 7. Eds. Reinhart Koselleck, Conze, Werner., Brunner, Otto. Stuttgart: Klett-Cotta, 1992. 141–431.
https://www.landtag.nrw.de/portal/WWW/GB_II/II.1/OeA/Haus_des_Landtags/Karavan.jsp (26 February 2017).
Liebreich, Leon J. "The Songs of Ascents and the priestly blessing." *Journal of Biblical Literature* 74.1 (March 1955): 33–36.
Lorberbaum, Yair. *In God's Image: Myth, Theology, and Law in Classical Judaism*. New York: Cambridge University Press, 2015.
Misrach - Ort der friedlichen Begegnung, April 2005. http://www.infob.de/index.php?to=misrach (26 February 2017).

Omer, Mordechai. "Die Verbindung von Gegenwart und Vergangenheit – Zum Oeuvre Dani Karavans." Karavan, Dani., Jacobi, Fritz., Omer, Mordechai., Reuter, Jule., and Karavan Cohen, Noa. *Dani Karavan: Retrospektive*. Berlin: Wasmuth, 2008. 12–27.

Restany, Pierre. *Dani Karavan*. Trans. Jean Marie Clarke and Caroline Beamish. Munich: Prestel-Verlag, 1992.

Rykwert, Joseph. *The Dancing Column: On Order of Architecture*. Cambridge, MA: MIT Press, 1996.

Scheps, Marc. "Preface." Restany, Pierre. *Dani Karavan* [Hebrew]. Tel-Aviv: Sifriat-Poalim and Tel-Aviv Museum of Art, 1990.

The History of the Germanisches National Museum. http://www.gnm.de/en/museum/history-and-architecture/ (26 February 2017).

Zertal, Idith. "'Tikkun Olam' – Die Welt heilen. Über Kunst und Politik im Werk Dani Karavans." Karavan, Dani, Fritz Jacobi, Mordechai Omer, Jule Reuter, and Noa Cohen. *Dani Karavan: Retrospektive*. Berlin: Wasmuth, 2008. 356–361.

Tal Hever-Chybowski
Mikan ve'eylakh (From this Point Onward)[1]
Translated by Rachel Seelig

"One who reads from this point onward has not lost out"
(Mishnah Berakhot 1:2)

World Hebrew

There is an apparent contradiction between the Hebrew subtitle "Gatherer of World Hebrew"[2] (*Me'asef le'ivrit 'olamit*) and the English subtitle "Journal for

---

[1] Translator's note: Tal Hever-Chybowski points out that the original Hebrew title, *Mikan ve'eylakh,* can be translated as both "from now on" and "from here and beyond," conveying a temporal and spatial connection. He attributes the journal's "diasporic position" in part to the influence of *doikeyt* (Yiddish for "here-ness,") a term used by early twentieth century diaspora nationalists to refer to the ideal of rootedness throughout the diaspora, which was often contrasted with the Zionist emphasis on a "return" to the ancestral biblical homeland in the Land of Israel. I have chosen to retain the original title in the translation and to offer parenthetically the translation "From this Point Onward," which captures both temporal and spatial dimensions.
[2] Translator's note: The Hebrew word *me'asef* (literally "gatherer" or "collector") occupies a seminal role in Hebrew literary history. Hever-Chybowski associates this word with the name *Kohelet* (Ecclesiates), pointing out that Moses Mendelssohn offered two interpretations of that name: "the gatherer" (*der Sammler*), "for he [that is, King Solomon] gathered [*hikhil*] wisdoms, moral sayings and many poetic phrases," and "the preacher" (*der Prediger*), "for he spoke his words in public [*be-hakhel*]." According to Hever-Chybowski, "Mendelssohn's understanding of "Kohelet" as a word that links the collecting of knowledge (wisdoms, moral sayings, etc.) with the gathering of people, the task of a preacher," was the intellectual foundation for his earliest Hebrew work, considered the first modern Hebrew journal and one of the earliest works of the Haskalah, published in the 1750s under the title *Kohelet musar* ("gatherer/preacher of morality"). Mendelssohn's short-lived enterprise was followed by another Enlightenment Hebrew journal, first published in Königsberg in 1784, *Ha-me'asef* ("the gatherer"). Hever-Chybowski argues that the title of *Ha-me'asef* suggests that the purpose of this journal (like that of *Kohelet musar* before it), was not only to enlighten the Jews through the gathering (and dissemination) of articles, poems, allegories, letters, biographies etc., but also to bring them closer together as a people, "not in territory or in a state, but around general knowledge, science, aesthetics and literacy in Hebrew." Accordingly, the term *me'asef* in the Hebrew subtitle of *Mikan ve'eylakh* (From this point Onward) may be interpreted both in the sense of "gathering" (texts) and of "assembling" (people), not in a physical place, but around a shared cultural practice (Tal Hever-Chybowski, "The 'Zamlers' Scholarly Model: Mobilizing the East-European Jewish Masses for Philological Projects," lecture delivered at the conference *Nineteenth and Twentieth Century Philological Encounters*, organized by the research group *Zukunftsphilologie* in Leiden [4–5 June 2014]).

Diasporic Hebrew." Yet the point of contact between *world Hebrew* and *diasporic Hebrew* is precisely the point of departure for this enterprise. Those who affirmed the worldwide dispersion of Hebrew during the modern era used the noun *'olam* (world) and the related adjective *'olami* (universal, eternal)[3] in a partly similar and partly broader sense than what will be termed here "diaspora" and "diasporic." The representative example for the use of this adjective as an affirmation of Hebrew in the diaspora is the "World Hebrew Union," established in Berlin in 1931. In an article that appears here, David N. Myers discusses this organization and the other Hebrew projects of its founder, Simon Rawidowicz (1896–1957).[4] Ambiguity surrounds the term "world" in the name "World Hebrew Union." If it were possible to ask Rawidowicz whether he wished to establish a "world union for Hebrew" or a "union for world Hebrew," he undoubtedly would respond positively to both formulations, since his choice of the term evidently stemmed from its double-meaning.

To avoid any doubt, the adjective contained in the phrase "world Hebrew" is not intended as a translation of "global," "cosmopolitan," or "international," but rather is taken from the ancient Hebrew concept "world" (*'olam*), which has a double-meaning – referring to both space and time – as demonstrated, for instance, in one of the names for the Jewish people, "people of the world" (*'am 'olam*). In the introduction to the Hebrew version of the book *World History of the Jewish People*, known in Hebrew as *Chronicles of a World People*,[5] Simon Dubnow (1860–1940), Rawidowicz's admired teacher, writes that *'am 'olam* is a people

> whose home is the entire world. This is the literal meaning, which fits the reality of the Jewish people in all lands [...]; yet there is another interpretive possibility: the Jewish people is called *'am 'olam* in the sense of eternity, since this people is unusually wide-reaching not just in space but also in *time*, in its existence on the stage of history from antiquity until the present day.[6]

---

3 Translator's note: The Hebrew word *'olami*, which could be translated as "worldwide," "universal," or "eternal," carries a variety of connotations that are inevitably obscured in English translation. First and foremost, the association with *'am 'olam* (a traditional name for the Jewish people that means either "eternal people" or "people of the world") implies that *'ivrit 'olamit* has both a metaphysical dimension and an inherent connection with Jews and Judaism.
4 David N. Myers, "Rawidowicz in Berlin," here, 49–52.
5 Translator's note: The Hebrew translation of the work is titled *Divre yemey 'am 'olam* ("Chronicles of a world people"). Written in Russian and first published in German translation (1925–1929), Dubnow's ten-volume magnum opus is known in English translation as *World History of the Jewish People*. I have translated here from the Hebrew version that appears in the original essay.
6 Simon Dubnow, "Author's Introduction," in *Chronicles of a World People: From Its Origins to the Eve of the Second World War* (Tel Aviv: Devir, 1961), iii (in Hebrew), emphasis in the original.

Just as the Jewish people is a people of the world (and of eternity), so too Hebrew is an eternal world tongue. Insofar as its "worldness" (*'olamiut*) is not new,[7] the question arises as to why the need emerged in the modern era to emphasize this inherent trait. The affirmation of world Hebrew became necessary precisely because this trait was negated and denied, initially in the temporal sense, and later also in the spatial sense. The negation of the eternity of Hebrew, which preceded (and in a significant sense even laid the groundwork for) the negation of its spatial dimension (i.e. the negation of the diaspora), became manifest in *the myth of the death of Hebrew*.[8]

Elad Lapidot's article in this journal opens with Aristotle, who defined humans as living beings with language.[9] Roughly two thousand years later, Italian humanists turned Aristotle's definition on its head and described the languages of humans as living beings. The school of Dante Alighieri (1265–1321), Pietro Bembo (1470–1547), and Benedetto Varchi (1502–1565) refined the organic metaphor, which attributed life, on the one hand, to vernacular languages, and, death, on the other hand, to classical written languages.[10] "At the time when the title of dead languages was conferred on Latin and Greek," wrote the sociolinguist Max Weinreich (1894–1969), "Hebrew too was stamped as dead, and the *maskilim* introduced this evaluation into the Jewish milieu."[11] In time, however, the figurative character of the metaphor was forgotten, and the death of Hebrew came to be understood by many, even today, as a historical fact.

Indeed, the death of Hebrew thesis translates into the negation of its worldness, since a language that is capable of dying cannot be an eternal

---

[7] Translator's note: The word *'olamiut*, in the context of this essay, is intended to reinforce the multiplicity of meanings inherent to the Hebrew concept *'olam*, as discussed above. I have introduced the neologism "worldness" because no existing English word captures this multiplicity of meanings.

[8] In his lecture "Modern Hebrew: The Uncanny Story of the Life and Death of and Undead Language," delivered at the conference *Semitic Philology within European Intellectual History*, organized by the research group *Zukunftsphilologie* in Berlin (19–21 June 2013), Ya'ar Hever offered a Freudian interpretation of the metaphor of life and death in relation to the Hebrew language in the tradition of modern Hebrew linguistics. A Hebrew version of the lecture will be published in the next issue of this journal.

[9] Elad Lapidot, "The Deformed Tongue: Phenomenology of the Holy Language," here, 57.

[10] I am grateful to Sonia Yampolskaya for sending me her article, "The Concept of a 'Dead Language' as Exemplified by Hebrew," forthcoming in the journal *Vestnik of Saint Petersburg University*.

[11] Max Weinreich, *History of the Yiddish Language*, Vol. 1, trans. Shlomo Nobel (New Haven and London: Yale University Press, 2008), 252. Original: Max Weinreich, *History of the Yiddish Language: Concepts, Facts, Methods*, Vol. 1 (New York: YIVO, 1973), 256 (in Yiddish).

language. Yet from the negation came forth an affirmation: the thinkers who opposed the description of Hebrew as a dead language were the first to extoll its worldness, in terms of both time and space, in terms of both time and space, and established the theoretical foundation for what is conceptualized here as "world Hebrew."

An early example of the affirmation of Hebrew's "world character" appears in *Well of Judgement* (*Eyn mishpat*, 1867), by Sholem Yankev Abramovitch (1836–1917), known as Mendele Moykher-Sforim:

> It is true that the sacred tongue is not a spoken language, yet it is not dead like the languages of other ancient peoples. When the Chaldean language ceased to be spoken, for instance, the Chaldeans ceased to exist; they assimilated among the nations and learned their customs and laws. Their language is the meager legacy of a nation that had become extinct and removed from the realm of the living. But the Jewish people lives on; it has not splintered and withered: though it is scattered and dispersed among the nations, its flavor will endure and its fragrance will not be diminished; though it has gone into exile, it hath not settled on its lees (Jeremiah 48:11). The Jewish people thrives because of its faith and because of the Torah of its God. While the gods of other peoples lie down in sorrow (Isaiah 50:11), and the Greek idols sleep on Olympus, the place of their slumber, behold, He that keepeth Israel shall neither slumber nor sleep (Psalms 121:4)! [The Jewish people] has not lost its eternity. It lives on because of its Torah, the Torah of life, which grants the people a soul and spirit to all the dispersed people of Judah to be one nation on earth.[12]

The claim that Hebrew was a dead language led Abramovitch repeatedly to assert the opposite argument.[13]

For Abramovitch, the life of Hebrew was tied to the life of Israel. He did not reject the organic metaphor in relation to language, and he did not hesitate to declare the death of the Chaldean language, Aramaic. Yet his affirmation of the life (and the *eternity*) of Hebrew and of the Jewish people led him also to affirm the *space* within which they exist. In his assertion that Hebrew has not "settled on its lees" we find an affirmation of the diaspora *avant la lettre*,[14] that

---

[12] Sholem Yankev Abramovitch, *Well of Judgement* (Zhitomir: A.S. Shadav, 1867), 4 (in Hebrew).
[13] See Ibid, 5 and 23. For Abramovitch the *maskil*, the question of the life and death of Hebrew was ultimately less important than its usefulness in education: "Whether [the language] lives or dies, this is not of our concern; we only know that it is a good and reliable tool for the enlightenment of the children of Israel" (Ibid, 26).
[14] See, for example, Simon Dubnow, "The Affirmation of the Diaspora," in *Nationalism and History: Essays on Old and New Judaism*, ed. Koppel S. Pinson (Philadelphia: Jewish Publication Society of America, 1958), 182–191. The article was first published in May 1909 in the Russian journal *The Jewish World* (Еврейский мир).

is, decades before the diaspora was completely and explicitly negated. Therefore, even if Abramovitch did not use the term "world" (*'olam*), his words invoke the merging of time ("it has not lost its eternity") and space ("all the dispersed people of Judah" in the sense of "one nation on earth," i.e. throughout the world) that brings us closer to the concept of "world Hebrew."

The negation of Hebrew's world character was expressed not only in the claim of its death but also in the declaration of its revival in recent generations. At this stage, the simple *organic* metaphor of life and death was transformed into a new and more sophisticated metaphor: *the resurrection of the dead* – a kind of realization of Ezekiel's prophecy, the ascent of the Messiah from his grave, or even an act of sorcery. Although this wondrous and unnatural metaphor does not align with common sense,[15] here too figurative language seems to have been forgotten to such a degree that the resurrection of "Modern Hebrew" came to be accepted by many as an unproblematic idea, a known fact, as it were.[16]

The myth of the revival of Hebrew relies on the premise that Hebrew was a dead language, and thus on the negation of its worldness, its eternity. In this case, too, the negative intellectual reaction contributed to the theoretical refinement of the concept of "world Hebrew," which became more and more necessary. In his essay "Neuhebräisch?" (New Hebrew?) of 1925, Franz Rosenzweig (1886–1929) renounced the separation of "Modern Hebrew" from the Hebrew that preceded it, as well as the distinction between "Hebrew" and "the sacred tongue" (*lashon-hakodesh*).[17] He rejected the association between sacredness and stagnation and emphasized the vitality of Hebrew from its beginnings and throughout the generations:

> The holiness of the Hebrew language never signified holiness in the original sense of "seclusion," a meaning which has been overcome in classic Judaism. The holy language, the language of God, has always drawn strength for renewal from the spoken language, from the spoken languages of man; and this was so not only in the times of Moses and Isaiah. In other words, holy though it was, Hebrew never stiffened into something rigid and monumental; it always stayed alive.[18]

---

15 Cf. Ron Kuzar's point of view, as presented by Lapidot in "The Deformed Tongue," 60.
16 This point is influenced by Ya'ar Hever's lecture (see footnote 8).
17 Franz Rosenzweig, "Classical and Modern Hebrew: A Review of a Translation Into the Hebrew of Spinoza's Ethics," in *Franz Rosenzweig: His Life and Thought*, ed. Nahum H. Glatzer, trans. Francis C. Golffing (New York: Schocken Books, 1961), 263–271. Original: Franz Rosenzweig, "Neuhebräisch? Anläßlich der Übersetzung von Spinozas *Ethik*," in *der Morgen: Monatsschrift der Juden in Deutschland* (1925), 105–109.
18 Rosenzweig, "Classical and Modern Hebrew," 266.

Mira Balberg's essay in this volume sheds light on the expressions that Rosenzweig employs: "the holy language" (*die heilige Sprache*) and "the language of God" (*die Sprache Gottes*).[19] In a brilliant philosophical move, Rosenzweig invokes precisely the sacredness of Hebrew in order to suggest a non-dichotomous model of fruitful interaction between writing and speech, while rejecting the humanistic paradigm that distinguishes between a living spoken language and a dead written language. Rosenzweig insisted, it is worth noting, that forces of renewal flow into the sacred tongue not just from *one* spoken language (Hebrew) but from *many* "spoken languages." He elaborates:

> ...the spoken Hebrew of time immemorial, the common Aramaic of the Persian era, the Greek of the times of the Diadochi, then – stronger and more enduring than all – the Aramaic of the Palestinian and Babylonian academies, and, simultaneously, the language of the armies and law courts of Rome and that of the rulers and subjects of the new Persian empire, the Arabic of the physicians and philosophers of Islam, and the languages of Europe, developing their own structures in the shadow of the widespread tree of the Latin of the universal church. By the fabric of language so wrought, the Holy of Holies of this sacerdotal people is both veiled from and indicated to the eyes of the peoples of the world.[20]

According to Rosenzweig, the various linguistic apogees of Hebrew creativity in different times and places join together to form one unified language:

> The Hebrew of the Torah and of the Book of Esther, the majesty of the great central prayers, the exquisite proportions of the Mishnah, the baroque of Kalir, the classicism of the great Spanish authors, the pious sobriety of Maimonides, Rashi's serene yet impassioned instruction, the absence of linguistic scruples of the Tibonides, the crudeness of the Shulhan Arukh, the historicism of the Haskalah in the historical nineteenth century – all this is Hebrew.[21]

Up until this point, Rosenzweig's way of dealing with the myth of the death of Hebrew resembles that of Abramovitch. Like Abramovitch, Rosenzweig emphasized the "vitality" of the sacred language rather than reject the organic metaphor altogether. Moreover, his description of Hebrew as a living language

---

19 Mira Balberg, "From 'One Language' to 'One Mind:' The Tongue of the Holy and the Translation of the Torah," here, 53–55 (in Hebrew).
20 Rosenzweig, "Classical and Modern Hebrew," 266–267.
21 Ibid, 266.

that is renewed consistently,[22] nourished by the languages that surround it and by its earlier layers, led him to assert: "What differentiates this vitality from that of a profane living language is that nothing adopted [by Hebrew] can ever be discarded; the language becomes richer and richer."[23]

Indeed, Rosenzweig's adoption of the life metaphor in relation to language does not emerge from an attempt to prove that the sacred tongue resembles other languages. On the contrary, for Rosenzweig, if the organic metaphor is applicable in any way to the sacred tongue, this is because the sacred tongue is more alive than any other language. Ultimately, however, the organic metaphor proves unviable in relation to the unique sacred tongue and is therefore replaced by a different, more suitable metaphor to the "eternal language" (*die ewige Sprache*):

> It does not proceed in a sequence of deaths and resurrections, the only expedient whereby everything that lives on earth can prolong its span beyond what nature has allotted. It endures because it cannot, will not, and may not, die. Nothing that has become an integral part of it is every discarded. Its growth is not that of an organism but of a treasure....[24]

According to Rosenzweig, the portrayal of Hebrew as a treasure (in the original: *Hort* and *Schatz*) represents a more suitable metaphor for Hebrew. It is preferable to the organic metaphor, since Hebrew never ceased to accrue new layers of language in different time periods and places, layers that never fade and whither but rather remain within the language eternally. For Rosenzweig, even the language known as "Modern Hebrew" and the language spoken in the new *yishuv* are only part of this world language (understood in terms of both time and space):

> The point is that one cannot simply speak Hebrew as one would like to; one must speak it as it is. And it is tied up with the past. It does have obligations to the rest of the world [*weltverpflichtet*], even when spoken by the youngest child in the most recently founded settlement.[25]

---

22 Cf. Abramovitch's reference to "the wise Christian" Franz Delitsch, who wrote that even "the tasteful Herder was unaware that the Hebrew language is not dead but rather undying and continuously rejuvenated" (*Well of Judgement*, 5). Original: "Dass die hebräische Sprache nie gestorben sei, sondern in unsterblicher Jugendfrische fortlebe, wusste selbst der geschmackvolle Herder nicht," Franz Delitzsch, "Vorrede," in *Zur Geschichte der jüdischen Poësie, vom Abschluss der heiligen Schriften alten Bundes vit auf die neueste Zeit* (Leipzig: Karl Tauschnitz, 1836), vi. On Herder's relationship to Hebrew, see Ofri Ilany's article, "Siona Sulamith: German Hebraism and the Beginning of Modern Hebrew Poetry," here, 82–85, 93–96.
23 Rosenzweig, "Neuhebräisch," 106–107. Original: "Der Unterschied dieser Lebendigkeit von der einer profanlebendigen Sprache ist nur, daß hier nichts, was einmal aufgenommen wurde, verloren gehen kann; die Sprache wird immer reicher."
24 Ibid.
25 Ibid, 268–269.

Diasporic Hebrew

The term "diaspora" refers to the dispersal of groups of people, in the sense of sowing and germinating (the Greek word διασπορά stems from the verb σπείρειν – *speírein* – which means "to sow"). The recurrence of this word in the Septuagint (but never as a translation of "exile" [*galut* or *golah*])[26] is responsible for the association of this ancient Greek term with the Jewish experience in particular. However, since the 1970s the term has been expanded and used outside of the Jewish context in reference to an increasing number of groups that experience dispersion not only in different places but also in different senses of the term – a kind of diaspora of the concept itself.[27] At the turn of the twenty-first century, diaspora theorists began to propose alternatives to the center/periphery model and sought to emphasize the positive, productive and radical aspects of the term "diaspora" in general and of individual diasporas in particular. The theoretical elaborations of the concept reached a new apex in the work of Daniel Boyarin, whose lectures in Berlin in 2012 and 2013 had a profound impact on this diasporic endeavor.[28] Diaspora "need not imply trauma, an original scene of forced dispersion, a longing for a homeland, or even the existence of a myth of one homeland," writes Boyarin.[29] Yet within the negative definition (of what diaspora need not necessarily be) a positive definition of diaspora emerges as

> a synchronic cultural situation applicable to people who participate in a doubled cultural (and frequently linguistic) location, in which they share a culture with the place in which they dwell but also with another group of people who live elsewhere, in which they have a local and a trans-local cultural identity and expression at the same time.[30]

Boyarin refers here to groups of people, but if we apply his theory also to language we may conclude that, in all the different places in which it resides, Hebrew is nourished by the various cultures and languages with which it comes into contact (just as Rosenzweig argued in the quotation above). This diasporic cross-fertilization is particularly pronounced in places where Hebrew is a minority

---

[26] The term "exile" (*galut*), whether in the Jewish context or not, is relevant and even useful in the context of the present discussion. On this topic see Edward Said's lecture, "Intellectual Exile: Expatriates and Marginals," here, 39–47.
[27] Roger Brubaker, "The 'Diaspora' Diaspora," in *Ethnic and Racial Studies* 28.1 (2005), 1–19.
[28] These lectures served as the foundation of the book: Daniel Boyarin, *A Traveling Homeland: Babylonian Talmud as Diaspora* (Philadelphia: University of Pennsylvania Press, 2015).
[29] Boyarin, "A Traveling Homeland," here, 43; Cf. Boyarin, *A Traveling Homeland*, 19.
[30] Ibid.

language.³¹ The poems and stories published in this journal attest to the manifest influence exerted upon Hebrew by majority cultures and languages in places like Warsaw,³² Paris,³³ Los Angeles,³⁴ and New York.³⁵ The local context has a decisive role in the *Hebrew Berlin of today,* where most of the articles and literary texts gathered here were written and edited.³⁶ At the same time, the aforementioned cities are connected to Berlin through a shared language and similar conditions of minority existence. The *duality* between the local presence and the trans-local presence of Hebrew, which this journal seeks to express, facilitates a minor, hybrid, heterogeneous Hebrew: a *diasporic Hebrew*.

In the Tents of Yiddish

Another component of Boyarin's diaspora theory is cultural *partnership* (specifically in the joint custody of the text).³⁷ Coincidentally (or perhaps not), partnership was also one of the central concepts in the teaching of Simon Rawidowicz, the greatest theorist of the Hebrew diaspora in the twentieth century.³⁸ The application of Boyarin's diaspora theory to Hebrew allows us to acknowledge not only linguistic partnerships among groups dispersed in different places but also the possibility of a diaspora between languages themselves. As Boyarin stresses, the duality of diaspora can often be expressed through a doubled linguistic location.

---

31 Existing as a minority is not a prerequisite of Diaspora, as Boyarin suggests in *A Traveling Homeland*, p.152, n. 66, but minority status (which is not necessarily traumatic) can be useful for diaspora. See "Hommage to the Draft Evaders of the First World War in Hebrew Literature," here, 172 (in Hebrew).
32 Boris Gerus, "Copernicus," here, 123–127 (Hebrew).
33 Gilles Rozier, "Poems for Harel," here, 147 (Hebrew).
34 Zvi Ben-Dor Benite, "Potato with Sauce," here, 107–113 (Hebrew).
35 Sami Shalom Chetrit, "Sun in a Plastic Bottle," here, 145 (Hebrew).
36 See in this issue the articles of Ofri Ilany and Elad Lapidot, Sharon Horodi's story, and the poems of Ya'ar Hever and Admiel Kosman, as well as the translations of Gadi Goldberg ("To Sleep" by Isolde Kurz), Rimo Lomes ("Death Fugue" by Paul Celan), and my translations ("A Traveling Homeland" by Daniel Boyarin; "Intellectual Exile" by Edward Said, and "Europe" by Victor Klemperer). See also the texts included at an event organized in Berlin on August 1, 2014, which appear at the end of this issue under the title "Hommage to the Draft Evaders of the First World War in Hebrew Literature."
37 See Boyarin, *A Traveling Homeland*, 29–32.
38 Myers, "Rawidowicz in Berlin," 51.

For this reason, the present Hebrew enterprise, nourished by its local context in Ashkenaz,[39] views itself as a link in the chain of historical partnership between *Hebrew and Yiddish*. Each of these languages has had and remains in contact with many partner-languages, but the close relationship between the two languages here in Ashkenaz for roughly one thousand years makes them *sister languages*. Among the numerous historical, literary, linguistic, and political contexts that they share, what stands out in particular is their shared historical destiny over the last two hundred years, during which both languages were dispersed across a vast geographical space. These two minority languages, whose place is the world, flourished and produced literatures so intimately intertwined that the literary critic Bal-Makhshoves (the penname of Isidor Yisroel Eliashev, 1873–1924) declared them "two languages – one literature."[40]

The shared destiny of Hebrew and Yiddish in the modern era can also be observed in the fact that both blossomed in the shadow of their denial. The very same early *maskilim* who declared the death of Hebrew also rejected Yiddish as "a miserable jargon" not worthy of being called a "language."[41] This tendency intensified in the following generations, since the *maskilic* movement that tried to "revitalize" Hebrew relied ideologically on a dual linguistic negation, as Lewis Glinert has observed:

> And just as the desire to revitalize Hebrew has ubiquitously been bound up with the desire to be rid of Yiddish, so too it has sought to reject the "old-style" Hebrew of Ashkenaz, its sound and words – and the knowledge of it.[42]

---

39 Translator's note: The biblical name "Ashkenaz" came to be associated during the Middle Ages with the geographical area of the Rhineland, where Jewish communities began to take root in the eleventh century. These communities, which began migrating eastward during the late Middle Ages, came to be known as "Ashkenazi," a term widely applied to Jews of European origin, in contrast to "Sephardi" (literally "Spanish"), the term applied to Jews descended from the Iberian Peninsula who became dispersed after 1492 throughout North Africa and the Ottoman Empire.
40 Bal-Makhshoves (Dr. Eliashev), "Two Languages – One Literature," in *Collected Writings*, Vol. 2 (Warsaw: *Bikher*, 1929), 57–64 (in Yiddish).
41 Just as the representations of Hebrew as a world language emerged as a response to the negation of its eternity, so it seems that the phrase "the Yiddish language" (*di yidishe shprakh*) frequently used by Yiddishists until today emerged as a reaction to the claim that Yiddish is not a true language.
42 Lewis Glinert, "Preface," in *Hebrew in Ashkenaz: A Language in Exile*, ed. Lewis Glinert (New York: Oxford University Press, 1993), viii.

The shared destiny of Hebrew and Yiddish reached its apex during the years of destruction (*khurbn*)[43] of the twentieth century, when Nazi Germany and its allies began to cut off the branches and pull up the roots of both languages throughout Europe. The appearance of *Mikan ve'eylakh* here, in Berlin and Paris, attests to the fact that these roots will not, or cannot, be torn assunder. The decision to publish it under a Yiddish roof is intended to emphasize the choice of a partnership between these two languages rather than the relation of rivalry and enmity that has harmed both languages in the past. Like the pioneering Yiddish journal *Kol mevaser* (1862), published as a supplement to the Hebrew journal *Hamelits*, it is no coincidence that the Hebrew journal *Mikan ve'eylakh* found its place with a Yiddish publisher: the Medem Library in Paris (*Parizer-yidish-tsenter – Medem-bibliyotek*).[44]

---

[43] In Yiddish, the word *khurbn* refers to the Holocaust. The term is taken from the traditional Hebrew word usually associated with the destruction of the Temple (*ḥurban beyt-hamikdash*).
[44] Full disclosure: the editor of this journal is the director of the Paris Yiddish Center – Medem Library. In this case, the search for diasporic Hebrew in Ashkenaz led us to Yiddish, and not the other way around.

Mati Shemoelof
The Berlin Prize for Hebrew Literature
Translated by Rachel Seelig

(excerpt from a novel in progress)

1

The air was stale at Urbanstrasse Hospital on the southern bank of the Landwehr Canal. An exhibit of photographs adorned the hallway with colorful fish, including the type Helena had seen in the Red Sea when she went diving at Bir Suwair with that shabby red snorkel. Beneath the photographs running the length of the wall was a summery yellow stripe. Third floor, area 1B, building 6, room 145, where pregnant women leave behind fluids and discharge in the bathroom to the left of the examination room. Detergents had lost the fight against bodily secretions. The result was putrid. No wonder Helena refused to remain there under medical observation.

But now it was all behind her and she was sinking into warm water tinged green by foaming pine tree oil. Usually she bathed on weekends, not Tuesday evenings. But she had to rinse off the smells and stale impressions from the morning that now seemed an eternity away. Perhaps she had made a mistake telling Chezi the truth, but she had to get it out, let him know what a hypocrite he was. He didn't even call to thank his own father for the story, just left him to wither in that cheap old age home on Yitzhak Bar Moshe Street in Yahud. Helena was afraid of the future that was quickly approaching. Is that what their home would be like? Full of squabbles, with her unable even to ask for her husband's help? Lately it was one fight after the other; it seemed they couldn't get through a single day without yelling at each other. She asked herself whether Chezi could survive the truth. After all, her truth was one of the reasons she had always avoided serious relationships. One thought led to another and she was unable to answer the question. She tried to focus on her breathing, to forget the chaos that engulfed her, stretching her nerves thin.

She got up to go to the bathroom and began dripping all over the carpet, a small stream flattening tufts of dust. What would her parents say if they knew that she'd become pregnant, she wondered. Helena had thought about getting in touch many times and even made an attempt a while back. But Easter dinner fell apart after her father's remark about "those Arab immigrants" who are to blame for the rise of sexual assaults, not to mention anti-Semitic attacks. Her mother tried to make contact a few times, but Helena couldn't forgive her father, initially for what he'd said to her and later because he gave interviews on the subject to the press. She suffered the fallout wherever she went. Her surname was a disaster. Recently her mother had begun sending appeasing text messages and emails about her father's poor health, practically begging Helena to come visit. Helena didn't want any contact with him, or with her. Not least because of the rumor she heard. One afternoon on Boppstrasse she ran into Brigitte, the downstairs neighbor from Stuttgart, who was in town visiting her son Mark. Brigitte told her the secret: Helena's mother had become a rightwing fanatic who wanted out of the European Union – "Gerxit" – in order to prevent more immigrants from entering Germany. Helena could not believe it. She blamed her dad for brainwashing her mom, who used to be a liberal. Once, her mother even put up a family of Vietnamese refugees for an entire summer – the summer Helena lost her virginity to Mark. He was fifteen at the time, she was sixteen-and-a-half. Her father texted her about a surprise party for her mother in just a few days, asking her to come. She didn't answer.

Helena feared she had miscarried the first time because she was nearing forty. To make matters worse, Chezi avoided the subject and didn't know how to handle the pain of losing the longed-for pregnancy. She didn't want to go back to work, having already prepared for a long maternity leave. Soon her coworkers would know about the miscarriage and she would return to her mindnumbing job.

2

Chezi had overslept. He woke up in a panic, worried that Helena might have already checked out of the hospital before he had even managed to call or help her home. It occurred to him that he had forgotten to ask Johannes Birne, the piano tuner, to drop by. Helena was supposed to come home to a tuned piano so that she wouldn't need to tune it herself. Chezi was disappointed in himself. He put on his clothes without even brushing his teeth and rushed off to the *Späti*.

The roses at the exit to the building opened up in front of him and he couldn't resist, plucked a few red blossoms, cupping them close to his nose, and took in the fragrance of an especially serene evening.

Helena called just as he was standing in line to pay at the only open late-night grocery store in the neighborhood. As Chezi glanced at his cell phone a Facebook invitation popped up for the Or Yehuda High School reunion. Behind Chezi in line stood a man, perhaps German, perhaps foreign, with small gray eyes, a chubby face, and bluish stubble on a tattooed face, who had placed on the black rubber conveyer belt a sausage resembling a dissected penis, a gleaming eggplant, and some sort of spaghetti sauce that Chezi had never seen before; in front of him was a foreign woman with a large piercing, tiny bits of silver-plated iron fastened to her cheeks, a chain that looped through her eyebrow and descended to the outer edge of her lip. Chezi was repulsed by this fashion of holes in one's face and wondered what might happen if the small iron bars were to be removed from her delicate ivory skin. A man joined the back of the line, his skin covered in tattoos, with only the whites of his innocent eyes standing out, causing every shade of the greenish tattoo surrounding them to resemble a warrior from another era, perhaps from outer space.

Chezi was glad to see Helena's name appear on his screen. He listened carefully to the nuances in her voice, checked how she was feeling and when she woke up. Helena asked him to buy a specific type of cabbage that's known to be particularly healthy and prepare it for her for when she returned from the recovery room at Urbanstrasse Hospital. She mentioned the name of the cabbage in German twice, but Chezi couldn't quite make it out. He had tried to learn the local language but was dyslexic and struggled. Helena repeated the word again and again: *Grünkohl*. He heard *Grukol*. She repeated it again – *Grünkohl* – as he reached the front of the line and noticed the cashier, Rosa Luxemburg, staring at him, irritated. Chezi was hesitant to deal with her. During their many previous encounters Rosa had spoken with such speed that the translation mechanism in his brain short-circuited. He looked behind him and realized the entire line was staring back at him impatiently, but unlike the convenience store in Or Yehuda, no one said a word. Rosa had no patience for the linguistic difficulties of immigrants. She said "*Bitte*" a few times and signaled him to move forward. Chezi glanced at her and then at the long line behind him. He lifted his cell phone to his ear and asked Helena quietly not to yell at him. (That was a trick he learned from her. She often asked him to lower his voice when speaking with her.) "Text me the name," he whispered to Helena in English, and wondered whether he still had time to find the cabbage, leaving behind on the conveyer belt all the items with barcodes that the cashier was eagerly preparing to scan. Chezi asked Rosa in broken German to wait a moment and then turned to the crowd, interlacing his fingers as he lifted and lowered his hands, and mumbled in English, "I am sorry." For a moment he thought they might not understand and switched to German: "Tur mir Leid." The crowd groaned and didn't exactly consent, nor did they protest, aside from Rosa, perhaps, who frowned dramatically.

Chezi smiled like a silly child, ran through the aisles in search of the vegetable, and finally found an empty box emblazoned with the name of the salubrious cabbage. He returned in a sweat. By then Rosa had lost it and was yelling loudly at him for holding everyone up. Nervously, Chezi put his phone down on the conveyer belt just as it lit up, displaying an email from a known address. The orange juice bottle fell out his hand and broke. Rosa got up to clean the mess, shaking her head continuously. All eyes were on Chezi. Rosa returned to her black chair silently, calmly scanned his groceries and dismissed him. Still no one said a word.

Chezi decided the road was too dangerous for a morning like this. He stepped onto the sidewalk built of large square stones and walked toward his apartment. Along the way he passed the name of the prolific German-Jewish anarchist Erich Mühsam peering at him from among the worn, brass *Stolpersteine*, "stumbling stones" covered in a thin layer of dust. In the early morning of March 28, 1933, the sun just beginning to emerge, Mühsam had been arrested by the Nazis for an unknown transgression. Josef Goebbels, the Nazi Minister of Propaganda, labeled Mühsam, then at the peak of his career, a subversive Jew, and claimed that he planned to escape to Switzerland (why not, come to think of it?!). Over the course of the next seventeen months Mühsam was imprisoned in the concentration camps of Sonnenburg, Brandenburg, and finally Oranienburg, where he was tortured, beaten, and eventually found hanged. Chezi had been to Brandenburg, and to Oranienburg, and found it difficult to imagine that these quiet places could have contained such evil and wickedness, and so many bitter enemies.

With his left hand Chezi put his conversation with Helena on speakerphone. She was eager to know whether had had found the cabbage, and he didn't care that the entire street could hear them. And with his right – he almost got a heart attack – he opened the incoming email that informed him he had one the Berlin Prize for Hebrew Literature. He knew that he had been nominated for the illustrious prize but was sure he didn't stand a chance of winning. Was he really going to make this big step up from the national league to the international major writers league? Authors big and small, famous and obscure sent in books from all over the world to the committee of The Berlin Prize for Hebrew Literature, the most significant prize in the world for writers of Hebrew (citizenship, religion, and territory didn't matter; the nominees could be non-Israelis, non-Jews, and citizens of any country in the world). The prize offered an enormous amount of money, translation into a dozen languages, including English, German, Spanish, Arabic, Portuguese, Chinese, and Russian, and a contract for one more book with the international publishing house of Else Lasker-Schüler. Perhaps the greatest advantage of The Berlin Prize for Hebrew Literature, at least compared with other major German literary prizes, was that translation was not a prerequisite for entry – Hebrew books could be submitted *in* Hebrew. What's more, the competition was open to all authors who write in Hebrew, and not just to those who actually manage to make a living from it. As it happens, it was Chezi's *To Remain in*

Baghdad that won big. The words at the center of the email appeared in bold: "The ceremony will take place in six days, on June 5, 2016."

3

Chezi stormed into the house, tossed the groceries on the small wooden table that Helena had brought from her apartment, the table he saw as a symbol of honest Christian labor, entirely devoid of opulence and ornamentation. Helena had come home from the hospital just minutes before him. She asked him to help her remove her faux leather boots as she lay down on the white shag rug in the bedroom. He tugged off the right boot, and as he shifted to the left foot, blurted out suddenly, "I won The Berlin Prize for Hebrew Literature – can you believe it?!"

"Is it for the first book or the second?" she asked, nudging him with her toes to remove the boot from her other foot.

"The second." Chezi suddenly felt worthy, even though he had been certain just moments before reading the email that he'd never make the final cut. His second book had earned him a grant to spend a year writing in Berlin, but he had no idea what the following year would bring. He would probably have to apply for more writer-in-residence programs and pray for something to come through. "That's not a way to live," Chezi thought, "especially not with a pregnant wife. Don't you want to be able to support a baby, buy a house, give your wife and child a future?" But everything was different now. The generous grant provided by The Berlin Prize for Hebrew Literature was about to relieve him, at least for a few years, of all existential fear. And, who knows? Perhaps it would even put him in the champions' league of literature.

Fate had decided that he would win the prize. Fate crowned him and fate looked after him. It wasn't luck, he liked to think, but hard work that had come to fruition, creativity and talent that allowed his words to ascend the biggest ladder of all, climbing toward their glorious apogee before Chezi, like all other mortals, would pass on to the world to come. In soccer the trophy goes to the player that scores the largest number of goals in the European league, and yet here was Chezi Morad from Or Yehuda taking the Golden Shoe thanks to his measly second book. All of life's challenges, growing up under the poverty line, the constant feeling of not fitting in and doubts about his writing – gone.

Nobody in Germany is interested in yet another Israeli author who writes in Hebrew. Immigrants belonged in the immigrant ghettoes. The big German publishing houses gambled only on authors with prior success in Israel. And what about the Israeli community in Berlin? *Quatsch,* they were nothing. *Gurnisht.*

Not worth translating, unless of course they offer German readers an insider's perspective on Israeli culture. But Chezi didn't write about Israel. The situation in Israel, meanwhile, wasn't all that different. No author from Or Yehuda had ever made it onto Israel's national literature team. Besides, Israelis saw Chezi as an emigrant and interloper, a traitor who had abandoned his country and boasted brazenly about life in Germany. But now everything would change. Chezi Morad would show them! Chezi would prove that it's possible to live in Berlin and win prizes in the diaspora based on his Baghdadi origins. He was the first writer the Germans recognized as capable of writing about Baghdad while remaining part of an Israeli establishment that wins prizes.

Helena excused herself to change her clothes and go to the bathroom while Chezi waited patiently on the couch in the living room. A moment before wiping herself, she noticed drops of crimson blood on the white toilet sink. Her underwear was drenched with brownish red blood. The pad she had been given at the hospital hadn't held up. She wondered whether they had just been cutting costs or had in fact purchased defective materials – was this intentional or accidental? She recalled the ultrasound that revealed damage to the amniotic sac. Bed rest hadn't been sufficient. When she finally emerged from the bathroom she asked for water. Something about her pale complexion wasn't normal. She said she felt weak, lay down, and asked Chezi to let her sleep. But then she shot up, nearly vomited and couldn't calm down, so he drew her a bath with healing oils. They met in the kitchen.

"That's not the vegetable I wanted you to buy."
"I'm sorry. It's all they had."
"Honey, I should have explained it in English."
"No, no, it's good that you speak to me in German."

Helena returned to the bathroom and Chezi ducked into the office momentarily to check his email and refresh his Facebook page, dying to find out whether people had heard the news. Should he share the email he received, he wondered? He could hear Helena writhing uncomfortably as she yelled to him to bring the green bath oil.

The sound of her favorite concerto emanated from the bathroom, Bach's Brandenburg No. 5, written for the Duke of Brandenberg in 1719 upon the composer's return from Berlin. Chezi located the foam on the top shelf of the high cupboard next to the shower and began to dribble it into the water when the cork came loose, causing the fluid to gush uncontrollably into the bathtub.

"Why did you do that?" Helena asked.
"I'm sorry. I didn't mean to."

"Why don't you answer when I call you?"

"I'm sorry. I needed to check if anyone had written about the prize." Chezi looked at the filthy floor, rolls of dust mixed with water, his dark hairs entangled with her light ones.

"I'm not feeling well and I need you to come quick if something happens, okay?" Helena looked at him impatiently, trembling.

"Yes, my love, *neshama*, I'm sorry." Chezi looked at himself in the cloudy mirror.

"I really don't feel well." Helena gently splashed the water that came up to her breasts.

"Poor thing." He lowered the volume of the music and looked at how she had changed as she lay in the water. Something childlike coursed through her and he wanted to jump into the bathtub with her.

"I don't want your pity. It's just– I've been thinking a lot about us lately."

"Let's talk about it later on."

"I had a strange dream,"

"Tell me later. Right now let's just play a game."

"Let me guess, the one where you imitate me? No. I don't want to play that. Not now."

"Come on, please?"

"No."

"Please, please, please?"

"It's not the right time. Even now you refuse to take 'no' for an answer."

Helena reluctantly complied and changed her voice to sound like Chezi.

"I'm the great Chezi Morad, I won the Berlin Prize for Fucking Literature. And you're a big failure. You lost our child. But don't worry, my Helenushka, I'll buy you a child with the money I won, I'll take you on vacations, buy you a house, everything I was always unable to afford because I was a writer living from hand to mouth. All that time I kept saying, 'Just wait, it'll happen.' And now look! It happened! I won enough money to take care of us. And the money isn't just mine, Helena, it's also yours. Because you were there by my side and you're the love of my life. So there, Helena, now you should feel wonderful, fabulous, elated, because your partner is no longer a loser who can't even take care of his teeth or buy a car.... Thank you very much, kind audience. Thanks for the money. I always knew I was worth it. I promise to spend it with reckless abandon out of respect for the capitalist values of the donors, judges and respected audience. And while we're at it, thank you for the antisemitism and for the new trend of philosemitism, and, last but not least, thanks for giving me an *Ausländer* visa for artists." Helena had slipped out of her acting mode and was no longer impersonating Chezi's deep voice.

Chezi smirked and began imitating Helena: "Poor me, I'm Helena. I lost my first child. I, the one who fantasizes about a big family full of kids, want to thank Chezi for winning that prize. Maybe we can use it to buy children from third-world families who are in desperate need of money and are willing to live with the biggest trauma of all in order to supply fertility to wealthy countries with an abundance of every resource other than children."

"Stop it. You're a lot nastier than me." Helena pleaded, her face drained, eyes nearly shut.

Chezi wiped his nose with the toilet paper next to the sink. On each square of paper were three green hearts arranged in a diagonal row. Yet another excellent purchase from 'Edefa', the supermarket chain known for its soft, comfortable, ecofriendly and efficient toilet paper.

"Your dad called. I told him you'd gone grocery shopping." Helena's lake blue eyes gazed into Chezi's forest-green ones.
"I love you," he said. "I think that's enough of that game for today. You need to get well."
"I love you. And I'm asking you to help me, okay? Now maybe you call your dad to tell him the news?"
"If you call your dad, I'll call mine."
"Don't be silly, *Schatzi*."

About the Authors

Yael Almog is a fellow at the Lichtenberg-Kolleg at the Georg-August-Universität Göttingen. She concurrently teaches Jewish Studies at the Technical University of Berlin. Upon receiving her PhD in German Studies from the University of California, Berkeley in 2014 she became a member of the Center for Literary and Cultural Research in Berlin. Almog's book project, "Biblical Reminiscences: Global Religion in the Age of Hermeneutics," describes the emergence of modern interpretation as contingent upon the universalization of the Hebrew Bible in the late German Enlightenment.

Maya Barzilai is Assistant Professor of modern Hebrew and Jewish culture at the University of Michigan. She received her PhD in Comparative Literature from UC Berkeley in 2009. Her book, *Golem: Modern Wars and Their Monsters*, appeared with NYU Press in 2016. She has published essays on Hebrew-German literary relations and translations in *Prooftexts*, *Naharaim*, *The Journal of Jewish Identities*, and *The Yearbook of Comparative and General Literature*.

Amir Eshel is Edward Clark Crossett Professor of Humanistic Studies and Professor of German Studies and Comparative Literature at Stanford University, where he also co-directs the Poetic Media Lab at the Center for Textual and Visual Analysis (CESTA). He is the author of *Futurity: Contemporary Literature and the Quest for the Past* (University of Chicago Press, 2013), which appeared initially in German under the title *Zukünftigkeit: Die zeitgenössische Literatur und die Vergangenheit* (Suhrkamp Verlag, 2012). He co-edited *Hannah Arendt zwischen den Disziplinen* (Wallstein Verlag, 2014) together with Ulrich Baer and *Kurz hinter der Wahrheit und dicht neben der Lüge: Zum Werk Barbara Honigmanns* (Fink Verlag, 2013) together with Yfaat Weiss. His earlier work includes *Zeit der Zäsur: Jüdische Lyriker im Angesicht der Shoah* (Universitätsverlag, 1999).

Abigail Gillman is Associate Professor of Hebrew, German and Comparative Literature, and Interim Director of the Elie Wiesel Center for Jewish Studies, at Boston University. She is the author of *Viennese Jewish Modernism: Freud, Hofmannsthal, Beer-Hofmann and Schnitzler* (Penn State University Press, 2009). A second book, *A History of German Jewish Bible Translation*, will appear in 2017 with the University of Chicago Press. Her essay "Martin Buber's Message to Postwar Germany" won the 2015 Egon Schwarz Prize for an Outstanding Essay in the Area of German Jewish Studies.

Since retiring from the Department of Comparative and General Literature of the Hebrew University, Ruth Ginsburg has been an active translator of Freud from

German into Hebrew. She has published *Peirush ha-halom* [*Die Traumdeutung*] 2002; *Moshe ha-Ish ve-ha-Dat ha-Monoteistit* [*Der Mann Moses und die monotheistische Religion*], 2009; *Ha-Albeiti* [*Das Unheimliche*], 2012; *Totem ve-Tabu* [*Totem und Tabu*] 2013. Her present project is the translation of a collection of previously untranslated essays by Erich Auerbach. Her recent publications include essays on trauma and theoretical considerations of translation.

Tal Hever-Chybowski is the director of the Paris Yiddish Center – Medem Library (Maison de la culture yiddish – Bibliothèque Medem), founder and editor of *Mikan ve'eylakh: Journal for Diasporic Hebrew* (Berlin/Paris), editor of the Yiddish journal *Der yidisher tam-tam* (Paris), and a PhD candidate at the History Department of Humboldt University, Berlin. He holds a BA in History from the Hebrew University of Jerusalem and an MA in History from the Humboldt University. He translated into Hebrew Edward Said's *Representations of the Intellectual* (1993), Mikhal Dekel's *The Universal Jew: Masculinity, Modernity, and the Zionist Moment* (2014), and is the editor of Daniel Boyarin, *The Talmud – A Personal Take, Selected Essays* (forthcoming 2017).

Stefanie Mahrer competed her PhD in 2011 with an award-winning study on the history of Jewish watchmakers in 19th century Switzerland (published 2012, Böhlau Verlag). She is currently teaching modern Jewish history at Basel University, Switzerland, where she is about to finish her post-doctoral project, "Salman Schocken's Cultural Project and the Circle of German-Jewish Intellectuals in the First Half of the 20th Century."

Freddie Rokem is Professor (Emeritus) in the Department of Theatre at Tel Aviv University, where he was the Dean of the Faculty of the Arts (2002–2006), and is currently the Wiegeland Visiting Professor of Theater & Performance Studies at the University of Chicago. His more recent books are *Philosophers and Thespians: Thinking Performance* (Stanford University Press, 2010); *Jews and the Making of Modern German Theatre* (University of Iowa Press, 2010, co-edited with Jeanette Malkin); *Strindberg's Secret Codes* (Norvik Press, 2004) and the prize-winning book *Performing History: Theatrical Representations of the Past in Contemporary Theatre* (University of Iowa Press, 2000). He has been a visiting professor at many universities in the United States, Germany, Finland and Sweden, and is also a practicing dramaturge.

Na'ama Rokem is Associate Professor of Hebrew and Comparative Literature at the University of Chicago. Her book, *Prosaic Conditions: Heinrich Heine and the Spaces of Zionist Literature,* was published by Northwestern University Press in 2013. She has written articles about W.G. Sebald, H.N. Bialik, Theodor Herzl, Franz Kafka, Hannah Arendt, and Leah Goldberg, and is currently completing a book about the encounter and dialogue between Yehuda Amichai and Paul Celan.

About the Authors

Rachel Seelig is a fellow at the Frankel Institute for Advanced Judaic Studies at the University of Michigan. She has published essays on German-Jewish, Hebrew and Yiddish literatures in *Prooftexts, Modern Language Notes, Naharaim*, and *The Jewish Quarterly Review*. Her first book, *Strangers in Berlin: Modern Jewish Literature between East and West, 1919–1933*, was published by the University of Michigan Press in 2016.

Galili Shahar is professor of Comparative Literature and German studies and serves as the director of the Minerva Institute for German History at the Tel Aviv University.

Mati Shemoelof is a poet, author and editor. His writing is diverse, including newspaper columns, poems and prose, for which he won several prizes and scholarships. His latest collection of short stories was published by Kinneret Zmora (2014). "The Berlin Prize for Hebrew Literature" is an excerpt from a novel in progress. Today Shemoelof lives and writes as part of the growing Israeli diaspora in Berlin.

Giddon Ticotsky is a Hebrew literature scholar and the executive editor of Stanford's *Dibur Literary Journal*.